TAKING SIDES

Clashing Views in

Human Sexuality

TWELFTH EDITION

Selected, Edited, and with Introductions by

William J. Taverner
The Center for Family Life Education

Ryan W. McKee
Montclair State University

Connect
Learn
Succeed™

TAKING SIDES: CLASHING VIEWS IN HUMAN SEXUALITY, TWELFTH EDITION

Published by McGraw-Hill, a business unit of The McGraw-Hill Companies, Inc., 1221 Avenue of the Americas, New York, NY 10020. Copyright © 2012 by The McGraw-Hill Companies, Inc. All rights reserved. Previous edition(s) © 2010, 2008, and 2006. Printed in the United States of America. No part of this publication may be reproduced or distributed in any form or by any means, or stored in a database or retrieval system, without the prior written consent of The McGraw-Hill Companies, Inc., including, but not limited to, in any network or other electronic storage or transmission, or broadcast for distance learning.

Some ancillaries, including electronic and print components, may not be available to customers outside the United States.

Taking Sides® is a registered trademark of the McGraw-Hill Companies, Inc.
Taking Sides is published by the **Contemporary Learning Series** group within the McGraw-Hill Higher Education division.

1 2 3 4 5 6 7 8 9 0 DOC/DOC 1 0 9 8 7 6 5 4 3 2 1

MHID: 0-07-805020-0
ISBN: 978-0-07-805020-6
ISSN: 1095-5387

Managing Editor: *Larry Loeppke*
Senior Developmental Editor: *Jill Meloy*
Permissions Coordinator: *Rita Hingtgen*
Senior Marketing Communications Specialist: *Mary Klein*
Marketing Specialist: *Alice Link*
Project Manager: *Erin Melloy*
Design Coordinator: *Brenda A. Rolwes*
Cover Graphics: *Rick D. Noel*
Buyer: *Nicole Baumgartner*
Media Project Manager: *Sridevi Palani*

Compositor: MPS Limited, a Macmillan Company
Cover Image: Cover illustration by Dane Jefferson

Editors/Academic Advisory Board

Members of the Academic Advisory Board are instrumental in the final selection of articles for each edition of TAKING SIDES. Their review of articles for content, level, and appropriateness provides critical direction to the editors and staff. We think that you will find their careful consideration well reflected in this volume.

TAKING SIDES: Clashing Views in HUMAN SEXUALITY
Twelfth Edition

EDITORS

William J. Taverner
The Center for Family Life Education

Ryan McKee
Montclair State University

ACADEMIC ADVISORY BOARD MEMBERS

Editors/Academic Advisory Board continued

Editors/Academic Advisory Board continued

Preface

In few areas of American society today are clashing views more evident than in the area of human sexual behavior. Almost daily, in the news media, in congressional hearings, and on the streets, we hear about Americans of all ages taking completely opposite positions on such issues as abortion, contraception, fertility, same-sex marriage, teenage sexuality, and the like. Given the highly personal, emotional, and sensitive nature of these issues, sorting out the meaning of these controversies and fashioning a coherent position on them can be a difficult proposition. The purpose of this book, therefore, is to encourage meaningful critical thinking about current issues related to human sexuality, and the debates are designed to assist you in the task of clarifying your own personal values in relation to some common, and often polar, perspectives on the issues presented.

This twelfth edition of *Taking Sides: Clashing Views in Human Sexuality* presents 40 lively and thoughtful statements by articulate advocates on opposite sides of a variety of sexuality-related questions. Each issue includes:

- An Issue *Question* (e.g., Issue 1 asks, Is Sexting a Form of Safer Sex?);
- An *Introduction* that presents background information helpful for understanding the context of the debate and information on the authors who will be contributing to the debate;
- *Essays* by two authors—one who responds YES, and one who responds NO to the question; and
- A *Postscript* that poses additional questions to help you further examine the issues raised (or not raised) by the authors, including bibliographical resources.

It is important to remember that for the questions debated in this volume, the essays often represent but two perspectives on the issue. Remember that the debates do not end there—most issues have many shades of gray, and you may find your own values congruent with neither author. Since this book is a tool to encourage critical thinking, you should not feel confined to the views expressed in the articles. You may see important points on both sides of an issue and may construct for yourself a new and creative approach, which may incorporate the best of both sides or provide an entirely new vantage point for understanding.

As you read this collection of issues, try to respect other people's philosophical worldviews and beliefs and attempt to articulate your own. At the same time, be aware of the authors' potential biases, and how they may affect the positions each author articulates. Be aware, too, of your own biases. We all have experiences that may shape the way we look at a controversial issue. Try to come to each issue with an open mind. You may find your values challenged or strengthened after reading both views. Although you may disagree with one or even both of the arguments offered for each issue, it is important that you read each statement carefully and critically.

Changes to This Edition

This edition of *Taking Sides: Clashing Views in Human Sexuality* includes substantial changes from the previous edition, including 15 brand new articles in nine new or updated issues.

New Issues

- Is Sexting a Form of Safer Sex?
- Is There Academic Merit to Students Viewing Live Sexual Acts in College Courses?
- Is Pornography Harmful?
- Is Female Circumcision/FGM an Acceptable Practice?
- Do Reality TV Shows Portray Responsible Messages about Teen Pregnancy?

Issues with updated articles (note that some issues, not listed here, have questions that we have updated or rephrased):

- Can Sex be Addictive?
- Does Sexual Medicine Benefit Society?
- Should Same-Sex Marriage Be Legal?
- Should Pharmacists Have the Right to Refuse Contraceptive Prescriptions?

In all, more than one-third of the essays are brand-spanking new. In addition, introductions and postscripts have been revised and updated where necessary.

A Word to the Instructor

An Instructor's Manual, with issue synopses, suggestions for classroom discussions, and test questions (multiple-choice and essay) is available from McGraw-Hill/Dushkin. This resource, authored by Eli Green, makes a very useful accompaniment for this text. A general guidebook, *Using Taking Sides in the Classroom*, which discusses methods and techniques for integrating the pro/con approach into any classroom setting, is also available. An online version of *Using Taking Sides in the Classroom* and a correspondence service for Taking Sides adopters can be found at http://www.mhhe.com/cls.

Taking Sides: Clashing Views in Human Sexuality is one of the many titles in the Taking Sides series. If you are interested in seeing the table of contents for any of the other titles, please visit the Taking Sides Web site at http://www.mhhe.com/cls or by contacting the authors at sexedjournal@hotmail.com or ryan@ryanmckee.com. Ideas for new issues are always welcome!

Acknowledgments
Thanks from William J. Taverner

First and foremost, I wish to thank my family. Putting together a collection of pro and con essays is no easy task, and the many hours I worked on this book were also hours that my family waited patiently for me to be done for the day.

I thank my wife, Denise, and my children, Robert and Christopher, who always welcomed me with open arms whenever I was finished working. I thank my parents, Joan and Bill, and my brother and sister, Joey and Karen. My family's differing opinions about social issues is always a source for spirited discussion, and I love them all for their support and for their help in making me think critically about all these issues. I am amused to think how occasionally a member of the press will call for a quote about a sexual issue and accidentally reach the "other" William Taverner, and be surprised by the quote my father gives.

For the hard work that goes into this book, I am indebted to the expert publishing skills of all my colleagues at McGraw-Hill. Thank you, Larry Loeppke, for your encouragement. Thanks to Rita Hingtgen for handling all the permissions requests. Thanks to Jill Meloy for your patience and for giving sound advice on the new issues, carefully reviewing every article and giving excellent feedback on what to keep and what to cut.

Thanks to colleagues and friends who suggested new issues or pointed us in the direction of great articles, gave good advice, or just continue to inspire me. Thanks to my friend and colleague, Judith Steinhart, who several years ago introduced me to Ryan McKee. Judith insisted that I just *had* to meet Ryan, and I am glad I did. Ryan is a gifted researcher and writer whose thoughtful analysis shines in the commentaries that precede and follow many of the selections. Ryan and I have now had the opportunity to work together on several editions of *Taking Sides,* and it is always a thoughtful process in which I learn a great deal.

Thanks to Eli Green, a gifted writer who wrote the Instructor's Manual for this edition. Thanks also to Olivia Von Kohorn, who assisted with researching current trends and facts for the new issues, and to Allyson Sandak who assisted with issues that appeared in the previous edition.

Thanks also to my old friends who passed away earlier in the decade: Tim Cummings and Pete Kasenchak. Tim and Pete were two of the smartest people I knew and could debate the night away.

Finally, I wish to thank two colleagues who have been both mentors and friends for many years: Peggy Brick and Robert T. Francoeur. Peggy and I have collaborated on numerous sexuality education manuals, and I value her advice dearly. She is a patient and generous mentor who constantly inspires me to think critically about all matters, not just those related to sexuality education. Bob edited or coedited the first seven editions of *Taking Sides: Clashing Views on Controversial Issues in Human Sexuality.* I have had the privilege of working with Bob on three previous editions of this book and was introduced to both *Taking Sides* and Bob when I took his international studies course in Copenhagen, Denmark, 20 years ago. I am grateful for his kind guidance over the years and honored to carry on his legacy. Everyone should be so lucky as to have such knowledgeable and caring mentors.

Thanks from Ryan W. McKee

Work on the past few editions of *Taking Sides* has coincided with many changes in my life that I would not have been able to navigate without the love and support of my family. To my parents, I want to say thanks for always being supportive no matter what direction my life takes. I thank my brothers, sisters, nephews, and niece for being a constant source of inspiration and motivation.

Thanks to William J. Taverner for again including me in this fascinating and challenging process. When he asked me to contribute to the Instructor's Manual of the 9th edition of *Taking Sides,* I never imagined it would open the doors to so many opportunities. His trust and support in having me on-board as a coeditor is an honor. His contributions to the field of human sexuality education are immeasurable, and I am fortunate to have him as a mentor, colleague, and friend. Thanks as well to Robert T. Francoeur, a former editor of *Taking Sides* and a brilliant sexologist, for giving me the opportunity to sit in on classes and follow in his footsteps at Fairleigh Dickinson. I am especially grateful to both Daphne Rankin and Judith Steinhart, mentors and friends who have treated me like family since we were first introduced. Their support and encouragement have been invaluable over the years.

Thanks to the folks at McGraw-Hill, including Larry Loeppke and Rita Hingtgen. Special thanks to Jill Meloy for all the hours she put into reviewing issues and articles, providing feedback, and for keeping us on track. Many thanks are due to the brilliant Eli Green for writing the Instructor's Manual for the current edition. Thanks are also due to Olivia Von Kohorn for assisting with research in this edition. Thanks to Dane Jefferson for providing the cover illustration and nearly 20 years of friendship. You can see more of his amazing work at http://artistdane.blogspot.com.

Extra special thanks to my friends and colleagues in the Human Sexuality Education program at Widener University. My fellow students at Widener are incredibly gifted and dedicated to making the world a better place through their contributions in research, education, and the helping professions. The future of sexology is bright thanks to their efforts. Thanks also to my professors at Widener, including Dr. Dyson, Dr. Sitron, Dr. Crane, Dr. Stayton, Dr. Kellogg-Spadt, and Amelia Hamarman, who have provided me with the best educational opportunities anyone in the field of human sexuality education could ask for.

Finally, I would like to thank Alison Bellavance for her love, support, and encouragement throughout this process. Alison is the hardest working person I know, and she has inspired me to accomplish things I never dreamed possible. She is brilliant, kind, caring, and forgiving. I am fortunate to be a part of her life and family.

Contents In Brief

Contents

UNIT 1   UNDERSTANDING SEXUAL EXPRESSION   1

Brent Satterly, Professor and Program Director at Widener University's Center for Social Work Education, acknowledges the risks involved in sexting while criticizing fear-based media coverage of the phenomenon. He argues in favor of harm-reduction strategies to reduce the risks associated with sexting rather than continuing the trend of panicked reactions to the expression of youth sexuality. Donald Dyson, Associate Professor and Director of Doctoral Studies in the Center for Education at Widener University, examines sexting through the lens of the World Health Organization's definition of sexual health and determines that the risks inherent in the digital transmission of sext messages is not a form of safer sex.

Rebecca Hagelin, author and public speaker on family and culture, argues that sex education promotes casual sex and that schools and parents should do more to protect children. Lara Riscol, an author who explores the connections between society and sexuality, counters that blaming sex education is an oversimplification while arguing that sexuality has always been openly expressed throughout human history.

Patrick Carnes, considered by many to be an expert on sexual addiction, answers some common questions about this phenomenon, as featured on the Web site http://www.sexhelp.com/. Carnes discusses the nature of sexual addiction and ways in which it might be manifested, and offers suggestions for treatment. Sex therapist Lawrence Siegel and sex therapist/ educator Richard Siegel counter that sexual addiction is grounded in "moralistic ideology masquerading as science." They argue that although some sexual behaviors may be dysfunctional, the term "sexual addiction" pathologizes many common forms of sexual expression that are not problematic.

Connie Newman, an endocrinologist and adjunct associate professor of Medicine at New York University School of Medicine, explores the definitions and causes of sexual dysfunction and explains how sexual medicines can improve sexual response. Leonore Tiefer, author and clinical associate professor of psychiatry at New York University School of Medicine, counters that the rise of "sexual medicine" brings with it risks that should not be ignored.

Sexuality educator Rhonda Chittenden says that it is important for young people to expand their narrow definitions of sex and understand that oral sex *is* sex. Chittenden offers additional educational messages about oral sex. Sexuality trainer Nora Gelperin argues that adult definitions of oral sex are out of touch with the meaning the behavior holds for young people. Rather than impose adult definitions of intimacy, educators should be seeking to help young people clarify and understand their own values.

Sex educator Wayne Pawlowski provides an explanation of BDSM and describes it as a normal, healthy expression of sexuality. J. Paul Fedoroff describes BDSM as a disorder and a pathology and links BDSM to criminal activity.

UNIT 2 SEX AND SOCIETY 121

Susan Milstein, associate professor in the Health Department at Montgomery College and advisory board member for Men's Health Network, argues that while the legalization of prostitution will not stop all of the social problems associated with the institution, the benefits of legalization make it the best option. Donna Hughes, professor at the University of Rhode Island and leading international researcher on trafficking of women and children, counters that the criminalization of prostitution not only reduces demand, but also slows the spread of international sex trafficking.

Fuambai S. Ahmadu, associate professor at the University of Chicago, in an interview with Richard A. Shweder, argues that studies reporting traumatic effects of female circumcision have been greatly exaggerated and that opposition to the practice represents an ethnocentric bias among researchers and policy makers. The World Health Organization, the directing and coordinating authority for health within the United Nations system, details the common procedures and reasons for the practice of FGM, while arguing that the health risks and social implications deem the practice a violation of basic human rights.

The Human Rights Campaign (HRC), America's largest gay and lesbian organization, explains why same-sex couples should be afforded the same legal right to marry as heterosexual couples. Timothy J. Dailey, senior fellow for policy at the Family Research Council, argues that allowing same-sex marriage would go against thousands of years of human social norms and would be a "counterfeit" version of traditional, other-sex marriage.

Charalambos Siristatidis, an obstetrician, and Mark Hamilton, a gyneco-logist, advocate for restrictions on the number of embryos implanted during IVF, arguing the reduction of risk to mother and child. William Saletan, national correspondent for slate.com and author, acknowledges the risks of multiple embryo transfer but argues that any attempts to legislate the practice must consider women's reproductive autonomy.

Law professor John A. Robertson argues that preimplantation genetic diagnosis (PGD), a new technique that allows parents-to-be to determine the gender of their embryo before implantation in the uterus, should be permissible. Robertson argues that it is not sexist to want a baby of a particular sex and that the practice should not be restricted. Marcy Darnovsky, associate director of the Center for Genetics and Society, argues that by allowing PGD for sex selection, governments are starting down a slippery slope that could create an era of consumer eugenics.

Correlation Guide

The *Taking Sides* series presents current issues in a debate-style format designed to stimulate student interest and develop critical thinking skills. Each issue is thoughtfully framed with an issue summary, an issue introduction, and a postscript. The pro and con essays—selected for their liveliness and substance—represent the arguments of leading scholars and commentators in their fields.

Taking Sides: Clashing Views in Human Sexuality, 12/e is an easy-to-use reader that presents issues on important topics such as *sexual expression, sex and society,* and *sex and reproduction.* For more information on Taking Sides and other McGraw-Hill Contemporary Learning Series titles, visit www.mhcls.com.

This convenient guide matches the issues in **Taking Sides: Human Sexuality, 12/e** with the corresponding chapters in three of our best-selling McGraw-Hill Psychology textbooks by Hyde/DeLamater, Kelly, and Miller/Perlman.

Taking Sides: Human Sexuality, 12/e by Taverner/ McKee	Understanding Human Sexuality, 11/e by Hyde/ DeLamater	Sexuality Today, 10/e by Kelly	Intimate Relationships, 6/e by Miller/ Perlman
Issue 1: Is Sexting a Form of Safer Sex?	**Chapter 14:** Variations in Sexual Behavior **Chapter 19:** Ethics, Religion, and Sexuality	**Chapter 12:** Solitary Sex and Shared Sex **Chapter 16:** Sexual Consent, Coercion, Rape, and Abuse **Chapter 17:** Sexually Transmitted Diseases, HIV/AIDS, and Sexual Decisions	**Chapter 9:** Sexuality
Issue 2: Has Sex Become too Casual?	**Chapter 1:** Sexuality in Perspective **Chapter 10:** Sexuality and the Life Cycle: Adulthood **Chapter 11:** Attraction, Love, and Communication **Chapter 18:** Sexually Transmitted Infections	**Chapter 7:** Adult Sexuality and Relationships **Chapter 8:** Sexual Individuality and Sexual Values **Chapter 9:** Sexuality, Communication, and Relationships **Chapter 12:** Solitary Sex and Shared Sex **Chapter 14:** The Spectrum of Human Sexual Behavior **Chapter 17:** Sexually Transmitted Diseases, HIV/AIDS, and Sexual Decisions	**Chapter 1:** The Building Blocks of Relationships **Chapter 6:** Interdependency **Chapter 9:** Sexuality
Issue 3: Can Sex be Addictive?	**Chapter 4:** Sexual Anatomy **Chapter 8:** Sexual Arousal **Chapter 14:** Variations in Sexual Behavior **Chapter 15:** Sexual Coercion **Chapter 17:** Sexual Disorders and Sex Therapy	**Chapter 2:** Female Sexual Anatomy and Physiology **Chapter 3:** Male Sexual Anatomy and Physiology **Chapter 4:** Human Sexual Arousal and Response **Chapter 12:** Solitary Sex and Shared Sex **Chapter 14:** The Spectrum of Human Sexual Behavior **Chapter 16:** Sexual Consent, Coercion, Rape, and Abuse **Chapter 18:** Sexual Dysfunctions and Their Treatment	**Chapter 9:** Sexuality

(Continued)

Taking Sides: Human Sexuality, 12/e by Taverner/McKee	Understanding Human Sexuality, 11/e by Hyde/DeLamater	Sexuality Today, 10/e by Kelly	Intimate Relationships, 6/e by Miller/Perlman
Issue 4: Does Sexual Medicine Benefit Society?	**Chapter 7:** Contraception and Abortion Hormonal Methods **Chapter 17:** Sexual Disorders and Sex Therapy **Chapter 18:** Sexually Transmitted Infections	**Chapter 10:** Reproduction, Reproductive Technology, and Birthing **Chapter 11:** Decision Making about Pregnancy and Parenthood **Chapter 17:** Sexually Transmitted Diseases, HIV/AIDS, and Sexual Decisions **Chapter 18:** Sexual Dysfunctions and Their Treatment	
Issue 5: Is Oral Sex Really Sex?	**Chapter 8:** Sexual Arousal **Chapter 14:** Variations in Sexual Behavior **Chapter 19:** Ethics, Religion, and Sexuality	**Chapter 4:** Human Sexual Arousal and Response **Chapter 8:** Sexual Individuality and Sexual Values **Chapter 12:** Solitary Sex and Shared Sex **Chapter 14:** The Spectrum of Human Sexual Behavior	**Chapter 9:** Sexuality
Issue 6: Is BDSM a Healthy Form of Sexual Expression?	**Chapter 8:** Sexual Arousal **Chapter 14:** Variations in Sexual Behavior	**Chapter 4:** Human Sexual Arousal and Response **Chapter 8:** Sexual Individuality and Sexual Values **Chapter 14:** The Spectrum of Human Sexual Behavior **Chapter 16:** Sexual Consent, Coercion, Rape, and Abuse **Chapter 18:** Sexual Dysfunctions and Their Treatment	**Chapter 9:** Sexuality **Chapter 12:** Power and Violence
Issue 7: Is 'Gender Identity Disorder' an Appropriate Psychiatric Diagnosis?	**Chapter 5:** Sex Hormones, Sexual Differentiation, and the Menstrual Cycle **Chapter 9:** Sexuality and the Life Cycle: Childhood and Adolescence **Chapter 12:** Gender and Sexuality **Chapter 13:** Sexual Orientation: Gay, Straight, or Bi? **Chapter 14:** Variations in Sexual Behavior **Chapter 17:** Sexual Disorders and Sex Therapy	**Chapter 4:** Human Sexual Arousal and Response **Chapter 5:** Developmental and Social Perspectives on Gender **Chapter 6:** Sexuality in Infancy, Childhood, and Adolescence **Chapter 7:** Adult Sexuality and Relationships **Chapter 8:** Sexual Individuality and Sexual Values **Chapter 13:** Same-Gender Orientation and Behavior **Chapter 14:** The Spectrum of Human Sexual Behavior **Chapter 18:** Sexual Dysfunctions and Their Treatment	**Chapter 1:** The Building Blocks of Relationships **Chapter 9:** Sexuality

Taking Sides: Human Sexuality, 12/e by Taverner/ McKee	Understanding Human Sexuality, 11/e by Hyde/ DeLamater	Sexuality Today, 10/e by Kelly	Intimate Relationships, 6/e by Miller/ Perlman
Issue 8: Should Sex Ed Teach about Abstinence?	**Chapter 6:** Conception, Pregnancy, and Childbirth Conception **Chapter 7:** Contraception and Abortion Hormonal Methods **Chapter 9:** Sexuality and the Life Cycle: Childhood and Adolescence **Chapter 18:** Sexually Transmitted Infections	**Chapter 6:** Sexuality in Infancy, Childhood, and Adolescence **Chapter 8:** Sexual Individuality and Sexual Values **Chapter 10:** Reproduction, Reproductive Technology, and Birthing **Chapter 11:** Decision Making about Pregnancy and Parenthood **Chapter 16:** Sexual Consent, Coercion, Rape, and Abuse **Chapter 17:** Sexually Transmitted Diseases, HIV/AIDS, and Sexual Decisions	
Issue 9: Is There Something Wrong with the Content of Comprehensive Sex Education Curricula?	**Chapter 6:** Conception, Pregnancy, and Childbirth Conception **Chapter 7:** Contraception and Abortion Hormonal Methods **Chapter 18:** Sexually Transmitted Infections	**Chapter 10:** Reproduction, Reproductive Technology, and Birthing **Chapter 11:** Decision Making about Pregnancy and Parenthood **Chapter 16:** Sexual Consent, Coercion, Rape, and Abuse **Chapter 17:** Sexually Transmitted Diseases, HIV/AIDS, and Sexual Decisions	
Issue 10: Is There Academic Merit to Students Viewing Live Sexual Acts in College Courses?	**Chapter 1:** Sexuality in Perspective **Chapter 3:** Sex Research **Chapter 19:** Ethics, Religion, and Sexuality	**Chapter 1:** Cultural, Historical, and Research Perspectives on Sexuality **Chapter 15:** Sex, Art, the Media, and the Law	**Chapter 9:** Sexuality
Issue 11: Should Libraries and Other Places That Provide Public Wi Fi Restrict the Sexual Content?	**Chapter 1:** Sexuality in Perspective **Chapter 14:** Variations in Sexual Behavior **Chapter 15:** Sexual Coercion **Chapter 16:** Sex for Sale **Chapter 19:** Ethics, Religion, and Sexuality **Chapter 20:** Sex and the Law	**Chapter 1:** Cultural, Historical, and Research Perspectives on Sexuality **Chapter 15:** Sex, Art, the Media, and the Law **Chapter 16:** Sexual Consent, Coercion, Rape, and Abuse	

(Continued)

Taking Sides: Human Sexuality, 12/e by Taverner/ McKee	Understanding Human Sexuality, 11/e by Hyde/ DeLamater	Sexuality Today, 10/e by Kelly	Intimate Relationships, 6/e by Miller/ Perlman
Issue 12: Is Pornography Harmful?	**Chapter 1:** Sexuality in Perspective **Chapter 3:** Sex Research **Chapter 14:** Variations in Sexual Behavior **Chapter 16:** Sex for Sale **Chapter 19:** Ethics, Religion, and Sexuality **Chapter 20:** Sex and the Law	**Chapter 1:** Cultural, Historical, and Research Perspectives on Sexuality **Chapter 4:** Human Sexual Arousal and Response **Chapter 8:** Sexual Individuality and Sexual Values **Chapter 12:** Solitary Sex and Shared Sex **Chapter 15:** Sex, Art, the Media, and the Law	**Chapter 9:** Sexuality
Issue 13: Should Prostitution be Legalized?	**Chapter 10:** Sexuality and the Life Cycle: Adulthood **Chapter 16:** Sex for Sale **Chapter 19:** Ethics, Religion, and Sexuality **Chapter 20:** Sex and the Law	**Chapter 7:** Adult Sexuality and Relationships **Chapter 8:** Sexual Individuality and Sexual Values **Chapter 15:** Sex, Art, the Media, and the Law **Chapter 16:** Sexual Consent, Coercion, Rape, and Abuse **Chapter 17:** Sexually Transmitted Diseases, HIV/AIDS, and Sexual Decisions	**Chapter 9:** Sexuality
Issue 14: Is Female Circumcision/FGM an Acceptable Practice?	**Chapter 1:** Sexuality in Perspective **Chapter 4:** Sexual Anatomy **Chapter 8:** Sexual Arousal **Chapter 9:** Sexuality and the Life Cycle: Childhood and Adolescence **Chapter 10:** Sexuality and the Life Cycle: Adulthood **Chapter 12:** Gender and Sexuality **Chapter 19:** Ethics, Religion, and Sexuality	**Chapter 1:** Cultural, Historical, and Research Perspectives on Sexuality **Chapter 2:** Female Sexual Anatomy and Physiology **Chapter 4:** Human Sexual Arousal and Response **Chapter 5:** Developmental and Social Perspectives on Gender **Chapter 6:** Sexuality in Infancy, Childhood, and Adolescence **Chapter 7:** Adult Sexuality and Relationships **Chapter 16:** Sexual Consent, Coercion, Rape, and Abuse	**Chapter 9:** Sexuality **Chapter 12:** Power and Violence

Taking Sides: Human Sexuality, 12/e by Taverner/ McKee	Understanding Human Sexuality, 11/e by Hyde/ DeLamater	Sexuality Today, 10/e by Kelly	Intimate Relationships, 6/e by Miller/ Perlman
Issue 15: Should Same Sex-Marriage Be Legal?	**Chapter 1:** Sexuality in Perspective **Chapter 2:** Theoretical Perspectives on Sexuality **Chapter 12:** Gender and Sexuality **Chapter 13:** Sexual Orientation: Gay, Straight, or Bi? **Chapter 14:** Variations in Sexual Behavior **Chapter 19:** Ethics, Religion, and Sexuality **Chapter 20:** Sex and the Law	**Chapter 1:** Cultural, Historical, and Research Perspectives on Sexuality **Chapter 7:** Adult Sexuality and Relationships **Chapter 8:** Sexual Individuality and Sexual Values **Chapter 13:** Same-Gender Orientation and Behavior **Chapter 15:** Sex, Art, the Media and the Law	**Chapter 1:** The Building Blocks of Relationships **Chapter 3:** Attraction **Chapter 8:** Love **Chapter 9:** Sexuality
Issue 16: Do Reality TV Shows Portray Responsible Messages about Teen Pregnancy?	**Chapter 1:** Sexuality in Perspective **Chapter 7:** Contraception and Abortion Hormonal Methods **Chapter 9:** Sexuality and the Life Cycle: Childhood and Adolescence	**Chapter 6:** Sexuality in Infancy, Childhood, and Adolescence **Chapter 10:** Reproduction, Reproductive Technology, and Birthing **Chapter 11:** Decision Making about Pregnancy and Parenthood **Chapter 15:** Sex, Art, the Media and the Law	
Issue 17: Should Pharmacists Have the Right to Refuse Contraceptive Prescriptions?	**Chapter 6:** Conception, Pregnancy, and Childbirth Conception **Chapter 7:** Contraception and Abortion Hormonal Methods **Chapter 19:** Ethics, Religion, and Sexuality	**Chapter 10:** Reproduction, Reproductive Technology, and Birthing **Chapter 11:** Decision Making about Pregnancy and Parenthood	
Issue 18: Is Abortion Moral?	**Chapter 7:** Contraception and Abortion Hormonal Methods **Chapter 19:** Ethics, Religion, and Sexuality	**Chapter 10:** Reproduction, Reproductive Technology, and Birthing **Chapter 11:** Decision Making about Pregnancy and Parenthood **Chapter 16:** Sexual Consent, Coercion, Rape, and Abuse	

(Continued)

Taking Sides: Human Sexuality, 12/e by Taverner/McKee	Understanding Human Sexuality, 11/e by Hyde/DeLamater	Sexuality Today, 10/e by Kelly	Intimate Relationships, 6/e by Miller/Perlman
Issue 19: Should There Be Restrictions on the Number of Embryos Implanted during In-Vitro Fertilization?	**Chapter 6:** Conception, Pregnancy, and Childbirth Conception **Chapter 7:** Contraception and Abortion Hormonal Methods **Chapter 19:** Ethics, Religion, and Sexuality	**Chapter 10:** Reproduction, Reproductive Technology, and Birthing **Chapter 11:** Decision Making about Pregnancy and Parenthood **Chapter 18:** Sexual Dysfunctions and Their Treatment	
Issue 20: Should Parents Be Allowed to Select the Sex of Their Baby?	**Chapter 6:** Conception, Pregnancy, and Childbirth Conception **Chapter 19:** Ethics, Religion, and Sexuality	**Chapter 10:** Reproduction, Reproductive Technology, and Birthing **Chapter 11:** Decision Making about Pregnancy and Parenthood	

Topics Guide

This topic guide suggests how the selections in this book relate to the subjects covered in your course. You may want to use the topics listed on these pages to search the Web more easily. On the following pages a number of websites have been gathered specifically for this book. They are arranged to reflect the units of this *Taking Sides* reader. You can link to these sites by going to http://www.mhhe.com/cls. **All the articles that relate to each topic are listed below the bold-faced term.**

Abortion

17. Should Pharmacists Have the Right to Refuse Contraceptive Prescriptions?
18. Is Abortion Moral?

Adulthood, Later

 5. Is Oral Sex Really Sex?
12. Is Pornography Harmful?
15. Should Same-Sex Marriages Be Legal?
16. Do Reality TV Shows Portray Responsible Messages about Teen Pregnancy?
17. Should Pharmacists Have the Right to Refuse Contraceptive Prescriptions?
18. Is Abortion Moral?
19. Should There Be Restrictions on the Number of Embryos Transferred during In-Vitro Fertilization?

Adulthood, Middle

 5. Is Oral Sex Really Sex?
12. Is Pornography Harmful?
15. Should Same-Sex Marriages Be Legal?
16. Do Reality TV Shows Portray Responsible Messages about Teen Pregnancy?
17. Should Pharmacists Have the Right to Refuse Contraceptive Prescriptions?
18. Is Abortion Moral?
19. Should There Be Restrictions on the Number of Embryos Transferred during In-Vitro Fertilization?

Adulthood, Young

 2. Has Sex Become Too Casual?
 5. Is Oral Sex Really Sex?

 9. Is There Something Wrong with the Content of Comprehensive Sex Education Curricula?
 8. Should Sex Ed Teach about Abstinence?
16. Do Reality TV Shows Portray Responsible Messages about Teen Pregnancy?
17. Should Pharmacists Have the Right to Refuse Contraceptive Prescriptions?
18. Is Abortion Moral?

Contraception

17. Should Pharmacists Have the Right to Refuse Contraceptive Prescriptions?
18. Is Abortion Moral?

Culture

 1. Is Sexting a Form of Safer Sex?
 2. Has Sex Become Too Casual?
 9. Is There Something Wrong with the Content of Comprehensive Sex Education Curricula?
10. Is There Academic Merit to Students Viewing Live Sexual Acts in College Courses?
12. Is Pornography Harmful?
14. Is Female Circumcision/FGM an Acceptable Practice?
16. Do Reality TV Shows Portray Responsible Messages about Teen Pregnancy?

Desire

 3. Can Sex Be Addictive?
 6. Is BDSM a Healthy Form of Sexual Expression?
12. Is Pornography Harmful?

(Continued)

Reproduction

Sex Education

Sexual Dysfunctions and Treatments

Technology

Transgender/Transsexual Identities

Introduction

Sexual Attitudes in Perspective

To many, America can seem like one seriously divided country, with a blue northern and coastal perimeter and a bright red center! On television and in print media, this is the overly simplified caricature of American politics and social attitudes. Are you from a *red state*, perhaps Utah, or maybe Texas? Then surely you supported the GOP in the most recent elections. You also oppose abortion and same-sex marriage, and you probably love hunting and NASCAR. Are you from a *blue state,* perhaps California, or maybe Massachusetts? Then surely you are a Democrat who votes the party line every chance you get. You support a woman's right to choose, are a staunch supporter of civil rights, and maybe have plans to attend a friend's same-sex wedding. Oh, and you are also a vegan who bikes to work to reduce greenhouse gas emissions!

If you are scratching your head thinking that neither profile describes you, you are not alone. Texas and Utah may be "red states," but how do we reconcile the fact that millions of Americans in these two states vote for democrats in general elections? Or that millions of other people voted for in favor of conservative candidates in the "blue state" of California? Moreover, what about voters in the so-called "swing states," who have the power to sway elections in favor of one party or the other from term to term? And what do we know about those who choose not to vote? It is an important question as these nonvoters make up nearly 100 million Americans! The reality is that our opinions, attitudes, and values on social and sexual issues are as diverse as we are. They are formed by numerous factors that we will explore in this *Introduction*.

As you examine the 20 controversial issues in human sexuality in this volume, you will find yourself unavoidably encountering the values you have absorbed from your society, your ethnic background, your religious heritage and traditions, and your personal experiences. Because these values will influence your decisions, often without being consciously recognized, it is important to actively think about the role these undercurrent themes play in the positions you take on these issues.

How Social and Ethnic Factors Influence Our Values

American society is not homogeneous, nor is it even red or blue! People who grow up in rural, suburban, and large urban environments sometimes have subtle differences in their values and attitudes when it comes to gender roles, marriage, and sexuality, or trends that may reflect the views of the majority of people in communities. Growing up in different areas of the United States can influence one's views of sex, marriage, and family. This is also true for men and women who were born or raised, in another country and culture.

Many researchers have found that values can be affected by one's family income level and socioeconomic status. Researchers have also indicated that one's occupation, educational level, and income are closely related to one's values, attitudes, sex role conceptions, child-rearing practices, and sexual identity. Our values and attitudes about sex are also influenced by whether we are brought up in a rural, suburban, or large urban environment. Our ethnic background can also be an important influence on our values and attitudes.

An example of differing ethnic values is the issue of single motherhood. In ethnic groups with a strong tradition of extended matrilineal families, the concept of an "illegitimate" child born "out-of-wedlock" may not even exist. Unmarried mothers in these cultures do not carry the same stigma often associated with single mothers in other, less matrilineal cultures. When "outsiders" who do not share the particular ethnic values of a culture enter into such a subculture, they often cannot understand why contraception and sexuality education programs do not produce any substantial change in attitudes. They overlook the basic social scripting that has already taken place. Gender roles also vary from culture to culture. Muslim men and women who grow up in certain parts of the Middle East and then emigrate to the United States have to adapt to the much greater freedom women have in the United States. Similarly, American men and women who have served in the armed forces in Afghanistan, Iraq, Saudi Arabia, and other parts of the Middle East found they had to adapt to very different Muslim cultures that put many restrictions on the movement and dress of women in the military.

A boy who grows up among the East Bay Melanesians in the Southwestern Pacific is taught to avoid any social contact with girls from the age of three or four, even though he may run around naked and masturbate in public. Adolescent Melanesian boys and girls are not allowed to have sex with each other, but boys are expected to have sex both with an older male and with a boy of his own age. Their first heterosexual experiences come with marriage. In the Cook Islands, Mangaian boys are expected to have sex with many girls after an older woman teaches them about the art of sexual play. Mangaians also accept and expect both premarital and extramarital sex. These are all examples of differing cultural attitudes toward sexual norms. Although these norms may seem peculiar to many Americans, it is important to consider that American norms may seem just as strange to those in other societies.

But one does not have to look to exotic anthropological studies to find evidence of the importance of ethnic values. Even within the United States, one can find subtle but important differences in sexual attitudes and values among the diverse population of its native people, and of those who immigrated from all over the world.

Religious Factors in Attitudes toward Sex

In the Middle Ages, Christian theologians divided sexual behaviors into two categories: behaviors that were "natural" and those that were "unnatural." Since they believed that the natural function and goal of all sexual behavior and relations was reproduction, masturbation was unnatural because it frustrated the natural goal of conception and continuance of the species. Rape certainly was considered illicit because it was not within the marital bond, but since it was procreative, rape was also considered a "natural" use of sex. The same system of distinction was applied to other sexual relations and behaviors. Premarital sex, adultery, and incest were "natural" uses of sexuality, while oral sex, anal sex, and contraception were "unnatural." Homosexual relations were both illicit and unnatural. These religious values were based on the view that God created man and woman at the beginning of time and laid down certain rules and guidelines for sexual behavior and relations. This view is still very influential in our culture, even for those who are not active in any religious tradition.

In recent years, several analysts have highlighted two philosophical or religious perspectives that appear throughout Judeo-Christian tradition and Western civilization. These perspectives have been synthesized into a model proposed by Dr. Robert T. Francoeur, coeditor of the *International Encyclopedia of Sexuality*. Understanding these two perspectives, or "worldviews," is important in any attempt to debate controversial issues in human sexuality.

Two Major Sexual Value Systems

Fixed or Absolutist World View

- Sexuality is basically an animal passion and must be controlled.
- The main goal of sex is marriage and reproduction. Sex is only acceptable in heterosexual marriages.
- Masturbation, oral sex, anal sex, and other nongenital sex all impede God's purpose for sex. They are forbidden.
- Same-sex relationships are forbidden.
- Gender roles are strictly defined and the male is superior in relationships.
- The emphasis of sex should be on genital acts.

Process or Relativist World View

- Sexuality is a natural and positive life force with both sensual and spiritual aspects.
- Pleasure, love, and celebration of life are goals in themselves. Sex does not have to be confined to marriage.
- The purpose of sex is to celebrate life; masturbation, oral sex, anal sex, and other nongenital sex can express the celebratory and communal nature of sex.
- Same-sex relationships are accepted.
- Gender roles are equal and flexible.
- The emphasis should be on people and their relationships, rather than on what they do sexually.

Adapted from a summary of the work of sexologist and biologist Robert T. Francoeur by Linda L. Hendrixson.

Judeo-Christian tradition allows us to examine two distinct worldviews, the *fixed worldview* and the *process worldview*. The fixed worldview says that morality is unchanging. Right and wrong are always right and wrong, regardless of the situation or circumstances. The fixed worldview relies on a literal interpretation of its religious or ethical teachings, without regard for context. The process worldview examines issues of morality in an ever-changing world. What is right or wrong may require a contextual examination, and rules and ethics must constantly be reexamined in light of new information and the world's evolving context.

Take for example the question of masturbation. Where does the Christian prohibition of masturbation come from? If you search the words of the Bible (the wonderful Web site www.biblegateway.com allows for such searches), you will discover that the words "masturbate" and "masturbation" are never mentioned! Yet, much of what has been taught in Christianity regarding masturbation comes from the story of Onan:

> Then Judah said to Onan, "Go in to your brother's wife and perform the duty of a brother-in-law to her, and raise up offspring for your brother." But Onan knew that the offspring would not be his. So whenever he went in to his brother's wife he would waste the semen on the ground, so as not to give offspring to his brother. And what he did was wicked in the sight of the Lord, and he put him to death also.
>
> Genesis 38:8–10, English Version

Many theologians point to this passage as evidence for a masturbation prohibition. The passage describes how Judah asked his brother Onan to help him to bear a child, and how Onan had sexual intercourse with his sister-in-law, but "waste[ed] his semen on the ground." This phrase has been interpreted literally by fundamentalist Christians to say that semen must never be wasted, that is, no masturbation. Indeed, Catholic theologians in the middle ages even examined whether or not sperm cells had souls! This interpretation led to prohibitions on masturbation and other sexual behaviors that do not produce pregnancy. The fixed worldview is that God did not want any semen wasted—what Onan did was "wicked," and so masturbation will always be wicked.

Process worldview Christians may read the same passage differently. They might ask, "What was the thing Onan did that was 'wicked in the sight of the Lord'?" Was God condemning the wasting of semen? Or was God angry at Onan's selfishness—or disobedience—with his intentional failure to produce a child for his brother, as was his traditional obligation at the time? A process worldview Christian might also point out that even if the passage is to be interpreted as a masturbation prohibition because of the spilling of one's seed, the passage says nothing about female masturbation, which involves no release of any seed. Is female masturbation therefore permissible?

This example only serves to illustrate only two possible values related to the sometimes controversial issue of masturbation. It may be tempting to stop there and look only at two perspectives, but consider that there are many other reasons people may support or oppose masturbation. The ancient Chinese Tao of love and sex advises that semen should be ejaculated very rarely, for reasons related to mental and physical (not moral) health. Masturbation aside, the Tao advises that males should only ejaculate one time per every 100 acts of intercourse, so that female—not male—pleasure is maximized! Another position on masturbation may be its functionality, as viewed by sex therapists, for treating sexual dysfunction. Another perspective is to evaluate the morality of masturbation on whether or not it causes physical harm. Since masturbation—a very common behavior, from birth to death—causes no physical harm, it might be regarded as a healthy sexual alternative to other behaviors that may be dishonest or exploitative. There are many perspectives on this one topic, and there are similarly many perspectives beyond the two articles presented for every issue in this book.

Consider a non-Western, non-Christian example from recent history: the Islamic cultures of the Middle East and the politics of Islamic fundamentalists. On the fixed worldview side are fundamentalist Muslims who believe that the Muslim world needs to return to the unchanging, literal words of Mohammed and the Koran (the sacred book of the teachings of Allah, or God). Again, there is no gray area in a fixed worldview—what Allah revealed through Mohammed is forever the truth, and the words of the Koran must be taken as literally as the day they were first recorded. There is no room for mitigating factors or new or unique circumstances that may arise.

On the other side are Muslims who view the world through a process worldview—an ever-changing scene in which they must struggle to reinterpret and apply the basic principles of the Koran to new situations. They consider as progress the new rights that some Muslim women have earned in recent years, such as the right to education, the right to vote, the right to election of political office, the right to divorce their husbands, the right to contraception, and many other rights.

The fixed and process worldviews are evident throughout the history of American culture. Religious fundamentalists believe that Americans need to return to traditional values. This worldview often shares a conviction that the sexual revolution, changing attitudes toward masturbation and homosexuality, a tolerance of premarital and extramarital sex, sexuality education in the schools, and the legality of abortion are contributing to a cultural decline and must be rejected.

At the same time, other Americans argue for legalized abortion; civil rights for gays, lesbians, and transgender individuals; and the decriminalization of prostitution. For a time, the process worldview gained dominance in Western cultures, but renewed influences of such fixed world groups as the Moral Majority and Tea Party have manifested in the recent elections of conservative and other fundamentalist politicians.

The two worldviews described here characteristically permeate and color the way we look at and see everything in our lives. One or the other view will influence the way we approach a particular political, economic, or moral issue and the way we reach decisions about sexual issues and relationships. However, one must keep in mind that no one is ever fully and always on one or the other end of the spectrum. The spectrum of beliefs, attitudes, and values proposed here is an intellectual abstraction. Real life is not that simple. You may find yourself holding fixed worldviews on some issues and process worldviews on others. Your views may represent neither worldview. Just like there are no pure blue and red states, there are no absolutes when it comes to sexual values. There is a continuum of values, with the fixed worldview on one end, and the process worldview on the other. Your sexual values for each issue presented in this text will likely depend on the issue, your personal experiences with the subject matter, and the values and beliefs that you have accumulated by important sources within your own life.

Personal connection with an issue may be a strong indicator of one's sexual values. If you are among the millions of Americans who have had a sexually transmitted infection, that firsthand experience will likely affect what you believe about condom availability programs or sexuality education. If a family member whom you love and respect taught you that pornography is wrong, it may be difficult for you to accept the proposition that it is not harmful. As we are all sexual beings, so many of the issues presented here provide an opportunity for a personal connection to an issue beyond a simple academic exercise.

As you plunge into the 20 controversial issues selected for this volume, try to be aware of your own predispositions toward certain topics and try to be sensitive to the kinds of ethnic, religious, social, economic, and other factors that may be influencing the position a particular author takes on an issue. Understanding the roots that support a person's overt position on an issue will help you to decide whether or not you agree with that position. Take time to read a little bit about the authors' biographies, too, as their affiliations may reveal something about their potential biases. Understanding these same factors in your own thinking will help you to articulate more clearly and convincingly your own values and decisions.

Many thanks to Robert T. Francoeur for his insights on this Introduction, parts of which are repeated from previous editions of Taking Sides when Francoeur was editor.

Internet References . . .

That's Not Cool

That's Not Cool is a joint effort of the Family Violence Prevention Fund, the Department of Justice's Office on Violence Against Women, and the Advertising Council. It aims to prevent teen dating abuse by understanding digital and online boundaries.

http://www.thatsnotcool.com

SexHelp.com

This Web site showcases resources championed by Patrick J. Carnes, authority on sexual addiction, and provides links for further reading, self-assessments, discussion forums, and more.

http://www.sexhelp.com/

Sexual Intelligence

Sexual Intelligence provides information and commentary on contemporary sexual issues, written by sex therapist Dr. Marty Klein.

http://www.sexualintelligence.org

National Coalition for Sexual Freedom

A resource that provides information about psychotherapeutic, medical, and legal services from "kink-aware" professionals.

www.ncsfreedom.org

The Gender Identity Project

Started by The Lesbian, Gay, Bisexual and Transgender Community Center in NYC, the Gender Identity Project supports transgender and gender non-comforming individuals in the NY area and beyond.

http://www.gaycenter.org/gip

Go Ask Alice!

Go Ask Alice is the health question and answer Internet service produced by Columbia University's Health Promotion program. The service provides reliable, accessible information about health, including sexuality, sexual health, and relationships.

www.goaskalice.columbia.edu

FSD Alert

FSD Alert is an educational campaign that challenges myths promoted by the pharmaceutical industry and calls for research on the causes of women's sexual problems. Visitors will find developing information on Intrinsa at this Web site.

http://www.fsd-alert.org

International Society for Sexual Medicine

Established In 1982 to promote erectile dysfunction research, the ISSM today encourages research and education across a broad spectrum of human sexual functioning. The ISSM publishes the *Journal of Sexual Medicine*.

www.issm.info

Understanding Sexual Expression

Robert T. Francoeur, author of the Complete Dictionary of Sexology, calls sexuality a "bio-psycho-socio and cultural phenomenon." Humans are sexual beings from birth through death, and our sexuality is shaped by our physical makeup (biological), our thoughts, feelings, and perceptions of our sexuality (psychological), and the way we interact with our environment (sociological and cultural). In many ways, sexuality may be as subjective as the individual who expresses it.

Defining "sex" is no more universal. One of our favorite classroom activities is to ask students to take out their cell phones, call or text a few friends and family members, and ask them what "sex" means. The varied responses illustrate the many different viewpoints people have about the nature of sex.

This unit examines the very nature of sex by presenting debates on issues related to sexual definitions, how we understand sexual behavior, and how sexual problems are addressed.

- Is Sexting a Form of Safer Sex?
- Has Sex Become Too Casual?
- Can Sex Be Addictive?
- Does Sexual Medicine Benefit Society?
- Is Oral Sex Really Sex?
- Is BDSM a Healthy Form of Sexual Expression?
- Is "Gender Identity Disorder" an Appropriate Psychiatric Diagnosis?

ISSUE 1

Is Sexting a Form of Safer Sex?

YES: Brent A. Satterly, from "Sexting, Not Infecting: A Sexological Perspective of Sexting as Safer Sex," an original essay written for this volume (2011)

NO: Donald A. Dyson, from "Tweet This: Sexting Is NOT Safer Sex," an original essay written for this volume (2011)

ISSUE SUMMARY

YES: Brent Satterly, Professor and Program Director at Widener University's Center for Social Work Education, acknowledges the risks involved in sexting while criticizing fear-based media coverage of the phenomenon. He argues in favor of harm-reduction strategies to reduce the risks associated with sexting rather than continuing the trend of panicked reactions to the expression of youth sexuality.

NO: Donald Dyson, Associate Professor and Director of Doctoral Studies in the Center for Education at Widener University, examines sexting through the lens of the World Health Organization's definition of sexual health and determines that the risks inherent in the digital transmission of sext messages is not a form of safer sex.

The rise in cell phone usage, as well as the increased quality of cameras installed in the devices, has given rise to a new outlet for sexual expression—sexting. Sexting is the nickname given to the sending of sexual messages or pictures via text message. Although teens engaging in steamy conversations is nothing new, the ability to send, receive, and forward messages and images in an instant presents parents and authorities with new challenges in regard to the understanding and managing of adolescent sexuality. Media coverage of the phenomenon highlighted the perceived harm done to young victims of the sexting trend. Over the past several years, scandals involving underage teens snapping and sending nude pictures of themselves have resulted in child pornography charges being filed against teens in several areas across the United States. In other cases, shared images or messages have been used to bully or embarrass the sender. Media scrutiny, with headlines like "Girl, 15, Faces Porn Charges for Sexting" (CBSnews.com, 2009) and "Think Your Kid Isn't Sexting? Think Again" (Quaid, 2009), has led many to feel that sexting has reached epidemic levels.

Research into sexting, however, tells a different story. A 2009 Pew Research study found that, while some young people text nude and seminude images for a variety of reasons, only 4 percent have actually sent an image of themselves to someone they know. Only 15 percent of young people report having received such an image via text (Lenhart, 2009). Another research on sexting, which looked at text messages as well as additional means of image sharing including e-mail and services like Facebook, found only slightly higher percentages of young people participation (Associated Press & MTV, 2009; National Campaign to Prevent Teen and Unplanned Pregnancy & Cosmo Girl, 2008). These statistics present a different story than the sensational headlines and media coverage of the topic.

The controversy has presented sexologists an opportunity to question the "sext-panic" that has clouded the dialogue around sexting and examine what place, if any, the behavior has in sexuality education, and if sexting could be a form of safer sex. In the following essays, two professors from Widener University's Center for Education do just that. Brent Satterly argues that while sexting does not carry the same risks as exchanging bodily fluids, similar harm-reduction strategies applied to physical behaviors can reduce the risks involved in sexting and translate into dialogue and opportunities that will assist teens in navigating sexual scenarios in the future. Donald Dyson applies the definition of "healthy sexuality" developed by the World Health Organization to sexting and finds that qualities inherent in the behavior dictate that it is, in fact, unhealthy and therefore cannot be considered a form of safer sex.

References

Associated Press & MTV, "A thin line: 2009 AP-MTV Digital Abuse Study," accessed at http://www.athinline.org/MTV-AP_Digital_Abuse_Study_Executive_Summary.pdf (2009).

CBSnews.com, "Girl, 15, Faces Porn Charges for Sexting," accessed at http://www.cbsnews.com/stories/2009/02/20/national/main4816266.shtml (February 20, 2009).

A. Lenhart, "Teens and Sexting," accessed at http://www.pewinternet.org/~/media//Files/Reports/2009/PIP_Teens_and_Sexting.pdf (2009).

National Campaign to Prevent Teen and Unplanned Pregnancy & Cosmo Girl, "Sex and Tech: Results from a Survey of Teens and Young Adults," accessed at http://www.thenationalcampaign.org/sextech/PDF/SexTech_Summary.pdf (2008).

L. Quaid, "Think Your Kid Isn't Sexting? Think Again", accessed at http://www.msnbc.msn.com/id/34257556/ns/technology_and_science-tech_and_gadgets/ (December 3, 2009).

YES

Brent A. Satterly

Sexting, Not Infecting:
A Sexological Perspective
of Sexting as Safer Sex

According to the Pew Research Center (2009), the use of cell phones to text has become a primary mode of communication among adolescents. Over the course of the last few years, there has been a growing concern over how adolescents are using their texting capabilities around sexual expression. Sexting, the infamous phenomenon where individuals—usually assumed to be adolescents—share naked or partially naked pictures (a.ka. "pics") or sexually explicit conversations with others, is often touted as a severely dangerous practice that can have far reaching negative outcomes for those who do so. The question of whether or not this practice is "safer sex" simply because it doesn't involve the exchange of bodily fluids is a misnomer. I would posit that it is indeed safe sex [not only] for that reason, but also because parents, educators, and public health officials can teach adolescents about how to reduce the potentially negative risks that sexting may involve.

Incidence

This practice has received wide public "sex-panic" oriented media coverage primarily focusing on adolescents (White, 2009). While this "kids these days" approach conveniently neglects to include the wide numbers of adults who engage in the same behavior, it still remains, however, primarily considered an adolescent phenomenon. The Pew Research Center conducted a 2009 survey citing that:

- 4% of 12–17 year olds who own cell phones have sent nude photos of themselves to someone;
- 15% of 12–17 year olds who own cell phones have received nude photos of someone;
- 8% of 17-year-olds who own cell phones have sent nude photos of themselves;
- 30% of 17-year-olds who own cell phones have received nude photos of someone.

Additionally, a MTV-Associated Press poll found that 1 out of 10 young adults between 14 and 24 have at some point shared nude photos of themselves with others (2009). Whether one considers a 24-year-old as an adolescent is another question entirely.

Is Sexting New?

"There's nothing new about using technology to get sex" (Joannides, 2009, p. 393). Sharing naked pictures or having sexually explicit conversations with others is not a new practice (Joannides, 2009). From naked Polaroids to dirty love letters to phone sex to lustful emails to dirty instant messaging, cell phones have made sexually explicit exchanges more accessible with their prominence (White, 2009).

Potential Negative Outcomes of Sexting?

Regardless of history and the populations who practice this behavior, there are potential negative outcomes for the sender based upon what the recipients of such photos or explicit texts do with it. In the immediate, this may include the public exposure of a nude picture by an angry ex who decides to send the picture to a number of other friends or post it online in an effort to humiliate the original sender. It can also have unintended legal consequences where the sender and/or receiver can be charged with various illegalities, including distribution or possession of child pornography and/or registration as a sex offender depending on state law (Ostrager, 2010).

For example, in the state of Pennsylvania, 17 students were threatened with being charged with child pornography possession or dissemination as a result of sending or receiving nude pictures of two female adolescents (Sexting Girls Facing Porn Charge Sue D.A.). The families of the two female teens countersued the local district attorney stating that since the pictures were distributed with their consent, they could not be charged accordingly. The potential far-reaching effects of this are evident.

While all of this is true, it nevertheless reinforces the quest to control American teen sexuality. Since this "sex-panic" effort to legislate and eliminate teen sexuality is fueled by such frightening incidents as the one previously mentioned, often parents or caregivers recount them as evidence for renewed efforts to squash teenage sexual expression. While this sex-panic bleeds over into how adult sexuality is viewed, ultimately the fear is for children. "Because not only are adults increasingly treated as children—incapable, where sex is concerned, of thinking with anything more elevated than their genitals: but the touchstone for policy in an adult world is increasingly 'what would happen if children got hold of this?'" (Fae, 2011, para. 6). A parental blog from America OnLine exemplifies such fear:

> The intention doesn't matter—even if a photo was taken and sent as a token of love, for example, the technology makes it possible for everyone to see your child's most intimate self. In the hands of teens, when

revealing photos are made public, the subject almost always ends up feeling humiliated. Furthermore, sending sexual images to minors is against the law, and some states have begun prosecuting kids for child pornography or felony obscenity. There have been some high profile cases of sexting. (*Parentdish*, 2009, para 1.)

While one may assume that parents' desire here is to protect their adolescent, the result is the same as touting the fear-based abstinence-only message of sexuality education. "Just don't do it because bad things will happen to you" is an insufficient message for teens for behavior change.

Christopher White (2009) addresses such media-based sex-panic of sexting as blaming the victim. He reframes this fear-based reactivity as finger-pointing resulting in further harm:

Sending photos out to friends and family members or posting them online without the consent of the other person is an assault on that individual in an attempt to cause them great harm and suffering and is where we should be focusing our greatest efforts at stopping a behavior, if that is the action most needed. Instead, certain groups are pointing their finger at the person whose photo was distributed without her permission and putting the blame on the victim. (2009, para. 3)

We cannot control adolescents; rather, we must understand adolescents and help adolescents understand themselves. Hence, the efforts public health officials and sexologists should be centered around is a developmentally-appropriate comprehensive sexuality education approach starting from very young. Again, White (2009) poses a poignant solution by encouraging us to redirect our efforts toward working with adolescents around decision-making to safe-guard themselves:

Rather than focusing on how harmful and dangerous sexting is, we should be talking to young people about healthy sexual behaviors including the difference between consensual and nonconsensual acts. We should provide them with the truth about possible unintentional consequences and issues related to trust and dating in relationships. (2009, para. 5)

Is Sexting a Form of Safer Sex?

To frame sexting as a form of safer sex is a misleading question. Sexting, in and of itself, does not necessitate an exchange of bodily fluids. It is a digital exchange of pics and/or texts. The Pew Research Center states that sexting usually occurs within the context of three scenarios: (1) between romantic partners; (2) between partners that share the pics outside of the relationship, and (3) between individuals who aren't in relationship, but would like to be. Each context here carries its own risk of potential exploitation or harm, just as any kind of sexual behavior with another person carries a certain degree of risk, depending upon the variables. Many a sexuality educator has uttered the standard phrase, "What is the only 100% risk-free way to not get pregnant or [to not] get a sexually-transmitted infection?" The only acceptable answer is, of course, abstinence.

The same logic holds true for sexting. If an adolescent simply doesn't engage in the behavior, he or she is subsequently abstaining from sexting; therefore, the teen is free of risk of exploitation or harm from someone using a pic, the teen previously sent against them. (This does not account for those individuals who have pictures taken of them without their consent, of course.) If, however, the adolescent is engaging in some kind of sexting behavior, most typically within one of the three aforementioned contexts, she or he needs to consider reducing the risk of potential harm. Teaching healthy decision-making within a comprehensive sexuality education curriculum will aid the teen in considering the risks and benefits of such a behavior.

In the column *Go Ask Alice!,* a reader posed a question about how to become more comfortable with using sexting as a means of bridging the distance between she and her long-distance boyfriend. "Alice" responded with a series of both critical thinking questions and recommendations to reduce risks and increase sensuality. These included consideration of (1) who may view the sext, (2) the potential emotional outcomes should someone else see it, and (3) the level of trust of the recipient of the sext (Go Ask Alice!, para 3.). Alice continues, "If you're comfortable with the potential risks, sexting . . . [is a] great way to explore new and unique ways to sexual satisfaction. If you're not comfortable with the privacy concerns, you may want to let this sexual adaptation of technology slide"(para. 4). She adds some additional points to bear in mind:

- **Character limits.** Sexting a Shakespeare sonnet may callous your fingers and require 30 texts before you even get "there", so you may need to keep it short and sweet.
- **Different sense of time.** If one or both sexters are multitasking, response times may vary from seconds to days. If you're looking for more instant gratification from a distance, phone sex or cyber sex may be quicker. If you're looking for something that fits into a busy schedule, this may be your sexual medium while you're physically away.
- **Beep beep!** If you're expecting a heavy flow of incoming sexts, you may want to switch your mobile device to vibrate or silent to not gather a crowd's attention or disturb bystanders.
- **Keep it discreet.** If you're in a public space, consider stepping aside as your face blushes, heart races, or breaths get deeper. Having a concerned stranger ask if you're hyperventilating may create some awkward moments.
- **Secure the messages.** Consider setting up the security and privacy features of your phone to minimize curious friends . . . and strangers from accessing your sexts. (Go Ask Alice!, para. 5)

Conclusion

Avoiding fear-based and controlling approaches to squashing teen sexuality is an important consideration by which to address the very real risks of sexting. In this rapidly changing world of technology, taking a comprehensive sexuality education-based approach to develop healthy decision-making skills for adolescents around sexting may just allow teens to apply such skills in their lives as a whole.

References

Go Ask Alice! (2010, October 15). *Sexting.* Retrieved from http://www.goaskalice.columbia.edu/11238.html.

Fae, J. (2011, February). *Sex is dangerous. Again.* Sexual Freedom, Retrieved February 24, 2011 from http://www.freedominapuritanage.co.uk/?p=1475.

Joannides, P. (2009). *The guide to getting it on* (6th ed.). Portland, OR: Goofy Foot Press.

MTV-AP Digital Abuse Study, Executive Summary. (September, 2009). AThinLine.org. http://www.athinline.org/MTV-AP Digital Abuse Study Executive Summary.pdf. Retrieved from Pewinternet.org.

Ostrager, B. (2010). SMS. OMG! LOL! TTYL: Translating the law to accommodate today's teens and the evolution from texting to sexting. *Family Court Review, 48*(4), 712.

Parentdish. (February 21). RE: Sexting and your kids [Web log message]. Retrieved from ProQuest Central. (Document ID:2272244681).

Sexting Girls Facing Porn Charge Sue D.A. (2009, March 27). CBS.com. Retrieved from http://www.cbsnews.com/stories/2009/03/27/earlyshow/main4896577.shtml

White, C. (May, 2009). Teen sex panic: Media still freaking out about "sexting". Retrieved from Alternet.org.

Donald A. Dyson  **NO**

Tweet This: Sexting Is NOT Safer Sex

In their publication Mobile Access 2010 (Smith, 2010), the Pew Internet and American Life Project identified the current trends in cell phone usage. At the time of the report, 82% of all adults (age 18+) in the United States owned a cell phone. Of those people, 76% used their cell phone to take pictures, 72% used text messaging, and 54% had sent photos or videos using their cell phone.

Leading the charge toward a fully wired populace, the 18–29 year olds in that survey scored higher across the board in their wireless technology utilization. In this age bracket, 90% of the overall population owned cell phones, with 93% of those individuals taking pictures, 95% texting, and 81% sending photos and videos.

Consider as well that the average age for young people to own their first cell phone has decreased dramatically. In the latest data available from Pew on adolescent cell phone use from 2009 (Lenhart, 2009), 58% of 12 year olds owned a cell phone. This number was up dramatically from 18% in 2004.

While ownership has increased, the available technology has moved ahead light years as well. Touch screens with incredible definition join with faster networks to easily facilitate the sharing of pictures and videos from phone to phone. Facetime features allow individuals to live video chat between similarly equipped smartphones. Add to this the increase of smartphone applications (apps) that connect random strangers for live video chat, and the implications are staggering.

For decades, professionals in the technology field have accepted the fact that pornography, in many ways, drives technological innovation (Johnson, 1996). This innovation, often moving faster than the development of ethical guidelines, creates new opportunities for sharing and expressing oneself, including one's sexual self. According to Coopersmith (2009), these technologies offer users the ability to create and share information with both a sense of privacy and with user-friendly interfaces. In essence, it is quick and easy to create and send sexual images in a way that feels, to the user, like it is safe from the judgment and oversight of others.

Out of this technological morass has come the phenomenon popularly referred to as "sexting," or the sending and receiving of sexually explicit text messages (including words, symbols, pictures and videos) using an individual's cell phone.

In the 2009 Pew data of teen cell phone users between 12 and 17, four percent (4%) had sent a sexual image (nude or nearly nude) of themselves to someone via text message and 15% had received such an image. In 17 year olds, those numbers literally doubled, with eight percent (8%) having sent and 30% having received such images (Lenhart, 2009).

Little research has been done on these patterns in adult users, but it is safe to assume that turning 18 years old does not immediately change an individual's behavior, and these trends are likely to continue as technology users get older. As a result, we must begin to acknowledge that sexting is a phenomenon that not only exists, but also exists with little or no oversight and little or no ethical study to guide its use.

Within this experience, some advocates for sexual freedom and expression along with some dedicated to the prevention of sexually transmitted infections, HIV, and unintended pregnancies have begun to consider whether or not sexting can be considered the new "safer sex". Consider the origin of the safer sex terminology. Rising out of the HIV pandemic, first as "safe sex" then as "safer sex," the term has come to be associated with sexual practices that do not risk spreading disease or creating an unintended pregnancy.

With this definition, sexting would certainly seem to be a natural fit. To date, it is not possible to pass human viruses or semen from one mobile device to another through a wireless network.

At issue here, though, is the narrow and reductionist view of sexuality that has too often been embraced as the guiding principle of sex in the current millennium. Ask most high-school sexuality educators for the core concepts of their curricula, and you are likely to get "safer sex" from almost every one. Lessons about condoms and contraception are surely included if allowed by the administration and school board.

In fact, the abstinence-only education movement succeeded in narrowing the debate about sexuality education to the extent that often, when advocates fight for "comprehensive sexuality education," what they are fighting for is the inclusion of medically accurate information about condoms and contraception (Collins, Alagiri & Summers, 2002).

It is important in this discussion, however, to consider a more holistic approach to sexuality. In response to the global need for a clear construction of what it means to be sexually healthy, the World Health Organization (WHO, 2002) created the following definition:

> A state of physical, emotional, mental and social wellbeing in relation to sexuality; it is not merely the absence of disease, dysfunction or infirmity. Sexual health requires a positive and respectful approach to sexuality and sexual relationships, as well as the possibility of having pleasurable and safe sexual experiences, free of coercion, discrimination and violence. (p. 10)

In this larger context, disease prevention is clearly a part of the physical wellbeing identified. As such, it is certainly an important consideration in sexual decision-making. However, it is far from the only consideration necessary. In fact the definition clearly defines health as beyond mere disease prevention. Using the WHO definition, in order to consider a behavior "safe," one would have to consider the emotional, mental, and social implications associated with the behavior as well.

Briefly consider the act of sexting in the framework provided by the WHO. To do this, one must remember that electronic images sent from one device to another have a few unique qualities. First, they have the potential to remain intact and available for years. Second, because of this longevity, they can be transferred from one device to another and can exist in multiple locations at the same time. Third, this potential for multiplication makes sending or showing them to people who were not the intended recipients remarkably easy.

Now, consider the WHO framework. Is sexting safe physically? Yes, from disease. And while images cannot physically harm an individual, a jealous lover in a fit of rage can certainly cause serious physical harm after seeing a sexual image of another person on a partner's cell phone or computer. Also consider the reality that in some municipalities in the United States, minors who are sending images of themselves, their friends, or their classmates are being charged with both creating and distributing child pornography. This offense can lead to incarceration as well as to inclusion in sex offender registries (Lenhart, 2009). Neither are "safe" locations.

Is sexting safer emotionally? This is a more difficult issue to parse out. Sexting can be flirtatious, fun, and bring an individual a great deal of emotional joy. It is also possible for those images to be kept over time, to be shown to unintended recipients, to be used to blackmail, bully, intimidate, and harass. Imagine the jilted lover who sends your seminude picture to your workplace, or the divorcee who uses stored sexts in a custody battle. The potential for emotional harm certainly needs to be acknowledged.

Is sexting safer mentally? While social networking has changed the nature of privacy in today's online world, sexual images of one's self are still generally considered to be private, and shared with those with whom an individual chooses. The nature of digital communication removes the power of choice from the individual, allowing others the freedom to determine who does and does not have access to these very personal images. That powerlessness, combined with anxiety about the possible unintended recipients of the images, can certainly cause an individual mental anguish.

Finally, consider the "freedom from coercion, discrimination and violence" clause. It is clear that the images captured in sexting can be used for all of those things.

In short, sexting is not and cannot be the new "safer sex." In and of itself, it is NOT safe, and framing it as such teaches individuals to ignore the potential harm that may come from engaging in the behavior. Would you tell your 11-year-old niece that sexting was safe?

In the end, it is far wiser to consider sexting to be like most other sexual behaviors: a mixed bag. It can be fun, flirtatious, exciting, and contribute to some wonderful sexual experiences. It also has risks associated with it, and those risks are beyond mere disease transmission or pregnancy. The key is to educate people about the potential risks, help them to consider how those risks fit into their life, and to make individual choices about their willingness to accept those risks.

References

Collins, C., Alagiri, P., & Summers, T. (2002). Abstinence only vs. comprehensive sex education: What are the arguments? What is the evidence? AIDS Policy Research Center & Center for AIDS Prevention Studies, AIDS Research Institute, University of California, San Francisco. Retrieved April 1, 2011, from http://ari.ucsf.edu/pdf/abstinence.pdf

Coopersmith J. (2000). Pornography, Technology and Progress, ICON 4, 94–125.

Johnson, P (November 1996). *Pornography Drives Technology: Why Not to Censor the Internet.* Federal Communication Law Journal 49(1).

Lenhart, A. (2009). *Teens and Sexting.* Pew Internet & American Life. Retrieved from http://www.pewinternet.org/~/media//Files/Reports/2009/PIP_Teens_and_Sexting.pdf

Smith, A. 2010. *Mobile access 2010.* Washington, DC: Pew Internet & American Life Project.

World Health Organization. (2002). *Defining sexual health: report of a technical consultation on sexual health,* 28–31, January 2002, Geneva. Retrieved April 1, 2011, from www.who.int/reproductivehealth/publications/sexualhealth/defining_sh.pdf.

POSTSCRIPT

Is Sexting a Form of Safer Sex?

Much of the dialogue surrounding sexting has focused on the controversy and risks involved. Many sexuality educators have questioned the fear-based response and challenged the assumption that sexting is always unhealthy. At its core, sexting is a form of communication, and communication about sexual thoughts and desires is not, in and of itself, a bad thing. Does the digital mode of communication change this? Does the history of messages stored in phones make sexual communication riskier than sharing feelings in face-to-face conversation? Do images need to be shared in order for a text message to become a sext message?

And what about the images themselves? How much skin needs to be shown for a flirtatious message to become a full-on sext? Does a male sharing a shirtless picture of himself or female sharing a shot of herself in a bikini count as sexting? Or must there be exposed genitals in the frame? Is it safer for a person to snap and share an image of his or her genital area if his or her face (or other identifying features like tattoos) is not visible in the frame?

In his essay, Satterly presents strategies for reducing the risks involved in sexting. Do you think these steps make sexting a safe practice? Or is it still too risky for teens to engage in the practice? Are there things that are easier to say via text than in person? Can sexting make communication about sexual desires or boundaries easier? Can sexting contribute to healthy sexual dialogue and expression of feelings? Or are the risks still too great? Dyson examines sexting through the World Health Organization's description of "healthy sexuality" and comes to the conclusion that it is not safe. Do you agree with his conclusions? Why or why not? He states that describing sexting as a form of safer sex "teaches individuals to ignore the potential harm that may come from engaging in the behavior." Do you agree? Finally, Dyson asks, "Would you tell your 11-year-old niece that sexting is safe?" What is your answer to this question?

Most of the attention given to sexting has focused on adolescents. But sexting is not limited to the keypad-savvy thumbs of teens. Adults also engage in the practice, and the high-profile sexting mishaps of celebrities and politicians have received media attention as well. Are there different risks for adults who sext as opposed to teens? Why might adults consider sexting a problem for youth while engaging in the practice themselves? What does this say about the risks, benefits, and meaning behind the trend?

Lastly, have you ever sent or received a sext message? What were the reasons behind your actions? How did you feel when you clicked the send button or opened the message? Did you talk with your partner about what should happen to the images or messages once the sexting conversation stopped? Are

13

there things that are easier for you to express via nonverbal communication like text messages? Did you consider both the risks and benefits involved? In the end, what shaped your final decision? Do you think the conclusions you came to about sexting are the same conclusions everyone should come to? Should sexting be discussed in conversations of safer sex options?

Suggested Readings

K. Jaishankar, "Sexting: A New Form of Victimless Crime?" *International Journal of Cyber Criminology* (vol. 3, no. 1, 2009).

S. Shafron-Perez, "Average Teenager or Sex Offender? Solutions to the Legal Dilemma Caused by Sexting," *The John Marshall Journal of Computer and Information Law* (February 2009).

ISSUE 2

Has Sex Become Too Casual?

YES: Rebecca Hagelin, from "Parents Should Raise the Bar for Their Kids," http://townhall.com/columnists/RebeccaHagelin/2009/03/10/parents_should_raise_the_bar_for_their_kids (March 10, 2009)

NO: Lara Riscol, from "Purity, Promiscuity or Pleasure?" an original essay written for this volume (2009)

ISSUE SUMMARY

YES: Rebecca Hagelin, author and public speaker on family and culture, argues that sex education promotes casual sex and that schools and parents should do more to protect children.

NO: Lara Riscol, an author who explores the connections between society and sexuality, counters that blaming sex education is an oversimplification while arguing that sexuality has always been openly expressed throughout human history.

It seems that every generation envisions the younger, emerging generation as more permissive than itself. This pattern of observation can be seen at least throughout the past century. In the late 1800s, the mass production of the *bicycle* worried many adults who thought that this would allow young people to ride far away and engage in sexual trysts, free of the watchful eyes of their parents. Similarly, the growing automobile industry gave young people new opportunities to be alone and led to concerns among many adults that younger generations were becoming sexually permissive. In the "roaring '20s," "flappers"—women who drank, danced, voted, and wore their hair short—were regarded by their elders as being especially permissive. In the 1930s–1950s, the growing number of movie theaters, dance halls, and coed universities worried adults that sex was becoming more and more casual.[1]

Adults looked to the televised hip gyrations of Elvis Presley as a signal of emerging sexual permissiveness, and in the 1960s and 1970s, many adults did not know what to make of young people and the sexual revolution, particularly with its "free love" messages. Some critics still point to the sexual revolution as being the originator of a "casual sex" mentality. Sociologist Ira Reiss refutes this notion by observing that it was not sexual *behaviors* that changed so much during this period; rather, the *attitudes* people expressed about sex began to change.[2]

Still, modern commentators continue to describe sex as more casual than ever. Some have remarked on the high volume of sexual content on television, in the movies, on the Internet, and so forth, which often has no marital or relationship context. Others look to the surge of Web sites through which people often meet to arrange for sexual encounters, from Craigslist.org to AdultFriendFinder.com and OnlineBootyCall.com.

Is sex more casual today? In the following selections, author and commentator Rebecca Hagelin blames sex education for promoting casual sex and says that parents and schools should expect more of their children, instilling "concepts of self-worth," "basic morality," and abstinence education. Author Lara Riscol criticizes the Far Right for oversimplifying the issue and responds by comparing the social and sexual norms today to those at other times in history, noting that in many instances, the norms today are better than the norms of the past.

Notes

1. Special thanks to Dr. Robert T. Francoeur, coeditor of the *International Encyclopedia of Sexuality,* for his extensive notes on sexual customs in American history.
2. I. L. Reiss, *An Insider's View of Sexual Science Since Kinsey* (Lanham, MD: Rowman & Littlefield, 2006).

Parents Should Raise the Bar
for Their Kids

Spring break is in full swing for many college students across the country. And believe me, when I say "full swing," I mean full-rockin', rollin' party-hearty swinging!

But given that nearly all of these students' lifestyles are still funded by their parents, and that nearly all are still under the legal drinking age, it makes me wonder: What are their parents thinking?

As a mom of two college men I actually find it fairly easy to boldly proclaim: "If you are livin' on my dime, then you are livin' by my rules."

My rules for them as adults are actually filled with freedom, coupled with the principle of "self government." They were raised with this consistent theme, and they understand that my husband and I practice the "abuse and lose" approach. (I.e., they have both freedom and our full support as long as they follow basic rules that provide for their safety, moral development, and future.)

Of course, I can hear the naysayers now: "But they're adults. You can't tell adult children what to do." To this I simply answer, "BALONEY!"

I am a much older adult, and I understand that an employer can impose certain codes and expectations for my behavior on me. That's the deal in life—you work for someone, you have to play by their rules. (Of course, I know they can't trample your basic rights, deny civil liberties, etc. So don't go there. You know what I'm talking about.)

The young college men in my life—of whom I am so very proud and blessed to be called their "mom"—also know that my husband and I are fully committed to them as individuals and will provide plenty of opportunities for good, safe fun.

Let's get back to Spring Break as an example. Instead of shrugging our shoulders and letting them go off to some distant beach where mayhem, alcohol, and "Girls Gone Wild" abound, I booked a house at our favorite beach, which is located on a barrier island on Florida's Gulf Coast. With no bridge (you have to get here by boat) and no bars, this break is a lot safer and a lot more meaningful than what many are experiencing.

One of my dear friends has a house nearby and her daughter, also on Spring Break, has brought about nine of her "best friends" too. So, there's plenty of social activity, fun, and friendship without the nonsense. The kids go back and forth between our houses, so my friend and I both get to spend time with them and listen to their entertaining—and interesting—chatter.

Last night the gang was at my friend's house and the main topic of conversation proved an eye-opening, mind-numbing experience for her.

Most of the girls on this trip are freshmen, and somehow the conversation led to a shared humiliating experience now common at most college campuses: the mandatory co-ed, sex-ed course they all attended during their first few weeks on campus. They described the graphic nature of the class, and how embarrassed and outraged they were when they were shown how to put a condom on a banana.

But then it got worse—they were all encouraged to do the condom/banana exercise, too. The girls spoke of how a couple of their fellow students seemed to take great pride at their skill in demonstrating what seemed an all-too-familiar maneuver. However, my young friends said they were mortified and left the course feeling "trashy" and belittled by administration officials who expect them to all behave like wild animals in heat. "They seemed to be encouraging us to be sexually active," one member of the volleyball team said. "I was insulted and offended by the entire experience."

This particular young co-ed had gone to a private Christian high school, so she had managed to escape the low expectations that many educators bring to today's youth. She and her mom weren't aware that in today's public schools, millions of boys and girls are now, indeed, treated as if they are going to be sex-crazed creatures and, therefore, are actually encouraged to engage in risky behavior.

Face it: When an adult in authority stands in front of the classroom and directs graphic discussions of sex in every form, forces boys and girls to sit by each other throughout the humiliating lectures, and then further violates the child's natural tendencies to be private or modest, then you end up with kids who follow what they've been taught. On the other hand, when kids are treated with dignity, taught the value of abstinence, and how to avoid placing themselves in compromising situations in the first place, the research shows that more of them do, indeed, respond by adopting a lifestyle of self-control and more responsible behavior than those drowning in "sex ed". Also critical to the delayed on-set of sexual activity is parental involvement. I can not overstate the influence that loving, connected parents have on their teens and young adult children. You'll find loads of data and research on both points at www.abstinenceclearinghouse.com and www.familyfacts.org.

Which, once again, brings me back to the plethora of wild Spring Break "pah-tays" going on around the country as you read this. I wonder: If more public junior high and high schools joined hands with more parents in teaching abstinence education, the concepts of self-worth, and basic morality, wouldn't our nation's kids have a higher view of themselves and rise to meet the expectations?

And if colleges and parents expected better of our kids, wouldn't more of them choose the higher ground? If more parents took the effort to provide safer—but still "way fun"—supervised beach trips and other options for college kids, would more of them opt for something other than the drunken orgies that many Spring Break trips have become? In short, are older adults getting exactly the type of behavior from young adults that we expect?

Granted, my personal "focus group" is small. But the data, my experience, and the e-mails I receive from thousands of people tell me this: Young adults are still malleable, still looking for direction, and still crave to rise above the status quo. But they need help and encouragement. They need to be told that they can be self-controlled people of strong character, and they need to be provided with opportunities to thrive, have fun, and become men and women they can be proud of.

Young adults rise or fall to the expectation levels set for them. Will you help raise the bar?

Purity, Promiscuity or Pleasure?

"**Y**ou would watch the girls give each other oral sex, do themselves with dildos, place cigars in their vaginas and rectums, suck on each others' breasts, and lick freshly poured beer off of one another's vulvas while their legs were tucked behind their necks." Often one fellow would get to have sex with one of the three performers directly before leering and cheering men.

No, this is not another spring break outrage making the latest round on cable news, but business as usual back in the good ol' days when live sex shows were easier to find than now. And I don't mean the '50s glory days of traditional values when *Ozzie and Harriet* reigned and the United States teen pregnancy rate hit an historic high, but in the prostitution heyday of the 1800s when feminists and medical experts warned against women riding bicycles lest the seat stir "libidinousness and immorality."

In the latest hot and seminal *Guide to Getting It On,* author Paul Joannides' longest chapter, "Sex in the 1800s," reminds us that the more things change, the more they stay the same. He compares the sexual contradictions of then "hardcore live sex shows and concerns about bicycle seats for adult women" to now "abstinence-only sex education and porn-filled Websites on the Internet." As today's technology flings sex front and center, in your face, round the clock, no escape, get me off of this d——n merry-go-round spinning ever faster into an erotic yawn of Girls Gone Wild, prostitots, MILFs, Bang Bus, booty call, and endless multimedia overexposures—America, "Land of the Free," remains stuck in a sexual schizophrenia of smut and sanctimony.

My first mental flash when reading about the famous centuries-ago sex show was VH1's latest season premiere of *Rock of Love Bus with Bret Michaels,* where Pamela Anderson wannabes vie for the lead singer of '80s hair band Poison. When one drunken contestant takes a vagina shot of booze from another, even a nonbeliever can fear the Apocalypse is near. Minus historical context and nuanced reasoning, I feel the appeal of Chicken Little conservatives crying the decline of Western civilization due to the sexual revolution and liberal moral relativism.

It's cheap and easy to dump hypersexualized floaties from our unfettered free market society on those who reject retro reactions to today's growing sexual, reproductive, gender, relationship, and family complexities. But could our nation's unmatched trouble with sex—runaway rates of teen and unplanned pregnancy, single parenthood, abortion, HIV and STDs, sexual "addiction," alienation and desire discrepancies, divorce—really be a black-and-white case of purity or promiscuity? How to reach the glorious human heights of pleasure—sacred to silly—when laden by potent conflicting forces intent on commercializing and politicizing sex?

Our dominantly Christian nation's schizophrenic approach to sex has deep roots. Likely former Governor Elliot Spitzer wouldn't have been so disgraced for feeding his costly call girl fetish in 1870, when New York City's second-largest economy was commercial sex. Yet America's prostitution-powered era wouldn't have tolerated a women's studies graduate auctioning off her virginity to finance her master's in family and marriage therapy, à la Natalie Dylan. Women weren't allowed the same transgressions as men. Of course women weren't allowed the same opportunities. Traditionalists argued that the intellectual rigors of higher education would shrink female reproductive organs and deny a real woman's one true calling: motherhood.

The God-fearing Victorian era of presumed moral restraint was nearly as sex segregated as Afghanistan today. Hooking up isn't so easy when you don't school, work, or socialize together. Young men routinely staved off masturbation at brothels where prepubescent virgins were in high demand; women were deemed unnatural if they displayed sexual desire, though ads for birth control abounded. Gender and sexuality has evolved along with technologies like automobiles, birth control, the Internet, economic shifts, and social equality. America, grounded in equality and plurality, rises from the right to life, liberty, and the pursuit of happiness. Our national stability and family honor doesn't rest on hypocritical sexual traditions like enforcing female virtue.

But that doesn't stop opportunistic purity posturing by family values conservatives, such as wedge-issue Republicans, the religious right, and Fox News, which airs so much B-roll of pulsating female flesh, while morally bloviating it inspired the NSFW FoxNewsPorn.com. The head of the "Biblically based" policy group Concerned Women for America says that proponents of sexual health education are financially motivated to encourage kids' having sexually transmitted diseases and abortions. A Morality in Media press release, "Connecting the Dots: The Link Between Gay Marriage and Mass Murders," links secular values, the sexual revolution, and the decline in morality to the gay rights movement, all sexual ills, including rape and the sexual abuse of children, and naturally the recent spate of mass murders.

Fox News megastar Bill O'Reilly, who a few years ago paid millions to make a sexual harassment suit go away, makes millions as lead culture-war bugle for traditional values against deviant secular progressives out to destroy America. In a recent column, "Kids Gone Wild," he decries the supposed sidelining of "Judeo-Christian principles of right and wrong" in policymaking. He shamelessly makes a slippery slope case against nuanced responses to sexual controversies by conflating child rape, unfettered abortion, gay marriage, and sexting—the latest shame name for teenagers and younger sharing provocative photos of themselves via cell phone, mostly girls sending and guys receiving.

But with child porn charges against juveniles now in at least five states, our sense of right and wrong can't be vindicated when we scar a kid as sex offender for a naughty consensual exchange. Some of the girls dragged into our criminal justice system posed in bikinis or thick, white bras. Flailing before budding sexuality and uncontainable technology, alleged adults lose all moral sense and lump the heinous crime of child pornography with a developing person's playful physical expression. Forget addressing the real potential harm to a child's well-being, such as high-tech bullying when a jerk "friend" recklessly or vindictively distributes private communication.

Yes, times are rapidly changing, and there's no going back to that elusive simpler time when men were predators and women gatekeepers, and anyone in between stayed in the closet. Despite hyperventilating sex-frenzied traditionalists, societal breakdowns go way beyond gay marriage, the hookup generation, Bill Clinton, or even Hugh Hefner. Although the "anything-goes, if it feels good do it" '60s is a tattered punching bag, liberalism not only ushered in free-love rebels, but also groundbreaking equality for women, queers, and ethnic minorities. Life can feel out of control as technology accelerates, rules of the game change, and our salacious 24/7 infotainment highway takes us to the edge of tolerance, but we face much graver threats today than friends with benefits, condoms on a banana, or two grooms in a tux.

With sexual debate stuck in such demonizing reductionism of traditional vs. secular, conservative vs. liberal, purity vs. perversion, abstinence vs. condoms, good vs. evil, no wonder we can't budge beyond nostalgia-fed moral panics to sane responses to modern challenges. A politically potent, multibillion-dollar industry of chastity crusaders seeks to save our national Gomorrah by corralling sex back into the procreative marital bedroom. But with virtually all of us doing some version of the dirty deed before, outside, between, or after marriage, America must expand the sexual conversation beyond purity balls or rainbow parties.

The two authors of the book, *Hooked: How Casual Sex Is Harming Our Kids*, recently lectured at a broadcast forum by the Christian-right Family Research Council, the powerful lobbying arm of media empire Focus on the Family. Beyond the usual physical dire consequences, Joe McIlhaney and Freda Bush stated the irreparable emotional damage of one having multiple sex partners. Dr. Bush drove home their scientific claims by describing how adhesive tape loses its sticky power after pulling it apart more than once. Like used adhesive tape, the more you have sex with someone other than your spouse, the more you lose your ability to bond. Oh, and sex means anything that incites physical arousal; no word on masturbation. Bottom line is there are only two types of sex: married (good) and unmarried (bad).

Their conclusion supports the absolutist agenda of the synergistic family values, traditional marriage and abstinence-only movements that push the conservative ideal of sex confined to a heteronormative lifetime of marital fidelity, to the exclusion of all other sexual expressions. But hawking sexual purity as a salve for personal ills and tonic for a stronger America amounts to selling snake oil.

For many, a magic pill to make bad and scary things go away sounds nice. But if prescribing to dogmatic absolutes worked, then the most religious and conservative red states wouldn't have the highest rates of teen pregnancy, divorce, and porn consumption. And the fallen Colorado megachurch Pastor Ted Haggard, former head of the National Association of Evangelicals, frequent

President George W. Bush confidant, and fierce opponent of same sex marriage, wouldn't have betrayed his family by spending three years with a male prostitute and crystal meth.

Ignoring the human frailties of adults and the capitalistic pornification of our public square, conservatives offer only one denial standard for all kids aged 8 to 28 if unmarried. Maybe in the Obama era, we're ready to grow up and stop making the most vulnerable ground zero in our lose–lose, sex-obsessed culture war. For the past eight years, we've been demonizing sexual science, distorting sex education, limiting access to information and health care services, and denying civil rights all for the sake of the children. Consequences be damned, we resist lessons of holistic sexual openness from our far sexually healthier Western allies. Instead we champion the A & B only of the "Abstinence, Be Faithful, Use Condoms" HIV campaign launched by war torn, polygamist Uganda, which now rewards virginal new brides with TV sets instead of goats.

Steeped in raunch culture that shames or sensationalizes young sex, we grasp onto Disney offerings of purity no matter how often or far our sexy virgins fall (Britney Spears, Jessica Simpson, Mandy Moore), and as long as new ones keep us afloat (Miley Cyrus, Jonas Brothers). But sustaining the virgin–whore dichotomy after all these centuries perverts smart decision making for all. You can't answer a high-tech free society's hypersexualized reality with fictionalized extremism? As I wrote in a 2001 column, "The Britney and Bob Challenge," about America's sexual schizophrenia and refusal to move beyond sexuality's marital ideal or commodified reality: neither excess nor repression develops into sexual intimacy or connection, let alone responsibility.

In *17 Again,* Disney's *High School Musical* heartthrob Zac Efron dresses down sexy cheerleaders, saying boys don't respect them, and rebukes a condom-distributing teacher with "abstinence is best," he knows. Well his character knows because he's really his dad who lost his basketball scholarship because he knocked up his high school sweetheart and chose teen marriage and fatherhood. So even though abstinence-only didn't work any more for him than for Bristol Palin, the lesson remains "no sex unless married," not responsible sexual choices like protection or non-coital play.

In real life, Zac Efron dates his HSM co-star Vanessa Hudgens, who suffered momentary embarrassment when earlier sexy photos surfaced online. But after celebrating her 20th birthday, she and Zac comfortably posed when shopping at a Los Angeles sex-toy shop.

The *Today Show* recently pitted the feminist author of *The Purity Myth: How America's Obsession with Virginity is Hurting Young Women* against international abstinence advocate Lakita Garth, who promotes her success to staying a virgin until marriage at 36. Jessica Valenti points out that a women's worth is more than her hymen, and most fall between girls gone wild or chaste virgin. Like Zac and Vanessa versus their Disney image, most of us figure out how to achieve a full life *while* expressing our sexuality, married or not.

I saw Lakita Garth keynote an Abstinence Clearinghouse conference themed, "Abstinence: It's a Black and White Issue," as in "allowing no gray area between sexual integrity and irresponsibility." The flashy multimedia conference took me back to high school pep rallies and my cheerleader senti-mentality. Watching a bejeweled and stylin' Garth flash photos of herself with President Bush as she bragged about her virginity-won "bling," I momentarily felt sexually inadequate for my life's choices before marrying at almost 32. After all, I don't have any photos with a United States president. But by Star Parker, a self-described former welfare queen and abortion regular, reducing all of America's problems to the denial of God's sexual truth, I kept from getting further swept away by the idealism and heartfelt talent of the "Abstinence Idol" competition.

Though Kelly Clarkson, a self-proclaimed Christian virgin, won *American Idol's* first season, this year's likely winner, Adam Lambert, doesn't deny rumors of his being gay or bisexual. When Internet photos circulated of him kissing other men and dressed in drag, he responded, "I have nothing to hide. I am who I am." Other successful *American Idol* contestants include Clay Aiken, who finally came out as gay when he announced becoming a father with his male "friend," and Fantasia, a young single mom.

Oh, I like being an American and am glad my six-year-old son, husband, and I have so many more sexual and gender options today than in the 1800s or 1950s. The virginal ideal of the 1950s was beautiful, bubbly movie icon Sandra Dee, whose reality was as an incest survivor, divorced at 22, and with a lonely life of anorexia, alcoholism, and depression.

Because my son is so precious, I'll protect him by preparing him to make healthy sexual decisions throughout his life. I'm not going to feed him more of the same parental "do as I say, not as I do or did" crap, but will teach him moral reasoning over absolutes. I'll teach him to be is own moral agent, to value himself, to choose pleasure no matter how much purity or promiscuity extremes are forced upon him. I'll teach him that this is the United States of America and his sex does not belong to the church or state.

To reach humanity's highest ideals, permission trumps repression. With rights come responsibilities. My son may mess up, as I have, and will have to deal with consequences with respect and dignity. And I'll work for a world that uses all of its modern resources to ameliorate harm. As Mahatma Gandhi said, "Freedom is not worth having if it does not include the freedom to make mistakes."

POSTSCRIPT

Has Sex Become Too Casual?

Some commentators who view sex as having become too casual today point to explicitly sexual lyrics in popular music for sexualizing modern culture. Consider three sets of sexually explicit lyrics by different composers.

1. A composer encourages his listeners to shake their bodies "like a Polaroid Picture," and the accompanying music video on YouTube makes it clear that the performer is referring to the shaking of one's buttocks and/or breasts.
2. A second composer processes her sexual encounter with another female while considering the consequences on her relationship with her boyfriend.
3. A third composer describes a woman tricking her boyfriend into performing analingus (mouth-to-anus sexual contact) on her.

Which of these three lyrical pieces would you consider to be the most promoting of casual sex? If you chose #1, you charged the contemporary group Outkast with promoting casual sex in their smash hit, "Hey Ya." Sample lyrics follow:

> *"Shake it, shake, shake it, shake it (OHH OH)*
> *Shake it, shake it, shake, shake it, shake it, shake it (OHH OH)*
> *Shake it, shake it like a Polaroid Picture, shake it, shake it*
> *Shh you got to, shake it, shh shake it, shake it, got to shake it*
> *(Shake it Suga') shake it like a Polaroid Picture"*[1]

If you chose #2, you decided that Katy Perry was the most promoting of casual sex in her popular song from 2008, "I Kissed a Girl." Read on for an excerpt.

> *"I kissed a girl and I liked it,*
> *the taste of her cherry chapstick.*
> *I kissed a girl just to try it,*
> *I hope my boyfriend don't mind it.*
> *It felt so wrong,*
> *it felt so right.*
> *Don't mean I'm in love tonight.*
> *I kissed a girl and I liked it (I liked it)."*[2]

If you chose #3—the piece describing analingus—then you thought that the lyrics of Geoffrey Chaucer, written more than 600 years ago, were the most promoting of casual sex. An excerpt from "The Miller's Tale" in *The Canterbury Tales* follows, in which Absalom's girlfriend gives him quite a surprise.

> *"And through the window she put out her hole.*
> *And Absalom no better felt nor worse,*
> *But with his mouth he kissed her naked arse*
> *Right greedily, before he knew of this."*[3]

Although many other examples of casual, sexually explicit passages can be found in some of the world's great literature—from ancient Greece's Aristophanes to William Shakespeare to the modern day—it still seems to many who would agree with Hagelin that today's society is more casual than ever about sex. What is it about modern-day society that fosters these impressions? Is Hagelin right that sex has become way too casual, and parents and schools need to take greater responsibility in raising the bar of expectation for children? Is Riscol right that sexual values have been depraved at other times in history? How does Riscol's understanding of moral depravity differ from Hagelin's? With whom do you agree? After considering the viewpoints of both Hagelin and Riscol, how would you describe the sexual norms at your college in comparison with what you know about other generations or other times in history?

Notes

1. Source: www.azlyrics.com
2. Source: www.azlyrics.com
3. Source: www.litrix.com/canterby/cante004.htm

Suggested Readings

D. Herzog, Sex in Crisis: *The New Sexual Revolution and the Future of American Politics* (New York: Basic Books, 2007).

M. Klein, *America's War on Sex* (Santa Barbara, CA: Praeger, 2006).

J. McIllhaney and F.M. Bush, *Hooked: New Science on How Casual Sex Is Affecting Our Children* (Chicago, IL: Moody Publishers, 2008).

J.A. Sherman and N. Tocantins, *The Happy Hook-Up. A Single Girl's Guide to Casual Sex* (Berkeley, CA: Ten Speed Press, 2004).

B. Taverner, "Behind the Music: Music Literacy and Healthy Relationships," in S. Montfort and P. Brick, eds., *Unequal Partners: Teaching About Power and Consent in Adult-Teen and Other Relationships* (Morristown, NJ: The Center for Family Life Education, 2007).

ISSUE 3

Can Sex Be Addictive?

YES: Patrick J. Carnes, from "**Frequently Asked Questions,**" 2011, accessed at http://www.sexhelp.com/addiction_faq.cfm

NO: Lawrence A. Siegel and Richard M. Siegel, from "Sex Addiction: Semantics or Science," an original essay written for this volume (2011)

ISSUE SUMMARY

YES: Patrick Carnes, considered by many to be an expert on sexual addiction, answers some common questions about this phenomenon, as featured on the Web site http://www.sexhelp.com/. Carnes discusses the nature of sexual addiction and ways in which it might be manifested and offers suggestions for treatment.

NO: Sex therapist Lawrence Siegel and sex therapist/educator Richard Siegel counter that sexual addiction is grounded in "moralistic ideology masquerading as science." They argue that although some sexual behaviors may be dysfunctional, the term "sexual addiction" pathologizes many common forms of sexual expression that are not problematic.

$\mathbf{T}$he name Tiger Woods once conjured images of competitions, championships, and million-dollar endorsements. The champion golfer was on pace to win more major tournaments than anyone in history. But after his multiple extramarital affairs were revealed, his name became synonymous with one term—"sex addict." Woods sought to keep much about his situation private, but apologized to family and fans at a press conference. Questions and diagnoses were tossed about from television studios to dining rooms worldwide. "Why would he risk his family and fortune?" "He MUST be addicted to sex!" "Sex wasn't his problem, hubris was!"

Although Woods' behavioral addiction was blamed by many in the general public, the concept of sex addiction is a controversial subject among experts in the fields of sexology and sex therapy. At the heart of the controversy is a seemingly simple question that has no easy answer: *How much sex is too much?*

Consider this exchange from the 1977 Woody Allen movie, *Annie Hall*. Two characters, Alvy and Annie, have just been asked by their therapists if they have sex "often."

Alvy: Hardly ever. Maybe three times a week.

Annie: Constantly. I'd say three times a week.

Whether or not one can have (or is having) too much sex might be a matter of perspective, as it seems to be for Alvy (wanting more) and Annie (wanting less). On the other hand, some members of the sexological community will clearly tell you that there is a point at which sex can become too much.

Another important consideration is how a person defines sex. Does it include masturbation? Does it include oral or anal intercourse, in addition to vaginal intercourse? Are nongenital touching behaviors, like kissing or massage, sexual in nature? And how about the viewing of erotic material or the reading of an erotic passage? Is sex outside of a committed relationship or marriage necessarily a sign of addiction? Answers will depend on who you ask.

Much of modern understanding of sexual addiction comes from the work of Patrick J. Carnes, who authored *Don't Call It Love: Recovery from Sexual Addiction*. Carnes cofounded the Society for the Advancement of Sexual Health in 1987, an organization dedicated to "helping those who suffer from out of control sexual behavior." Today, Carnes is considered a leading authority on sexual addiction, in a field that includes prevention services, treatment services (including a 12-step recovery model), professional conferences, an academic journal (*Sexual Addiction and Compulsivity*), and more.

The Web site for Sex Addicts Anonymous (www.sexaa.org) states that addicts are "powerless over our sexual thoughts and behaviors and that our preoccupation with sex was causing progressively severe adverse consequences for us, our families, and our friends. Despite many failed promises to ourselves and attempts to change, we discovered that we were unable to stop acting out sexually by ourselves," and points the visitor to links for additional resources and meeting information.

Many sexologists, however, call the whole idea of sexual addiction nonsense, stating that the very term "sexual addiction" invites comparison to other addictions in which the object of addiction (heroin, nicotine, alcohol, gambling, etc.) is inherently harmful. They explain that sex, as a normal biological drive, should not be placed in the same category. Efforts to create an addiction out of sex do nothing more than feed a hungry new addiction treatment industry that is erotophobic at its core.

In the YES selection, Patrick J. Carnes explains the nature of sexual addiction, signs of possible sexual addiction, codependency, and different types of treatment. In the NO selection, sex therapists Lawrence Siegel and Richard Siegel reject the notion of "sexual addiction" as unscientific and moralistic.

YES

Patrick J. Carnes

Frequently Asked Questions

"Like an alcoholic unable to stop drinking, sexual addicts are unable to stop their self-destructive sexual behavior. Family breakups, financial disaster, loss of jobs, and risk to life are the painful themes of their stories.

Sex addicts come from all walks of life—they may be ministers, physicians, homemakers, factory workers, salespersons, secretaries, clerks, accountants, therapists, dentists, politicians, or executives, to name just a few examples. Most were abused as children—sexually, physically, and/or emotionally. The majority grew up in families in which addiction already flourished, including alcoholism, compulsive eating, and compulsive gambling. Most grapple with other addictions as well, but they find sex addiction the most difficult to stop.

Much hope nevertheless exists for these addicts and their families. Sex addicts have shown an ability to transform a life of self-destruction into a life of self-care, a life in chaos and despair into one of confidence and peace."

—Patrick J. Carnes, Ph.D.
Author of *Out of the Shadows*, 1992

What Is Sexual Addiction?

Sexual addiction is defined as any sexually-related, compulsive behavior which interferes with normal living and causes severe stress on family, friends, loved ones, and one's work environment.

Sexual addiction has been called sexual dependency and sexual compulsivity. By any name, it is a compulsive behavior that completely dominates the addict's life. Sexual addicts make sex a priority more important than family, friends, and work. Sex becomes the organizing principle of addict's lives. They are willing to sacrifice what they cherish most in order to preserve and continue their unhealthy behavior.

No single behavior pattern defines sexual addiction. These behaviors, when they have taken control of addicts' lives and become unmanageable, include: compulsive masturbation, compulsive heterosexual and homosexual relationships, pornography, prostitution, exhibitionism, voyeurism, indecent phone calls, child molesting, incest, rape, and violence. Even the healthiest forms of human sexual expression can turn into self-defeating behaviors.

What Is Sexual Anorexia?

Sexual anorexia is an obsessive state in which the physical, mental, and emotional task of avoiding sex dominates one's life. Like self-starvation with food or compulsive dieting or hoarding with money, deprivation with sex can make one feel powerful and defended against all hurts. As with any other altered state of consciousness, such as those brought on by chemical use, compulsive gambling or eating, or any other addiction process, the preoccupation with the avoidance of sex can seem to obliterate one's life problems. The obsession can then become a way to cope with all stress and all life difficulties. Yet, as with other addictions and compulsions, the costs are great. In this case, sex becomes a furtive enemy to be continually kept at bay, even at the price of annihilating a part of oneself.

Specialists in sexual medicine have long noted the close parallels between food disorders and sexual disorders. Many professionals have observed how food anorexia and sexual anorexia share common characteristics. In both cases, the sufferers starve themselves in the midst of plenty. Both types of anorexia feature the essential loss of self, the same distortions of thought, and the agonizing struggle for control over the self and others. Both share the same extreme self-hatred and sense of profound alienation. But while the food anorexic is obsessed with the self-denial of physical nourishment, the sexual anorexic focuses his or her anxiety on sex. As a result, the sexual anorexic will typically experience the following:

- A dread of sexual pleasure
- A morbid and persistent fear of sexual contact
- Obsession and hyper vigilance around sexual matters
- Avoidance of anything connected with sex
- Preoccupation with others being sexual
- Distortions of body appearance
- Extreme loathing of body functions
- Obsessional self-doubt about sexual adequacy
- Rigid, judgmental attitudes about sex
- Excessive fear and preoccupation with sexual diseases
- Obsessive concern or worry about the sexual activity of others
- Shame and self-loathing over sexual experiences
- Depression about sexual adequacy and functioning
- Self-destructive behavior to limit, stop, or avoid sex

Sexual anorexics can be men as well as women. Their personal histories often include sexual exploitation or some form of severely traumatic sexual rejection or both. Experiences of childhood sexual abuse are common with sexual anorexics, often accompanied by other forms of childhood abuse and neglect. As a result of these traumas, they may tend to carry dark secrets and maintain seemingly insane loyalties that have never been disclosed. In fact, sexual anorexics are for the most part not conscious of the hidden dynamics driving them.

Dr. Carnes book, *Sexual Anorexia*, focuses on the suffering of the sexual anorexic. Sexual anorexia is as destructive as the illnesses that often accompany it, and behind which it often hides, such as alcoholism, drug addiction, sexual addiction, and compulsive eating. It resides in emotion so raw that most sufferers would wish to keep it buried forever were it not so painful to live this way. Sexual anorexia feeds on betrayal, violence, and rejection. It gathers strength from a culture that makes sexual satisfaction both an unreachable goal and a nonnegotiable demand. Our media focus almost exclusively on sensational sexual problems such as rape, child abuse, sexual harassment, or extramarital affairs. When people have problems being sexual, we are likely to interpret the difficulty as a need for a new technique or a matter of misinformation. For those who suffer from sexual anorexia, technique and information are not remotely enough. Help comes only through an intentional, planned effort to break the bonds of obsession that keep anorexics stuck.

This book is intended as a guide to support that effort. The early chapters help the reader understand sexual anorexia: how it starts, and how it gathers such strength. The last twelve chapters present a clinically tested and proven plan for achieving a healthy sexuality. This program has worked for many, many people. It is safe. It is practical. It works if the sufferer follows the guidelines and has the appropriate outside support. It will not be easy because the obsession was created in the first place by intimate violations and shattered trust. Yet step by step, healing can be effected so that the sufferer can learn to trust the self as well as others.

Recognition of Sexual Addiction by the Professional Health Care Community

Sexual addiction was first brought to the forefront in Dr. Patrick Carnes' 1983 book, *Out of the Shadows: Understanding Sexual Addiction* (Hazelden). Since then, thousands of people have come forward seeking help, and more and more professionals are being trained to identify and treat sexual addiction.

The Society for the Advancement of Sex Health was created in 1987 to serve as an independent clearing house for information on sexual addiction and treatment options. One of SASH's missions is to decrease the stigma surrounding sexual addiction problems and treatment. They may be contacted at:

The Society for the Advancement of Sex Health
P.O. Box 725544
Atlanta, Georgia 31139
1-770-541-9912
e-mail-sash@sash.net

Medical and clinical research appears each quarter in *Sexual Addiction and Compulsivity; The Journal of Treatment and Prevention* published by Taylor and Francis. For further information contact:

Taylor and Francis
1101 Vermont Ave., N.W., Suite 200
Washington, DC
1-800-272-7737

Sexual Dependency vs Other Addictions

Sexual addiction can be understood by comparing it to other types of addictions. Individuals addicted to alcohol or other drugs, for example, develop a relationship with their "chemical(s) of choice"—a relationship that takes precedence over any and all other aspects of their lives. Addicts find they need drugs merely to feel normal.

In sexual addiction, a parallel situation exists. Sex—like food or drugs in other addictions—provides the "high" and addicts become dependent on this sexual high to feel normal. They substitute unhealthy relationships for healthy ones. They opt for temporary pleasure rather than the deeper qualities of "normal" intimate relationships.

Sexual addiction follows the same progressive nature of other addictions. Sexual addicts struggle to control their behaviors, and experience despair over their constant failure to do so. Their loss of self-esteem grows, fueling the need to escape even further into their addictive behaviors. A sense of powerlessness pervades the lives of addicts.

How Many People Are Affected by Sexual Addiction?

Estimates range from three to six percent of the population.

What Are Multiple Addictions?

National surveys revealed that most sexual addicts come from severely dysfunctional families. Usually at least one other member of these families has another addiction (87%).

Dual addictions include sexual addiction and:

- Chemical Dependency (42%)
- Eating Disorder (38%)
- Compulsive Working (28%)
- Compulsive Spending (26%)
- Compulsive Gambling (5%)

Sexual Addiction and Abuse

Research has shown that a very high correlation exists between childhood abuse and sexual addiction in adulthood.

Sexual addicts, both men and women, who have reported experiencing:

- Emotional Abuse (97%)
- Sexual Abuse (83%)
- Physical Abuse (71%)

There is a growing body of evidence that early child abuse, especially sexual, is a primary factor in the onset of sex addiction. It appears that biological shifts occur in the brain which heightens the brain's arousal mechanisms as well as limiting the ability to inhibit behavior.

Are More Sex Addicts Male or Female?

It remains unclear whether one gender has a higher incidence of sexual addiction than the other. Research by Dr. Carnes shows that approximately 20–25% of all patients who seek help for sexual dependency are women. (This same male-female ratio is found among those recovering from alcohol addiction, drug addiction, and pathological gambling.)

As once was the case with alcohol addiction, many people cannot accept the reality that women can become sexual addicts. One of the greatest problems facing female sexual addicts is convincing others that they have a legitimate problem.

The great irony is that sex addiction in women appears to be increasing. In recent, very large studies of on-line behavior, 40% of those struggling with sexually compulsive behavior are women.

Why Don't Sexual Addicts "Just Stop" Their Destructive Behavior?

Sexual addicts feel tremendous guilt and shame about their out-of-control behavior, and they live in constant fear of discovery. Yet addicts will often act out sexually in an attempt to block out the very pain of their addiction. This is part of what drives the addictive cycle. Like other forms of addiction, sex addicts are out of control and unable to stop their behaviors despite their self-destructive nature and potentially devastating consequences.

Key to understanding loss of control in addicts is the concept of the "hijacked brain." Addicts essentially have rewired their brains so that they do behaviors (drinking, drug use, eating, gambling, and sex) even when they are intending to do something quite different. The triggers to these maladaptive responses are usually stress, emotional pain, or specific childhood scenarios of sexual abuse or sexual trauma. Breakthrough science in examining brain function is helping us to understand the biology of this disease.

What About AIDS and the Sexual Addict?

As a function of their denial system, sexual addicts often ignore the severe emotional, interpersonal, and physical consequences of their behavior. Addicts are so entrenched in maintaining their behaviors that environmental cues which would signal caution and danger to most non-addicted people are lost to them. Such has been the case with the HIV virus and other dangerous sexually transmitted diseases (STDs).

Sexual addicts are focused on getting a sexual "fix." They may occasionally consider the possible consequences of their activities, but in the throes of the addictive cycle, rational thinking is seldom, if ever, present. Often dismissing the potential danger of their behavior, addicts will embrace an anxiety-laden situation to enhance their sexual high. Avoiding reality and disregarding personal safety and health are typical symptoms of sexual addiction, and they put sexual addicts at grave risk for contracting one of the many disabling STDs, including HIV.

Fear of being infected with the HIV virus and developing AIDS is not enough to stop an addict intent on being anonymously sexual, picking up prostitutes, or having multiple affairs with unsafe sex partners. Even the potential of infecting a loved one with a[n] [S]TD is often not enough to stop addicts from acting out. In fact, sexual addicts may find ways to act out even more intensely after such sexual practices in order to help drown out the shame and guilt of an overloaded and repressed emotional life.

Despite the frequency and range of their acting-out experiences, sexual addicts are often poorly informed about sexuality in general. An important part of their recovery process is learning about healthy sexual practices: behaviors which are connecting and affirming rather than shaming and guilt inducing. In addition, sexual addicts often need to be taught about safe sexual practices, basic self-care, and health concerns.

How Is Sexual Addiction Diagnosed?

Often sexual addicts don't know what is wrong with them. They may suffer from clinical depression or have suicidal tendencies. They may even think they are losing their minds.

There are, however, recognizable behavior patterns which indicate the presence of sexual addiction. Diagnosis should be done by a mental health professional trained in carrying out such diagnoses.

To help professionals determine whether a sexual addiction is present, Dr. Carnes has developed the Sexual Addiction Screening Test (SAST), an assessment tool specially designed for this purpose. It is available for self-assessment on www.sexhelp.com.

What Are the Behavior Patterns Which May Indicate Sexual Behavior?

While an actual diagnosis for sexual addiction should be carried out by a mental health professional, the following behavior patterns can indicate the presence of sexual addiction. Individuals who see any of these patterns in their own life, or in the life of someone they care about, should seek professional help.

1. Acting out: a pattern of out-of-control sexual behavior
   Examples may include:
   - Compulsive masturbation
   - Indulging in pornography
   - Having chronic affairs
   - Exhibitionism
   - Dangerous sexual practices

- Prostitution
- Anonymous sex
- Compulsive sexual episodes
- Voyeurism

2. Experiencing severe consequences due to sexual behavior, and an inability to stop despite these adverse consequences
   Some of the losses reported by sexual addicts include:
   - Louse of partner or spouse (40%)
   - Severe marital or relationship problems (70%)
   - Loss of career opportunities (27%)
   - Unwanted pregnancies (40%)
   - Abortions (36%)
   - Suicide obsession (72%)
   - Suicide attempts (17%)
   - Exposure to AIDS and venereal disease (68%)
   - Legal risks from nuisance offenses to rape (58%)

3. Persistent pursuit of self-destructive behavior
   Even understanding that the consequences of their actions will be painful or have dire consequences does not stop addicts from acting out. They often seem to have a willfulness about their actions, and an attitude that says, "I'll deal with the consequences when they come."

4. Ongoing desire or effort to limit sexual behavior
   Addicts often try to control their behavior by creating external barriers to it. For example, some move to a new neighborhood or city, hoping that a new environment removed from old affairs will help. Some think marriage will keep them from acting out. An exposer may buy a car in which it's difficult to act out while driving.
   Others seeking control over their behavior try to immerse themselves in religion, only to find out that while religious compulsion may soothe their shame, it does not end their acting out.
   Many go through periods of sexual anorexia during which they allow themselves no sexual expression at all. Such efforts, however, only fuel the addiction.

5. Sexual obsession and fantasy as a primary coping strategy
   Through acting out sexually can temporarily relieve addicts' anxieties, they still find themselves spending inordinate amounts of time in obsession and fantasy. By fantasizing, the addict can maintain an almost constant level of arousal. Together with obsessing, the two behaviors can create a kind of analgesic "fix." Just as our bodies generate endorphins, natural anti-depressants, during vigorous exercise, our bodies naturally release peptides when sexually aroused. The molecular construction of these peptides parallels that of opiates like heroin or morphine, but are many times more powerful.

6. Regularly increasing the amount of sexual experience because the current level of activity is no longer sufficiently satisfying
   Sexual addiction is often progressive. While addicts may be able to control themselves for a time, inevitably their addictive behaviors will return and quickly escalate to previous levels and beyond. Some addicts begin adding additional acting out behaviors. Usually addicts will have three or more behaviors which play a key role in their addiction—masturbation, affairs, and anonymous sex, for instance.

In addition, 89% of addicts reported regularly "bingeing" to the point of emotional exhaustion. The emotional pain of withdrawal for sexual addicts can parallel the physical pain experienced by those withdrawing from opiate addiction.

7. Severe mood changes related to sexual activity

Addicts experience intense mood shifts, often due to the despair and shame of having unwanted sex. Sexual addicts are caught in a crushing cycle of shame-driven and shame-creating behavior. While shame drives the sexual addicts' actions, it also becomes the unwanted consequence of a few moments of euphoric escape into sex.

8. Inordinate amounts of time spent obtaining sex, being sexual, and recovering from sexual experiences

Two sets of activities organize sexual addicts' days. One involves obsessing about sex, time devoted to initiating sex, and actually being sexual. The second involves time spent dealing with the consequences of their acting out: lying, covering up, shortages of money, problems with their spouse, trouble at work, neglected children, and so on.

9. Neglect of important social, occupational, or recreational activities because of sexual behavior

As more and more of addicts' energy becomes focused on relationships which have sexual potential, other relationships and activities—family, friends, work, talents, and values—suffer and atrophy from neglect. Long-term relationships are stormy and often unsuccessful. Because of sexual over-extension and intimacy avoidance, short-term relationships become the norm.

Sometimes, however, the desire to preserve an important long-term relationship with spouse or children, for instance, can act as the catalyst for addicts to admit their problem and seek help.

What Is the Role of Cybersex?

Today over 70% of sex addicts report having problematic on-line sexual behavior. Two-thirds of those engaged have such despair over their internet activities that have had suicidal thoughts. Sexual acting out online has been shown to manifest in similar off-line behavior. People who already were sex addicts find the internet accelerates their problem. Those who start in the on-line behavior quickly start to act out in new ways off-line. One of the pioneering researchers of this problem, the late Dr. Al Cooper, described on-line sexual behavior as the "crack-cocaine" of sexual compulsivity.

What Help Is There for Sexual Addiction or Sexual Anorexia?

1. Take our online test, the *SAST*
2. Contact a Certified Sex Addition Therapist (CSAT) for help. You can find a therapist in your area by calling 800-708-1796 or by visiting www. sexhelp.com

3. Twelve step programs
4. Visit GentlePath.com to browse the online catalog for books and tapes which will help you understand sex addiction and sexual anorexia.

Getting Help: The First Step

The first step in seeking help is to admit to the problem. Though marital, professional, and societal consequences may follow, admission of the problems must come, no matter the cost. Fear of these consequences unfortunately keeps many sexual addicts from seeking help.

Many sources of help are available to provide information, support, and assistance for sexual addicts trying to regain control of their lives. These include inpatient and outpatient treatment, professional associations, self-help groups, and aftercare support groups.

Sex Addicts Anonymous (SAA)
P.O. Box 70949
Houston, TX 77270
1-800-477-8191
e-mail: webmaster@saa-recovery.org

SASH
P.O. Box 725544
Atlanta, GA 31139
1-770-541-9912
e-mail: info@SASH.net

Sex Compulsives Anonymous (SCA)
P.O. Box 1585
Old Chelsea Station
New York, NY 10011
(001)210-828-7900
email: info@slaafws.org

Sex and Love Addicts Anonymous (SLAA)
1550 NE Loop 410, Ste. 118
San Antonio, TX 78209
212-439-1123
email: info@slaafws.org

National Council for Couple and Family Recovery
P.O. Box 410586
St. Louis, MO 63141
314-997-9808
email: nccfr@hotmail.com

What Treatment Is Available for Sex Addiction?

Treatment programs for sexual addiction include patient, outpatient, and aftercare support, and self-help groups. Treatment programs also offer family counseling programs, support groups, and educational workshops for addicts and their families to help them understand the facets of belief and family like that are part of the addiction.

Unlike recovering alcoholics who must abstain from drinking for life, sexual addicts are led back into a normal, healthy sex life much in the way those suffering from eating disorders must relearn healthy eating patterns.

The staff at Gentle Path is trained to help individuals develop healthy, effective coping skills through interacting with others experiencing similar problems. Gentle Path is designed to set addicts on the road to recovery, to provide relapse prevention techniques, and to help them stay in recovery with the help of aftercare and Twelve Step recovery support groups.

Are Sexual Addicts Ever Cured?

Like other types of addicts, some sexual addicts may never be "cured." Sexual addicts achieve a state of recovery, but maintaining that recovery can be a life-long, day-by-day process. The Twelve Step treatment approach teaches addicts to take their recovery "one day at a time"—concentrating on the present, not the future.

Is There Any Help Available for the Partners of Sex Addicts?

Partners of sexual addicts, like partners of alcoholics, can also benefit from counseling and support groups. Normally these partners are codependents, and they, too, suffer from the extreme adverse effects of the addiction. Inpatient and outpatient programs, counseling, and support groups are all available to help them regain control of their lives and support the recovery of their partner.

**Lawrence A. Siegel and
Richard M. Siegel**

 **NO**

Sex Addiction: Semantics or Science?

With the dizzying blur of events that was 2010—from unprecedented economic turmoil and panic to our military continuing to be mired in Iraq and Afghanistan, and even the emergence of a new "Tea Party" movement and the most vitriolic bipartisanship in decades—it seems the year will most likely be remembered as the Year of the Tiger. And though it was, in fact, that very year in the Chinese calendar, we are of course talking about the golfer, Tiger Woods. And now, as we roll into 2011, Mr. Woods is slowly, slowly beginning to be thought of as a golfer again, rather than the latest and most notorious "poster boy" for the sex addiction industry—which, it should be noted, is enjoying a windfall of popularity and exponentially growing profit, as well as the predictable explosion of "experts" and "sex addiction therapists" swarming markets all over the country, offering vague promises of "recovery" from any one of a hundred forms of so-called "sex addiction."

Nevermind (as the public, the media, and the industry itself do) that there is no such medically or psychologically recognized diagnosis, and that an outrageously expensive and completely unproven "treatment" thrives without the slightest oversight or accountability. And despite the industry's assertions that the medical and psychological establishment has simply not caught up with what they just know to be true, there has still not been any scientific research conducted to either confirm such a diagnosis or show effectiveness of any kind of "sex addiction treatment."

The whole idea of "sex addiction" is a metaphor gone amuck, and is borne out of a moralistic ideology masquerading as science. It is a concept that seems to serve no other purpose than to relegate sexual expression to the level of shameful acts, except within the extremely narrow and myopic scope of a monogamous, heterosexual marriage. Sexual diversity? Interests in unusual forms or frequency of sexual expression? Choosing not to be monogamous? Advocates of "sex addiction" would likely see these as the uncontrollable acts of a sexually pathological individual; one who needs curing.

To be clear, we do not deny the fact that, for some people, sexual behavior can become problematic, even dysfunctional or unmanageable. Our objection is with the use of the term "sexual addiction" to describe a virtually unlimited array of—in fact, practically ANY—aspect of sexual expression that falls outside of the typically Christian view of marriage. We believe that the term contributes to a generally sex-negative, pleasure-phobic tone in American society, and it also tends to "pathologize" most forms of sexual expression that fall outside of a narrow view of what "normal" sex is supposed to look like. This is a point made clear by sex addiction advocates' own rhetoric. Three of the guiding principles of Sexaholics Anonymous include the notion that (1) sex is most healthy in the context of a monogamous, heterosexual relationship; (2) sexual expression has "obvious" limits; and (3) it is unhealthy to engage in any sexual activity for the sole purpose of feeling better, either emotionally or to escape one's problems. These principles do not represent either science or most people's experience. They, in fact, represent a restrictive and repressive view of sex and sexuality and reflect an arrogance that sex addiction proponents are the keepers of the scepter of morality and normalcy. Moreover, the concept of "sex addiction" comes out of a shame-based, arbitrarily judgmental addiction model and does not speak to the wide range of sexual diversity, both in and outside the context of a committed relationship.

A primary objection to the use of the term "sex addiction," an objection shared with regard to other supposed behavioral "addictions," is that the term *addiction* has long ago been discredited. Back in 1964, the World Health Organization (WHO) declared the term "addiction" to be clinically invalid and recommended in favor of dependence, which can exist in varying degrees of severity, as opposed to an all-or-nothing disease entity (as it is still commonly perceived) (1). This is when we began to see the terms *chemical dependency* and *substance abuse,* terms considered to be much more appropriate and clinically useful. This, however, did not sit well with the addiction industry. Another objection to the concept of "sex addiction" is that it is a misnomer whose very foundation as a clinically significant diagnosis is built on flawed and faulty premises. For example, a common assertion put forth by proponents of sex addiction states that the chemical actions in the brain during sexual activity are the same as the chemical activity involved in alcohol and drug use. They, therefore, claim that both sexual activity and substance abuse share reward and reinforcement mechanisms that produce the "craving" and "addictive" behaviors. This assertion is flawed on several levels, not the least of which is that it is based on drawing conclusions from brain scan imaging that are devoid of any real interpretive foundation, a "leap of faith," so to speak. Furthermore, it is somewhat of a stretch to equate the neurophysiological mechanisms which underlie chemical dependency, tolerance, and withdrawal with the underlying mechanisms of what is most often compulsive or anxiety-reducing behaviors like gambling, shopping, sex, and other so-called "process addictions."

Another example often cited by sex addiction proponents is the assertion that, like alcohol and drugs, the "sex addict" is completely incapable of controlling his or her self-destructive behavior. Of course, this begs the question of how, then, can one change behavior they are incapable of controlling? More importantly, however, is the unique excuse this "disease" model provides for abdicating personal responsibility. "It's not my fault, I have a disease." More often than not, it seems that "I can't stop" is the ultimate excuse for "I don't want to stop." Finally, a major assertion put out by sex addiction advocates is that anyone who is hypersexual in any way (e.g., frequent masturbation, anonymous "hook ups," infidelity, and cybersex) must have been abused as children or adolescents. Again, the flaws here are obvious and serve to continue to relegate any type of frequent sexual engagement to the pathological and unseemly—Tiger Woods was merely one of a long list of celebrity indiscretions made public. But what made Mr. Woods' case unique was that he seemed to have been diagnosed by the media, based on assumptions made from rumors and leaked reports, along with a paparazzi's photograph of him outside a sex addiction treatment center in Mississippi. Confirmation of his admission, then, was proof enough of his "disease."

Of course, the seemingly never-ending parade of politician sex scandals, each with the requisite and routine news conference of "mea culpas" and high-profile treatment stays (some even the fodder for "reality television" shows like "Celebrity Sex Rehab") that have become *de rigueur* for any famous person caught having an affair.

This becomes even more troubling in light of the fact that many professionals in this industry rely on patients' self diagnosis, often giving legitimacy to the notion that if one feels they are an addict, then they are one. One would be hard pressed to find any other area of clinical management that is based on patients diagnosing themselves.

Every clinician knows that "addiction" is not a word that appears anywhere in the *Diagnostic and Statistical Manual,* or "DSM," the diagnostic guidebook used by psychiatrists and psychologists to make any psychopathological diagnosis. Nor does it appear in any of the International Classification of Diseases (ICD-10), codes used for classifying medical diagnoses. "Abuse" and "dependence" do appear in the DSM, relevant only to substance use patterns, but "addiction" does not. Similarly, there is an ICD-10 code for "substance dependence," but not addiction. Why? Perhaps because the word means different things to different people, especially when used in so many different contexts. Even without acknowledging the many trivial uses of the addiction concept, such as bumper stickers that proclaim, *"addicted to sports, not drugs,"* cookies that claim to be *"deliciously addicting,"* Garfield coffee mugs that warn *"don't talk to me until after my first cup,"* or T-shirts that say *"chocoholic,"* there aren't even consistent *clinical* definitions for the concept of addiction. A 1993 study, published in the *American Journal of Drug and Alcohol Abuse,* compared the diagnostic criteria for substance abuse and dependence between the DSM and ICD-10. The results showed very little agreement between the two (2).

Pharmacologists, researchers who study the effects of drugs, define addiction primarily based on the presence of tolerance and withdrawal. Both of these phenomena are based on pharmacological and toxicological concepts of "cellular adaptation," wherein the body, at the very cellular level, becomes accustomed to the constant presence of a substance, and readjusts for "normal" function; in other words, whatever the "normal" response was before regular use of the substance began returns. This adaptation first accounts for tolerance, wherein an increasing dose of the substance to which the system has adapted is needed to maintain the same level of "normal." Then it results in withdrawal, wherein any discontinuation of the substance disrupts the "new" equilibrium the system has achieved and symptoms of "withdrawal sickness" ensue. This is probably most often attributed to addiction to opiates, such as heroin, because of its comparison to "having a monkey on one's back," with a constantly growing appetite, and its notorious "cold turkey" withdrawal. But perhaps it is most commonly observed with the chronic use of drugs with less sinister reputations, such as caffeine, nicotine, or alcohol.

Traditional psychotherapists may typically define addiction as a faulty coping mechanism, or more accurately, the *result* of using a faulty coping mechanism to deal with some underlying issue. Another way to consider this is to see addiction as the symptom, rather than the disease, which is why the traditional therapist, of any theoretical orientation, is likely to want to find the causative issue or issues, and either teach the patient more effective coping mechanisms or resolve the unresolved issue(s) altogether. This is backed up by a number of studies which show that the vast majority of so-called "sex addicts" display an extremely high co-morbidity rate with mood, anxiety, and personality disorders. Keep in mind that psychotherapists are legally and ethically bound to adhere to established and accepted standards of diagnosis and treatment, regardless of whatever cultural fads may be enjoying popularity.

Another definition of addiction has emerged, and seems to have taken center-stage, since the development of a pseudo-medical specialty known as "addictionology" within the last twenty or so years. Made up primarily of physicians, but including a variety of "addiction professionals," this field has helped to forge a treatment industry based on the disease model of addiction that is at the core of 12-Step "fellowships," such as Alcoholics Anonymous and Narcotics Anonymous. Ironically, despite the resistance to medical or psychiatric treatment historically expressed in AA or NA, their philosophy has become the mainstay of the addictionological paradigm. This becomes especially ironic considering these programs also eschew any attempt to empirically validate their rhetorical effectiveness, seeking validation only on the basis of recommending the program to others.

If the concept of chemical addictions, which have a neurophysiological basis that can be measured and observed, yields no clinical consensus, how, then, can we legitimize the much vaguer notion that individuals can be "addicted" to behavior, people, emotions, or even one's own brain chemistry? Other than to undermine responsibility and self-determination, we really can't. It does a tremendous disservice to our clients and patients to brand them with a label so full of judgment, arbitrary opinion, and fatuous science. It robs individuals of the ability to find their own levels of comfort and, ultimately, be the determining force in directing their own lives. There is a significant and qualitative difference between the person who acts because he or she can't (not a choice, but a position of default) and the person who is empowered to choose not to. As clinicians, we should loathe sending our clients and patients down such a fearful, shameful road.

In 1989, Patrick Carnes, founder of the sex addiction movement, wrote a book entitled *Contrary to Love*. The book is rife with rhetoric and personal ideology that reveals a lack of training, knowledge, and understanding of sexuality and sexual expression, not surprising for someone whose background is solely in the disease model of alcoholism. To illustrate the importance of understanding that perspective, we will simply paraphrase the oft-quoted Abraham Maslow: If the only tool in your toolbox is a hammer, then everything begins to look like a nail. This, while seemingly a harsh judgment, is clearly reflected in the Sex Addiction Screening Test (SAST). Even a cursory glance at the items on the SAST shows a deep-seated bias against most forms of sexual expression. Unlike other legitimate screening and assessment tools, there is no scientific foundation that would show this tool to be credible (i.e., tests of reliability and validity). Instead, Carnes developed this "test" by simply culling his own ideas from his book. Annie Sprinkle, America's first adult-film-star-turned-PhD-Sexologist, has written a very good web article on the myth of sex addiction. In it, she also describes some of the shortcomings of the SAST. While not describing the complete test here, a listing of some of the assessment questions are listed below, along with commentary (3).

1. *Have you subscribed to sexually explicit magazines like* Playboy *or* Penthouse? This question is based in the assumption that it is unhealthy to view images of naked bodies. Does that mean that the millions of people who subscribe to or buy adult magazines are sex addicts? Are adolescent boys who look at the *Sports Illustrated Swimsuit* edition budding sex addicts? By extension, if looking at *Playboy* or *Penthouse* is unhealthy and pathological, then those millions of people who look at hardcore magazines or Internet porn should be hospitalized!

2. *Do you often find yourself preoccupied with sexual thoughts?* This is totally nebulous. What does "preoccupied" mean? How often does one have to think about sex in order to constitute preoccupation? Research has shown that men, on average, think about sex every eight seconds; does that mean that men are inherently sex addicts?

3. *Do you feel that your sexual behavior is not normal?* What is normal? What do they use as a comparison? As sexologists, we can state unequivocally that the majority of people's sexual concerns relate, in one way or another, to the question "Am I normal?" This is incredibly vague, nebulous, and laughably unscientific.

4. *Are any of your sexual activities against the law?* This question is also steeped in a bias that there is only a narrowly acceptable realm of sexual expression. It assumes that any sexual behavior that is against the law is bad. Is being or engaging a prostitute a sign of pathology? What about the fact that oral sex, anal sex, and woman-on-top sex are illegal in several states?

5. *Have you ever felt degraded by your sexual behavior?* Again, there is a serious lack of quantification here. Does regretting a sexual encounter constitute feeling degraded? Does performing oral sex for your partner, even though you think it's degrading, constitute a pathology or compromise? What if one's partner does something during sex play that is unexpected and perceived as degrading (like ejaculating on someone's face or body)? What if someone enjoys feeling degraded? This question pathologizes at least half of the S/M and B/D communities. Moreover, anyone who has had a long and active sexual life may likely, at one point, to have felt degraded by something they've done. It is important to note that this question does not ask

if one consistently puts oneself in a position of being degraded and later experiences intense guilt and shame but, rather, have you ever felt degraded. We suspect that most people can lay claim to that, to some degree or another.

6. *Has sex been a way for you to escape your problems?* Is there a better way to escape one's problems temporarily? This is a common bias used against both sex and alcohol use: using sex or alcohol to provide relief from anxieties or problems is inherently problematic. It also begs the question: why are things like sex and alcohol not appropriate to change how one is feeling but Zoloft, Paxil, Xanax, and Klonopin are? The truth of the matter is that sex is often an excellent and healthy way to occasionally experience relief from life's stressors and problems, more often working better than any medication.

7. *When you have sex, do you feel depressed afterwards?* Sex is often a great way to get in touch with one's feelings. Oftentimes, people do feel depressed after a sexual experience, for any number of reasons. Furthermore, this doesn't mean that sex was the depressing part! Perhaps people feel depressed because they had dashed expectations of the person they were involved with. Unfulfilled expectations, lack of communication, and inattentiveness to one's needs and desires often result in post-coital feelings of sadness and disappointment. In addition, asking someone if they "feel depressed" is arbitrary, subjective, and clinically invalid.

8. *Do you feel controlled by your sexual desire?* Again, we are being asked to make an arbitrary, subjective, and clinically invalid assessment. There is an undercurrent here that seems to imply that a strong sexual desire is somehow not normal. Human beings are biologically programmed to strongly desire sex. Our clients and patients might be better served if we addressed not their desires, but how and when they *act* upon them.

It is worth further noting that the concept of "sex addiction" is one with very little clinical relevance or usefulness, despite its popularity. Healthy sexual expression encompasses a wide array of forms, functions, and frequency, as well as myriad emotional dynamics and personal experiences. Healthy behavior, in general, and sexual behavior, in particular, exists on a continuum rather than as a quantifiable point. Using the addiction model to describe sexual behavior simply adds to the shame and stigma that is already too often attached to various forms of sexual expression. Can sexual behaviors become problematic? Most certainly. However, we must be careful to not overpathologize even problematic sexual behaviors because, most often, they are symptomatic expressions rather than primary problems.

For many years, sexologists have described compulsive sexual behavior, where sexual obsessions and compulsions are recurrent, distressing, and interfere with daily functioning. The actual number of people suffering from this type of sexual problem is relatively small. Compulsive sexual behaviors are generally divided into two broad categories: *paraphilic* and *non-paraphilic* (4). Paraphilias are defined as recurrent, intensely arousing fantasies, sexual urges, or behaviors involving non-human objects, pain and humiliation, or children (5). Paraphilic behaviors are usually non-conventional forms of sexual expression that, in the extreme, can be harmful to relationships and individuals. Some examples of paraphilias listed in the DSM are pedophilia (sexual attraction to children), exhibitionism (exposing one's genitals in public), voyeurism (sexual excitement from watching an unsuspecting person), sexual sadism (sexual excitement from dominating or inflicting pain), sexual masochism (sexual excitement from being dominated or receiving pain), transvestic fetishism (sexual excitement from wearing clothes of the other sex), and frotteurism (sexual excitement from rubbing up against or fondling an unsuspecting person). All of these behaviors exist on a continuum of healthy fantasy play to dangerous, abusive, and illegal acts. A sexologist is able to view these behaviors in varying degrees, knowing the difference between teacher-student fantasy role play and cruising a playground for victims; between provocative exhibitionist displays (including public displays of affection) and illegal, abusive public exposure. For those with a "sex addiction" perspective, simply having paraphilic thoughts or desires of any kind is reason to brand the individual a "sex addict."

The other category of compulsive sexual behavior is non-paraphilic or "normaphilic," and generally involves more conventional sexual behaviors which, when taken to the extreme, cause marked distress and interference with daily functioning. This category includes a fixation on an unattainable partner, compulsive masturbation, compulsive love relationships, and compulsive sexuality in a relationship. The most vocal criticism of the idea of compulsive sexual behavior as a clinical disorder appears to center on the overpathologizing of these behaviors. Unless specifically trained in sexuality, most clinicians are either uncomfortable or unfamiliar with the wide range of "normal" sexual behavior and fail to distinguish between individuals who experience conflict between their values and sexual behavior, and those with obsessive sexual behavior (6). When diagnosing compulsive sexual behavior overall, there is little consensus even among sexologists. However, it still provides a more useful clinical framework for the professional trained in sexuality and sexual health.

To recognize that sexual behavior can be problematic is not the same as labeling the behaviors as "sexually compulsive" or "sexual addiction." The reality is that sexual problems are quite common and are usually due to non-pathological factors. Quite simply, people make mistakes (some more than others). People also act impulsively, not always making good sexual choices. When people do make mistakes, act impulsively, and make bad decisions, it often negatively impacts their relationships; sometimes even their lives. Moreover, people do often use sex as a coping mechanism or, to borrow from addiction language, a "medicating behavior" that can become problematic. While this can be a useful metaphor, it has been taken literally by proponents of the "sex addiction" approach. Thus, an entire field has as its foundation a metaphor run amuck.

However, this is qualitatively different from the concept that problematic sexual behavior means the individual is a "sexual addict" with uncontrollable urges and potentially dangerous intent. Most problematic sexual behavior can be effectively redirected (and cured) through psycho-sexual education, counseling, and sex therapy. According to proponents of "sex addiction," problematic sexual behavior cannot be cured. Rather, the "sex addict" is destined for a life of maintaining a constant vigil to prevent the behavior from reoccurring, often to the point of obsession, and will be engaged in a lifelong process of a fear-based "recovery." Unfortunately, as with its chemical counterparts, it is just not the reality for most people. More unfortunately, this view causes people to live in fear of that ever-present "demon" lurking around every corner: themselves.

References

1. Center for Substance Abuse Treatment (CSAT) and Substance Abuse and Mental Health Services Administration (SAMHSA). Substance use disorders: A guide to the use of language. 2004.

2. Rappaport M, Tipp J, Schuckit M. A comparison of ICD-10 and DSM-III criteria for substance abuse and dependence. American Journal of Drug and Alcohol Abuse. June, 1993.

3. Sprinkle, A. Sex addiction. Online article. Accessed 11/5/06 from www.anniesprinkle.org.

4. Coleman E. What sexual scientists know about compulsive sexual behavior. Electronic series of the Society for the Scientific Study of Sexuality (SSSS). Vol 2(1). 1996. Accessed 11/5/06 from www.sexscience.org.

5. American Psychiatric Association. Diagnostic and Statistical Manual of Mental Disorders. 4th edition, TR. Washington: American Psychiatric Publishing. June, 2000.

6. Coleman E. What sexual scientists know about compulsive sexual behavior. Electronic series of the Society for the Scientific Study of Sexuality (SSSS). Vol 2(1). 1996. Accessed 11/5/06 from www.sexscience.org.

POSTSCRIPT

Can Sex Be Addictive?

The framing of sex as a compulsive and addictive behavior is nothing new. The idea that masturbation and frequent intercourse could send a person into a downward spiral of unhealthiness was presented in advice columns, "health" journals, and other periodicals during the Victorian Era and the early 1900s. Consider the following excerpt about masturbation from John Harvey Kellogg's *Plain Facts for Old and Young,* written in 1891:

> As a sin against nature, it has no parallel except in sodomy. It is known by the terms self-pollution, self-abuse, masturbation, onanism, voluntary pollution, and solitary or secret vice. The habit is by no means confined to boys; girls also indulge in it, though it is to be hoped, to a less fearful extent than boys, at least in this country. Of all the vices to which human beings are addicted, no other so rapidly undermines the constitution, and so certainly makes a complete wreck of an individual as this, especially when the habit is begun at an early age. It wastes the most precious part of the blood, uses up the vital forces, and finally leaves the poor victim a most utterly ruined and loathsome object.
>
> Suspicious signs are: bashfulness, unnatural boldness, round shoulders and a stooping position, lack of development of the breasts in females, eating chalk, acne, and the use of tobacco.

Nineteenth-century preacher Sylvester Graham also described a litany of ailments that would affect the masturbator, or anyone who had "frequent" intercourse before age 30. If the names Kellogg and Graham ring a bell, it may be because the food products they created, cornflakes and graham crackers, were made because they would supposedly help to suppress the sexual urges of some of the earliest "sex addicts" (which could have been just about anyone)!

More recently, attempts at measuring sexual addiction have taken on a more scientific tone, although critics of this term pose that it is simply the same old Victorian idea, repackaged for a new century. At the heart of this controversy, however, is the true meaning of a word many have trouble defining: addiction.

Think of the many things that might be considered addictive—alcohol, caffeine, tobacco, other drugs—and assess whether or not they are part of your life, or the lives of your family or friends. What makes something addictive? Is it how often a person indulges in it? Is it the degree to which it seems recreational or compulsive? Is it how much control a person has in deciding whether or not to engage in it? Or, is addiction more about what might be considered a social vice?

How about nonchemical behaviors that some might consider compulsive? Are people who surf the Internet for hours "addicted"? How about a political "junkie" who constantly scours newspapers and blogs for new information, the person who never misses an episode of his or her favorite TV crime fighting drama, or teens (and adults) who play video games for hours at a time? What about the person who spends every Sunday glued to the TV watching football, or the one who builds his or her life around his or her favorite soaps, or the person who constantly checks and updates his or her Facebook or Twitter account? Can a person be addicted to his or her artistic or musical pursuits or fitness and exercise? Are these harmless habits—ways to relax and blow off steam? Which behaviors escape the realm of "addiction" because they are more socially functional?

Does something become addictive only when it is undesired or otherwise interferes with one's life? Does this apply to spending more time with one's hobbies than a significant other, family, or job might like? Does skipping class to play video games or engage in online gambling put one at the cusp of addiction? Considering sexual behaviors, is it possible to be addicted to masturbation or other sexual behaviors, as Carnes asserts? Is looking at online porn for hours different than playing an online game for hours? Is skipping class to have intercourse with a partner a sign of addiction? Is there a line between healthy sexual expression and compulsion or addiction? And if so, where is that line drawn?

Did you agree with Carnes' examples of behaviors that may indicate sexual addiction? Do you agree or disagree with Siegel and Siegel's critiques of Carnes' assessment criteria? Is sex addiction a serious problem, as Carnes asserts? Or is the assigning of an "addiction" status to otherwise healthy and consensual activities simply adding to the modern trend of the medicalization of sexuality, while recalling an era when sexuality was simply demonized?

Suggested Readings

P. Carnes, *Out of the Shadows: Understanding Sexual Addiction* (Compcare Publications, 1992).

B.J. Dew and M.P. Chaney, "Sexual Addiction and the Internet: Implications for Gay Men," *Journal of Addictions & Offender Counseling,* (vol. 24, 2004).

B. Dodge et al., "Sexual Compulsivity Among Heterosexual College Students," *The Journal of Sex Research* (vol. 41, 2004).

C. Holden, "Behavioral Addictions Debut in Proposed DSM-V," *Science* (February 2010).

M. Klein, *America's War on Sex* (Praeger, 2006).

S. Levine, "What Is Sexual Addiction?" *Journal of Sex & Marital Therapy* (vol. 36, no. 3, 2010).

C. Samenow, "Classifying Problematic Sexual Behaviors—It's All in the Name," *Sexual Addicion & Compulsivity* (vol. 17, no. 3, 2010).

M.F. Schwartz, "Sexual Addiction: An Integrated Approach," *Archives of Sexual Behavior* (vol. 33, 2004).

ISSUE 4

Does Sexual Medicine Benefit Society?

YES: **Connie Newman**, from "Pharmacological Treatment for Sexual Problems: The Benefits Outweigh the Risks," an original essay written for this volume (2011)

NO: **Leonore Tiefer**, from "Beneath the Veneer: The Troubled Past and Future of Sexual Medicine," *Journal of Sex and Marital Therapy* (vol. 33, 2007)

ISSUE SUMMARY

YES: Connie Newman, an endocrinologist and adjunct associate professor of medicine at New York University School of Medicine, explores the definitions and causes of sexual dysfunction and explains how sexual medicines can improve sexual response.

NO: Leonore Tiefer, author and clinical associate professor of psychiatry at New York University School of Medicine, counters that the rise of "sexual medicine" brings with it risks that should not be ignored.

If you watch much television, chances are you have seen ads for VIAGRA, a drug that treats erectile dysfunction in men. In fact, 2008 marked the 10-year anniversary of the "little blue pill." Since its release, several additional erectile dysfunction drugs, including LEVITRA and CIALIS, have made the process of getting erections much easier for millions of men around the world. The products have been so successful that pharmaceutical companies have, for years, been attempting to replicate their success with medications for a variety of sexual dysfunctions in women (including hypoactive sexual disorder, otherwise known as low libido). Authors of a study from 1999 found that 43 percent of women between the ages of 18 and 59 had some type of sexual dysfunction (Laumann et al., 1999). Pharmaceutical companies invested billions of dollars into research for elusive remedies. It was thought that the profits from women's treatments would rival, if not surpass, those of male treatments.

Clinical trials of a women's version of VIAGRA, as well as several other potential medications, ended with mixed results. Intrinsa, a testosterone patch designed to increase women's libido, showed promise, but was denied Food and Drug Administration (FDA) approval (the patch was approved in several European countries, however). The desire for the product was there; the desired results, on the other hand, were not.

Why has the search for a women's prescription treatment proven so challenging? If men can have some of their sexual issues taken care of with a prescription medication, critics argue, why have women's sexual problems proven so difficult to treat? Some women's health advocates take issue over the disparity between FDA-approved drugs available for men and women. Some saw sexism and a fear of women's sexuality at play in the FDA's decisions. Others theorized there were subtle differences between the ways men and women experienced arousal. A pill may have a difficult time differentiating between such body–mind nuances.

Another camp holds that pharmaceutical treatments for such complex issues (for both men and women) may be off base to begin with. Many therapists and sexologists warn against what they see as the "medicalization" of sexual problems. An overreliance on prescription drugs is seen as a one-size-fits-all approach that ignores larger issues. Some point to the far more common psychogenic causes of sexual dysfunction that cannot be treated by medication. They contend that nonmedical treatments (improving partner communication, for example) would be far more effective. They charge that pharmaceutical companies are making a hefty profit through the "medicalization" of sexuality. Still others argue that the estimated number of sexual dysfunction cases is inflated, and that the vast majority of real cases of both female and male sexual dysfunction are caused by psychological or interpersonal factors that are better treated with nonmedical intervention.

In the following selections, Connie Newman describes the common problem of sexual dysfunction in both men and women and explores the ways in which sexual medicines may alleviate these problems. Leonore Tiefer argues that pharmaceutical companies aim not to solidify a holistic approach to sexual health, but rather increase profits for drug companies.

Reference

E. Laumann, et al., "Sexual Dysfunctions in the United States," *Journal of the American Medical Association* (vol. 281, pp. 537–544, 1999).

YES

Connie B. Newman

Pharmacological Treatment for Sexual Problems: The Benefits Outweigh the Risks

Introduction

In the past decade considerable controversy has emerged over whether medicines that improve sexual function are truly needed. In fact, some experts have accused the pharmaceutical industry of creating sexual diseases in order to profit from new medicines specifically designed for these "invented" diseases (1, 2). In November 2010, while at a sex education conference sponsored by The Center for Family Life Education (The CFLE), I had the opportunity to preview the movie *Orgasm Inc.*, a documentary about the development of therapies to improve women's sex lives. The movie questioned whether female sexual dysfunction was a real disorder or a pseudo-disease created by the pharmaceutical industry in order to develop and market sex-enhancing medicines for women. In doing this, the movie made light of the real sexual problems that some women have. It did not explain the nature of the highly regulated drug development process, which requires pharmaceutical companies to adhere to strict standards in developing safe and effective medicines. It also put forth a distorted image of practicing doctors, showing them to be too eager to fix their patients' problems by prescribing medications.

To my surprise many people in the audience seemed to believe every word in the film and did not understand that there might be another side to this story. I am writing this article to explain the other point of view, or at least a more balanced point of view. Sexual dysfunction is a real disorder that occurs in women, especially as they age, as well as in men. Women's sex problems can have a physiological as well as a psychological basis, and are not solely due to lack of sex education, poor relationships, or working long hours. Sexual medicines that enhance sexual performance can benefit individuals and society. Pharmaceutical companies are interested in making a profit (after all they would not be in business if they did not), but in addition many scientists who work in pharmaceutical companies want to help people have healthier and more satisfied lives. Doctors prescribe medicines for patients only after a diagnosis is reached by evaluation of the patient's history, symptoms, physical findings and laboratory tests, and after consideration of the benefits and risks of available therapies.

This article assesses the benefits and risks of using pharmacological treatments (sexual medicines) for individuals with sexual dysfunction. The following topics will be considered: the definitions and causes of sexual dysfunction in men and women, the prevalence of sexual dysfunction, therapeutic options for individuals with sexual problems, and an analysis of currently available medicines for sexual dysfunction.

Changing Definitions of Sexual Dysfunction: A Shift from Psychological Factors to Combined Organic and Psychological Causes

Sexual dysfunction is a broad general term that includes abnormalities in libido (sex drive), erections, orgasms, and ejaculation in men, and in sexual desire, arousal, orgasm in women, as well as painful intercourse and vaginal spasm. The sexual response cycle differs in men and women (3). In men, sexual desire often occurs before sexual stimuli and subsequent arousal. In contrast, women, especially those in established relationships, often engage in sex with their partners for reasons other than desire (3). Data suggest that sexual desire, as expressed by fantasizing, anticipating sexual experiences, and spontaneously thinking about sex in a positive way, varies in frequency among women and may be infrequent in many women who have normal sexual function (3, 4). In women, desire can be triggered during the sexual encounter (5), and desire then follows sexual arousal.

In both men and women many hormones, peptides, and neurotransmitters have a role in sexual desire and arousal. One of these hormones, testosterone, and its potential therapeutic uses, will be discussed later. Various medical conditions can adversely affect sexual responsiveness, as can depression, other psychiatric diseases, and psychological and social factors. In addition, medications including antidepressant agents can cause sexual problems as a side effect.

Defining sexual dysfunction has been difficult because of incomplete understanding of sexual disorders, especially in women. Classification of sexual disorders has been based on the *Diagnostic and Statistical Manual of Mental Disorders, 4th Ed.* (*DSM-IV*), a manual published by the American Psychiatric Association, reflecting the long-held belief that most sexual problems are psychologically based (6). This in itself might explain some of the resistance to pharmacological therapies that is still present today. *DSM-IV* recognized five disorders in female sexual function: hypoactive sexual desire disorder (reduced desire for sexual activity), female sexual arousal disorder, female orgasmic disorder, dyspareunia (genital pain associated with sexual intercourse), and vaginismus (spasm of the muscles of the outer third of the vagina that interferes with sexual intercourse). *DSM-IV* classified sexual disorders in men into the following main categories: erectile disorder, orgasmic disorder, premature ejaculation, hypoactive sexual desire disorder, and dyspareunia due to general medical condition. A new, revised manual of sexual disorders, with more precise definitions, is targeted for publication in 2012.

Prevalence of Sexual Disorders: What Do We Really Know?

It is difficult to know the true prevalence of sexual disorders in different age groups because most of the information comes from large surveys, rather than from detailed assessment by interviews. Although both the Food and Drug Administration (FDA) and the American Psychiatric Association require personal distress as part of the definition of sexual dysfunction, some of the older studies did not specifically evaluate this parameter. In the following section, data from the following surveys are presented: Massachusetts Male Aging Study (MMAS) in 1,709 men ages 40–70 years (7) and in 847 men ages 40–69 years (8); National Health and Social Life Survey (NHSLS) in 1,749 women and 1,410 men ages 18–59 years (9); National Social Life, Health and Aging Project (NSHAP) in 1,550 women and 1,455 men ages 57–85 years (10); Prevalence of Female Sexual Problems Associated with Distress and Determinants of Treatment (PRESIDE) in 31,581 women ages 18–102 years (11).

Estimates of Prevalence of Sexual Disorders in Men

Premature ejaculation is the most prevalent sexual disorder in young adult men and is defined by *DSM-IV* as "persistent or recurrent ejaculation with minimal sexual stimulation, before, upon, or shortly after penetration and before the person wishes it." In addition, the disturbance must cause marked distress or interpersonal difficulty. This definition of premature ejaculation has been criticized because it is not precise and is dependent upon the judgment of the clinician as well as the patient (12). The exact prevalence is unknown because of the lack of a universally accepted definition and the fact that, like most data on sexual function, the available data are self-reported. In NHSLS, early climax was reported by 30% of men between the ages of 18 [and] 29 years, and by 28–32% of men in the older age groups: 30–39, 40–49, 50–59 (9). Performance anxiety was less common than premature ejaculation, and was reported by 19% of men in the youngest age group, and 14% of men in the oldest age group.

Erectile dysfunction also occurs in younger men, although less frequently than in older men. How much of this is related to performance anxiety in younger men is not known. In NHSLS (9), difficulty in maintaining an erection was reported in less than 10% of the youngest men (18–29 years), and in 18% of men between the ages of 50 [and] 59 years. As men are more likely to overstate than understate their sexual capacity, these percentages are probably underestimates. Among older men the most prevalent sexual problem is erectile dysfunction (7, 8, 10), which increases with age and disease. In MMAS (7, 8), 52% of men between the ages of 40 [and] 70 years reported some degree of erectile dysfunction. With more advanced age, the prevalence of erectile dysfunction increases, affecting as many as 75% of men over the age of 80.

Lack of interest in sex is a less frequent complaint for men than either premature ejaculation or erectile dysfunction. In NHSLS, about 15% of men reported lack of interest in sex (9). In NSHAP, in older men between the ages of 57 and 85 years, lack of interest in sex was reported by 28% of respondents (10).

Estimates of Prevalence of Sexual Disorders in Women

There is uncertainty about the overall prevalence of sexual problems in women. NHSLS concluded that in women aged 18–59 years the prevalence of sexual dysfunction was 43%. More recently, PRESIDE, a survey of about 31,000 women (age 18–102 years, mean age 49), found that while 43% had at least one sexual problem, only 22% reported sexually related personal distress (11). The most common sexual problems reported by women are low desire, low sexual arousal, and inability to achieve an orgasm (9–11). In PRESIDE, 27% of women in the youngest age group reported any of these sexual problems, compared with about 45% of middle-aged women, and 80% of women 65 years of age or older (11). In NHSLS, in the youngest women studied (ages 18–29), 32% reported lack of interest in sex, 26% reported inability to achieve orgasm, 21% reported pain during sex, and 16% reported performance anxiety (9). In PRESIDE low desire was the most common sexual problem reported by 39% of the entire group; less common were low arousal (26%) and orgasm difficulties (21%) (11). Distressing sexual problems were more common in middle-aged than in younger or older women. Women with depression had more than twice the chance of having distressing sexual problems. This may be due in part to the adverse sexual side effects of antidepressant drugs, which can interfere with the ability to have an orgasm.

Taking all these data into consideration, it appears that at least one-third of men and women of all ages report sexual problems. In younger men, premature ejaculation is the most commonly reported problem, and in younger women, the most commonly reported problems are low desire, low arousal, and difficulty achieving an orgasm. Problems due to low libido and orgasm difficulties in women and to erectile dysfunction in men increase with age.

Therapeutic Options for Sexual Dysfunction

The "VIAGRA Revolution"

As noted by Segraves (6), after the publication of *Human Sexual Inadequacy* by William Masters and Virginia E. Johnson (13) the majority of sexual problems were considered to be treatable by psychologically based methods. Psycho-sexual counseling to reduce performance anxiety, develop sexual skills, change sexual attitudes, and improve relationships became first line therapy for sexual dysfunction, regardless of cause (3). The introduction of sildenafil (VIAGRA) in 1998, dramatically changed the therapeutic approach to men with erectile problems. VIAGRA quickly became accepted as first line therapy for male patients with erectile dysfunction. Now doctors had available an oral medication that was effective in about 70% of men with this problem, effective both in those with organic (vascular and neurologic disease) and psychological causes. The use of VIAGRA and similar medications changed the emphasis of treatment for erectile dysfunction from psychological and behavioral therapies to medicinal interventions. Improved sexual performance increases self-confidence and improves interpersonal relationships. Thus, in individuals with a psychological basis for erectile dysfunction, pharmacological treatment may be used together with psychological therapies.

Medicines for Men

Table 1 lists approved medicines that are used to treat disorders of sexual function in men along with the approved indications. Information about potential side effects may be found in the Patient Information and Important Safety Information brochures (available on the medication's website). Although all of these medicines are approved by the FDA, not all are approved for use in sexual dysfunction. Premature ejaculation is the most prevalent sexual dysfunction in men aged 18–59 years, but there is no FDA-approved medication for premature ejaculation. Ejaculation is regulated by serotonin, and similar chemicals produced by the brain that are responsible for good feelings (14, 15). This has led to the off-label use of some medications that block serotonin, known as "selective serotonin reuptake inhibitors" (SSRIs), including fluoxetine (PROZAC), sertraline (ZOLOFT), and escitalopram (LEXAPRO) for the treatment of premature ejaculation.

Table 1

Medical Therapies for Sexual Dysfunction in Men

Drug (Brand Name)	Therapeutic Use	Approved Indications in United States
Sildenafil (VIAGRA) Vardenafil (LEVITRA) Tadalafil (CIALIS)	Erectile dysfunction, Selective Serotonin Uptake Inhibitor (SSRI)—induced sexual dysfunction*	Erectile dysfunction
Alprostadil [intraurethral (MUSE), intracavernosal]	Erectile dysfunction	Erectile dysfunction due to neurogenic, vasculogenic, psychogenic, or mixed etiology
Fluoxetine (PROZAC, SARAFEM) Sertraline (ZOLOFT) Paroxetine (PAXIL) Escitalopram (LEXAPRO) Citalopram (CELEXA)	Premature ejaculation*	Depression, obsessive compulsive disorder, panic attacks, post traumatic stress disorder, social anxiety disorder, premenstrual dysphoric disorder, generalized anxiety disorder
Bupropion (WELLBUTRIN, ZYBAN)	SSRI-induced sexual dysfunction*	Depression, seasonal affective disorder, smoking cessation
Testosterone[†]	Hypoactive sexual desire disorder when low testosterone is present	Replacement therapy in men with deficiency or absence of endogenous testosterone

Information is from the United States Product Circulars for the medications listed. Approved indications may not apply to all drugs in that class. Information about possible side effects can be found in the "Patient Information" for each drug, and the" Important Safety Information" which are available on each product's website.

[*]Off-label use in the United States SSRIs include fluoxetine, sertraline, paroxetine, escitalopram, citalopram.

[†]Preparations include injectable testosterone, transdermal gels, transdermal patches, buccal tablets, implantable pellets.

Conversely, the use of SSRIs for depression and other psychiatric diseases has led to sexual side effects such as difficulty in reaching orgasm and difficulty maintaining an erection. SSRI-induced sexual dysfunction is often treated with VIAGRA and similar medications, although VIAGRA is approved for use in erectile dysfunction but not for orgasmic difficulties.

Although libido is not completely understood in either men or women, the hormone testosterone is necessary for sexual desire in men and is also believed to contribute to sexual desire and function in women. The average testosterone level in premenopausal women is about 10% of the average male level. Hypoactive sexual desire disorder in men, commonly known as decreased libido or lack of sexual interest, can have many causes including depression, medications, and chronic illness, but may also be due to deficiency of testosterone (16, 17), especially in older men. A variety of testosterone preparations are available for treating men with low levels of testosterone, and this treatment usually restores libido. Testosterone is not recommended for use in men with normal levels of testosterone or in men who simply want to increase their sexual desire, as levels above normal increase the risk of prostate cancer.

Medicines for Women are Lacking

Unfortunately, there are few medications available for the sexual disorders that affect women (Table 2). This is particularly true for younger women who most commonly suffer from low desire, low arousal, or difficulty with orgasm. More research is needed. Presently, the only FDA-approved medications for treating sexual dysfunction in women are estrogen preparations for dyspareunia related to vulvovaginal atrophy (a post-menopausal condition that is associated with vaginal dryness, irritation, soreness, urinary frequency and urgency, and pain during intercourse).

The clinical success of VIAGRA in men increased interest in finding pharmacological treatments for women with sexual dysfunction. However, trials of VIAGRA in women failed to show significant benefit and the drug development program for this indication has been discontinued. Unfortunately, the quest for medications to help women with sexual problems has led to criticisms of both the pharmaceutical industry and physician-experts who consult for the industry. Despite the epidemiological data, which shows that a significant proportion of women have sexual dysfunction, these critics insist that female sexual dysfunction is an illness created by doctors under the influence of their pharmaceutical industry allies.

Many factors—biological, psychological, and social—contribute to sexual response in women, and it is challenging to find an abnormality that can be corrected with medication. Thus, behavioral, cognitive, and sexual therapies continue to be the main therapies for sexual dysfunction in women (3). While some studies have found varying degrees of improvement with non-pharmacological therapies [with response rates varying from 37% to 82% in 9 studies reviewed by Basson (3)], outcome data evaluating these non-pharmacological approaches are severely limited by the different durations of

Table 2

Medical Therapies for Women with Sexual Dysfunction

Drug (Brand Name)	Therapeutic Use	Approved Indications in United States
Estradiol vaginal tablets (VAGIFEM); Conjugated estrogens vaginal cream (PREMARIN vaginal cream); Estradiol vaginal ring (ESTRING)	Vaginal atrophy in menopausal women (vaginal dryness, pain during sexual intercourse, vaginal itching)	Vagifem: atrophic vaginitis in menopausal women. Estring: moderate to severe symptoms due to postmenopausal vaginal atrophy (dryness, burning, itching, and pain during intercourse) and for urinary urgency/pain with urination
Bupropion (WELLBUTRIN, ZYBAN)	Selective serotonin uptake inhibitor (SSRI)—induced sexual dysfunction*	Depression, seasonal affective disorder, smoking cessation
Testosterone†	Hypoactive sexual desire disorder (low libido) usually when low testosterone is present*	Not approved for use in women in the United States INTRINSA (transdermal testosterone patch) is approved in the European Union for treatment of hypoactive sexual desire disorder in women with surgically induced menopause receiving estrogen therapy

Information in this table is from the United States Product Circulars for the medications listed and from the EU Summary of Product Characteristics for INTRINSA. Information about possible side effects can be found in the "Patient Information" for each drug, and the "Important Safety Information" which are available on each product's website.

*Off label use in the United States SSRIs include fluoxetine, sertraline, paroxetine, escitalopram, citalopram.

†Preparations approved in the United States for men include injectable testosterone, gels, patches, buccal tablets (absorbed through the gums), implantable pellets.

treatment and follow-up, different methods for assessing the benefits of treatment, and the fact that not all studies are controlled (3, 18).

Clearly there is still a need for safe and effective sexual medicines that can be used in younger as well as older women. Fortunately research efforts continue. Investigational drugs which act upon neurotransmitters, increasing dopaminergic and decreasing serotoninergic activity, are postulated to have a favorable effect on sexual responsiveness (19), and several compounds are under evaluation in younger women (20).

Should Testosterone Be Used to Treat Low Sexual Desire or Low Arousal in Women?

It should be pointed out that testosterone is a promising treatment for older, postmenopausal women with decreased libido and low levels of testosterone. Testosterone, long considered the "male hormone" because of its role in the development of secondary sex characteristics in men (deeper voice, facial hair, etc.), is also produced in women and is thought to have an important role in female sexual function. Some but not all studies in women have found a direct correlation between testosterone levels, sexual desire, and frequency of sexual intercourse (21).

To date efforts to gain regulatory approval for testosterone use in post-menopausal women have been unsuccessful in the United States, but more successful in Europe. A testosterone patch, INTRINSA, for surgically menopausal women (women who had had their ovaries and uterus surgically removed) with hypoactive sexual disorder (low libido) was rejected by the FDA in 2005, and subsequently approved by regulatory authorities in the European Union in 2006 for specific use in surgically menopausal women with hypoactive sexual desire disorder who were also taking estrogen therapy. In the United States, some experts had concerns over the cardiovascular safety of this medication, because heart attacks in men occur at a much younger age than in women. However, it should be pointed out that in women who use the testosterone patch, blood levels of testosterone increase only to levels seen in pre-menopausal women (22), which are far lower than testosterone levels in men (22). In a recent review of potential safety issues in women taking testosterone because of symptoms of testosterone deficiency, Mathur and Braunstein found no good evidence for adverse cardiovascular effects, nor for increased risk of breast cancer (21).

The testosterone patch was subsequently studied in naturally menopausal women with hypoactive sexual desire disorder, showing benefit both in women taking estrogen and in women not taking estrogen (23). Use of the testosterone patch in naturally menopausal women has not as yet been approved by regulatory authorities in the United States or Europe. Nevertheless, despite the fact that in the United States, testosterone is not approved for use in women, about 2 million prescriptions of testosterone annually are written for women (24). Unfortunately, some of these preparations are prepared by pharmacies that mix testosterone with other ingredients to create topical creams, lozenges, oral gels, and drops. The standardization of such therapies is in question and therefore experts in the field do not encourage their general use (21).

However, some physicians with expertise in reproductive endocrinology (the study of hormones as it relates to fertility and the menopause) prescribe low doses of testosterone (by gel applied to the skin) on a case by case basis to individual patients with decreased libido who are postmenopausal, have low testosterone levels, and have not responded satisfactorily to treatment with estrogens. For many of these patients, especially those who are in healthy relationships and have suffered from loss of libido and markedly diminished sexual satisfaction with aging, the benefits of testosterone supplementation are worth the potential risks. As with many medications there are as yet no long-term safety data for this treatment. The main adverse effects include acne, oily skin, and increased hair growth at the site of application of testosterone. Virilization (the development of unwanted male sex characteristics such as facial hair, baldness, deepened voice) is rare. Women who take testosterone should be made aware of the potential benefits and potential risks of therapy, and should be told that the treatment is not approved by the FDA at this time. Also, serum levels of total and free testosterone should be monitored to keep these levels in the normal range for young women.

One might ask whether testosterone would benefit younger premenopausal women with decreased sexual desire if such women had low levels of testosterone. There are few clinical trials evaluating this. However, one placebo-controlled study in 51 women of reproductive age with low testosterone levels due to pituitary gland disease found a positive effect of the testosterone patch on some but not all parameters of sexual function, including a positive effect on arousal (25).

Summary and Conclusions

Sexual dysfunction is a common problem of men and women and may have both organic and psychological components. Abnormalities such as vascular or neurologic disease in men with erectile dysfunction, low levels of testosterone in men and some women with decreased sexual desire (hypoactive sexual desire disorder), and possibly alterations in neurotransmitters in women with low desire and low arousal may be the initial cause of the problem. The evaluation of patients with sexual problems should take into account organic and psychological factors, and treatment should combine medical and psychosocial therapies, as appropriate for the individual patient. The introduction of VIAGRA for men with erectile dysfunction, which is often due to vascular or neurogenic causes, has dramatically improved the prognosis of men with erectile dysfunction. Nevertheless psychological factors may still need to be addressed in patients who respond to VIAGRA and similar treatments. When choosing a medicine for an individual patient, as with any treatment, the benefit/risk balance must be taken into account and the patient should be fully informed about potential benefits as well as potential side effects. When there are no medications approved for use for a sexual disorder, such as premature or early ejaculation, the doctor and patient may sometimes cautiously use medications that are approved for other uses, but have been found effective in that particular sexual disorder.

There are very few medicines for sexual dysfunction in women. For women with low libido (hypoactive sexual disorder) and low levels of testosterone, the testosterone preparations that are available for men are not approved for use in women in the United States Yet, physicians may prescribe testosterone in some women because the clinical trial data support the effectiveness of testosterone replacement, and both physician and patient perceive that the benefit/risk balance is acceptable. The lack of approved medications for women with sexual problems is of concern and argues for more research to understand the appropriate drug targets for women with sexual problems such as low desire, low arousal and difficulties with orgasm.

References

1. Goldbeck-Wood, S. (2010). Commentary: Female sexual dysfunction is a real but complex problem. *BMJ, 341*, p. c5336.
2. Moynihan, R. (2010). Merging of marketing and medical science: female sexual dysfunction. *BMJ, 341*, p. c5050.

3. Bhasin, S. and Basson, R. (2008). Sexual Dysfunction in Men and Women. In: Kronenberg H, Melmed, S, Polonsky, K, Larsen, PR ed. *Williams Textbook of Endocrinology, 11th edition.* 11th ed. Philadelphia: Saunders Elsevier; pp. 701–737.

4. Basson, R. (2006). Clinical practice. Sexual desire and arousal disorders in women. *N. Engl J. Med, 354,* pp. 1497–1506.

5. McCall, K. and Meston, C. (2007). Differences between pre- and postmenopausal women in cues for sexual desire. *J Sex Med, 4,* pp. 364–371.

6. Segraves, R.T. (2010). Considerations for diagnostic criteria for erectile dysfunction in DSM V. *J Sex Med, 7,* pp. 654–660.

7. Feldman, H.A, Goldstein, I., Hatzichristou, D.G., Krane, R.J., McKinlay, J.B. (1994). Impotence and its medical and psychosocial correlates: results of the Massachusetts Male Aging Study. *J Urol, 151,* pp. 54–61.

8. Johannes, C.B., Araujo, A.B., Feldman, H.A., Derby, C.A., Kleinman, K.P., McKinlay, J.B. (2000). Incidence of erectile dysfunction in men 40 to 69 years old: longitudinal results from the Massachusetts male aging study. *J Urol, 163,* pp. 460–463.

9. Laumann, E.O., Paik, A., Rosen, R.C. (1999). Sexual dysfunction in the United States: prevalence and predictors. *JAMA, 281,* pp. 537–544.

10. Lindau, S.T., Schumm, L.P., Laumann, E.O., Levinson, W., O'Muircheartaigh C.A., Waite, L.J. (2007). A study of sexuality and health among older adults in the United States. *N Engl J Med, 357,* pp. 762–774.

11. Shifren, J.L., Monz, B.U., Russo, P.A., Segreti, A., Johannes, C.B. (2008). Sexual problems and distress in United States women: prevalence and correlates. *Obstet Gynecol, 112,* 970–978.

12. Segraves, R.T. (2010). Considerations for an evidence-based definition of premature ejaculation in the DSM-V. *J Sex Med, 7,* pp. 672–679.

13. Masters, W., Johnson, V. (1970). Human Sexual Inadequacy. Boston: Little, Brown, and Company.

14. Waldinger, M.D., Olivier, B. (2004). Utility of selective serotonin reuptake inhibitors in premature ejaculation. *Curr Opin Investig Drugs, 5,* pp. 743–747.

15. Waldinger, M.D., Zwinderman, A.H., Olivier, B. (2003). Antidepressants and ejaculation: a double-blind, randomized, fixed-dose study with mirtazapine and paroxetine. *J Clin Psychopharmacol, 23,* pp. 467–470.

16. Diaz, V.A. Jr., Close, J.D. (2010). Male sexual dysfunction. *Prim Care, 37,* pp. 473–489, vii–viii.

17. Bhasin, S., Cunningham, G.R., Hayes, F.J., Matsumoto, A.M., Snyder, P.J., Swerdloff, R.S., Montori, V.M. (2010). Testosterone therapy in men with androgen deficiency syndromes: an Endocrine Society clinical practice guideline. *J Clin Endocrinol Metab, 95,* pp. 2536–2559.

18. Heiman, J.R. (2002). Psychologic treatments for female sexual dysfunction: are they effective and do we need them? *Arch Sex Behav, 31,* pp. 445–450.

19. Pfaus, J.G. (2009). Pathways of sexual desire. *J Sex Med, 6,* pp.1506–1533.

20. Nappi, R.E., Martini, E., Terreno, E., Albani, F, Santamaria, V., Tonani, S., Chiovato, L., Polatti, F. (2010). Management of hypoactive sexual desire

disorder in women: current and emerging therapies. *Int J Womens Health, 2,* pp. 167–175.

21. Mathur, R., Braunstein, G.D. (2010). Androgen deficiency and therapy in women. *Curr Opin Endocrinol Diabetes Obes, 17,* pp. 342–349.

22. FDA. (2004). Transcript, FDA Advisory Committee for Reproductive Health Drugs, December 2, 2004.

23. Davis, S.R., Moreau,M., Kroll, R., Bouchard, C., Panay, N., Gass, M., Braunstein, G.D., Hirschberg, A.L., Rodenberg, C., Pack, S., Koch, H., Moufarege, A., Studd, J. (2008).Testosterone for low libido in postmenopausal women not taking estrogen. *N Engl J Med, 359,* pp. 2005–2017.

24. Snabes, M.C., Simes, S.M. (2009). Approved hormonal treatments for HSDD: an unmet medical need. *J Sex Med, 6,* pp.1846–1849.

25. Miller, K.K., Biller, B.M., Beauregard, C., Lipman, J.G., Jones, J., Schoenfeld, D., Sherman, J.C., Swearingen, B., Loeffler, J., Klibanski, A. (2006). Effects of testosterone replacement in androgen-deficient women with hypopituitarism: a randomized, double-blind, placebo-controlled study. *J Clin Endocrinol Metab, 91,* pp. 1683–1690.

Leonore Tiefer

NO

Beneath the Veneer: The Troubled Past and Future of Sexual Medicine

My presidential address to the International Academy of Sex Research in 1993, 5 years *before* VIAGRA was released to the world, was entitled "Three Crises Facing Sexology" (Tiefer, 1994). One of the crises, a subject on which I had been publishing since 1986, 12 years before VIAGRA, was the medicalization of sexology (Tiefer, 1986). Ah, the joys of being ahead of one's time! Using sociological notions of medicalization and disease-mongering (Conrad, 2007; Payer, 1992), I have analyzed, over the past 20 years, how urologists, funded by an ambitious pharmaceutical industry assisted by favorable government policies such as direct-to-consumer advertising and poor oversight of conflicts of interest, created a new but thin subspecialty, "sexual medicine" (Tiefer, 2004, 2006a).

In the present essay under comment, Rowland (2007) errs in regarding this new "sexual medicine" as if it were an established clinical subspecialty, rather than merely the brand-name for a product being aggressively promoted by a multi-billion dollar industry. His analysis of the weaknesses of "sexual medicine" would be alarming if not for this fundamental error. It's as if he went to extraordinary lengths to analyze the advantages and disadvantages of alchemy. Over the past decade the pharmaceutical industry has spent billions to persuade professionals and the public that its leaden sex research is actually gold, in fact "gold standard." Much of the research in Rowland's figures is the result of this industry pseudoscience. Fortunately, the huge marketing machine of sponsored research, sponsored professional continuing education, sponsored lunches, sponsored organizations, sponsored dinner talks, sponsored workshops, sponsored awards, sponsored speakers' bureaus, sponsored conferences, sponsored journals, and other forms of gifts and entanglements by which the pharmaceutical industry pushes its brands is at last beginning to unravel (Abramson, 2004; Angell, 2004; Avorn, 2004; Critser, 2005; Kassirer, 2005; Moynihan, 2003a, 2003b; Moynihan & Cassels, 2005).

The rising tide of regulatory reform promises effectively to limit industry-expert entanglements and end direct-to-consumer drug advertising, off-label prescribing, and the epidemic of conflicts-of-interest among scientists and physicians. I expect that, then, the new subspecialty of sexual medicine will rapidly deflate in size and prominence. I hope the American Psychiatric Association will awaken to the biases at the heart of the human sexual response

From *Journal of Sex & Marital Therapy*, vol. 33, October 2007, pp. 473–477. Copyright © 2007 by Routledge/Taylor & Francis Group. Reprinted by permission via Rightslink.

cycle model and eliminate its list of specific sexual dysfunction disorders. As sex drugs continue to multiply, and there I agree with Rowland that the future will be full of more and more drugs (legal, illegal, prescription, nutraceutical, herbal, and over-the-counter, delivered through skin, nose, mouth, and all other orifices), sexologists will find their true calling in multi-method sexuality research, community-based sex coaching and education, academic and professional sex education, and treatment of people whose sex lives have been damaged by traumatic events, media hype, drug side effects, and false promises of all sorts.

In 1994, without the perspectives on advertising, conflicts of interest, sponsorship, etc. offered by the recent investigative work cited above, I called for rapprochement between sex research promoting a psychobiosocial model and that promoting a reductionistic view of sexuality (what Rowland calls "the medical model"). I called for multi-modal research to carve out "a complex middle ground" against "the medical juggernaut" (Tiefer, 1994, p. 373). Such rapprochement didn't happen, and eventually I understood that I had fallen into a fundamental error that I believe Rowland currently makes. What I hadn't grasped was that the medical juggernaut was not about developing good science or problem management from a biomedical perspective, but that the medical juggernaut was fundamentally about biological reductionism and pharmaceutical promotion. Too often, social and psychological research was used as window dressing to add a veneer of psycho-bio-social sophistication, but it remained unintegrated into research design or teaching materials in any meaningful way. While every organ, disease, and function system in the body was linked to sexual problems with a page or paragraph of its own, mental and social factors would repeatedly be summed up in one "psychological factors" paragraph as "anxiety" or "communication problems." No matter how much lip service was given to the importance of psychological factors, drug prescription was the first and often the only recommendation. This was the clear evidence that we were in the land of veneer, not multi-disciplinary integration. Recently, in the new sexual medicine organizations and journals, lip service is again being paid to collaboration and rapprochement, but the same oversimplifications reveal the same motives.

It is true that sexual problems are legion in our violent, inequitable, anxious, and speeded-up world, but fortunately we already have a sufficient armamentarium to help people relax, gain insight, develop skills, overcome trauma, and strengthen their capacities for cooperation, sensuality, pleasure, and intimacy. New diagnostic language is not needed, adequate research models are already available, and in my opinion, energy might be better spent at this point in preventing sexual problems than in developing new treatments. The quest for the "new" is probably more related to marketing than therapeutics, and truly useful work for sexologists might be to lend our professional clout to the politics of comprehensive sex education, reliable contraception and abortion services, parent education, and anti-stigma human rights training.

Although Rowland omits any mention of this, there are enormous new developments in sexuality scholarship over the past two decades in the new cultural studies of sexuality emerging from the social study of gender, as exemplified by journals like The Journal of the History of Sexuality (started in 1990) and books on men and masculinity. An obsessive focus on clinical trials research has allowed clinical sexologists to avoid familiarization with theoretical and empirical contributions arising from science and technology studies, globalization studies, gay and lesbian studies, the sociology of sexual identities and institutions, qualitative research on sexual meanings in diverse sexual cultures, and the impact of sexualized media (e.g., Seidman, Fischer, & Meeks, 2006). The disastrous substitution of clinical trials for genuine research and theoretical development in sexology since the mid-1990s may give rise to significant intellectual lacunae for many years to come. I hope it does not prove to have been a fatal choice.

This opportunity to comment on Rowland's essay rings one other historical bell for me, and I think it is important to take a little space to recognize stages in the process of medicalization.1 A watershed event in the progress of the medicalization of sexuality and the dismantling of the psycho-bio-social approach was the National Institutes of Health (NIH) Consensus Development Conference on "Impotence" held in 1992 (Impotence, 1992). Although this was the first (and to the date only) NIH Consensus Conference on a sexual topic, it signaled a urology agenda to build a new specialty of "sexual medicine."

The scientific evidence prepared for the conference was compiled in a 1986–1992 bibliography of 956 items (Beratan, 1992). Of the 19 database search strategies described, only three included anything clearly sexological (e.g., "psychosexual disorders" or "libido"). All the others had to do with "penis," "impotence," "erection," various diseases (e.g., diabetes), or medical treatments. The 21 "experts" speaking at the conference, each allotted 20 minutes, included five sexologists, one epidemiologist, and 15 urologists or basic scientists whose research focus was the biology of the penis. Three urologists (one, Goldstein, now founding editor of the Journal of Sexual Medicine) gave eight of the 27 presentations. The panel of "nonexperts" who heard the presentations and prepared the final report consisted of 14 members, including 6 urologists and 1 sexologist.

Inevitably, the final NIH report was suffused with a medical model orientation that reified "impotence" and exhaustively investigated details of physiology. It threw psychological factors into long nontechnical lists of "risk factors" such as "lack of sexual knowledge, poor sexual techniques, inadequate interpersonal relationships" (Impotence, 1992, p. 11). The report mentioned the patient's sexual partner only in passing and discussed nothing about differences among partners. It dealt with erectile troubles as an individual man's problem, and recommended that diagnostic evaluations be multi-disciplinary, "when available" (p. 13). The triumph of biological reductionism was the message of the 1992 report.

I suggested to Arnold Melman, then co-editor of the International Journal of Impotence Research, that the NIH Consensus Conference final report be published in his journal along with comments from sexologists and urologists.I hoped that the 31 sexologists whose names I provided would weigh in with trenchant commentaries about the dangers of the rush towards medicalization, but only 14 chose to respond, and they were generally polite in pointing out omissions and biases. The 18 invited urologists, by contrast, understandably, were generally euphoric. More to the point, sexologists took no concerted action to limit or rechannel the medicalization juggernaut. Fast forward 15 years and we have the current situation Rowland describes.

The creation of "sexual medicine" was the result of an unhindered confluence of events and social trends which Rowland should acknowledge (Tiefer, 2004, 2006b). Urologists needed a new subspecialty as new biotechnologies eliminated most kidney stone and benign prostate surgeries. Government policies promoting new academic–industry partnerships encouraged applied science on university and medical campuses, and escalated industry sponsorship of research and professional education. Government regulations relaxed drug approval and advertising policies as the result of industry lobbying and AIDS activism, and the industry shifted towards lifestyle drug development to reach the baby boomer market. Health and science media discovered the popularity of explicit sexual subjects. Conservative policies limited comprehensive sex education and cut back social science sexological funding.

I do not believe that sex therapy "stagnated" so much as it existed in an apolitical bubble, unaware of and uninterested in the many social trends poised to limit its development. It celebrated "objective" science and therapeutics, oblivious to the fact, extensively examined in the new sexuality studies, that sex is permanently political. It would be nice to hope that increased awareness of the current dilemmas identified by Rowland, and attention to the many factors that have brought it about, will lead to new directions. The New View Campaign is an educational network of sexologists and allies promoting just such new directions.

POSTSCRIPT

Does Sexual Medicine Benefit Society?

In her essay, Newman explains, "Sexual dysfunction is a common problem of men and women and may have both organic and psychological components." Since it is not only a psychological problem, it should not be treated only with psychosexual therapy. Treatment needs to combine medical and psychosexual therapies "as appropriate for the individual patient." She also notes that men have a variety of medications available to treat sexual dysfunctions, but there are few such medical options for women. More research is needed to develop safe and effective sexual medicines for women. Why do you think there are few medical treatments available for women? Newman also notes that there is some clinical evidence for the success of testosterone treatments in women with low libido, and that doctors and patients must weigh the potential benefits and risks of any treatment.

Tiefer takes a strong stance against the idea of sexual medicine as a valid field. Does the fact that much of the research on sexual dysfunction is sponsored by pharmaceutical companies, as Tiefer states, make the field of sexual medicine "merely the brand name for a product being aggressively promoted by a billion-dollar industry?" Are dysfunctions being created to make billions? Or is the neophyte field of sexual medicine simply trying to understand which dysfunctions are and are not best treated through prescription drugs?

One of the most interesting, yet least discussed, aspects of the controversy over the medicalization of sexuality is the future of sex therapy. If people are able to have their sexual issues treated chemically by their general practitioners, OB-GYNs and urologists, what role will the therapist fill? Newman suggests that pharmacological and psychological treatments can coexist and can even be used together.

How comfortable would you be taking medications for sexual problems? Would you rather deal with these issues through counseling first? Or would you be more comfortable raising the issue in doctor's office than on a therapist's couch?

In their new book, *Older, Wiser, Sexually Smarter*, sexuality educator Peggy Brick and her colleagues argue that many of the physical changes that people experience related to their sexuality as they grow older are not inherently problematic and may not necessarily require medication or therapy. Rather, they necessitate a new understanding of one's sexuality and, perhaps, new sexual behaviors that may not be quite the same as when they were aged 18 years. What do you think of this viewpoint? Can sexuality be experienced differently as one grows older?

Suggested Readings

J.R. Berman, L.A. Berman, and K.A. Kanaly, "Female Sexual Dysfunction: New Perspectives on Anatomy, Physiology, Evaluation and Treatment," *Female Urology* (vol. 1, no. 3, pp. 166–177, 2003).

P. Brick, J. Lunquist, A. Sandak, and B. Taverner, *Older, Wiser, Sexually Smarter: 30 Sex Ed Lessons for Adults Only* (Morristown, NJ: The Center for Family Life Education, 2009).

J.E. Frank, P. Mistretta, and J. Will, "Diagnosis and Treatment of Female Sexual Dysfunction," *American Family Physician* (vol. 77, no. 5, pp. 635–642, 2008).

B. Green, "The Quick Fix: Orgasm Inc. Examines the Treatment of Female Sexuality," *Honolulu Weekly* (May 4, 2011).

S. Katz, "Return of Desire: Fighting Myths about Female Sexuality," *AlterNet* (July 23, 2008).

L. Lyon, "Women Lacking Libido Aren't Sick," *U.S. News & World Reports* (March 27, 2008).

L. Tiefer, *Sex Is Not a Natural Act & Other Essays* (Westview Press, 2008).

ISSUE 5

Is Oral Sex Really Sex?

YES: Rhonda Chittenden, from "Oral Sex *Is* Sex: Ten Messages about Oral Sex to Communicate to Adolescents," *Sexing the Political* (May 2004)

NO: Nora Gelperin, from "Oral Sex and Young Adolescents: Insights from the 'Oral Sex Lady,'" *Educator's Update* (September 2004)

ISSUE SUMMARY

YES: Sexuality educator Rhonda Chittenden says that it is important for young people to expand their narrow definitions of sex and understand that oral sex *is* sex. Chittenden offers additional educational messages about oral sex.

NO: Sexuality trainer Nora Gelperin argues that adult definitions of oral sex are out of touch with the meaning the behavior holds for young people. Rather than impose adult definitions of intimacy, educators should be seeking to help young people clarify and understand their own values.

In 1998, President Bill Clinton famously stated, "I did not have sexual relations with that woman, Miss Lewinsky." As it later became evident that the president, in fact, did have *oral* sex with intern Monica Lewinsky, a national debate raged over the meaning of sex. What, people asked, does "sexual relations" mean? What about "sex?" Do these terms refer to vaginal intercourse only, or are other sexual behaviors, like oral sex, included?

Some welcomed this unprecedented opportunity to have an open, national discussion about sex in an otherwise erotophobic, sexually repressed culture. Sexuality education professionals lent their expertise, offering suggestions to help parents answer their children's questions about the new term, "oral sex," they might hear on the evening news or at family gatherings. Others feared such openness would inevitably lead to increased sexual activity among teens. Perhaps the media viewed this as a foregone conclusion when they began airing hyped reports indicating a rise in teen oral sex, based on anecdotal, rather than research-based, evidence.

Feature reports, often intended to alarm viewers, have introduced even more new terms into our sexual lexicon. "Friends with benefits" describes a partner pairing based on friendship and casual oral sex. "Rainbow parties" involve events where girls wear different colors of lipstick and boys try to get as many colored rings on their penises as they can. But how much of this is really happening, and how much of this just makes for good television?

Even if *some* of what the reports say is true, many adults—parents, teachers, public health officials, and others—are concerned. Some are worried about the potential rise in sexually transmitted infections that can be passed orally as well as vaginally or anally. Others lament the inequity of oral sex as young people may experience it—with females *giving* oral sex far more than they are *receiving* it. Still others may have religious or other moral reasons that drive their concerns.

The apprehension among many adults is rooted in the very meaning of sex and oral sex. Since many adults hold oral sex to be an intensely intimate act—one that is even more intimate than vaginal intercourse—it is difficult for them to observe what they interpret as casual attitudes toward this behavior.

In the following selections, sexuality education professionals Rhonda Chittenden and Nora Gelperin examine the meaning of sex and oral sex in the context of giving young people helpful educational messages. Chittenden articulates several reasons why it is important for young people to know that oral sex is sex, and offers several other important messages for adults to convey to young people. Gelperin argues that it is not for adults to decide the meaning of such terms for young people. Rather, educators can help young people critically examine the meaning of such words and activities for themselves. She further argues against having overly dramatized media accounts dictate public health approaches.

YES

Rhonda Chittenden

Oral Sex *Is* Sex: Ten Messages about Oral Sex to Communicate to Adolescents

As a teen in the early-80s, I was very naïve about oral sex. I thought oral sex meant talking about sex with one's partner in a very sexy way. A friend and I, trying to practice the mechanics, would move our mouths in silent mock-talk as we suggestively switched our hips from left to right and flirted with our best bedroom eyes. We wondered aloud how anyone could engage in oral sex without breaking into hysterical laughter. In our naïveté, oral sex was not only hilarious, it was just plain stupid.

Twenty years later, I doubt most teens are as naïve as my friend and I were. Although the prevalence of oral sex among adolescents has yet to be comprehensively addressed by researchers,[1] any adult who interacts with teens will quickly learn that, far from being stupid or hilarious, oral sex is a common place activity in some adolescent crowds.

Some teens claim, as teens have always claimed about sex, that "everyone is doing it." They tell of parties—which they may or may not have attended—where oral sex is openly available. They describe using oral sex as a way to relieve the pressure to be sexual with a partner yet avoid the risk of pregnancy. Some believe oral sex is an altogether risk-free behavior that eliminates the worry of sexually transmitted infections. There is a casualness in many teens' attitudes towards oral sex revealed in the term "friends with benefits" to describe a non-dating relationship that includes oral sex. In fact, many teens argue that oral sex really isn't sex at all, logic that, try as we might, defies many adults. Most pointedly, teens' anecdotal experiences of oral sex reveal the continuing imbalance of power prevalent in heterosexual relationships where the boys receive most of the pleasure and the girls, predictably, give most of the pleasure.

Not willing to wait until research confirms what many of us already know, concerned adults want to address the issue of adolescent oral sex *now*. We know that young people long for straightforward and honest conversations about the realities and complexities of human sexuality, including the practice of oral sex. But where do we start with such an intimidating topic? The following ten messages may help caring and concerned adults to initiate authentic conversations about oral sex with young people.

1. Oral sex *is* sex. Regardless of how casual the behavior is for some young people, giving and receiving oral sex are both sexual behaviors. This is made obvious simply by defining the act of oral sex: Oral sex is the stimulation of a person's genitals by another person's mouth to create sexual pleasure and, usually, orgasm for at least one of the partners. It's that straightforward.

Even so, many young people—and even some adults—believe that oral sex is not "real sex." Real sex, they say, is penis-vagina intercourse only. Any other sexual behavior is something "other" and certainly not *real* sex. This narrow definition of sex, rooted in heterosexist attitudes, is problematic for several reasons.

First, such a narrow definition is ahistorical. Art and literature reveal human beings, across human history and culture, consensually engaging their bodies in loving, pleasurable acts of sex beyond penis-vagina intercourse.[2] In Western culture, our notions of sex are still shackled by religious teachings that say the only acceptable sex—in society and the eyes of God—is procreative sex. Of course, the wide accessibility of contraceptives, among other influences, has dramatically shifted our understanding of this.[3] Even still, many people are unaware that across centuries and continents, human beings have enjoyed many kinds of sex and understood those acts to be sex whether or not they involved a penis and a vagina.

Next, by defining sex in such narrow terms, we perpetuate a dangerous ignorance that places people at risk for sexually transmitted infections (STIs), including HIV. Many people, including teens, who define sex in such narrow terms incorrectly reason that they are safe from HIV if they avoid penis-vagina intercourse. Because saliva tends to inhibit HIV, it's true that one's chances of contracting HIV through oral sex with an infected partner are considerably small, compared to the risk of unprotected vaginal or anal sex. Of course, this varies with the presence of other body fluids as well as the oral health of the giver. However, if one chooses to avoid "real sex" and instead has anal sex, the risk for HIV transmission increases.[4] In reality, regardless of what orifice the penis penetrates, all of these sex acts are real sex. In this regard, the narrow definition of sex is troubling because it ignores critical sexual health information that all people deserve, especially those who are sexually active or intend to be in the future.

Finally, this narrow definition of sex invalidates the sexual practices of many people who, for whatever reasons, do not engage in penis-vagina intercourse. Obviously, these people include those who partner with lovers of the same sex. They also include people who, regardless of the sex of their partners, are physically challenged due to illness, accident, or birth anomaly. To suggest to these individuals that oral sex—or any other primary mode of shared sexual expression—is not real sex invalidates the range of accessible and sensual ways they can and do share their bodies with their partners.

Clearly, we must educate young people that there are many ways to enjoy sex, including the sensual placement of one's mouth on another person's genitals. Oral sex may be practiced in casual, emotionally indifferent ways, but this does not disqualify it as a legitimate sex act. Oral sex *is* sex—and, in most states, the law agrees.

2. Without consent, oral sex may be considered sexual assault. Adults who work with teens know that oral sex often takes place at parties where alcohol and other drugs are consumed. It's imperative, then, that when adults talk to teens about oral sex, we confront the legal realities of such situations. Of course, drinking and drug use are illegal for adolescents. In addition, according to Iowa law, if alcohol or drugs are used by either partner of any age, consent for oral sex (or any sex) cannot be given. Without consent, oral sex may be considered sexual assault.[5] Other states have similar laws.

While giving some adolescents reason to reflect on their substance use, this information may also help them to contextualize their past experiences of oral sex. It may affirm the often uneasy and unspoken feelings of some teens who feel they were pressured into oral sex, either as the giver or receiver. It may also illuminate other risks that often occur when sex and substance use are combined, especially the failure to use protection against pregnancy, and in the case of oral sex, sexually transmitted infections.

3. Practice safer oral sex to reduce the risk of sexually transmitted infections. Because many young people don't consider oral sex to be real sex, they don't realize that sexually transmitted infections that are typically transmitted through genital-genital contact can also be transmitted through oral-genital contact. Although some are more easily transmitted through oral sex than others, these infections include chlamydia, gonorrhea, herpes, and, in some cases, even pubic lice. The lips, tongue, mouth cavity, and throat, are all vulnerable to various sexually transmitted bacteria and viruses.[6] With pubic lice, facial hair, including mustaches, beards and eyebrows, can be vulnerable.[7]

Aside from abstaining from oral sex, young people can protect themselves and their partners from the inconvenience, embarrassment, treatment costs, and health consequences of sexually transmitted infections by practicing safer oral sex. The correct and consistent use of latex condoms for fellatio (oral sex performed on a penis) and latex dental dams for cunnilingus (oral sex performed on a vulva) should be taught and encouraged. Manufacturers of condoms, dental dams, and pleasure-enhancing lubricants offer these safer sex supplies in a variety of flavors—including mint, mango, and banana—to increase the likelihood that people will practice safer oral sex.[8] Certainly, adolescents who engage in oral sex should be taught about the correct, pleasure-enhancing uses of these products, informed of the location of stores and clinics that carry them, and strongly encouraged to have their own supply at hand.

4. Oral sex is a deeply intimate and sensual way to give sexual pleasure to a partner. Although casual references to oral sex abound in popular music, movies and culture, many young people have never heard an honest, age-appropriate description of the profoundly intimate and sensual nature of oral sex. Especially for the giver of oral sex, the experience of pleasuring a partner's genitals may be far from casual. Unlike most other sex acts, oral sex acutely engages all five senses of the giver.

As is suggested by the availability of flavored safer sex supplies, for the giver of oral sex, the sense of taste is clearly engaged. If safer sex supplies are not used, the giver experiences the tastes of human body fluids—perhaps semen, vaginal fluids, and/or perspiration. In addition, the tongue and lips feel the varied textures of the partner's genitals, and, depending on the degree of body contact, other touch receptors located elsewhere on the body may be triggered. With the face so close to their partner's genitals, the giver's nose can easily smell intimate odors while the eyes, if opened, get a very cozy view of the partner's body. Lastly, during oral sex the ears not only pick up sounds of voice, moaning, and any music playing in the background, they also hear the delicate sounds of caressing another's body with one's mouth. Obviously, if one is mentally engaged in the experience, it can be quite intense! Honest conversations with adolescents about the intimate and sensual nature of oral sex acknowledge this incredibly unique way human beings share pleasure with one another and elevate it from the casual references of popular culture.

5. Boys do not have to accept oral sex (or any sex) just because it is offered.   As I talked with a group of teenagers at a local alternative high school, it became painfully clear to me that some teen girls offer oral sex to almost any guy they find attractive. As a consequence of such easy availability, these teen boys, although they did not find a girl attractive nor did they desire oral sex from her, felt pressured to accept it simply because it was offered. After all, what real man would turn down sex? Popular music videos, rife with shallow depictions of both men and women, show swaggering males getting play right and left from eager, nearly naked women. These same performances of exaggerated male sexual bravado are mirrored on the streets, in the hallways, and in the homes of many boys who may, for various reasons, lack other more balanced models of male sexuality.

When I told the boys that they were not obligated to accept oral sex from someone to whom they were not attracted, it was clearly a message they had never heard. I saw open expressions of surprise and relief on more than a few young faces. This experience taught me that adults must give young men explicit permission to turn down oral sex—and any sex—they do not want. We must teach them that their manhood is not hinged on the number of sex partners they amass.

6. Making informed decisions that respect others and one's self is a true mark of manhood.   In May 2002, when Oprah Winfrey and Dr. Phil tried to tackle this subject on her afternoon talk show, they not only put the onus of curbing the trend of casual adolescent oral sex on the girls, they threw up their hands and said, "What do the guys have to lose in this situation? Nothing!"

Nothing? I would suggest otherwise. To leave teen boys off the hook in regard to oral sex fails them miserably as they prepare for responsible adult relationships. In doing so, we set up boys to miss out on developing skills that truly define manhood: healthy sexual decision making, setting and respecting personal boundaries, and being accountable for one's actions. We also leave them at risk for contracting sexually transmitted infections. In addition, although our culture rarely communicates this, men who accept oral sex whenever it is offered risk losing the respect of people who do not admire or appreciate men who have indiscriminate sex with large numbers of partners. Clearly, adults—and especially adult men—must be willing to teach boys, through words and actions, that authentic manhood is a complex identity that cannot be so simply attained as through casual sex, oral or otherwise.[9]

7. Giving oral sex is not an effective route to lasting respect, popularity or love. For some teen girls, giving oral sex is weighted with hopes of further attention, increased likeability, and perhaps even a loving relationship.[10] For them, giving oral sex becomes a deceptively easy, if not short-term, way to feel worthy and loved. Adults who care about girls must empower them to see beyond the present social situation and find other routes to a sense of belonging and love.

One essential route to a sense of belonging and love is the consistent experience of non-sexual, non-exploitive touch. Some adolescent girls seek sex as a way to find the sense of love and belonging conveyed by touch. If a girl's touch needs go unfilled by parents or other caregivers, sex is often the most available means for fulfilling them.[11] Adults who work with girls must acknowledge the deeply human need for touch experienced by some adolescent girls. Although outside the scope of this discussion, girl-serving professionals can provide creative ways for girls to experience safe, non-sexual touch as part of their participation in programs without violating program restrictions on physical touch between staff and clients.

On the other hand, it is possible—and developmentally normal—for teen girls to experience sexual desire. Although our cultural script of adolescent sexuality contradicts this, it may be that some girls, especially older teens, authentically desire the kind of sensual and sexual intimacy oral sex affords. If this is the case, it is essential that adults do not shame girls away from these emergent desires. Instead, they should explore the ways oral sex may increase one's physical and emotional vulnerabilities and strategize ways that girls can stay healthy and safe while acknowledging their own sexual desires.

8. Girls can refuse to give oral sex. Unlike Oprah and Dr. Phil, I do not believe the onus for curbing casual adolescent oral sex rests solely or even primarily on teen girls. Teen boys can and should assert firmer boundaries around participating in oral sex. The cultural attitudes that make girls and women the gatekeepers of heterosexual male sexual behavior, deciding when and if sex will happen, are unduly biased and burdensome. By perpetuating these attitudes, Oprah and Dr. Phil missed a grand opportunity to teach the value of mutuality in sexual decision-making and relationships, a message many young people—and adults—desperately need to hear.

That said, it is disturbing to hear stories of adolescent girls offering casual oral sex to teen boys. Again, the models of a balanced female sexuality in the media and in the lives of many girls are often few and far between. This, coupled with the troubling rates of sexual abuse perpetrated against girls in childhood and adolescence, makes the establishment of healthy sexual boundaries a problem for many girls.

Therefore, adults must go beyond simply telling girls to avoid giving oral sex for reasons of reputation and health, as was stressed by Dr. Phil. We must empower girls, through encouragement, role plays, and repeated rehearsals, to establish and maintain healthy boundaries for loving touch in their friendships and dating relationships, an experience that may be new to some. Moreover, we must be frank about the sexual double-standards set up against girls and women that make them responsible for male sexual behavior. And, we must create safe spaces where girls can encourage and support each other in refusing to give boys oral sex, thus shifting the perceived norm that "everyone is doing it."

9. Young women may explore their own capacities for sexual pleasure rather than spending their energies pleasuring others. Some girls will argue that oral sex is just another exchange of friendship, something they do with their male friends as "friends with benefits." I would argue, however, that, in most cases, the benefits are rather one-sided. Rarely do the teen boys give oral sex to the teen girls in exchange. Neither research nor anecdotal evidence indicates a trend of boys offering casual oral sex to girls. It seems that the attention the girls get *en route* to oral sex make it a worthwhile exchange for them, even as they are shortchanged on other "benefits."

If, indeed, girls are fulfilling their valid need for attention and acceptance through giving oral sex, and if they don't consider what they are doing to be "real sex," it stands to reason that many girls engaged in oral sex may not be experiencing genuine sexual desire or pleasure at all. It wouldn't be surprising if they're not. After all, few girls receive a truly comprehensive sexuality education, one that acknowledges the tremendous life-enhancing capacities for desire and pleasure contained in the female body. Our sex education messages are often so consumed by trying to prevent girls from getting pregnant and abused that we fail to notice how we keep them as the objects of other people's sexual behaviors. In doing so, we keep girls mystified about their own bodies and thus fail to empower them as the sexual subjects of their own lives.[12]

Adults can affirm girls' emerging capacities for desire and pleasure by, first, teaching them the names and functions of all of their sexual anatomy, including the pleasure-giving clitoris and G-spot. When discussing the benefits of abstinence, adults can suggest to girls that their growing sexual curiosity and desires may be fulfilled by learning, alone in the privacy of one's room, about one's own body—what touch is pleasing, what is not, how sexual energy builds, and how it is released through their own female bodies. If girls could regard themselves as the sexual subjects of their own lives rather than spending vast energies on being desirable objects of others, perhaps they would make healthier, firmer, more deliberate decisions about the sexual experiences and behaviors they want as adolescents.[13] Not only might girls make better decisions around oral sex, they may feel more empowered to negotiate the use of contraception and safer sex supplies, a skill that would serve them well through their adult years.[14]

**10. Seek the support and guidance of adults who have your best interests
at heart.**   Young people do not have to figure it all out on their own. Human
sexuality is complicated, and most of us, adults and adolescents, do better by
sometimes seeking out the support, guidance, and caring of others who want
to see us enjoy our sexualities in healthy, life-enhancing ways. Adults can let
young people know we are willing to listen to their concerns around issues of
oral sex. We can offer teens support and guidance in their struggles to decide
what's right for their lives. We can become skilled and comfortable in addressing risk-reduction and the enhancement of sexual pleasure together, as com-
panion topics. And, finally, adults can use the topic of oral sex as a catalyst to
dispel myths, discuss gender roles, and communicate values that affirm the
importance of mutuality, personal boundaries, and safety in the context of
healthy relationships.

References

1. L. Remez, "Oral Sex Among Adolescents: Is it Sex or Is It Abstinence?"
   Family Planning Perspectives, Nov/Dec 2000, p. 298.

2. R. Tannahill, *Sex in History* (New York: Stein and Day, 1980), pp. 58–346.

3. M. Carrera, *Sex: The Facts, The Acts, and Your Feelings* (New York: Crown,
   1981), pp. 49–51.

4. Centers for Disease Control and Prevention, "Preventing the Sexual Transmission of HIV, the Virus that Causes AIDS, What You Should Know about
   Oral Sex," Dec. 2000. . . .

5. Iowa Code, Section 709.1, Sexual abuse defined (1999). . . .

6. S. Edwards and C. Carne, "Oral Sex and the Transmission of Viral STIs,"
   Sexually Transmitted Infections, April 1998, pp. 95–100.

7. Centers for Disease Control and Prevention, "Fact Sheet: Pubic Lice or
   'Crabs'," June 2000. . . .

8. Several online retailers sell safer sex supplies, including flavored condoms
   and lubricants. . . .

9. P. Kivel, *Boys Will Be Men: Raising Our Sons for Courage, Caring and Community.*
   (Gabriola Island B.C., Canada: New Society, 1999), pp. 177–184.

10. S. Thompson, *Going All the Way: Teenage Girls' Tales of Sex, Romance, and
    Pregnancy* (New York: Hill & Wang, 1995), pp. 17–46.

11. P. Davis, *The Power of Touch* (Carlsbad, CA: Hay House, 1999), p. 71.

12. M. Fine, "Sexuality, Schooling, and Adolescent Females: The Missing Dis-
    course of Desire," *Disruptive Voices: The Possibilities of Feminist Research,*
    Ann Arbor: University of Michigan, 1992), pp. 31–59.

13. M. Douglass & L. Douglass, *Are We Having Fun Yet? The Intelligent Woman's
    Guide to Sex* (New York: Hyperion, 1997), pp. 170–171.

14. TARSHI (Talking About Reproductive and Sexual Health Issues), *Common
    Ground Sexuality: Principles for Working on Sexuality* (New Dehli, India:
    TARSHI, 2001), p. 13.

Nora Gelperin

Oral Sex and Young Adolescents: Insights from the "Oral Sex Lady"

A Brief History

I've been the Director of Training at the Network for Family Life Education for three years, but recently I've become known as the "Oral Sex Lady." (My parents are so proud.) It all began when I started receiving more frequent calls from parents, teachers and the media concerning alleged incidents of 11–14-year-olds engaging in oral sex in school buses, empty classrooms or custodial closets, behind the gym bleachers and during "oral sex parties." People were beginning to panic that youth were "sexually out of control." Most people believe young teens should not engage in oral sex, but that's not our current reality. So in response, I developed a workshop about oral sex and young teens, which I have since delivered to hundreds of professionals throughout the country. This process has helped me refine my thinking about this so-called oral sex "problem." Now, when I arrive at a meeting or workshop I smile when I'm greeted with, "Hey, aren't you the Oral Sex Lady?!"

What's the "Problem"?

The 1999 documentary "The Lost Children of Rockdale County" first chronicled a syphilis outbreak in suburban Conyers, Georgia, due to a rash of sex parties. Since then, more anecdotal and media stories about middle school students having oral sex began to surface. Initially, a training participant would tell me about an isolated incident of a young girl caught performing oral sex on a boy in the back of the school bus. During a workshop in Minnesota, I was educated about "Rainbow Parties" in which girls wear different-colored lipstick and the goal for guys is to get as many different-colored rings on their penises by night's end. In Florida, there were stories of "chicken head" parties where girls supposedly gave oral sex to boys at the same time, thus bobbing their heads up and down like chickens. During a workshop in New Jersey, I learned that oral sex was becoming the ultimate bar mitzvah gift in one community, given under the table during the reception, hidden by long tablecloths. (At one synagogue, the caterer was ultimately asked to shorten the tablecloths as a method of prevention!) The media began to pick up on these stories and run cover stories in local and national newspapers and magazines. One could conclude from the media buzz that the majority of early adolescents are frequently having oral sex at sex parties around the country. But what was *really* going on and what can the research tell us?

What is missing from the buzz is any recent scientific data to support or refute the claims of early adolescents having oral sex at higher rates than in previous years. Due to parental rights, research restrictions, and lack of funding, there is no rigorous scientific data conducted on the behavior of early adolescents to establish the frequency or incidence of oral sex. So we are left with anecdotal evidence, research conducted on older adolescents, media reports and cultural hype about this "new" phenomenon. We don't know how frequent this behavior is, at what ages it might begin, how many partners a young teen might have, whether any safer sex techniques are utilized, or the reasoning behind a teen's decision to engage in oral sex. What is universal among the anecdotes is that girls are giving oral sex to boys without it generally being reciprocated and it's mostly the adults that find this problematic. But what can we learn from all this?

Major Questions to Consider

Is Oral Sex Really "Sex"?

One of the most common themes I hear during my workshop is that adults want to convince teens that oral sex is really "sex." The adult logic is that if we can just convince teens that oral sex is "really" sex, they will take it more seriously and stop engaging in it so recklessly. This perspective seeks to universally define oral sex from an adult perspective that is out of sync with how many teens may define it. Many teens view oral sex as a way to maintain their "virginity" and reduce their risk for pregnancy and infections. According to a recent Kaiser Family Foundation report, 33 percent of 15–17-year-old girls report having oral sex to avoid having intercourse. In the same report, 47 percent of 15–17-year-old girls and boys believe that oral sex is a form of safer sex. Most people believe that young adolescents should not engage in oral, anal, or vaginal sex. As a backup, we should make sure teens understand that if they are going to engage in sexual behaviors, oral sex is less risky for many infections than vaginal or anal sex if latex barriers like flavored condoms and sheer glyde dams[1] are used, and it cannot start a pregnancy.

If You've Only Had Oral Sex, Are You Still a Virgin?

From my experience facilitating workshops on oral sex, professionals really struggle with this question and many of the 32,000 teens per day who come to our *SEX, ETC.* Web site . . . do too. The concept of virginity, while troublesome to many adults, is still central to the identity of many teens, particularly girls. Many adults and teens define virginity as not having had vaginal intercourse, citing the presence or absence of the hymen. Some adults then wrestle with the idea of what constitutes actual intercourse—penetration of a penis into a vagina, orgasm by one or both partners, oral sex, anal sex, penetration of any body opening? For heterosexual couples, virginity is something girls are often pressured to "keep" and boys are pressured to "lose." The issue also becomes much more volatile when a teen may not have given consent to have intercourse the first time—does this mean that he/she is no longer a virgin? Gay and lesbian teens are also left out when virginity is tied to penis-vagina intercourse, possibly meaning that a gay or lesbian teen might always be a "virgin" if it's defined that way. Educators can help teens think more critically about their definitions of sex, intercourse, and virginity and the meanings of these words in their lives.

How Intimate Is Oral Sex?

Many adults in my workshops express their belief that oral sex is just as intimate as other types of penetrative sexual behaviors. Some adults believe oral sex is even *more* intimate than vaginal or anal intercourse because one partner is considered very vulnerable, it involves all of the senses (smell, taste, touch, sight, and sound) and requires a lot of trust. Many teens, although certainly not all teens, believe oral sex is *less* intimate than vaginal intercourse. Through my experience as an on-line expert for our *SEX, ETC.* Web site, I hear from hundreds of teens every month who submit their most personal sexual health questions. Some of these teens believe oral sex is very intimate and acknowledge the same issues that adults raise while others find it less intimate than vaginal intercourse. From a teen's perspective, it is less intimate because:

- oral sex doesn't require that both partners be nude;
- oral sex can be done in a short amount of time (particularly if performed on adolescent boys);
- oral sex can maintain virginity;
- oral sex doesn't involve eye contact with a partner;
- oral sex doesn't require a method of contraception;
- oral sex doesn't require a trip to the gynecologist; and
- most teens believe oral sex doesn't carry as much of a risk for sexually transmitted infections as vaginal or anal intercourse.

Some girls even feel empowered during oral sex as the only sexual behavior in which they have complete control of their partner's pleasure. Others feel pressured to engage in oral sex and exploited by the experience. So while many adults view oral sex as extremely intimate, some teens do not.

This dichotomy presents challenges for an educator in a group that may assign a different value to oral sex than the educator. Oral sex also requires a conversation about sexual pleasure and sexual response, topics that many educators are not able to address with young teens. The salient issue is how teens define behaviors, not how adults define behaviors, since we are operating in their world when we deliver sexuality education. I believe our definitions and values should be secondary to those of teens because ultimately teens need to be able to operate in a teen culture, not our adult world.

What Can an Educator Do?

As sexual health educators, our role is to provide medically accurate information and encourage all adolescents to think critically about decisions relating to their sexuality. We should ask middle school–age adolescents to sift through their own beliefs and hear from their peers, many of whom might not agree about oral sex, virginity, intimacy or the definition of sex. Finding ways to illuminate the variety of teens' opinions about oral sex will more accurately reflect the range of opinions instead of continuing to propagate the stereotype that "all teens are having oral sex." Additionally, instead of focusing exclusively on the ramifications of oral sex and infections, we should address the potential social consequences of having oral sex. Since early adolescents are not developmentally able to engage in long-term planning, focusing on the long-term consequences of untreated sexually transmitted infections (STIs) is not developmentally appropriate. Educators should be cognizant of what is developmentally appropriate for early adolescents and strive to include information about sexual coercion, correct latex condom and sheer glyde dam use, and infection prevention.

So Are They or Aren't They?

Without research, this question will remain unanswered and we must not rely on overly dramatized media accounts to dictate public health approaches. Instead we should focus on giving young adolescents developmentally appropriate information, consider their reasoning for wanting to engage in oral sex, explore their definitions of sex, virginity, and intimacy, and develop programs that incorporate all of these facets. We need to advocate for more research and reasoned media responses to what is likely a minority of early adolescents having oral sex before it becomes overly dramatized by our shock-culture media. Finally, we must not forget that the desire for early adolescents to feel sexual pleasure is normal and natural and should be celebrated, not censored. From my experience as the "Oral Sex Lady," teens are much more savvy than we adults think.

Note

1. Sheer glyde dams are squares of latex that are held in place on the vulva of a female during oral sex to help prevent sexually transmitted infections. They are the only brand of dental dam that is FDA approved for the prevention of infections.

POSTSCRIPT

Is Oral Sex Really Sex?

"Sex is more than sexual intercourse. This means teaching young people that there are many ways to be sexual with a partner besides intercourse, and most of these behaviors are safer and healthier than intercourse. The word 'sex' often has a vague meaning. When talking about intercourse, the word 'intercourse' [should be] used."

This statement is taken from a list of principles for sexuality education developed by The Center for Family Life Education, included in the United States chapter of the *International Encyclopedia of Sexuality*. Do you agree or disagree with this principle? How does it compare with your own definition of "sex"? Do you agree with Chittenden that young people need to recognize oral sex as "really sex"? Or are you inclined to side with Gelperin as she asserts that adult values and definitions should be secondary, and that young people need to form their own definition of oral sex?

Chittenden presents specific messages she believes young people need to hear about oral sex. What do you think about these messages? Are they messages you would want to give to a son or daughter, or to a younger sibling? What other advice would you want to give to a loved one who was thinking about having oral sex?

Whereas Chittenden identifies specific messages that need to be articulated to young people, Gelperin seems more inclined to advocate a values clarification process and educational strategies based on the developmental needs of a given audience. What merits do these different approaches have? Would you advocate a combination of these approaches? Or would your own educational approach be very different?

Gelperin expresses great concern about the hype surrounding media reports of oral sex. What do you think about such reports? How do they compare with the social climate in your schools or community as you were growing up?

Since both Chittenden and Gelperin are sexuality education professionals, you may have noticed several overlapping themes, such as the concern both expressed about condom use and protection from sexuality transmitted infections. What other similarities did you observe?

Is it more important to have a uniform definition of "sex," that includes (or does not include) oral sex, or for people to create their own personal definitions that have meaning for themselves and/or their partners? Some reproductive health professionals have ascertained that if you cannot define "sex," then you cannot define its supposed opposite, "abstinence." In other words, young people need to understand what sex is before they can determine what it is they are being encouraged to abstain from. How has a culturally vague notion of "sex" and "abstinence" contributed to the widespread failure of abstinence-only education programs?

Suggested Readings

C. Billhartz and C.M. Ostrom, "What's 'Real' Sex? Kids Narrow Definition, Put Themselves at Risk" *Seattle Times* (November 6, 2002).

K.L. Brewster and K.H. Tillman, "Who's Doing It? Patterns and Predictors of Youths' Oral Sexual Experiences," *Journal of Adolescent Health* (vol. 42, no. 1, pp. 73–80, 2008).

W.C. Chambers, "Oral Sex: Varied Behaviors and Perceptions in a College Population," *Journal of Sex Research* (vol. 44, no. 1, pp. 28–42, 2007).

G. D'Souza, et al., "Oral Sexual Behaviors Associated with Prevalent Oral Human Papillomavirus Infection," *Journal of Infectious Diseases* (vol. 199, pp. 1263–1269, 2009).

D.W. Freeman, "Oral Sex Is Now Main Cause of Oral Cancer: Who Faces Biggest Risk?" *CBS News* (February 23, 2011).

L.D. Lindberg, et al., "Noncoital Sexual Activities Among Adolescents," *Journal of Adolescent Health* (vol. 43, no. 3, pp. 231–238, 2008).

L. Remez, "Oral Sex Among Adolescents: Is It Sex or Is It Abstinence?" *Family Planning Perspectives* (November/December 2000).

R. Stein, "Oral Sex Isn't Keeping Kids Virgins," *Washington Post* (May 20, 2008).

P. Schehl, "Middle Schoolers Facing Tough Issues," *Mount Vernon News* (January 20, 2009).

J. Timpane, "No Big Deal: The Biggest Deal of All—Young Adults and the Oral Sex Code," *Philadelphia Inquirer* (October 28, 2002).

D. Trice, "Teens Have Sex But Don't Have the Facts," *Chicago Tribune* (March 17, 2008).

ISSUE 6

Is BDSM a Healthy Form of Sexual Expression?

YES: Wayne V. Pawlowski, from "BDSM: The Ultimate Expression of Healthy Sexuality," an original essay written for this volume (2009)

NO: J. Paul Fedoroff, from "Sadism, Sadomasochism, Sex, and Violence," *The Canadian Journal of Psychiatry* (vol. 53, no. 10, 2008)

ISSUE SUMMARY

YES: Sex educator Wayne Pawlowski provides an explanation of BDSM and describes it as a normal, healthy expression of sexuality.

NO: J. Paul Fedoroff describes BDSM as a disorder and a pathology and links BDSM to criminal activity.

Bondage/Discipline, Dominance/submission, and Sadism/Masochism (BDSM) all involve the eroticization of the exchange of power. For some, there is no bigger turn on than taking control in a sexual encounter. For others, giving away all power may be the ultimate thrill. These choices may manifest in many different ways. Bondage play involves the restriction of movement by rope, chains, or other instruments. Submission may take the form of being spanked or confined to a cage. A sadist may enjoy striking a submissive partner with an object like a whip or cane. To some, these behaviors may sound like an exhilarating Friday night. For others, the behaviors may seem extreme or even dangerous. There is even much debate among health care professionals and sexuality educators. The subjective nature of classifying behaviors and fantasies, along with the social stigma attached to BDSM, can make it difficult to find accurate and representative statistics on the subject. A 1993 study found that 14 percent of men and 11 percent of women had engaged in some sadomasochistic sexual activities in their lives (Janus & Janus, 1993). Much of what we know about those who practice BDSM comes from studies of those who attend BDSM clubs or functions, or who are members of BDSM organizations (Weinberg, 2006) rather than from studies of the general population.

According to the DSM-IV, the reference book used by psychiatrists to diagnose mental disorders, both sadism and masochism are considered paraphilias (sex-related disorders), as long as the thoughts or behaviors cause "clinically significant distress or impairment in social, occupational, or other important areas of functioning." Sadism is defined as the use of "sexual fantasies, urges, or behaviors involving infliction of pain, suffering, or humiliation to enhance or achieve sexual excitement"; and masochism is defined as the use of "sexual fantasies, urges, or behaviors involving being beaten, humiliated, bound, or tortured to enhance or achieve sexual excitement" (APA, 1994).

Despite the caveat that an interest in BDSM must cause "distress" in order to be considered a problem, many find hardly any interest in sadistic or masochistic sexuality to be unhealthy. Making for surprising bedfellows, conservatives and radical feminists have often found themselves on the same side of the argument against BDSM. The conservative group Concerned Women for America have pressured hotel chains to prevent BDSM organizations from holding conventions in their hotels (CWFA, 2003). Large BDSM groups like Black Rose in Washington, DC, often rent out entire hotels for weekend conventions that host hundreds of BDSM practitioners. Across the ideological spectrum, many radical feminists also criticize BDSM, holding that any form of sexual dominance reinforces sexual hierarchy, thereby contributing to the well-established patriarchal dominance.

But does sex play involving dominance and submission always signal violence and oppression? Are they dangerous? Or are they simply part of diverse sexual expressions?

In his essay, sexuality educator Wayne Pawlowski explains BDSM and describes it as a normal, healthy form of sexual expression. J. Paul Fedoroff describes BDSM as a disorder and a pathology and links BDSM to criminal activity.

Suggested Readings

American Psychiatric Association, *Diagnostic and Statistical Manual of Mental Disorders* (4th ed.) (Washington, DC: American Psychiatric Association, 1994).

Concerned Women for America (CWFA), "Cancel Sexual Torture Convention, CWA Urges Adam's Mark Chicago–Northbrook Hotel," press release accessed at http://www.cwfa.org/articledisplay.asp?id=3270&department=FIELD&categoryid=misc (2003).

M. Freedenberg, "Kink Dreams: Peter Acworth's Fetish Porn Empire Takes over the San Francisco Armory to Create a New Kind of Dot-com," accessed at http://www.sfbg.com/entry.php?entry_id=7161&catid=4&volume_id=398&issue_id=425&volume_num=43&issue_num=27 (2008).

R. Goldman, "Love Hurts: Sadomasochism's Dangers: Man Spends Three Days in a Coma after Kinky Sex—But Unsafe Play Can Result in Death." Accessed at http://abcnews.go.com/Health/story?id=4285958&page=1 (2008).

S. Janus and C. Janus, *The Janus Report on Sexual Behavior* (New York: Wiley, 1993).

D. Schoetz, "Wife Held in Kinky Hubby's Bondage Death: Police Say Woman Left Her Husband for 20 Hours Bound, Gagged Before He Suffocated." Accessed at http://abcnews.go.com/US/story?id=4703433 (2008).

T. S. Weinberg, "Sadomasochism and the Social Sciences: A Review of the Sociological and Social Psychological Literature," *Journal of Homosexuality* (vol. 50, pp. 17–40, May 2006).

YES

Wayne V. Pawlowski

BDSM: The Ultimate Expression of Healthy Sexuality

What is BDSM? We will get to definitions in a moment, but let's start off by saying that it (BDSM) is perhaps one of the most misunderstood forms of sexual expression today. It is not only misunderstood, it is feared; prosecuted as abuse/assault; depicted as something engaged in by mentally disturbed, sexual predators who torture, rape, kill, and dismember their victims; and the behaviors associated with it are classified as mental disorders in the psychiatric diagnostic criteria of the *Diagnostic and Statistical Manual of Mental Disorders* (commonly known as the DSM) and the *International Classification of Diseases* (ICD). Given all of this, individuals who engage in BDSM behaviors rarely talk about their interests with people outside of the "BDSM Community." The end result is that BDSM and BDSM behaviors remain "in the closet" and misunderstood.

It is known that BDSM behaviors occur among all genders, sexual orientations, races, ages, sexual identity groups, social groups, and economic groups. And, they have occurred throughout recorded history and across cultures. Beyond these general statements, however, there is very little solid and reliable research as to the number of individuals who engage in and/or who fantasize about BDSM behaviors. And, in part because of its secrecy, there is almost no research data describing the population of individuals who are regular or periodic BDSM "players" and/or who are members of the "BDSM Community." As a result, the misunderstanding and myths about BDSM continue to pervade the culture and the psychiatric view of BDSM behaviors.

Much has been written and discussed about:

- The weaknesses of the psychiatric diagnostic criteria for BDSM behaviors,
- The lack of research and data to back up the diagnostic criteria,
- The inaccurate and inconsistent application of diagnoses of BDSM behaviors,
- The gender bias in the diagnostic descriptions (overwhelmingly male),
- The discrepancies between the descriptions of BDSM behaviors in the *Diagnostic and Statistical Manual* and the *International Classification of Diseases,* and,

- The lack of a clear and consistently applied distinction between individuals who engage in BDSM behaviors *consensually and safely* versus those who force, rape, torture, and/or otherwise engage in non-consensual, violent behaviors.

The bottom line is that the *Diagnostic and Statistical Manual* is not a useful place to go to try to understand BDSM, or the people who engage in BDSM behaviors. In addition, as with other previously "pathologized" behaviors that the *Diagnostic and Statistical Manual* eventually "de-pathologized" (masturbation and same-sex sexual behavior, to name two), BDSM behaviors as they are engaged in by those who identify with the "BDSM Community" bear little to no resemblance to the behaviors described in the psychiatric diagnostic criteria. The subtleties and distinctions among BDSM behaviors as practiced and understood by those who engage in those behaviors (hereafter, for brevity sake, referred to as "practitioners") are lost on the majority of the psychiatric community (those who write the psychiatric diagnostic criteria), the legal community (police, courts, lawyers), and the culture as a whole.

So, in order to understand how BDSM and engaging in BDSM behaviors can be the ultimate, healthy expression of self and of sexuality we must first step away from the psychiatric diagnostic criteria and from the legal and cultural misperceptions and interpretations. Next we must clarify what BDSM is and isn't, then we must examine BDSM behaviors in the context of "normal," "conventional" behaviors, and lastly, we must try to let go of our preconceived biases and see the incredibly healthy aspects of how BDSM play is conducted and experienced.

What BDSM Is and Isn't

BDSM is an acronym for a wide range of behaviors, both sexual and non-sexual. It is actually a complex interplay of three separate and distinct "worlds" of behavior, none of which are inherently overtly sexual but most of which can and often do play out in powerfully erotic ways. BDSM includes the world of *BD*, the world of *Ds* and the world of *SM*. While these three worlds can and frequently do overlap (hence the acronym "BDSM"), they can and frequently do travel totally and completely separately from each other.

Recognizing that the language used to describe BDSM is in flux and that different regions of the US and the world will use different terms to describe the same behaviors, let us attempt to clarify the three "worlds" mentioned above.

BD is the world of "bondage and dominance," "bondage and domination," or "bondage and discipline" (remember, language varies from place to place and person to person so all three descriptions are simply different words used to define *BD*). *BD* always involves some sort of restraint—bondage—and is frequently, but not always, paired with some sort of domination and/or punishment/discipline.

Ds is the world of "Dominance and submission" or "Domination and submission." (Remember the note above about variations in language.) And, yes, the uppercase "D" and lowercase "s" are intentional. *Ds* involves some sort of "superiority" and "inferiority"; the domination of one individual over another and/or the submission of one individual to another.

SM is the world of "sadism and masochism" or "sadomasochism." *SM* involves some sort of playing with and/or giving (sadism) and receiving (masochism) of pain and/or other sensations.

So, BDSM encompasses a wide range of behaviors and activities. Common elements that are "played with" in most BDSM behaviors are power (exchanging it, taking it, and/or giving it up), the mind (psychology), and sensation (using or depriving use of the senses and working with the chemicals released by the body when pain and/or intense sensations are experienced).

BDSM play often occurs as much psychologically as it does physically so "using" the mind, the brain, and the imagination is a powerful and well-exercised skill among BDSM practitioners. It is the psychological aspect of BDSM that gives BDSM play its meaning and context. Sometimes, BDSM play is *primarily* psychology rather than physical. When it is, things like domination and submission may not look at all like what people expect. In fact, predominantly psychological BDSM "behaviors" may not be at all "visible" or evident to an observer even when they are occurring in a very public arena. More will be said about the psychological aspects of BDSM later in this article.

As with every other aspect of their lives, practitioners of BDSM make ongoing decisions about what role BDSM behaviors will play in their general lives and in their sexual lives. Their BDSM behaviors may be "real" or role play, one-time-only, 24/7, on-going, short-term, long-term, periodic, primarily erotically sexual, primarily non-sexual, a part of one relationship only, or a part of every relationship. There is no single way that BDSM behaviors are integrated into practitioners' lives, sexual lives, and/or love making in the same way that there is no single way that other more "conventional" behaviors are integrated into the lives, sexual lives, and/or love making of people in general.

Normal/Conventional or Abnormal/ Unconventional

For most non-practitioners, BDSM is viewed as "unconventional" and/or "exotic" behavior at best or abnormal and dangerous at worst. In fact, BDSM play is nothing more or less than an extension of the "normal," "conventional" behaviors that most "traditional" couples engage in with great frequency. Most behaviors in life are engaged in along a continuum from mild/gentle to moderate to extreme/intense. (See Figure 1.) BDSM is simply the more extreme/intense end of the continuum of normal, conventional behavioral expression.

Figure 1

Continuum of Expression of Conventional Behaviors

◀---▶

Mild   Moderate   Extreme

BD Behaviors

During love making it is not uncommon for one partner to "hold" the other partner "in place" at a particular moment (e.g., holding a partner's head in place during oral sex), or to tie a partner's hands with underwear or a scarf. Many couples view these behaviors as nothing more than playful and exciting ways to enhance their intimacy. Most would not view them as BDSM. They are, however, all forms of "restraint" and "restraint" in BDSM parlance is "bondage." These playful and exciting behaviors are simply the mild or gentle end of a continuum of behaviors that may, at the extreme end, involve having someone completely immobilized, caged, or chained to a wall. (See Figure 2.) The only difference between holding a person's head in place and having someone completely immobilized is the level of intensity and drama of the behaviors, the psychological meaning of the behaviors, the way the behaviors "look," and how the behaviors are experienced by the participants. The behaviors themselves are the same; one partner is restraining another. And, again, restraint is another word for bondage and bondage is a part of the world of *BD*.

Figure 2

Continuum of BD Behaviors

Partner's hands tied with scarf.	Partner handcuffed to bed.	Partner immobilized/caged.

◄---►

Mild	Moderate	Extreme

Ds Behaviors

A partner may playfully and lightheartedly say, "You get no sex from me unless you bring me a glass of wine and light some candles first!" This is a conventional, light-hearted occurrence among many "traditional" couples; sex is playfully "withheld" and later "granted" upon the completion of a task. As we saw with *BD*, this playful behavior is nothing less than the gentle end of *Ds*. It is servitude, "requiring" one partner to "serve" the other with sex as the "reward." The more intense end of this behavior might be a full-time live in "slave" who is "allowed" to have sex with the Dominant partner as a result of satisfactorily completing his/her chores. (See Figure 3.) Again, both of

Figure 3

Continuum of Ds Behaviors

No sex without a glass of wine.	Full-time live-in slave.

◄---►

Mild	Moderate	Extreme

---

these behaviors are essentially the same as they both involve servitude. What is different about them is the intensity and drama of the behaviors, their psychological meaning, how they "look," and how they are experienced by the participants.

SM Behaviors

A light slap on the buttocks or gently pinching a partner as orgasm nears is common "conventional" behavior among "traditional" couples. But, as with the *BD* and *Ds* examples, this light slap and gentle pinch are nothing less than the mild or gentle end of the *SM* continuum . . . playing with sensations. The moderate place on this continuum might be lightly spanking a partner. The extreme end of the continuum might be severely whipping or flogging a partner. (See Figure 4.) Again, all of these behaviors are the same in that they involve administering some sort of sensation to a partner in order to heighten erotic feeling. What is different about them is the intensity of the behaviors, their psychological meaning, how they "look," and how they are experienced by the participants.

Figure 4

Continuum of SM Behaviors

Light slap on buttocks	Light spanking	Severe whipping
◄ - ►		
Mild	Moderate	Extreme

Some readers might be horrified to think of or to interpret their "normal," "conventional," "vanilla," "ordinary" behaviors as BDSM behaviors . . . but in fact, they are just that. Perhaps they are the mild or gentle end of BDSM; but they are BDSM nonetheless. Or, to put it the other way, BDSM behaviors are nothing more than the extreme end of "normal," "ordinary," "conventional" behaviors.

The importance of the "psychological meaning" of behavior was mentioned earlier and it cannot be emphasized enough how important psychological meaning is to BDSM practitioners. The experience of any behavior and how the behavior "feels," comes directly from the meaning that has been given to the behavior by the people involved in it. It also comes from the context in which the behavior occurs. If a behavior is labeled and/or identified as a BDSM behavior for a particular couple, it will be EXPERIENCED as a BDSM behavior by that couple. If the exact same behavior is not given that label or identified in that way, it will be experienced completely differently; likely it will be experienced as ordinary, conventional behavior.

It was mentioned earlier that predominantly psychological BDSM behavior may not be visible even if it is occurring in a very public arena. An example of this is someone sitting alone on a park bench. That individual may well be doing nothing more or less than sitting alone on a park bench. However, if that individual is a submissive that has been ordered to sit there until his/her Dom returns, that submissive will be engaging in an intense and powerful BDSM experience. The behavior alone looks very conventional—sitting on a park bench—but the psychological meaning of that sitting is profoundly influenced by the meaning assigned to it by the individuals involved.

Healthy Sexuality and Healthy Relationships

Because the meaning of behavior comes from knowing and understanding its context, for BDSM behaviors to "work" they must be discussed, analyzed, clearly understood, and agreed upon. This means individuals must share with their partners their wants, needs, desires, fantasies, limits, fears, etc. It means they must *communicate* and *negotiate* in great detail and clarity about what they want, what they like, what they are willing to do, what they are not willing to do, what the relationship means to them right now, and what it might mean tomorrow; and, after-the-fact, they must communicate again about what the experience was like for them.

All of this requires the development of self-awareness, communication skills, listening skills, high self-esteem, awareness of boundaries (one's own and others'), awareness of personal likes and dislikes, negotiation skills, etc.

What could be healthier than for individuals to be encouraged to develop and practice all of these things? And then, what could be better for couples than to engage in this level of communication, negotiation, and feedback as they enter into and develop relationships?

As part of their belief in and need for communication, openness, and full consent, BDSM practitioners have developed a number of guiding principles which are taught and followed by the "community" and by those who seriously engage in BDSM activities. These principles include *SSC* (Safe, Sane, Consensual) and/or *RACK* (Risk Aware Consensual Kink), *Hurt Not Harm, Negotiation, Relationship of Equals, Safe Words, After Care, Self-Affirming Not Self-Destructive,* and *Never Under the Influence.*

This paper does not allow for a full explanation of each of these principles, but the list itself conveys the BDSM Community's interest in and desire to talk openly and honestly about safety, limits, can-do's, can't-dos, how to monitor and take care of each other while in the midst of play, how to take care of each other when play is done, etc. All of this illustrates the fact that BDSM practitioners are not the disturbed, compulsive, driven, dangerous individuals who engage in pathological behaviors as described in the *Diagnostic and Statistical Manual* and as seen on TV. Instead, in reality, they are serious, cautious, thoughtful, caring individuals who negotiate with equal partners to engage in behaviors that are mutually satisfying, mutually desired, and enacted as safely as possible. They believe that two people can only enter into a BDSM relationship if they both fully understand each other, they both fully understand what they are going to do together, and, they both fully and completely consent to what will happen before, during, and after the behavior. These beliefs, qualities, interactions, and behaviors epitomize healthy sexuality and sexually healthy relationships.

J. Paul Fedoroff

 **NO**

Sadism, Sadomasochism, Sex, and Violence

The true prevalence of sexual sadism (and its variants) is unknown. However, all clinicians will knowingly or unknowingly encounter patients with this disorder. Regretfully, few programs offer adequate education in normal sexuality and even less provide training in the assessment and treatment of pathologic sexual interests. This review synthesizes current theories about possible etiologies of criminal sexual sadism and the resulting implications for diagnosis and treatment of this sexual disorder. Included is a review of theories of criminally sadistic sexual motivations, response patterns, and physiology, including possible neurophysiologic factors and more complex interactions. This review focuses primarily on published English-language scientific studies of sexual sadism. It should be noted that my use of the term sadism refers to nonconsensual sexual aggression.

Highlights

- While some scientific evidence supports an interaction between sexual behaviours and aggression, the purported association between sex and violence in media reports is misleading. This is due to a focus on sensational cases, lack of consistency in diagnostic criteria, inconclusive study designs, overgeneralization, and reliance on opinion.
- Sexual arousal from consensual interactions that include domination should be distinguished from nonconsensual sex acts. Nonconsensual sex may be opportunistic, disinhibited, or sexually motivated. Often motivations are mixed.
- Future research needs to integrate studies to account for how neurophysiologic and neurohormonal events translate into psychologic experiences that in turn are modified by social variables within specific populations across the lifespan.
- The frequency of reported sex crimes is decreasing. The efficacy of treatment for paraphilias of all types is improving. Further research into the relation between sex and violence will aid in decreasing sex crimes but more importantly will aid in understanding how to facilitate safe, healthy, and happy sexuality for everyone.

Sadism and masochism occupy a special place among the perversions, for the contrast of activity and passivity lying at their bases belong to the common traits of the sexual life. —Sigmund Freud[1], p. 23

From *Canadian Journal of Psychiatry* by J. Paul Fedoroff, 53(10), October 2008, pp. 637–646.
Copyright © 2008 by Canadian Psychiatric Association. Reprinted by permission.

How one thing depends upon another is the greatest mystery about life in my opinion, and no doubt if we could see the network of cause and effect spun and spinning around us, it would be a very interesting and wonderful spectacle.[2], p. 1

The topics of sex and violence are of almost universal interest. A Google search using the word sex produces 687 million hits. A search linking sex with synonyms for violence results in 274 million searchable links. A more specific review of the scientific literature was conducted using SUM search, which combines a metasearch strategy with contingency searching of major databases including PubMed and PsycLIT. In our review, the following key words were linked with the word sexual: violence, sadism, homicide, coercion, and predator. This search, limited to human subject research published in the English language within the last 10 years, resulted in 4211 journal article citations. These citations were combined with 148 journal articles identified by the key word sadomasochism, followed up by referral to articles and books cited in the materials listed above.

To capture articles not yet cited within standard research databases, the results were combined with a recent review of the published literature on sexual violence.[3] Full details of the search strategies and results for this article are available on request.

Introduction

These incidence and prevalence of sex crimes in North America is declining,[4] and no one knows why.[5] In Canada, the rate of sexual assault in 2004 was 74 incidents per 100,000, representing a 33% drop from 1985. Since then, published rates report a further decrease to 72 per 100,000.[6]

Despite this welcome trend, the association between sexually motivated behaviours and violence is unknown. Sexual offences of all types result in devastating consequences, not only for victims but also for perpetrators (a third of whom are themselves victims of sexual abuse).[7] No clinician who cares for adult patients has the luxury of avoiding contact (knowingly or otherwise) with perpetrators and potential perpetrators whose activities may be modified to the extent that sex crimes can be prevented.

Appropriate interventions require adequate education. In a survey of 141 medical schools in North America, 54% provided 10 hours teaching on the general topic of sexual medicine[8]; however, most medical schools provided prospective physicians with less than 2 hours of sex education.[9] These numbers are important because physicians are often the first people confronted with situations in which clinical judgments are crucial. The vignette in Table 1 is an example of the questions posed during typical sexual attitude restructuring exercises advocated by experts in medical education.

The purpose of this review is to examine the relation between sex and violence, to explain some of the contradictory views of researchers, to provide a rational basis for answers to the questions posed in Table 1, and to advocate for evidence-based evaluation and treatment of men and women with potentially problematic sexual interests and behaviours. This review is intended primarily

ABBREVIATIONS USED IN THIS ARTICLE

BDSM	Bondage–Discipline, Dominance–Submission, Sadism–Masochism
DSM	Diagnostic and Statistical Manual of Mental Disorders
ICD	International Classification of Diseases
LH	luteinizing hormone
MRI	magnetic resonance imaging
PET	positron emission tomography
RCBF	regional cerebral blood flow

Table 1

Case History

You are a psychiatry resident on call in a busy downtown emergency room. A young patient is brought to the ER by ambulance with a fractured femur. Radiologic examination indicates this is a third fracture. You are asked whether a psychiatric consultation is indicated.

What is your answer if:

- The injuries were sustained during high school football games?
- The injuries were sustained during consensual, sadomasochistic sex play?
- The injuries were sustained during nonconsensual sexual activity?
- The patient is a child; is female; is intellectually disabled; does or does not think there is a problem?

Finally, what would your answer be in each case if the patient were the sexual partner of another individual with the same medical injury?

for psychiatrists in general practice. Reviews of topics of more interest to subspecialists are available, such as sexually aggressive women,[10] sexually aggressive juveniles,[11, 12] intellectually delayed sex offenders,[13] and neurological comorbidity in sexual violence.[14]

Diagnostic Criteria

DSM-IV-TR criteria for sexual sadism (302.84) are reproduced in Table 2.[15, p. 574] Examining the A criteria, several questions arise:

- Why 6 months?
- What does recurrent mean?
- What does intense mean?
- Is it meaningful to discuss sexual urges independent of sexual fantasies?

Table 2

DSM-IV-TR Criteria for Sexual Sadism (302.84)

Over a period of 6 months, recurrent, intense sexually arousing fantasies, sexual urges, or behaviors involving acts (real, not simulated) in which the psychological or physical suffering (including humiliation) of the victim is sexually exciting to the person.

The person has acted on these sexual urges with a non-consenting person, or the sexual urges or fantasies cause marked distress or interpersonal difficulty.[15, p. 574]

- Why distinguish between real and simulated acts?
- Appearing to be a fairly inclusive criteria, why is humiliation specifically identified in addition to psychological and physical suffering?

Few experts follow the DSM-IV-TR criteria.[16] For example, in a series of survey studies involving respected and experienced forensic psychiatrists, investigators found that "the diagnosis of sexual sadism was not being applied in the Canadian prison system in a way that matched any of the criteria identified in the literature."[17, p. 2]

These findings also applied to internationally renowned psychiatrists, in which a kappa coefficient for reliability across diagnosis was only 0.14.[18]

Table 3 lists the ICD-10 criteria for sadomasochism.[19] There are several obvious differences between these criteria and those of the DSM-IV-TR. First, the conditions of sexual sadism and sexual masochism are combined. Second, there is an indication that elements of sadomasochism may be present in so-called normal sexual life. Third, there is an explicit differentiation between sexually motivated sadomasochistic acts and those motivated by cruelty or anger in a sexual context.

The differences between the DSM and ICD diagnostic criteria underline a major cause of confusion in the literature as it is often hard to know what is meant by the term sadist. Also, most studies use samples of convenience consisting of men convicted of violent sexual crimes. Examination of samples of this type begs the question of the relation between sexual sadism and sexual violence.

Table 3

ICD-10 Criteria for Sadomasochism (F 65.5)

A preference for sexual activity that involves bondage or the infliction of pain or humiliation. If the individual prefers to be the recipient of such stimulation this is called masochism; if the provider, sadism. Often an individual obtains sexual excitement from both sadistic and masochistic activities.

Mild degrees of sadomasochistic stimulation are commonly used to enhance otherwise normal sexual activity. This category should be used only if sadomasochistic activity is the most important source of stimulation or necessary for sexual gratification.

Sexual sadism is sometimes difficult to distinguish from cruelty in sexual situations or anger unrelated to eroticism. Where violence is necessary for erotic arousal, the diagnosis can be clearly established. Includes: masochism, sadism.[19, p. 172]

Etiologic Theories

Sexual Motivation

In a recent paper,[20] 12 series of serial sexual murderers were reviewed.[20–31] The men in these surveys were judged to have shown evidence of "positive feelings of sexual pleasure, even exhilaration rather than anger or other unpleasant states . . ." that represented the "driving psychological force in the crimes."[20, p. 902]

On the basis of a review of studies on the sexual physiology in nonsadistic men, these authors assert that anger is incompatible with sexual arousal because sympathetic catecholamines associated with anger (for example, norepinephrine) are also associated with penile detumescence.[32, 33]

Unfortunately, all but one of the 12 reports involved reviewing historic cases, with several involving descriptions by authors with no clinical experience. It is possible that the descriptions of sexual pleasure as the prime motivating force may more accurately reflect the views of the reports' authors than those of the study's participants.

In addition, many sex crimes involve activities that do not require an erection.[34,35] The act of planning and carrying out a sex crime may itself be associated with subjective sexual arousal.[36] Presumably these phases of the crime are independent of penile tumescence and not incompatible with other emotions such as anger directed at the victim. Several studies have indicated that anger itself can be a major factor contributing to the commission of sex crimes.[37–39]

Sexual Fantasies, Experiences, and Behaviours

If serial violent sex offenders are primarily motivated by sexual arousal, how unique to offenders is sexual arousal in response to sadistic stimuli or scenarios? Meyers et al.'s review of 3 studies[20, p. 904] in which a percentage of presumably noncriminal male college students were aroused by fantasies of "infliction of pain on others"[40] and found pictures of women with "distressed faces"[41] more sexually arousing, and in which the degree of arousal increased together with the degree of distress depicted in pictures of "semi-nude women in bondage."[42]

These and other studies have been summarized.[43] Among the general male population, 39% have had fantasies of "tying up" and 30% of "raping a woman."[44, p. 571] Among male college students, 51%[44, p. 130] indicated they would rape a woman if they thought they could get away with it, and perhaps most controversially, 25%[44, p. 134] of the male and female college students in the sample thought women would enjoy being raped if no one knew about it.[45]

Most rapes involve the use of alcohol. In one representative study, according to 61% of the victims, the offender was under the influence of alcohol.[46] It is unknown whether the percentages of students apparently approving of rape in the previous study would have been higher had the surveys been done after the respondents had consumed alcohol.

One of the most influential studies of sexual murderers involved a sample of only 36 men, interviewed in custody by FBI special agents.[47] Authors of the FBI study hypothesized that offenders begin with deviant fantasies that graduate to minor crimes that in turn become increasingly serious. This "degeneration hypothesis" was originally advanced by Marquis Donatien-Alphonse Francois de Sade, after whom the term sadism was eponymously named.[48] This influential uncontrolled FBI study has supported the theory that men who commit extreme sex crimes can be identified and classified on the basis of unique characteristics, including deviant sexual fantasies.[40, 49, 51-53]

Problems with the sensitivity and specificity of sexual fantasies characteristic of sadistic sex offenders have been reviewed.[54] One study of 94 men with no history of sexual offences found 33% reported rape fantasies and 14.9% reported humiliation fantasies.[44] Although men far outnumber women convicted of sadistic sex crimes, surveys have found no difference in frequency of sadistic fantasies in men and women.[55-57] In fact, nonscientific reports indicate that women's fantasies may be becoming more sadistic even though the number of sadistic women convicted of sex crimes has remained constant or even dropped.[58] Variables identified as characteristic of criminal sadists by Burgess[49] were compared with frequencies of these variables in a sample of 18 undergraduate men and 32 undergraduate women. None of the university students were known to have committed crimes of any type. Among 11 childhood experiences identified as characteristic of criminal sadists, only a history of convulsions was more frequent in Burgess' criminal sadist group. Three childhood experiences were more common in the university group: daydreaming, accident proneness, and headaches. The university group also reported more adolescent experiences than the sexual sadists, including: poor body image, sleep problems, and headaches. Sexual sadists were more likely to report eneuresis and convulsions during adolescence. In adulthood, the university group continued to show more worrisome behavioural indicators than did Burgess' criminal sexual sadists: daydreaming, poor body image, sleep problems, and headaches.

A similar lack of specificity was found for the childhood behavioural indicators previously identified to be associated with criminal sadists. The only exceptions were self-identified compulsive masturbation and fire-setting, which were significantly more prevalent in the sadist group.

It should be noted that more differences emerged between the 2 groups during adolescence and adulthood. Unfortunately, data concerning the time of onset of criminal behaviour in the offender sample were not available. Still, the failure to find consistent clear differences between the criminal sadists and the university student group, even though the university student group consisted of both men and women, suggests that experiences and behaviours, at least as identified in the FBI sample, are unreliable.

Sexual Response Patterns

If criminal sadists cannot be reliably distinguished from noncriminal men on the basis of sexual fantasies, childhood experiences, or behaviours, can they be distinguished on the basis of laboratory testing of penile tumescence in response to stimuli designed to simulate or approximate sadistic scenarios? This possibility was also investigated.[59-65] Marshall[66] pointed out that results of these early studies have yielded inconsistent results when arousal in response to rape was compared between groups consisting of rapists and normal men. In response to rape stimuli, rapists were found to show penile tumescence responses that were either more than,[64, 67–69] equal to,[59, 60, 70–74] or less than[61] those of the control group. It may be that differences in results may be due to differences in the number of sadists in each group.[75, 76]

A second explanation for variance in ability to distinguish between rapist and nonrapists on the basis of penile tumescence testing may be due to the types of stimuli used in the test procedure.[77, 78] Two potentially important variations include the degree of brutality of the audiotape stimuli[79] or the degree of humiliation.[80] In all likelihood, an interaction exists between the degree of sadism in the man tested and the type of stimuli presented. In a group of rapists with few sadists, manipulation of sadistic elements in the stimuli presented during penile tumescence testing would not be expected to assist in discrimination from nonrapist, nonsadistic controls. This is in fact what was found.[81]

In a study involving[41] sexual offenders diagnosed with sexual sadism and 18 sexual offenders without sadism, Boer[65] found that on a "composite index" of phallometric responses, "only 17.1% of sadists appeared deviant and yet 44% of the so-called nonsadists displayed deviant responses."[p. 2] This raises the question of whether sadistic interest necessarily increases risk of sexual offences.

Penile tumescence (phallometric) testing is at best a crude measure of sexual interest because it measures only one aspect of sexual arousal (penile erection) and because it does not measure propensity to act on sexual interests.[82]

Physiology

More proximal measures of physiologic associations associated with sexual violence have been investigated. Testosterone is a hormone that has received great interest based on the observations that most sex offenders are male and that men have more testosterone than women. In a sample of 4462 male war veterans, serum testosterone was associated with antisocial behaviours.[83]

However, the only reported association with sexual behaviours was between high testosterone levels and "more than 10 sex partners in one year"[p. 210] and the association between high testosterone and antisocial behaviours was moderated by increases in socioeconomic status. An association between high salivary-free testosterone levels and aggression was also shown in a sample of 89 prison inmates.[84]

However, sexual aggression was not measured in this study. This deficiency was partially addressed in a third study, which included cross-validation with earlier samples of prisoners.[85] Although inmates with higher testosterone levels were described as more confrontational, only 5% of the 692 prisoners had committed a nonstatutory rape, and a total of 4% of men in this sample had been convicted for some type of child molestation. The percentage of sex offenders of both types was higher in the group of prisoners with the highest testosterone levels but the majority of men with high testosterone (86%) were not sex offenders.

These findings are consistent with an earlier study[86] specifically intended to investigate testosterone and violence involving 50 sex offenders in which no relation was found between plasma testosterone and violent sexual behaviour. In a review of the literature on testosterone and sexual behaviour in men, it was concluded that fluctuations in testosterone have little effect on sexual behaviour as long as the fluctuations are within the normal range and as long as a minimum amount of the hormone is present.[87]

In spite of the equivocal findings in the previously reviewed studies, considerable evidence supports the interrelation between high testosterone levels and social dominance and with low levels of social reciprocity. For example, testosterone levels in 2100 Air Force veterans decreased when they married but rose again when they divorced.[88] A more recent investigation examined serum testosterone levels in 501 adult male sex offenders.[89] Men with higher testosterone were reported to have historically committed the most invasive sex crimes and were reported to be more likely to recidivate.

However, the significance of testosterone in predicting sexual offence recidivism while controlling for age was absent in men who had completed treatment. Results of this study are hard to interpret for numerous reasons: while few in number, men with below average testosterone were excluded from the sample; high testosterone was defined as any level above the upper range (presumably even if within the standard error of the lab test); and recidivism rates were not reported for either group.

While the evidence supports some association between testosterone and aggression, a causal relation between testosterone and sexual violence has not been shown. (For a more extensive review of the association of testosterone and aggression, including a review of animal research, see Demetrikopoulos and Siegel.[90])

Until recently, most researchers have assumed that only free testosterone is biologically active.[91] However, boundtestosterone and gonadotropin-releasing hormones may also have important effects.[91] For example, in a new study examining the relation between aggression and both free and total testosterone levels in 848 convicted sexual offenders, a positive correlation was found for total testosterone, but a negative correlation was found between free testosterone levels and recidivism.[92] In addition, a significant correlation was found between LH and recorded violence of the index offence. These results are similar to those of another study that failed to find a significant correlation between testosterone and aggression or impulsivity in a sample of rapists but which did find a significant correlation with impulsivity.[93] LH, the hormone secreted by gonadotrope cells in the anterior pituitary, is significant to this discussion because it stimulates Leydig cells in the testes to produce testosterone. It may be that some offenders suffer from a breakdown in the normal hypothalamic—pituitary—testes biofeedback loop. This may explain LH elevation in the absence of recorded abnormalities in testosterone levels.

LH, other hormones, and bioamines were all implicated in normal sexual function in men and women.[94] Surprisingly, given the frequent descriptions of sadists as being heartless, cold-blooded, and loners (compare Brittain[95]), and given the presumed association of oxytocin with bonding (compare Carter[96]), there have been no investigations of this hormone in men and women with sadism and (or) psychopathy (another syndrome with similar descriptors).

Neurological Explanations and Investigations

Several surveys of sexual sadists have noted a high frequency of signs indicative of neurological abnormalities. The Gratzer survey[97] found 55% of the sadists in that sample had abnormal neurological findings, primarily suggestive of temporal lobe abnormalities. This is particularly significant because sexual arousal in males presented with visual stimuli has been shown to be associated with bilateral activation of the inferior temporal cortex, the right insular and inferior frontal cortex, and the left anterior cingulate cortex.[98] Considerable evidence supports the role of temporal—limbic neural pathways in sexual arousal[99] as well as in aggression (see Siegel[100] for a review).

Neuroimaging studies of violent offenders has been summarized in a chapter on brain imaging.[101] Among 8 studies, only one dealt explicitly with criminally sadistic offenders.[102] This study included 22 sadistic offenders, 21 nonsadistic sex offenders, and 36 nonviolent, nonsex offenders. Sadistic offenders were more likely than nonsadistic offenders or the control group to have right-sided temporal horn abnormalities (41%, compared with 11% and 13%, respectively).

However, significantly more nonsadistic offenders (61%) had neuropsychological impairments on the Luria-Nebraska test battery, compared with the sadists (17%) or the control group (17%). While the other studies reviewed in this series did not explicitly examine sadists, it is notable that temporal lobe abnormalities were also described in other sex offender groups.[103–105] Raine[101] also summarized 6 PET scan, regional cerebral blood flow, and MRI studies.

However, of these, only one studied a diagnosed sexual sadist. A flurodeoxglucose PET scan of a sexual sadist was compared with scans of 2 male university students with no known paraphilic interests.[106] All 3 men were presented with an erotic (nonsadistic) audiotape. Although all 3 men showed evidence of sexual arousal as evidenced by simultaneous circumferential penile plethysmography, the 2 men without sadism showed more right hemisphere lateralization than the man with sadism. Unfortunately, the investigators did not present the study participants with stimuli that were differentially sexual stimulating (for example, sexually sadistic materials).

As in other studies reviewed above, temporal lobe dysfunction was noted in one PET scan study involving violent patients[107] and in another, involving computed tomography, MRI scans of patients with organic brain syndrome who were violent.[108] In addition, neuroimaging studies showed selective frontal lobe dysfunction in murderers,[101] violent study participants,[107] and sex offenders including rapists.[105]

Complex Interactions

A frequently cited study compared offender and offence characteristics of 29 men known to have committed sadistic criminal offences with a control group consisting of 28 men with nonsadistic criminal sex offences.[97] These in turn were compared with a previously published uncontrolled sample of 30 men diagnosed sexual sadism.[50] Many characteristics listed in the Dietz et al. paper[50, p. 50] were found to occur with equal frequency in nonsadistic offenders.

The 4 characteristics found more frequently among sadists in both studies but not in the control group on nonsadistic offenders were: physical abuse in childhood; cross-dressing; history of peeping (voyeurism); and obscene phone calls or indecent exposure. With the exception of cross-dressing, which is a comparatively rarely reported activity among nonsadistic sex offenders, the other 3 characteristics are fairly high-frequency sex offences that are perhaps notable only for the fact that they often do not in themselves result in referral to specialized forensic assessment units.

Cross-dressing occurs with high frequency in 2 groups of men: those with gender identity disorder and those with transvestic fetishism.

Gender identity confusion in men with sadism has been noted in other descriptive studies (for example, see Langevin[38] and Langevin et al.[109]). Extreme cases of gender identity confusion were reported in men who have been described as sadists and whose crimes included dismembering female body parts, cannibalizing, and even attempting to wear body parts of their victims. Perhaps the most well known was Edward Theodore Gein, after whom the fictional sadistic killer in *The Silence of the Lambs* was modelled.[110]

The high frequency of transvestic fetishism (DSM-TR 302.3) is interesting for a different reason. Transvestic fetishism is a paraphilic sexual disorder characterized by sexual arousal from wearing clothes of the opposite sex.[111] Transvestic fetishism often cooccurs with sadomasochism. Evidence of both disorders is often found in men who fatally self-asphyxiate themselves.[112]

This finding is notable for 2 reasons. The first is the fact that criminal sexual sadists are often described as resorting to strangulation as a frequent or preferred method of incapacitating or killing their victims. In the Dietz study,[50, p. 50] cause of death in 130 victims was 32.3% by ligature strangulation, 26.1% by manual strangulation, 1.5% by hanging, and 0.8% by suffocation (although it should be noted that 57 of the murders by hanging or manual strangulation in this series were committed by 2 of the men in the study).

Is there a reason why criminal sadists appear to be so interested in asphyxia or strangulation? Obvious answers may be that these murder methods are compatible with sexual arousal from control of another person.

A second intriguing explanation results if the problem of sexual sadism is reformulated from one of problems owing to deviant sexual interest to one of problems arising from failure to become sufficiently aroused by conventional scenarios. In men with normal sexual function, at the time of orgasm, serum norepinephrine increases up to 12 times the baseline level.[113–115] Similar changes in biogenic amines were also shown in women at the time of orgasm.[116]

If an individual was unable to reach orgasm owing to insufficient autonomic sympathetic activity during sexual activity, it is conceivable that an individual might try to heighten release of norepinephrine. One of the most effective ways to do so is by breath holding or self-asphyxia. This strategy of purposefully engaging in dangerous or frightening activities to accentuate subjective simulation was noted in various paraphilic disorders including sexual sadism[117] and specifically transvestic fetishism.[118]

This theory gains some support from a study in which patients with Huntington disease were found to develop paraphilic behaviours only after the onset of inhibited orgasm.[119] For at least some sexual sadists, cruel or humiliating acts may produce sufficient autonomic arousal during sexual activity to facilitate or enhance orgasm thereby reinforcing the problematic behaviour.

Treatment

Reviews concerning the treatment of violent sex offenders, especially sexual sadists, tend to be pessimistic. However, this may be due more to the fact that convicted sadists are less likely than other offenders to be released from custody. The section of the Criminal Code of Canada dealing with applications for designation as a dangerous offender lists one of the criteria as the predicate crime was "of such a brutal nature as to compel the conclusion that the offender's behaviour in the future is unlikely to be inhibited by normal standards of behavioral restraint."[120]

Clinicians have been shown to be more likely to make a diagnosis of sadism if the patient had committed an offence that was brutal (compare Marshall and Kennedy,[16] Marshall and Hucker,[17] and Marshall et al.[18]). Therefore an offender with a diagnosis of sadism presumably is more likely to fulfill criteria for designation as a dangerous offender. This designation allows the sentencing judge to impose an indeterminate sentence, the most severe in Canadian law.

Offenders designated as dangerous offenders receive lower priority in treatment programs (as they are not likely to be released imminently). Therefore they are less likely to be able to show they have responded to treatment. Regretfully, the fact that treatment response has not been demonstrated is frequently misinterpreted as meaning that treatment is not available or effective.

In fact, available evidence suggests that at least some sexual sadists do respond to treatment. Case studies of successful treatment of sexually violent men with or without sadism have been published (for example, see Kafka[121]). One case report is of interest because it involved a man who entered treatment for a nonsexual and certainly nonsadistic problem.[122] After treatment with buspirone (prescribed for anxiety) he spontaneously reported that sadistic fantasies involving torture of his sister had disappeared. The fantasies had been clearly sadistic, focusing on humiliation and cruelty. He reported that he would fantasize about breaking his sister's bones while masturbating and that he would imagine the sound of her femur snapping at the time of orgasm.

Because he had kept a detailed and dated diary that included his fantasies, it was possible to independently verify that his sadistic fantasies had decreased in both frequency and severity in association with treatment. While case reports are usually of limited scientific value, this one is unique in that the medication was prescribed in a triple-blind fashion (that is, the prescribing physician did not know about the sexual disorder, the patient did not know the medication might help his sadistic fantasies, and neither knew the patient's diary would be used to assess his response to treatment).

Effective treatment of any condition is dependent on accurate diagnosis. A major issue in any assessment of treatment options is that sexual sadism (according to DSM-IV) and sadomasochism (according to ICD-10) explicitly require that the disorder must be of sufficient severity or kind to cause problems owing to nonconsensual harm of some type.

However, many individuals self-identify themselves as sadists or masochists while strongly advocating only consensual sexual activities. Examples of this issue come from self-identified members of the so-called BDSM community. BDSM is a portmanteau acronym for Bondage–Discipline, Dominance–Submission, as well as Sadism–Masochism. Clearly these headings define various sexual interests. As a side note, the Marquis de Sade, had he sought psychiatric attention, would have most likely been diagnosed as a sexual fetishist or paraphilias not otherwise specified rather than as a true sadist, as his primary preoccupation involved processes of elimination and because his writing appears to have been strongly motivated by his views on politics and religion rather than on sex.

In contrast to sadists as defined by the DSM-IV or ICD-10, most individuals who belong to BDSM communities repeatedly cite a rule concerning sexual relations: "safe, sane and consensual."[123, p. 3] While patients who meet psychiatric criteria for sexual sadism or sadomasochism may be sane (in the sense of not ordinarily meeting criteria for insanity defences), by definition, without treatment they are neither safe nor consensual. These and other issues concerning the noncriminal BDSM community have recently been summarized.[124]

Returning to Table 1, the diagnosis of sadism, based solely on observed behaviour is problematic, particularly if the behaviour is assessed without attention to the context in which the behaviours occurred and without regard to an assessment of the mental state of the patient. For example, individuals with intellectual disability (who often have impaired verbal ability to negotiate consent) are vulnerable to being misdiagnosed as sadistic (as the crucial characteristic of sadism is nonconsensual sexual activity). This concern has led to a reanalysis and proposed revision of DSM diagnostic criteria in this population.[125]

Recalling that the essential feature of sadism is nonconsensuality, prior to initiating treatment, other possible causes of nonconsensual behaviour should be investigated, including dis-inhibition (such as, owing to stroke or dementia), intoxication, personality disorders, and major psychiatric disorders. Nonpsychiatric conditions such as criminality should also be eliminated or at least accounted for.

Assuming the person being assessed meets diagnostic criteria for sadism after elimination of competing or complimentary explanations for observed or reported activities, treatment is similar to that of other sexually motivated problematic behaviours.

Several guidelines for treatment approaches have been published (compare Marshall et al.[126] and Serin[127] for reviews). The efficacy of these treatment options was also recently summarized.[128] A useful algorithm to assist in decisions about intrusiveness of intervention is also available.[129]

Table 4

Recommendations for Future Research

Study groups should be homogenous.

Study groups should be constituted in a way that allows generalization to clinical populations.

Sexual sadism should be distinguished from violence.

Studies should test falsifiable hypotheses.

Alternate or complimentary hypotheses should be entertained.

Summary

Recommendations for future research are summarized in Table 4.

This review indicates that sexual sadism, as currently defined, is a heterogeneous phenomenon. To date, research has often failed to clearly define the population under study and therefore conclusions are limited. This makes generalization from research findings to specific patients problematic. Of particular concern is the possibility that correlations and outcomes from studies consisting of samples of convenience may be interpreted as verified causal relations between unconventional sexual interests and nonconsensual sexual violence. Understanding the ways in which sexually sadistic interests are established and maintained will certainly aid not only in the development of increasingly effective treatments but also in the establishment of strategies to aid in the prevention of harmful sexual behaviours and the promotion of healthy and fulfilling lives for everyone.

Funding and Support

Dr Fedoroff's work on this manuscript was partially supported by the University of Ottawa Medical Research Fund, and the Canadian Institute of Health Research.

The Canadian Psychiatric Association proudly supports the In Review series by providing an honorarium to the authors.

Acknowledgments

Dr Fedoroff gratefully acknowledges the assistance of Ms Jennifer Arstikaitis and Ms Beverley Fedoroff, who both assisted with the literature search, and Dr J Bradford for his helpful editorial comments.

POSTSCRIPT

Is BDSM a Healthy Form of Sexual Expression?

In February 2008, a regular visitor at a New York City bondage club was found unconscious after being left alone while bound and partially suspended in air (Goldman, 2008). He spent three days in a coma before awaking in a nearby hospital. The following April, a Tennessee man died of suffocation after his wife left him alone, bound and gagged, for over 20 hours (Schoetz, 2008). It is unknown, however, how many people safely explored these or other BDSM-related fantasies during these months. To know this, we would first have to decide what behaviors or thoughts should be included under this umbrella. In fact, many who enjoy such acts may not identify as part of the scene or culture. Where, exactly, does one draw the line between being sexually aggressive and being "into" domination? Is the couple who occasionally play with pink fuzzy handcuffs necessarily "into" bondage? Does enjoying a smack on the behind make one a masochist, or must one be ritualistically paddled and scolded to carry that title?

Powlowski attempts to place BDSM behaviors along a continuum in order to cast them as merely less conventional expressions of common sexual activities. Do you agree with his analysis? Why or why not? He continues by attempting to counter the "pathology" label given by the DSM and "as seen on TV" depictions of BDSM. Do you feel any BDSM activities are pathological? Some? None? All? How did you decide?

Fedoroff focuses on the links between sadism and violent crime. Early in his article, Fedoroff stressed that his definition of sadism "refers to non-consensual sexual aggression." Why is this important? He presents several studies that support his arguments, including studies of college students. Did any of the research presented surprise you? Why or why not?

During recent tours, pop stars Britney Spears and Rihanna have incorporated steamy, bondage-inspired costumes and dance routines into their stage shows. When allegations of domestic violence arose between Rihanna and her partner, many online commentators pointed to her BDSM outfits as "evidence" of "risky" lifestyle choices. Critics also condemned Spears for allowing her own children to attend her shows. Are bondage-inspired costumes an outward expression of a troubled personality or relationship? Does an interest in BDSM reflect poorly on a person's ability to raise a child? Are the celebrities simply looking to push the envelope? Or is this type of entertainment merely a reflection of an increased public interest in BDSM? *Time* magazine, one of the nation's most popular weekly news magazines, ran an in-depth feature on BDSM in 2004. Kink.com, an online BDSM porn site, made over $16 million in

2007. Should we as a society be concerned about the apparent mainstreaming of BDSM, or "kink" culture? Or should we celebrate the growing visibility and acceptance of diverse sexual expressions?

The line between pleasure and pain has been the subject of erotic writings for centuries. Centuries-old artwork from around the world depicts sadistic and masochistic sexual acts. Is this proof that BDSM is a natural expression of our sexuality? Or simply is it proof that sexual exploitation is not a modern phenomenon? People of all genders have written about and enjoyed the erotic overtones of power exchange. While some feminists have brought attention to power imbalance in dominant/submissive relationships, do these same critiques apply to same-sex couples? To submissive males with female partners? Does the eroticization of power (or the lack thereof) signify sexual enlightenment or disordered thinking?

Suggested Readings

L. Alison, P. Santtila, N.K. Sandnabba, and N. Nordling, "Sadomasochistically Oriented Behavior: Diversity in Practice and Meaning," *Archives of Sexual Behavior* (vol. 30, no. 1, pp. 1–12, 2001). Accessed March 1, 2009, from SpringerLink database.

P.J. Kleinplatz and C. Moser (eds.), *Sadomasochism: Powerful Pleasures* (New York, NY: Harrington Park Press, 2006).

A. Moore, "Rethinking Gendered Perversion and Degeneration in Visions of Sadism and Masochism, 1886–1930," *Journal of the History of Sexuality* (vol. 18, no. 1, 2009). doi: 10.1353/sex.0.0034.

S. Newmahr, *Playing on the Edge: Sadomasochism, Risk, and Intimacy* (Bloomington: Indiana University Press, 2011).

B.J. Sagarin, B. Cutler, N. Cutler, K.A. Lawler-Sagarin, and L. Matuszewich, "Hormonal Changes and Couple Bonding in Consensual Sadomasochistic Activity," *Archives of Sexual Behavior* (vol. 38, 2008). doi: 10.1007/s10508-9374-5.

ISSUE 7

Is "Gender Identity Disorder" an Appropriate Psychiatric Diagnosis?

YES: Mercedes Allen, from "Destigmatization Versus Coverage and Access: The Medical Model of Transsexuality" at http://dentedbluemercedes .wordpress.com/2008/04/05/destigmatization-versus-coverage-and-access-the-medical-model-of-transsexuality/ (2008)

NO: Kelley Winters, from "GID Reform Advocates: Issues of GID Diagnosis for Transsexual Women and Men," http://www.gidreform .org/GID30285a.pdf (2007)

ISSUE SUMMARY

YES: Mercedes Allen, educator, trainer, and founder of AlbertaTrans. org, recognizes the bias in the DSM's classification of Gender Identity Disorder as a mental disorder, but argues that changes run the risk of leaving the trans community at risk of losing medical care and treatment.

NO: Kelley Winters, writer and founder of GID Reform Advocates, argues the inclusion of Gender Identity Disorder in the DSM adds to the stigma faced by transpersons and that reclassification is necessary in order to adequately address the population's health care needs.

Gender identity can be a difficult concept to describe. Many people have probably never given much thought to questions of how they feel about themselves in terms of maleness or femaleness. It is assumed that most people have a gender identity that is congruent with their anatomical sex. While some men may feel more (or less) masculine than others, the majority strongly *identify* as male. The same could be said for most women—regardless of how feminine they feel (or don't feel), the majority *identify* as women. If asked, most women would probably say they feel like a woman. Most men simply feel like a man. But what does it mean to "feel" like a woman or a man? What is it to "feel" feminine or masculine? Is there only one type of femininity? One style of masculinity?

What about those who feel that their gender identity, their feeling of maleness or femaleness, doesn't match their birth sex? For those whose gender does not match societal expectations for a person of their anatomical sex, gender identity can be hard to ignore. Their gender identities do not fit the binary gender system that is firmly in place in American society. Because of this, a diagnosis of Gender Identity Disorder (GID) has been applied to those who identify as transgender or transsexual. This diagnosis can be found in the *Diagnostic and Statistical Manual of Mental Disorders,* commonly referred to as the DSM, published by the American Psychiatric Association.

In 2012, an updated fifth edition of the DSM will be published (Melby, 2009). Over the years, new editions have been greatly anticipated to see what changes occur. With each edition, new disorders have been identified, adding to the list of mental illnesses. Diagnostic criteria for others have been refined and some behaviors, once defined as disordered, have been removed because they no longer meet the criteria for diagnosis as a mental illness. An example of this is homosexuality. In the DSM-II, published in 1968, homosexuality was considered a mental illness. The 1973 publication of the DSM-III did not list homosexuality as a disorder. This declassification erased some of the stigma associated with same-sex attraction and provided a boost to the gay rights movement in the United States (Melby, 2009).

As the release of the DSM-V draws closer, experts from various fields, appointed to an array of work groups, are holding meetings to discuss what should be added, revised, or removed. For those interested in the field of human sexuality, much attention is being given to the status of GID. There has even been controversy over those appointed to the Sexual and Gender Identity Disorders Work Group (National Gay and Lesbian Task Force, 2008). The changes made to the upcoming DSM-V concerning GID, or the lack thereof, could have great impact on the lives of transgender individuals.

In an essay entitled "Destigmatization Versus Coverage and Access: The Medical Model of Transsexuality," Mercedes Allen argues that the removal of Gender Identity Disorder from the DSM would put access to mental health care, hormonal treatments, and surgeries needed by some transsexual individuals at risk of being denied. Kelly Winters, in an essay titled "Issues of GID Diagnosis for Transsexual Women and Men," argues that the inclusion of GID in the DSM only serves to stigmatize the transgender and transsexual community, but fails to promote hormonal or surgical treatments as medical necessities.

References

T. Melby, "Creating the DSM-V," *Contemporary Sexuality* (vol. 43, no. 3, 2009).

National Gay and Lesbian Task Force, "Task Force Questions Critical Appointments to APA's Committee on Sexual and Gender Identity Disorders," accessed at http://www.thetaskforce.org/press/releases/PR_052808 (2008).

YES

Mercedes Allen

Destigmatization Versus Coverage and Access: The Medical Model of Transsexuality

In recent years, the GLB community has been more receptive to (and even energized in) assisting the transgender community, but regularly asks what its needs are. One that is often touted is the "complete depathologization of Trans identities" (quoting from a press release for an October 7, 2007, demonstration in Barcelona, Spain) by removing "Gender Identity Disorder" (GID) from medical classification. The reasoning generally flows in a logic chain stating that with homosexuality removed from the Diagnostic and Statistical Manual (DSM, the "bible" of the medical community) in 1974, gay and lesbian rights were able to follow as a consequence—and with similar removal, we should be able to do the same. Living in an area where GRS (genital reassignment surgery) is covered under provincial Health Care, however, provides a unique perspective on this issue. And with Presidential candidates proposing models for national health care in the United States, it would obviously be easier to establish GRS coverage for transsexuals at the ground floor, rather than fight for it later. So it is important to note, from this "other side of the coin," how delisting GID could do far more harm than good.

Granted, there are concerns about the current classification as a "mental disorder," and certainly as a transgender person myself, it's quite unnerving that my diagnosis of GID puts me in the same range of classification as things such as schizophrenia or even pedophilia. And when the emotional argument of "mental unfitness" can lead to ostracism, discrimination in the workplace or the loss of custody and/or visitation rights of children, there are some very serious things at stake. But when the lobbies are calling for a reclassification—or more dramatically a total declassification—of GID, one would expect that they had a better medical and social model to propose. They don't.

Basic Access to Services

The argument for complete declassification is a great concern, because unlike homosexuals, transgender people—especially transsexuals—do have medical needs and issues related to their journey. Genital reassignment surgery (GRS), mastectomies and hysterectomies for transmen, tracheal shave, facial hair removal and breast augmentation for transwomen . . . there are clear medical applications that some require, even to the point of being at risk of suicide from the distress of not having these things available (which is an important point to keep in mind for those in our own communities who assume that GRS is cosmetic surgery and not worthy of health care funding). And we need to use caution about taking psychiatry out of the equation: GID really does affect us psychologically, and we do benefit from having a central source of guidance through the process that keeps this in mind, however flawed and gated the process otherwise might be.

Declassification of GID would essentially relegate transsexuality to a strictly cosmetic issue. Without being able to demonstrate that GID is a real medical condition via a listing in the Diagnostic and Statistical Manual (DSM), convincing a doctor that it is necessary to treat us, provide referrals or even provide a carry letter that will enable us to use a washroom appropriate to our gender presentation could prove to be very difficult, if not impossible. Access to care is difficult enough *even with* the DSM-IV recommending the transition process—imagine the barriers that would be there without it weighing in on that! And with cases regarding the refusal of medical services already before review or recently faced in California, Ontario and elsewhere, the availability of services could grow overwhelmingly scarce.

A Model of Medical Coverage

And then there is health care coverage, which often causes a lot of issues of itself, usually of the "not with my tax money" variety. But no one just wakes up out of the blue and decides that alienating themselves from the rest of the world by having a "sex change" is a good idea. Science is developing a greater understanding that physical sex and psychological gender can, in fact, be made misaligned, causing a person to be like a stranger in their own body. In extreme cases (transsexuals), this often makes it impossible to function emotionally, socially, sexually, or to develop any kind of career—and often makes one constantly borderline suicidal. The medical community currently recognizes this with the existing medical classification, which is why GRS surgery is the recognized treatment, and why it (GRS, that is, and usually not things like breast augmentation) is funded by some existing health plans.

Canada provides an interesting model on this, as the nation has universal health care, and several provinces fund GRS with some limitations (British Columbia, Newfoundland, Saskatchewan and Quebec fund vaginaplasty, hysterectomy and breast reduction for FTMs, Alberta funds those plus phalloplasty, and Manitoba funds 60% of GRS-related costs). Funding may be restored in Ontario and gained in Nova Scotia, pending some ongoing activism.

This exists specifically because it is classified as a medical issue, and is treated according to the recommendations of WPATH. There are some idiosyncracies, of course—a diagnosis of Intersex, for example, overrides a diagnosis of GID, and if someone is diagnosed as IS, the treatment is different (namely, GRS is not covered). Phalloplasty and metoidioplasty (FTM surgeries) are not covered in several areas because they are considered "experimental." Some provinces insist on treatment only in publically-funded hospitals, resulting in the rather unusual situation of Quebec sending patients to the United States or overseas, even though one of the top-rated (but privately-owned) GRS clinics in the world is located in Montreal. And many provinces direct transsexuals to the notoriously restrictive and obstacle-laden Clarke Institute (CAMH in Toronto) for treatment. Waiting lists can be long, and only a select few GID-certified psychiatrists are able to be a primary signature on letters authorizing surgery and funding. Still, the funding provides opportunity that many non-Canadian transsexuals would leap at within a moment, if they could.

Future Considerations

This possibility, remote as it may seem, is also out there for future American transsexuals. Both Democratic Presidential nominees have discussed developing a national health care program. The time is now for the trans, gay/lesbian/bisexual and allied communities to lobby insurance companies to develop policies that cover GRS. The time is now to lobby companies to seek out group policies for their employees with such coverage, and with more emphasis than the HRC's impossibly easy Corporate Equality Index (CEI), in which providing mastectomies for breast cancer patients qualifies as "transgender-related surgeries." The more prevalent health care coverage is for transgender persons when a national program is developed, the more effective the argument is that a national program should include it. Certainly, it will be much harder to lobby to have it specifically added later.

This possibility, remote as it may seem, exists because of the current classification. Even some existing coverage of and access to hormone treatment is called into question in a declassification scenario. And certainly, where coverage is not available, it is the impoverished, disenfranchised and marginalized of our community—who quite often have more to worry about than the stigma of mental illness—who lose the most.

So a total declassification is actually not what's best for the transgender community. Too, if anyone had been thinking that proclaiming that "transsexuality is not a mental disorder" would magically change the way that society thinks about transfolk, then they are spectacularly and embarrassingly wrong.

The Question of Reclassification

At some point in the future, I expect that we will find more biological bases for GID, and that transgender people will perhaps become a smaller part of the larger intersex community (rather than the other way around). Recent studies in genetics have demonstrated some difference in chromosomal structure in male brains versus female brains, and the UCLA scientists who conducted the study have also proposed that their findings demonstrate gender dysphoria as a biological characteristic. Other studies into endocrine disrupting chemicals (EDCs) could open new discoveries related to variance in gender correlation. A reassessment of GID is almost certainly something that will be on the medical community's table at some point in the future, but it definitely needs to be in the DSM somewhere. But for now, GID is not something that can be determined by a blood test or an ultrasound, and is not easy to verifiably place with biological conditions. The science is not there; the evidence and solutions are not yet at hand.

This is why reclassification is not yet feasible. It's difficult to convince scientific and medical professionals to move a diagnosis when the current model is workable in their eyes (even if not perfect), while the alternatives are not yet proven, cannot be demonstrated as more valid than the current listing, and no modified treatment system has been devised or proposed. Any move of the diagnosis is not likely to be very far from the current listing, and from the literature I've seen, I doubt that those in the community who advocate to changing or dropping the current classification would be happy with that. For some, even listing it as a "physical disability" could constitute an "unwanted stigma." I have heard one WPATH doctor suggest the term "Body Morphology Disorder"—for many, I suspect, this would still be too "negative."

"Unnecessary Mutilation"

That's not to say that complacency is an answer. In the face of conservative reluctance and new activism on the left by the likes of Julie Bindel, claiming that GRS is "unnecessary mutilation," we need to demonstrate the necessity of treatments, in order to ensure that any change would be an improvement on the existing model, rather than a scrapping of it. This is, of course, something that affects a small portion of the transgender community in the full umbrella stretch of the term, but the need for those at the extreme on the spectrum is profound—not simply a question of quality of life, but often one of living at all—or at least a question of being able to function. If and when a reclassification occurs, it will need to be this sense of necessity that will determine the shape of what will be written into any revision.

The solution isn't to destroy the existing medical model by changing or eliminating the current classification of "Gender Dysphoria." Collecting data, demonstrating needs, fighting for inclusion in existing health plans, examining verifiable and repeatable statistics on transgender suicide and success rates and other information relevant to the medical front is where medical-related activism should be focused, for the moment.

 **NO**

GID Reform Advocates

Issues of GID Diagnosis for Transsexual Women and Men

Gender Identity Disorder in Adolescents or Adults, 302.85

**Section: Sexual and Gender Identity Disorders
Subsection: Gender Identity Disorders**

"Gender Identity Disorder" (GID) is a diagnostic category in the *Diagnostic and Statistical Manual of Mental Disorders* (DSM), published by the American Psychiatric Association (APA, 1994). The DSM is regarded as the medical and social definition of mental disorder throughout North America and strongly influences the *The International Statistical Classification of Diseases and Related Health Problems* (ICD) published by the World Health Organization. GID currently includes a broad array of gender variant adults and children who may or may not be transsexual and may or may not be distressed or impaired. GID literally implies a *"disordered"* gender identity.

Thirty-four years after the American Psychiatric Association (APA) voted to delete homosexuality as a mental disorder, the diagnostic categories of "gender identity disorder" and "transvestic fetishism" in the *Diagnostic and Statistical Manual of Mental Disorders* continue to raise questions of consistency, validity, and fairness. Recent revisions of the DSM have made these diagnostic categories increasingly ambiguous, conflicted and overinclusive. They reinforce false, negative stereotypes of gender variant people and at the same time fail to legitimize the medical necessity of sex reassignment surgeries (SRS) and procedures for transsexual women and men who urgently need them. The result is that a widening segment of gender non-conforming youth and adults are potentially subject to diagnosis of psychosexual disorder, stigma and loss of civil liberty.

A Question of Legitimacy

The very name, Gender Identity Disorder, suggests that cross-gender identity is itself disordered or deficient. It implies that gender identities held by diagnosable people are not legitimate, in the sense that more ordinary gender identities are, but represent perversion, delusion or immature development.

This message is reinforced in the diagnostic criteria and supporting text that emphasize difference from cultural norms over distress for those born in incongruent bodies or forced to live in wrong gender roles.

Under the premise of "disordered" gender identity, self-identified trans-women and trans-men lose any rightful claim to acceptance as women and men, but are reduced to mentally ill men and women respectively.

DIAGNOSTIC CRITERIA (APA 2000, P 581)

A. A strong and persistent cross-gender identification (not merely a desire for any perceived cultural advantages of being the other sex). In adolescents and adults, the disturbance is manifested by symptoms such as a stated desire to be the other sex, frequent passing as the other sex, desire to live or be treated as the other sex, or the conviction that he or she has the typical feelings and reactions of the other sex.

B. Persistent discomfort with his or her sex or sense of inappropriateness in the gender role of that sex. In adolescents and adults, the disturbance is manifested by symptoms such as preoccupation with getting rid of primary and secondary sex characteristics (e.g., request for hormones, surgery, or other procedures to physically alter sexual characteristics to simulate the other sex) or belief that he or she was born the wrong sex.

C. The disturbance is not concurrent with a physical intersex condition.

D. The disturbance causes clinically significant distress or impairment in social, occupational, or other important areas of functioning.

Specify if (for sexually mature individuals) Sexually Attracted to Males, . . . Females, . . . Both, . . . Neither.

Maligning Terminology

Of the disrespectful language faced by gender variant people in North America, none is more damaging or hurtful than that which disregards their experienced gender identities, denies the affirmed gender roles of those who have transitioned full time and relegates them to their assigned birth sex. Throughout the diagnostic criteria and supporting text, the affirmed gender identities and social role for transsexual individuals is termed "other sex." In the supporting text, subjects are offensively labeled by birth sex and not their experienced affirmed gender. Transsexual women are repeatedly termed "males," and "he." For example,

> For some _males_ . . . , the individual's sexual activity with a woman is accompanied by the fantasy of being lesbian lovers or that _his_ partner is a man and _he_ is a woman. (APA, 2000, p. 577, emphasis noted by underline)

Perhaps most disturbing, the term "autogynephilia" was introduced in the supporting text of the DSM-IV-TR to demean lesbian transsexual women:

> Adult <u>males</u> who are sexually attracted to females, . . . usually report a history of erotic arousal associated with the thought or image of oneself as a woman (termed *autogynephilia*). (p. 578, emphasis noted by underline)

The implication is that all lesbian transsexual women are incapable of genuine affection for other female partners but are instead obsessed with narcissistic paraphilia. The fact that most ordinary natal women possess images of themselves as women within their erotic relationships and fantasies is conspicuously overlooked in the supporting text.

Medically Necessary Treatment of Gender Dysphoria

Gender Dysphoria is defined in the DSM-IV-TR as:

> A persistent aversion toward some or all of those physical characteristics or social roles that connote one's own biological sex (APA, 2000, p. 823).

The focus of medical treatment described by the current World Professional Association for Transgender Health Standards of Care is on relieving the distress of gender dysphoria and not on attempting to change one's gender identity (WPATH, 2001). Yet, the DSM-IV-TR emphasizes cross-gender identity and expression rather than the distress of gender dysphoria as the basis for mental disorder. While criterion B of Gender Identity Disorder may imply gender dysphoria, it is not limited to ego-dystonic subjects suffering distress with their born sex or its associated role. Ego-syntonic subjects who do not need medical treatment may also be ambiguously implicated. In failing to distinguish gender diversity from gender distress, the APA has undermined the medical necessity of sex reassignment procedures for transsexuals who need them. It is little wonder that the province of Ontario and virtually all insurers and HMOs in the United States and have denied or dropped coverage for sex reassignment surgery (SRS) procedures. Since gender dysphoria is not explicitly classified as a treatable medical condition, surgeries that relieve its distress are easily dismissed as "cosmetic" by insurers, governments and employers.

The transgender community and civil rights advocates have long been polarized by fear that access to SRS procedures would be lost if the GID classification were revised. In truth, however, transsexuals are poorly served by a diagnosis that stigmatizes them unconditionally as mentally deficient and at the same time fails to establish the medical necessity of procedures proven to relieve their distress.

Overinclusive Diagnosis

Distress and impairment became central to the definition of mental disorder in the DSM-IV (1994, p. xxi), where a generic clinical significance criterion was added to most diagnostic categories, including criterion D of Gender Identity Disorder. Ironically, while the scope of mental disorder was narrowed in the DSM-IV, Gender Identity Disorder was broadened from the classification of Transsexualism in prior DSM revisions and combined with Gender Identity Disorder of Adolescence or Adulthood, Nontranssexual Type (GIDAANT) from the DSM-III-R (1987, pp. 74–77).

Unfortunately, no specific definition of distress and impairment is given in the GID diagnosis. The supporting text in the DSM-IV-TR lists relationship difficulties and impaired function at work or school as examples of distress and disability (2000, p. 577) with no reference to the role of societal prejudice as the cause. Prostitution, HIV risk, suicide attempts and substance abuse are described as associated features of GID, when they are in truth consequences of discrimination and undeserved shame. The DSM does not acknowledge the existence of many healthy, well-adjusted transsexual or gender variant people or differentiate them from those who could benefit from medical treatment. These are left to the interpretation of the reader. Tolerant clinicians may infer that transgender identity or expression is not inherently impairing, but that societal intolerance and prejudice are to blame for the distress and internalized shame that transpeople often suffer (Brown, 1995). Intolerant clinicians are free to infer the opposite: that cross-gender identity or expression by definition constitutes impairment, regardless of the individual's happiness or wellbeing. Therefore, the GID diagnosis is not limited to ego-dystonic subjects; it makes no distinction between the distress of gender dysphoria and that caused by prejudice and discrimination. Moreover, the current DSM has no clear exit clause for transitioned or post-operative transsexuals, however well adjusted. It lists postsurgical complications as "associated physical examination findings" of GID (2000, p. 579).

Pathologization of Ordinary Behaviors

Conflicting and ambiguous language in the DSM serves to confuse cultural nonconformity with mental illness and pathologize ordinary behaviors as symptomatic. The Introduction to the DSM-IV-TR (2000, p. xxxi) states:

> Neither deviant behavior ... nor conflicts that are primarily between the individual and society are mental disorders unless the deviance or conflict is a symptom of dysfunction...

However, it is contradicted in the Gender Identity Disorder section (p. 580):

> Gender Identity Disorder can be distinguished from simple nonconformity to stereotypical sex role behavior by the extent and pervasiveness of the cross-gender wishes, interests, and activities.

The second statement implies that one may deviate from social expectation without a diagnostic label, but not too much. Conflicting language in the DSM serves the agendas of intolerant relatives and employers and their medical expert witnesses who seek to deny transgender individuals their civil liberties, children and jobs.

In the supporting text of the Gender Identity Disorder diagnosis, behaviors that would be ordinary or even exemplary for ordinary women and men are presented as symptomatic of mental disorder on a presumption of incongruence with born genitalia. These include passing, living and a desire to be treated as ordinary members of the preferred gender. For example, shaving legs for adolescent biological males is described as symptomatic, even though it is common among males involved in certain athletics. Adopting ordinary behaviors, dress and mannerisms of the preferred gender is described as a manifestation of preoccupation for adults. It is not clear how these behaviors can be pathological for one group of people and not for another.

POSTSCRIPT

Is "Gender Identity Disorder" an Appropriate Psychiatric Diagnosis?

It is important to realize that, while both Allen and Winters take opposing sides to the question presented, both oppose the labeling of transgender or transsexual individuals as mentally ill. To a certain extent, the debate over the inclusion, reclassification, or exclusion of GID in the upcoming edition of the DSM exemplifies the phrase "You're damned if you do, you're damned if you don't." To remove GID from the DSM would in all likelihood help to reduce some of the stigma attached to transsexuality. However, many transsexual individuals need a diagnosable condition in order to receive adequate coverage for medical care. Could there possibly be a "correct" answer in this situation?

Allen's essay, which acknowledges the stigma attached to the label of mental disorder and notes the possible benefits of re- or declassification of GID, focuses on the issue of access to medical care. The point is made that declassification would impact transgender and transsexual individuals in much different ways than the declassification of homosexuality affected gay men and lesbians. Unlike other sexual minorities, "transgender people—especially transsexuals—do have medical needs and issues related to their journey," Allen states. What would be the risks of removing GID from the upcoming DSM? Why would some transgender advocates argue for its continued inclusion? Allen also mentions the impact of nationalized health care on the GID debate. How would the discussion be different if the United States implemented health care coverage for all citizens?

Winters focuses on deconstructing the current diagnosis of GID. Despite recent revisions, she states, the diagnostic criteria are "increasingly ambiguous, conflicted and overinclusive." After reading the most recent DSM criteria for GID, included in her essay, would you agree? Fears that a revised classification would endanger medical care for the transgender community are essentially moot, states Winters, given the fact that the current diagnosis "fails to establish the medical necessity of procedures proven to relieve their distress." With the criteria put in place by the DSM, Winters argues, many insurers are already refusing to cover treatments, dismissing surgeries as "cosmetic" in nature, rather than necessary for treatment.

In 2010, the APA released the preliminary results of the GID task force for public review. Among their recommendations was the relabeling of GID in children, adolescents, and adults as gender incongruence (though GID nonspecified remained a classification option). Critics, including Allen and Winters, say that while this is a step in the right direction, the classification focuses too much on the issue of gender rather than the issue of distress. Additionally, the inclusion focuses on the "desire" to be the other sex rather than acknowledging feelings of "being" other sexed. It also ignores the issue of those whose gender identities challenge the gender binary of strictly male and female.

Do you feel that total declassification is the correct step to take? Or would a revision of the current classification be more appropriate? What if these changes resulted in the denial of access to medical care for transgender or transsexual individuals? Is there a middle ground that reduces stigma while maintaining access to medical treatment?

Suggested Readings

M. Allen, "Reflections on the Proposed DSM5 Revisions and the Role of Community Consultation," *sexgenderbody*, accessed at http://99.192.136.36/content/reflections-proposed-dsm5-revisions-and-role-community-consultation (February 11, 2010).

P.T. Cohen-Kettenis, "The Treatment of Adolescent Transsexuals," *Journal of Sexual Medicine* (vol. 5, no. 8, 2008).

R. Ehrbar, "Clinical Judgment in the Diagnosis of Gender Identity Disorder in Children," *Journal of Sex and Marital Therapy* (vol. 34, no. 5, 2008).

K. Hausman, "Controversy Continues to Grow over DSM's GID Diagnosis," *Psychiatric News* (vol. 38, no. 14, 2003), accessed at http://pn.psychiatryonline.org/cgi/content/full/38/14/25.

S.R. Vance, Jr., et al., "Opinions about the DSM Gender Identity Disorder Diagnosis: Results from an International Survey Administered to Organizations Concerned with the Welfare of Transgender People," (vol. 12, no. 1, 2010).

K. Winters, "DSM-V Task Force Releases Proposed Diagnostic Criteria," *GID Reform Weblog,* accessed at http://gidreform.wordpress.com/2010/02/10/dsm-v-task-force-releases-proposed-diagnostic-criteria/ (February 10, 2010).

Internet References . . .

Sexuality Information and Education Council of the United States (SIECUS)

The SIECUS advocates for the right of all people to accurate information, comprehensive education about sexuality, and sexual health services.

http://www.siecu.org/

The National Campaign to Prevent Teen Pregnancy (NCPTP)

The NCPTP's mission is to prevent teen pregnancy while also reducing the high number of unplanned pregnancies in adults.

http://www.thenationalcampaign.org/

The Media Awareness Network

This Canadian non-profit organization is dedicated to increasing media and digital literacy through educational programs.

http://www.media-awareness.ca/

The Female Genital Cutting Education and Networking Project (FGCENP)

The FGCENP acts as an online clearinghouse and network for those dedicated to the issue of female genital mutilation around the world.

http://www.fgmnetwork.org/index.php

Electronic Frontier Foundation

The Electronic Frontier Foundation works to educate the press, policymakers, and the general public about civil liberties issues related to technology.

http://www.eff.org/

The Coalition Against Trafficking in Women—International

This international organization focuses on ending sexual exploitation, including the sex trafficking of women and girls.

http://www.catwinternational.org/

Human Rights Campaign

The Human Rights Campaign is America's largest gay and lesbian organization. It seeks to increase public understanding through education and communication.

http://www.hrc.org/

The Family Research Council

This organization promotes Christian values in policy research, grassroots mobilizing, and lobbying efforts in government.

http://www.frc.org

Sex and Society

*C*ompeting *philosophical forces drive concerns about human sexuality on a societal level. Some are primarily focused on the well-being of individuals (or groups of individuals) and their right to individual expression versus their protection from harm; others are mainly concerned with either maintaining or questioning established social norms; still others are engaged to the extent to which the law should impose on a citizen's privacy. This section examines nine such questions that affect our social understanding of sexuality.*

- Should Sex Ed Teach about Abstinence?
- Is There Something Wrong with the Content of Comprehensive Sex Education Curricula?
- Is There Academic Merit to Students Viewing Live Sexual Acts in College Courses?
- Should Libraries and Other Places That Provide Public Wi-Fi Restrict the Sexual Content?
- Is Pornography Harmful?
- Should Prostitution Be Legalized?
- Is Female Circumcision/FGM an Acceptable Practice?
- Should Same-Sex Marriage Be Legal?
- Do Reality TV Shows Portray Responsible Messages about Teen Pregnancy?

ISSUE 8

Should Sex Ed Teach about Abstinence?

YES: William J. Taverner, from "Reclaiming Abstinence in Comprehensive Sex Education," *Contemporary Sexuality* (2007)

NO: Maureen Kelly, from "The Semantics of Sex Ed: Or, Shooting Ourselves in the Foot as We Slowly Walk Backwards," *Educator's Update* (2005)

ISSUE SUMMARY

YES: William J. Taverner, sexuality educator and editor of *Taking Sides*, argues that sexuality education should teach about abstinence, and introduces a new model to replace problematic abstinence education models of the past.

NO: Sexuality educator Maureen Kelly argues that the framing of abstinence by conservatives has essentially made the term politically volatile, and that the one-size-fits-all definition has rendered the term useless to educators.

Should sex education teach students about abstinence? It sounds like a fairly straightforward question. Many who favor an abstinence-only approach to sex education might say, "Yes! Abstinence is the only 100 percent effective method for preventing pregnancy and the transmission of sexually transmitted infections (STIs). It should be the only thing we teach our students!" Others, who favor a comprehensive approach, might say, "Well, abstinence is an important concept, and we should include it in the discussion, as well as addressing other contraceptive methods and ways to prevent STIs." Some may say, "Since so many young people are already having sexual intercourse,

---

Editor's note: One of the arguments in this issue, "Should Sex Ed Teach about Abstinence?" is given by William J. Taverner, who is also an editor of this *Taking Sides*. For a fair and balanced examination of both the "YES" and "NO" perspectives, Ryan W. McKee is the sole writer of the Introduction and Postscript to this issue.

why bother teaching abstinence?" Still others may say, "Wait—what exactly do you mean by abstinence?"

Surprising as it may sound, the definition of abstinence isn't as clear-cut as one might think. And who holds the power to define the term at a particular point in time greatly adds to the confusion—and acceptance—of that definition. The strict, eight-point definition of abstinence education that *both* Taverner and Kelly reject says that federally funded abstinence-only-until-marriage education must:

1. Have as its exclusive purpose the teaching of the social, physiological, and health gains to be realized from abstaining from sexual activity;
2. Teach that abstinence from sexual activity outside of marriage is the expected standard for all school-age children;
3. Teach that abstinence from sexual activity is the only certain way to avoid out-of-wedlock pregnancy, sexually transmitted diseases, and other associated health problems;
4. Teach that a mutually faithful monogamous relationship in the context of marriage is the expected standard of human sexual activity;
5. Teach that sexual activity outside of the context of marriage may have harmful psychological and physical effects;
6. Teach that bearing children out of wedlock is likely to have harmful consequences for the child, the child's parents, and society;
7. Teach young people how to reject sexual advances and how alcohol and drug use increases vulnerability to sexual advances; and
8. Teach the importance of attaining self-sufficiency before engaging in sexual activity.

When the federal government supports sexuality education programs with funding, certain rules and restrictions must apply or the program risks losing that support. Sex educators often feel constrained by definitions and regulations handed down by agencies or governments. In some cases, they work within the system, following guidelines and adhering to definitions they may or may not agree with, but feel compelled to uphold. Others find creative ways to challenge definitions and expectations while still working within the specified framework. Some may disagree so strongly with the definitions that they reject them outright and actively seek systemic change. These are not uncommon occurrences in the paths of educational and social movements. Which tactic is more effective is generally a matter of debate among academics, activists, and historians.

In the following essays, William J. Taverner, the director of the Center for Family Life Education, outlines a new framework for teaching about abstinence as a vital component of sexuality education. Maureen Kelly, vice president for education and training for Planned Parenthood of the Southern Finger Lakes, maintains that the framing of abstinence by conservatives has essentially made the term politically volatile, and that the one-size-fits-all definition has rendered the term useless to educators.

YES

William J. Taverner

Reclaiming Abstinence in Comprehensive Sex Education

Two e-mails I received came from separate ends of the ideological universe, as it relates to the abstinence-only-until-marriage versus comprehensive sex education culture wars, but both had a similarly hostile tone. The subject of this electronic wrath was the new theoretical and pedagogical concepts introduced in a sex education manual I coauthored with Sue Montfort, *Making Sense of Abstinence: Lessons for Comprehensive Sex Education* (Taverner & Montfort, 2005).

The first e-mail followed a very short editorial in the *Wall Street Journal* that commented on one of the themes of the manual—that it was necessary to discuss with youth the way they *define* abstinence, so as to better help them be successful with this decision. The e-mail began as follows:

> *Dear Mr. Taverner:*
> *Abstinence means NO SEX. Only a pointy head liberal could think there was some other definition, and it is pointy headed liberals that give liberalism a bad name. It takes the cake that you would . . . write some papers on trying to define abstinence. I have done that in four words above.*

More later on this writer's comments about defining abstinence—and on my seemingly pointy head, too! The more recent e-mail followed the announcement of the annual sex ed conference of The Center for Family Life Education (CFLE) that went to thousands of sex educators by e-mail. Themed on the manual, the announcement was titled "The Abstinence Experience: Teaching about Abstinence in the Context of Comprehensive Sex Education." The conference featured sex education leaders from prominent organizations— Answer (Formerly the Network for Family Life Education), the California Family Health Council, Montclair State University, the Sexuality Information and Education Council of the United States (SIECUS), and trainers from the CFLE. This e-mail read, simply:

> *Please REMOVE my email address from this mailing list. I am 100% against ABSTINENCE!*

This is not the first time someone has asked to be taken off the e-mail list. People ask to be unsubscribed when they are no longer working in the field of sex education, or when they only do so peripherally, or when their inboxes are generally too clogged. Usually the request to unsubscribe is polite. But beyond the rude tone of this request, the last sentence stopped me in my tracks:

I am 100% against ABSTINENCE!

The capitalized ABSTINENCE was the writer's doing, not mine. Did I read this right? Or did he mean he was against abstinence *education?* Maybe he meant *abstinence-only-until-marriage education?* But I *did* read it correctly; in fact, I cut and pasted the writer's remarks to this article! He was against *ABSTINENCE.* How could that be? If a person chooses to abstain from sexual intercourse, or any other sexual behaviors, or drugs, alcohol, chocolate, or whatever, how could *anyone* be against that? And yet this is a common theme I have experienced since we wrote *Making Sense of Abstinence.* It seems some comprehensive sex educators and advocates are *turned off* by the word "abstinence." The atmosphere among some might best be described as anti-abstinence. The anecdotal evidence:

- Upon reviewing the final manuscript for our new abstinence manual, one well-respected reviewer asked not to be identified in the acknowledgments. She explained that while she thought the manual was great, she also thought it would be a bad career move to become too closely associated with the "world of abstinence."
- One prominent sex education leader urged us to reconsider the title of both our manual and our conference. He did not think we should be promoting abstinence, instead favoring the term "delaying intercourse." (Imagine a title such as *Making Sense of Delaying Intercourse—* what could more clearly illustrate the disconnect between adults and teens who *never* think of themselves as "delaying intercourse," but who *do* sometimes choose abstinence?)
- A CFLE educator having a casual conversation with a colleague asked if that colleague would be coming to our annual conference. The colleague said he had not yet received our flyer. The CFLE educator was surprised, since we had sent the flyers out over a month ago, and this individual had been on our mailing list for many years. Upon hearing the title of the conference, he replied, "That was *you*? I threw that out when I saw the word 'abstinence'! "

What was going on here? Sue Montfort and I spent a year and a half writing *Making Sense of Abstinence.* It was nominated for four sex ed awards, to date, winning two. It had been showcased by SIECUS at a Congressional Briefing in Washington, D.C. And yet while most colleagues were embracing this new model for abstinence education, some were clearly shunning the idea of *any* abstinence education.

My first real understanding of the distaste some sexologists have for the word "abstinence" came to light as I proudly stood by my "Making Sense of Abstinence" poster session at a conference of the American Association of Sexuality Educators, Counselors, and Therapists (AASECT). As colleagues walked by the four-panel poster that my intern, Laura Minnichelli, had created, many veered off their paths suddenly, as if the word "abstinence," would jump off the poster and bite them. Some looked briefly at the poster and gave a look of disgust, perhaps wondering how an "abstinence" poster infiltrated a sexology conference. Those who stopped to ask about it seemed puzzled initially. They saw the poster's worksheets on masturbation, outercourse, the lack of efficacy of virginity pledge programs, and they gradually came to recognize that this was a *different* type of abstinence program. As these thoughtful individuals left, they offered words of thanks and encouragement that there was *finally* a sex ed program out that there was reframing abstinence education.

There is no doubt that any self-respecting sex educator has good reason to be skeptical of a new abstinence manual. I can understand and even appreciate the sideways looks that sexologists give after ten years of federal funding for abstinence-only-until-marriage programs, and 25 years since the first "chastity education" federal funds were issued. Over $1 billion has produced curricula that are directive, simplistic, and insulting to teens—programs that want to tell teens *what to think,* not how to *think for themselves.*

Abstinence-only-until-marriage programs virtually ignore the nearly 50% of teens who *are* having intercourse (Centers for Disease Control, 2006). They tell these teens to get with the program, but have no advice, otherwise, for teens that *don't* get with the program. At worst, they give misleading or inaccurate information about condom and contraceptive efficacy. These programs ignore lesbian and gay teens (and their families) who are told to abstain until marriage, but who don't have a legal right to marry, except those who are residents of Massachusetts. These programs produce virginity pledge programs, where 88% of teens who pledge virginity fail to keep that pledge and are one-third less likely to use condoms at first intercourse (Brückner & Bearman, 2005).

There are many reasons to bemoan the current state of abstinence education, as it has been done so poorly. Just read Congressman Henry Waxman's report (United States House of Representatives, 2004). Perhaps consider the wisdom of Dr. Michael Carrera, who reminds us that expecting outcomes when we tell kids to "just say no," is no different than expecting a person's clinical depression to be treated by saying, "Have a nice day!" Or teacher/columnist Deborah Roffman, who compares abstinence-only education to the sex-hungry media: both, Roffman explains, tell teens exactly what to do. The media scream, "Always say yes," abstinence-only programs admonish, "Just say no," but *neither* encourage teens to *think* for themselves. That is, of course, the whole point of learning.

Certainly there are many reasons that justify the collective distaste for the current abstinence education paradigm among sex educators. The state of abstinence-only education is just awful, from the moralizing, shame, and fear-based tactics, to the sideshow industry that markets abstinence slogans on billboards, t-shirts, mugs, and even chewing gum. ("Abstinence gum—for *chewzing* an abstinent lifestyle.")

But all complaints about abstinence-only-until-marriage education aside, what is wrong with educating about the *choice* of abstinence? Doesn't the polling research say that American parents want their children to learn about abstinence? When comprehensive sex educators trumpet the latest polling data from groups like the Kaiser Family Foundation that says parents support comprehensive sex education, how do we miss the fact that the same polling data reveals parental desire for their kids to learn about abstinence? What are we doing about this, and how can we react to the word "abstinence" so negatively when we are supposedly teaching it as a *part* of comprehensive sex education?

A New Model

The pedagogical concepts introduced in *Making Sense of Abstinence* make it unlike any abstinence education manual produced to date. There are four key themes that are woven throughout the manual's sixteen lessons: (1) abstinence education needs to help young people *define* abstinence in ways that help them understand and apply their decisions in real life; (2) abstinence education needs to include decision-making, skills-building opportunities; (3) abstinence education is not just talking about which behaviors to *avoid*, but also the behaviors that are *permitted* in a person's decision; (4) abstinence education needs to help young people protect their sexual health and transition safely when they decide to no longer abstain.

Defining Abstinence

Remember the guy who called me a "pointy headed liberal"? Define abstinence? Well, DUH! Abstinence means "no sex," right? Next time you are with a group of professionals, or a group of students, ask them to take out their cell phones and call three people. Have their friends, colleagues, coworkers, children, parents, etc. define the terms "sex" and "abstinence." You will be amazed, as I always am, with the discordant results you get. Do the definitions address only vaginal intercourse? Oral or anal intercourse? Other touching behaviors? Masturbation? What reasons or motivations emerge? Religious? Parental? Pregnancy prevention? Prevention of sexually transmitted infections? Assessing one's readiness? Marriage? Protecting one's mental health? When one person defines "sex," as "a loving, intimate, physical connection between two people," does that mean that kissing is sex? And, thus, abstinence is no kissing? When one says, simply, that "abstinence means no sex," does this mean one must also avoid the aforementioned feelings of intimacy and love?

If this seems like a trivial exercise, consider the following definitions of abstinence printed or posted by a variety of health-promoting organizations:

> *"Abstinence is . . . not having sex with a partner. This will keep the sperm from joining the egg." . . .*

> *"Abstinence is . . . no intercourse. Not even any semen on the vulva. Pretty straight-forward."* (Kinsey Institute's Sexuality Information Service for Students)

> Hmmm. So abstinence means no *vaginal* intercourse. But wait . . .

> *"For protection against infection . . . abstinence means avoiding vaginal, anal, and oral-genital intercourse, or participating in any other activity in which body fluids are exchanged." . . .*

So, the motivation here is avoiding infections that may be transmitted via body fluid exchange. This could include oral, anal, or vaginal intercourse. It also seems to refer tacitly to another fluid through which HIV could be transmitted: breast milk. So, does one practice abstinence by not breastfeeding her child? From the *Dictionary of Sexology* (Francoeur, 1997):

> *"A definition of abstinence may include not engaging in masturbation."*

and

> *"The practices of tantric yoga recommend short periods of abstinence to concentrate one's sexual energy and prepare for more intense responses when sexual intercourse is resumed."*

Ah, so abstinence is periodic, for the purpose of making sex *better!* How about some input from abstinence-only programs:

> *"Abstinence is . . . voluntarily refraining from all sexual relationships before marriage in order to uplift your own self-worth and provide the freedom to build character, develop career potentials and practice true love."* (As cited by Kempner, 2001)

Abstinence for career potential? Never came up in my job interviews, but who knows today? Back to reality, Thoraya Obaid, executive director of the United Nations Populations Fund, reminds us that abstinence is not always a choice:

> *"Abstinence . . . is meaningless to women who are coerced into sex."*

As I collected all these definitions, I was surprised when glossaries on websites for lesbian, gay, bisexual, and transgender teens repeatedly came up empty on definitions for abstinence. I asked my friend and colleague, Lis Maurer, about this. Lis is the director of Ithaca College's Center for LGBT Education and Outreach Services, and she explained:

> *I remember a high school class where we were taught about abstinence. Afterward, several of us non-straight students got together and reacted. Some said, "OK—we're totally in the clear!" Others said, "No, we were ignored—they really don't know we exist!" and yet others were just completely confused, as if the lecture was in some other language.*

Finally, . . . sums up all this confusion quite nicely:

> *"Abstinence is . . . avoiding sex. Sex, of course, means different things to different people."*

Indeed. What might abstinence mean to a teen?

> *"I'm proud that my boyfriend and I have decided to be abstinent. We have oral sex, but definitely not real sex, you know?"*

The importance of helping teens define abstinence cannot be under-scored enough. A recent evaluation of one abstinence-only program found that teens developed more positive attitudes toward abstinence following the program. That seems like good news, but the study went on to explain that "abstinence" meant "abstaining from sexual intercourse," which meant, "the male's penis is in the female's vagina. Some slang names for sexual intercourse are 'having sex,' 'making love,' or 'going all the way.' " (Laflin et al., 2005). So while these teens were developing their positive feelings toward abstinence, they were learning nothing about how abstinence might *also* mean avoiding other sexual behaviors, including anal and oral intercourse that could transmit a sexually transmitted infection. The teen cited said earlier could easily have been a participant in this abstinence-only education program.

The evidence is clear that teens need opportunities to discuss what absti-nence means to them. They need worksheets, activities, and discussion oppor-tunities to reflect on their reasons for choosing abstinence, and specifically what behaviors they will avoid while abstaining. If they ultimately decide *not* to avoid oral sex, anal sex, etc., then they need further information about pro-tection from sexually transmitted infections.

Decision-Making, Skills-Building Lessons

Maybe you've seen a billboard sign that says, "VIRGIN: Teach Your Kid It's Not a Dirty Word!" Or maybe you're familiar with the slogan, "Quit your urgin', be a virgin!" One of the abstinence slogans that always gets a chuckle is "Good cowgirls keep their calves together." The list goes on and on, and many of them are cute, catchy, and memorable. But none of them speak to the complex decision-making skills that really need to be developed in young people to help them make decisions that are meaningful and responsible in their lives.

Young people need opportunities to develop concrete steps for "using" abstinence effectively. Abstinence is not just a state of being; it is a method to be *used*. This is an important distinction. The former implies passivity; i.e., no need to think about anything when abstinence is the foregone conclusion. The latter encourages young people to think about *how* they are going to be effective with their decisions, to develop the skills to be successful with their decisions, and to re-evaluate their decisions as need be.

Abstinence skills include learning to plan for sexual abstinence, and prac-ticing assertive communication, so that one can better stand up for one's deci-sions. It involves learning about sexual response, so that one can understand and manage their sexual feelings in ways that are consistent with their values and decisions. It involves negotiation and enforcing boundaries with one's partner. It involves so much more than "Just say no!" or other simplistic, "educational" approaches that are far more directive than they are educational.

A relatively new model, supported by the federal government seeks to improve upon abstinence-only programs by teaching an "ABC" model. ABC stands for "*A*bstinence," "*B*e faithful," and "*C*se Condoms," and unfortunately it is not much more comprehensive than its abstinence-only cousin. The United States exported its ABC's to Uganda for the purposes of HIV prevention. The hierarchical ABC approach stresses Abstinence first; while Be faithful reserved for those who can't seem to practice Abstinence; and Condoms are reserved strictly for the sex workers.

A closer look at this new sloganistic approach exposes a model that is devoid of critical thinking and skills building. For example, what if a person is using "B" but their partner isn't. That person is likely to learn about three new letters, "S," "T," and "D." Further, what if a person ditches "A," in favor of "B" without using C? Does anyone in these programs ever mention the possibility of an unplanned or unwanted "P"? Simplistic models like this continue to reveal the importance of helping young people think through their abstinence decisions and become effective abstinence users.

It's Not Just What You Avoid . . .

Why is it that we are not talking about masturbation when we are teaching about abstinence? Twelve years ago a United States surgeon general was fired for suggesting this might be a good idea. Masturbation is one of the safest sexual behaviors around, perhaps the safest. There is no risk of getting pregnant, no risk of getting a sexually transmitted infection, no risk of getting *anything*, except pleasure. As Woody Allen said, "Don't knock masturbation. It's having sex with someone you love!"

So why does masturbation have such a stigma in America. I have a clue that maybe it has something to do with the things that have been written about it. Sylvester Graham, a New York preacher, wrote in 1834 that a masturbator grows up:

> "with a body full of disease, and with a mind in ruins, the loathsome habit still tyrannizing over him, with the inexorable imperiousness of a fiend of darkness." (Graham, 1834)

And, in 1892, a prominent nutritionist, John Harvey Kellogg, wrote this:

> "As a sin against nature, [masturbation] has no parallel except in sodomy. The habit is by no means confined to boys; girls also indulge in it, though it is to be hoped, to a less fearful extent than boys, at least in this country. Of all the vices to which human beings are addicted, no other so rapidly undermines the constitution, and so certainly makes a complete wreck of an individual as this, especially when the habit is begun at an early age. It wastes the most precious part of the blood, uses up the vital forces, and finally leaves the poor victim a most utterly ruined and loathsome object.
>
> Suspicious signs are: bashfulness, unnatural boldness, round shoulders and a stooping position, lack of development of the breasts in females, eating chalk, acne, and the use of tobacco." (Kellogg, 1892)

No wonder the anxiety! It didn't matter that neither statement was true. People still flocked to buy the recommended antidotes, Sylvester's Graham crackers and Kellogg's Corn Flakes, both of which were supposed to suppress the urge to masturbate (and neither of which contained sugar or cinnamon in those days!).

More than a century later, our American culture still retains myths and misinformation. Perhaps if we can make young people feel a little less anxious about a behavior in which so many already engage, we can help them recognize masturbation as an important, safe *alternative* to intercourse.

Abstinence education needs to discuss other safe sexual behaviors, including outercourse, that get young people thinking about non-genital activities that are safe, and will keep them free of sexually transmitted infections and pregnancy. These behaviors—masturbation and outercourse—have inexplicably been omitted from abstinence-only curricula. It is as if we really think that if we don't mention these topics, teens won't think of it either! Have we really become that disconnected with our nation's youth? We really need to examine *why* information about masturbation and outercourse is omitted in abstinence education. Is it to keep information about sexual pleasure from young people? What gives educators the right to withhold *any* information from young people, especially information that might help keep them safe, while feeling positively about themselves?

Susie Wilson, who ran the Network for Family Life Education (now Answer), gave a review of *Making Sense of Abstinence,* and she put it better than I could have:

> "[Students] will learn that there is a long continuum of behaviors between "saying no" and "doing it" that will keep them safe, not sorry. Educators will feel more secure about teaching tough topics such as oral sex, masturbation and outercourse, when they see they are allied with discussion about personal values, decision-making and communication."

This is exactly what we are trying to do with our our model for abstinence education.

Help Young People Protect Themselves If/When Their Decisions Change

A final, critical part of abstinence education is the need to help young people protect themselves if and when their abstinence decisions change. It is no longer enough for us to bury our heads in the sand and just hope that teens remain abstinent through high school, college, and into young adulthood (or up until age 29, as the new federal abstinence-only guidelines suggest). We need to equip them with the skills to make that transition safely.

One way is to help them identify signs of *"sexual readiness"*. Students might read stories about other teens who are making sexual decisions, and assess and discuss how ready (or not) these teens are against any number of sexual readiness checklists. Consider these two teen quotes:

> "At times I get all hot with my partner and I feel like I really want to have sex. At other times, I know that I shouldn't have sex until I am ready. The problem is that sometimes I feel like I am ready and other times I feel like I am not ready. What should I do?"

and

"I've been going out with this guy—he's 18. Everything was romantic at first, but now he's gotten real pushy. Last time we were alone, he gave me a beer. I didn't feel like drinking, but he kept pushing it on me, so I drank it just to shut him up. Now he's pushing the sex thing on me. It's like we don't talk about anything but sex. I know he's tired of waiting for me, but I think things are getting out of hand, and I'm not sure I'm ready."

Both teens deserve much more than a catchy slogan. They need tools and discussion to help them identify how one knows when one is ready, and how to identify coercion in a relationship, and how to leave coercive relationships. We need to help young people actively think of their decisions in their sexual lives. Sexual intercourse is not something that people are just supposed to stumble into, without thinking of their decisions and their potential consequences. By contrast, the current culture of abstinence-only education supports teens making virginity pledges, which simply do not work. 88% of teens who make such a pledge break it! (Brückner & Bearman, 2005). And those teens are less likely to use protection, because they've never learned about condoms or contraceptives, or they've been taught only about failure rates.

In training teachers, I often say that "Sex education *today* is not necessarily for *tonight*." This is very applicable when it comes to abstinence education. We need to think about sex education in the context of a lifetime of sexual decision making, and abstinence as a conscious decision that is one's right to assert at anytime in their life. At the same time, we need to help teens gain knowledge and develop skills to protect their sexual health if and when they decide to no longer abstain, whether it is tonight, or in college, or when they celebrate a commitment ceremony, or after they walk down the aisle.

Young people need more from sex education. They need education that includes the *choice* to abstain. They need accurate information, not evasive, undefined terms, or misleading, or false information. Young people need and deserve respect, not to be subjected to scare tactics. They need to develop skills to be successful with abstinence; not to hear catchy slogans. They need to be met where they are, and recognized for their ability to make responsible decisions about their sexual lives. They need abstinence education, but they deserve better than what they've been getting so far.

References

Brückner, H. & Bearman, P. (2005). "After the promise: the STD consequences of adolescent virginity pledges," *Journal of Adolescent Health*, No. 36: 271–278.

Centers for Disease Control and Prevention. (2006). *Youth risk behavior surveillance—United States, 2005*. Atlanta, GA: Centers for Disease Control.

Francoeur, R.T. (1997). *The Complete Dictionary of Sexology*, New York: Continuum.

Graham, S. (1834). *A Lecture to Young Men on Chastity*. Boston, MA: Pierce.

Kellogg, J.H. (1892). *Plain Facts for Old and Young.* Burlington, IA: I.F. Segner.

Kempner, M.E. (2001). *Toward a Sexually Healthy America: Abstinence-Only-Until-Marriage Programs that Try to Keep Our Youth 'Scared Chaste.'* New York: Sexuality Information & Education Council of the United States.

Laflin, M.T., Sommers, J.M., & Chibucos, T.R., "Initial Findings in a Longitudinal Study of the Effectiveness of the *Sex Can Wait* Sexual Abstinence Curriculum for Grades 5–8," *American Journal of Sexuality Education,* 1(1):103–118.

Taverner, B. & Montfort, S. (2005). *Making Sense of Abstinence: Lessons for Comprehensive Sex Education.* Morristown, NJ: The Center for Family Life Education, Planned Parenthood of Greater Northern New Jersey.

U.S. House of Representatives, Committee on Government Reform (2004). *The Content of Federally Funded Abstinence-Only Education Programs,* prepared for Rep. Henry A. Waxman. Washington, DC: The House, December 2004.

Maureen Kelly

NO

The Semantics of Sex Ed: Or, Shooting Ourselves in the Foot as We Slowly Walk Backwards

Should Sex Ed Teach about Abstinence?

No. And when I say no, I need to add two important caveats. First, I need to add quotation marks around the word "abstinence" because my answer pertains to the word "abstinence" not the life-affirming concept of personal choice and sexual decision-making across a vast span of sexual possibilities (more coarsely and simplistically placed on a continuum from not-doing to doing "it," whatever "it" may be). Second, when I refer to "abstinence" I am specifically referring to the strict eight-point definition of what "abstinence education" must include which is laid out in the 1996 federal Welfare Reform Law's abstinence-only-until-marriage provision. One highlight on the list of target groups for abstinence-only-until-marriage programs is all unmarried people under the age of thirty. Federally funded abstinence education for unmarried thirty year olds? Just say no.

Why do I take such issue with a word? In the dozen-plus years that I have worked as a professional sex educator I have watched secrets and lies take a growing hold on sex ed policies and programs. The highjacking of the word "abstinence" and the claiming of the moral high ground by opponents to sex ed is a striking example.

It's almost a cliché how the whole sex ed vs. abstinence ed debate has unraveled. It's just one more intentionally crafted pro vs. anti political dichotomy that infiltrates citizen's daily lives and choices. And one of the more cunning aspects of the "abstinence" conversation in America is that the Friday-night-wrestling-smack-down nature of the debate does not acknowledge that, once again, a political debate completely misses the obvious and neglects to uncover the fact that the extreme permutations of the political concept of "abstinence" as applied to health information content and funding, is a failure. Seek out the data! Read the reports! What did Waxman say? Look to Western Europe for innovative and effective roadmaps! But please, don't succumb to fear and politics and allow "abstinence" to be the only right, moral, good choice to make or lesson to teach; take a risk. Stir the pot. We need to elevate this debate but I believe to do that we have to abandon the word "abstinence." However, when the pot is stirred, fear takes hold and people seem to freak out a bit.

When chatting about plans for an upcoming educational presentation, one teacher actually said, "I didn't want a controversy, so I invited the abstinence people in." There's just so much wrong with this! First, I am amazed that a certified teacher does not find the contrary controversial! Isn't it far more controversial to deny information to youth, mislead kids about health facts, and to hold all youth to a singular heterosexual standard? And the sneaky underlying assumption is also flawed. To assume that good sex educators do not talk about sexual decision-making (of which NOT doing "it" is always an option!) is just wrong. Talking about personal sexual choices and teaching tips and tools for making effective and responsible and safe sexual decisions—yes *and no* decisions—are cornerstones of good sex ed. Again, it's dirty politics that tarnish this conversation, that make us focus our energy and worry on words and perceptions and fear of controversy or repercussions, not on young people. They are the ones losing!

The problem here is language. Semantics. Let's look at *abstinence*. Now, as a concept, abstinence is without moral judgment, without coercion and does not withhold information. Abstinence is simply about *not doing something*. People abstain from a lot of things. Certain foods, voting, paying taxes, alcohol; the scope of *abstinence* as a concept is deep and broad and has a rich social, religious, and political history filled with social protest and acts of resistance. The "abstinence" vis-à-vis sex ed discussion certainly has all that too!

As you may notice, I've been pissed off about this word for a while now. My anger bubbles up from a place of disbelief about how some people can't see the truth. I am incensed when I see people who, once exposed to the truth, whatever that truth may be—the war, gay marriage, taxes, sex ed—don't act in accordance with that truth but rather, stick fiercely to their strongly held beliefs even when they are in direct conflict with the facts.

I am also deeply troubled by the reality that many of us—sex ed advocates and educators—have gotten sucked into the defensive, no-win abstinence debate. We have science, data, a majority of parents, common sense and all of Western Europe on our side in support of smart and sane sex ed but we are losing. We are losing because we are hemorrhaging from our defensive wounds.

And, thanks to George Lakoff (UC Berkeley linguistics professor and Rockridge Institute Fellow), I have shifted from a full pissed off boil to a smarter, more informed and productive simmer. Here's why: I've been mad at the wrong things. I have been mad at issues and people, not frameworks. Although I flirt with stepping above the fray and getting glimpses of why people act (and vote) the way they do, I haven't quite grasped the depth and breadth of the real battle being waged. What has facilitated this transformation are insights from Mr. Lakoff's 2004 book *Don't Think of an Elephant: Know Your Values and Frame the Debate—The Essential Guide for Progressives* combined with reactions and reflections about how the brilliance of framing—and reframing—can help us win the sex ed war.

First and foremost, we must begin by understanding the power of mental structures—the power of *frames*. Frames are the ties that bind; they are the unconscious connectors that define our actions, reactions, perceptions and worldview. Frames are about way more than just the words; ideas are the foundation for the frame and the words are the messengers that deliver the ideas. And simply enough, in order to change the world, we must understand and acknowledge the power of these frames—as words *and* ideas—and then go about the vital business of changing them; *reframing is social change*.

> Reframing is changing the way the public sees the world. It is changing what counts as common sense. Because language activates frames, new language is required for new frames. Thinking differently requires speaking differently.[1]

The progressive movement as a whole, and we, as sex ed advocates and educators, are caught in a defensive cycle marked by reaction to words and ideas and philosophies that do not represent our view, our thinking and what we know to be true and right. As we do this we are unwittingly giving credibility to a frame that we do not believe.

Our opponents brilliantly crafted a powerful frame around "abstinence" that conjures a happy, ideal fairyland where kids are safe and protected from the mean, scary and unpredictable world. Who the heck wouldn't want that? I *love* the idea of protecting the young people I care about from bad things; it's a natural urge. So, when I say "no, I am against abstinence" (as a political and social means of control and a troubling marriage of church and state) I am in essence rejecting their frame yet still defining myself through their frame. That's where it gets really confusing! By being opposed to their idea but using their words, I end up standing for nothing.

Because, when I say "I am against abstinence," I am in effect saying, "I want kids to be unsafe, unprotected and get exposed to mean, scary and unpredictable things" (because that's what happens when you make your argument based on your opposition's language rather than your own inspiration). And none of us want that! We are caught in a defensive loop trying to explain that, yes, we believe in abstinence (safe, happy protected kids) but we want abstinence-plus or abstinence-based education (if they do end up having sex, they should have access to information and supplies that protect them); this approach is totally wrong. We are, by default, accepting our opponents' framework while trying to add our own footnote. And we have forgotten that most people don't read footnotes.[2]

One particularly troubling outcome of our tacit acceptance of our opponent's framing of abstinence is that we can easily be dismissed as confused and inconsistent (if we are for abstinence, as their frame defines it, how in the world can we be for birth control education for youth as well?). We seem to forget that "abstinence" as used by our opponents is not at all akin to the actual definition of the word, but rather it evokes a feeling, a philosophy and an idea—a frame—that is diametrically opposed to our view. The simple act of using the word "abstinence"—*no mater how we might mean it*—activates their frame, not ours. We are shooting ourselves in the foot as we walk slowly backwards.

> This gives us a basic principle of framing, for when you are arguing against the other side; do not use their language. Their language picks out a frame—and it won't be the frame you want.[3]
> Framing is about getting language that fits your worldview. It is not just language. The ideas are primary—and the language carries those ideas, evokes those ideas.[4]

Another problem; our in-fighting divides us and keeps us vulnerable. Why are some of us taking abstinence money and others lobbying their States to give it all back to the Feds? Why do some of us want to feverishly reclaim the language of "abstinence" while others want to totally eradicate it from our parlance? We have to ask these questions, talk about them and commit to finding and applying a common approach. We must get beyond the "my way is the right way" division of our field. We are stuck and until we step above this soul sucking and divisive in-fighting to discover and capitalize on the unity of our movement, our fight will remain amongst ourselves and do little to change the world. As all this swirls around us, we are rendering our own work less and less effective, articulate and strong because *we are fighting among ourselves in service of their vision, not ours*. We must stop our own in-fighting, stop fighting their war for them, stop using the word "abstinence" and take a bold and brave step right off the battlefield and say, why the heck are we fighting here any way? It's a bad war, not based on truth and it's not good for our country or our kids, period.

So, what should we do about this? We need to intentionally and thoughtfully become the object-center of our debate; we need to reframe our arguments for and definitions of sex ed in reference to *our* values, vision and morality; not in reference to our opponents'. We must remember that when we attack our opponents' stance by disagreeing with it but building on it rather than offering a viable alternative, we fail to move our agenda forward. *Our agenda*? Yes! Our Agenda. We do have one and we need to talk about it more.

And to do that, we have to take one more step inside Lakoff's world. We need to understand the dynamic of the strict father vs. nuturant parent paradigm. It is this paradigm that exposes the stark differences of vision and value between our opponents and us. It is precisely why, when I listen to the rhetoric of our opponents, I cringe. Why? I don't subscribe to the Strict Father frame. I'm more of a nurturant chick. At my core, I don't buy into the Father Knows Best, teach kids what to think not how to think, pick-yourself-up-by-your-bootstraps, stop your crying or I'll give you something to cry about, one nation under god, don't have sex until you're married paradigm. Conversely, I'm more of a fan of empathy and nurturance, open, two-way communication, honesty, choice, trust, integrity, opportunity and freedom.

To be effective in re-framing our version of what sex ed should be, we must understand that we cannot simply borrow from the strict father foundation of the abstinence-only-until-marriage frame, but rather, we must create and propose new and radical ideas that evoke a distinct and powerful frame that encompasses the spirit of nurturance. By nature, that cannot be a frame based on an abstinence-plus message; in fact, to be most effective, it will be an antithetical concept compared to the spirit of current abstinence messages touted by the strict father moralists.

Our version of sex ed is about asking, choosing, discussing, considering, exploring, learning, and offering open, honest access to information and exposure to diverse options. Now, that's a real alternative to the abstinence-only-until-marriage model! Maybe ours is called the teach-me-trust-me-and-mentor-me model? Or maybe the Freedom, Opportunity and Awareness Act of 2007? To be successful in reframing our work, we must understand that the battle for sex ed is a sub-battle that shares values and vision with the progressive movement as a whole. And, as we get better at gathering around our common goals—and investing less in the self-defeating, chase your own tail, me-first conundrum that is identity politics—we will triumph. Our ideas resonate with people; we simply need to find the words that resonate as much as our ideas.

But fear sells. So, we need to tell the truth and bust the myth that "abstinence will save the world" because it's just not true. The fear is real and visceral for those who worry that if we talk to kids about sex they will transmogrify into sex-crazed, insatiable fiends without remorse, protection or forethought (sounds more like a member of congress than a teen who got honest and complete sex ed). The great irony is, that despite their hearts being in the right place *(we all want our kids to be OK, safe and smart!),* they have it all wrong. The fact is, the more we talk about sex in age-appropriate, frank, honest, accurate ways, the *safer our kids are.* Yes, despite the fears and worries of well-meaning people, *when we don't give our kids sex ed, we end up with much bigger problems than when we do.* Just look at our teen pregnancy, STD, and abortion rates for that evidence!

And then, take a look at western Europe as an example of what could be. Young people in Germany, the Netherlands and France are given a lot of education and access to information about s-e-x. But here's the kicker—these European kids that are getting all this sex ed early and often, they are having less sex, with fewer partners, at a later age than their US peers, with less negative outcomes, fewer abortions, fewer teen births, and fewer STDs.[5] No kidding. It seems that the more we take the shame and taboo-filled mystique from sex and help it assume a normal, natural, spoken about and human part of our lives, the better off we all are.

So what do I propose as alternatives to abstinence-only-until-marriage programming for our kids? Simple: teach the facts, tell the truth, and include everyone. We need to work side by side to remove the shame and secrecy that shrouds our conversation and education about sex. It's the shame and secrecy that truly put our kids at risk, not sex ed.

I would like to eradicate the use of the word "abstinence" while explicitly and frequently teaching about the concept of choice vis-à-vis sex. Teach about when or whether to have sex. Teach about sexual choices and safety and responsibility. Teach about saying yes and teach about saying no. Just TEACH!

The complexities of sex, relationships, and communication require depth and breadth in teaching style; not a one-size-fits-all-just-say-no approach.

We have to talk about it and prepare for it, because sex is a part of life.

Notes

1. Page xi, *Don't Think of an Elephant! Know Your Values and Frame the Debate: The Essential Guide for Progressives,* George Lakoff, Chelsea Green Publishing, 2004.
2. Just checking. . .
3. Page 3, op cit.
4. Page 4, ibid.
5. Advocates for Youth, . . . "European Approaches to Adolescent Sexual Behavior & Responsibility," 1999.

POSTSCRIPT

Should Sex Ed Teach about Abstinence?

The debate over abstinence-only-until-marriage education was highlighted recently after the Obama administration restored federal funding to comprehensive sexuality education programs while reducing the funds available for abstinence-only education. Conservative groups were furious that abstinence-only education would receive only a fraction of the previous funds. Supporters of comprehensive programs were frustrated that support for abstinence programs was not totally eliminated. Additional controversies over teen pregnancy, including Bristol Palin's post-pregnancy support for abstinence-only education, as well as the introduction of reality shows focusing on teen pregnancy (see Issue 16 in this edition for more on these shows) have added to the debate.

Academics, educators, and activists may often agree on a desired outcome, but may strongly disagree on the best approach to meet that end. In her essay, Maureen Kelly argues that sex educators' use of the "frame" of abstinence only helps to serve a conservative agenda promoting abstinence as the ONLY acceptable means of contraception and STI prevention. She challenges the way in which abstinence was defined by the federal government and rejects the use of the term. Taverner embraces the term while working to challenge its definition from within the existing structure. Is Taverner shooting himself, and the movement for comprehensive sex education, in the foot (as Kelly suggests) by using the terminology of a system he seeks to question? Should Kelly and other sex educators reclaim the language of abstinence as part of comprehensive sex education, as Taverner argues?

Most importantly, how do YOU define abstinence? What behaviors are off limits if a person is practicing abstinence? What behaviors are acceptable? What reasons might a person have for wanting to practice abstinence? What type of education, abstinence-only or comprehensive, do you feel is most effective? Should the government encourage abstinence only until marriage? How should a gay or lesbian person handle the message "abstinence until marriage" in a country that, except for a handful of states, makes same-sex marriages illegal?

Think back to your own sexuality education in high school. Did it include learning about abstinence, condoms, contraception, and other aspects of human sexuality? Or was it an abstinence-only program? If you had to give your high school sex education a grade, what would it be?

Suggested Readings

J. Blake, *Words Can Work: When Talking to Kids about Sexual Health* (Blake Works, 2004).

H. Brückner and P. Bearman, "After the Promise: The STD Consequences of Adolescent Virginity Pledges," *Journal of Adolescent Health* (no. 36, 2005).

J. Jemmott, L. Jemmott, and G. Fong, "Efficacy of a Theory-Based Abstinence-Only Intervention Over 24 Months," *Archives of Pediatrics and Adolescent Medicine* (vol. 164, no. 2, 2010).

R. Stein, "Obama Administration's Sex-Ed Program Criticized by Both Sides of Abstinence Debate," *Washington Post* (October 28, 2010).

B. Taverner and S. Montfort, *Making Sense of Abstinence: Lessons for Comprehensive Sex Education* (Morristown, NJ: The Center for Family Life Education, 2005).

U.S. House of Representatives, Committee on Government Reform, *The Content of Federally Funded Abstinence-Only Education Programs*, prepared for Rep. Henry A. Waxman (Washington, DC: The House, December 2004).

ISSUE 9

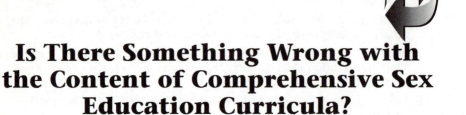

Is There Something Wrong with the Content of Comprehensive Sex Education Curricula?

YES: The Administration for Children and Families (ACF), Department of Health and Human Services (HHS), from "Review of Comprehensive Sex Education Curricula" (Washington, DC: United States Government Printing Office, 2007)

NO: Elokin CaPece, from "Commentary on the *Review of Comprehensive Sex Education Curricula* (2007)," *American Journal of Sexuality Education* (vol. 3, no. 3, 2007)

ISSUE SUMMARY

YES: The Administration for Children and Families, United States Department of Health and Human Services, presents their findings in a critical analysis of comprehensive sexuality education curricula.

NO: Elokin CaPece, Health Educator with Planned Parenthood Greater Memphis Region, disputes the research methods used and the findings of the report, highlighting what she sees as bias in the overall findings.

Since 1996, the United States has invested more than $1.5 billion in abstinence-only-until-marriage (AOUM) programs. These programs forbid providing accurate information about the use of contraceptives and condoms to prevent unplanned pregnancy and sexually transmitted infections, respectively. Concurrently, the federal government had also elected *not* to fund comprehensive sex education, which would have provided safer sex and contraceptive information, as well as other expert suggested age-appropriate information.

Initially, criticism of AOUM was largely ideological. "Why subject children to explicit information about sex when they should be waiting for marriage?" AOUM advocates would argue. "Why fund programs that withhold critical, potentially life-saving information from teens?" sexuality education advocates would respond. There were also concerns about using public funds—and public schools— to establish a singular moral (and, in some cases, religious) standard sexual behavior. *Only* in monogamous, heterosexual marriages taught AOUM programs.

As the battle waged, money continued to pour in for AOUM programs. The annual spending more than doubled during the administration of George W. Bush, rising from $97.5 million per year at the time of his election to

$242 million in his last year in office. This enormous amount of spending surprised many and American taxpayers who overwhelmingly support sexuality education were chagrined as the national economy tanked. During the administration of Barack Obama, AOUM funding continued but was substantially reduced. Obama also signed the Consolidated Appropriations Act of 2010, which marked that the first time the United States government funded teen pregnancy prevention programs and projects, and included $114.5 million in federal funds for the Teen Pregnancy Prevention Initiative (TPPI).

In the midst of the perennial debate over AOUM funding, a federally commissioned review of 13 AOUM curricula found that 80% of the curricula material provided "false, misleading, or distorted information about sexual health" (United States House of Representatives Committee on Government Reform, 2004). In some cases, the distortions were without reference, such as the assertion of one curriculum that "girls who have sex before marriage are six times as likely to commit suicide than virgins." (Taverner, 2008).

Research also found the programs to be ineffective. The independent research group Mathematica Policy Research, Inc. found that teens who participated in AOUM programs "were no more likely than control group youth to have abstained from sex." (Mathematica Policy Research, Inc., 2007). Doug Kirby, one of the nation's most respected researchers on adolescent sexual health, also found no impact of AOUM programs on teen sexual behavior. (Kirby, 2007). Two researchers found that AOUM programs were ineffective and potentially harmful. In a study of virginity pledge programs, the researchers found that 88% of those who made a pledge failed to keep that pledge, and one-third were less likely to use a condom during intercourse (Brückner and Bearman, 2005).

There was a backlash among conservatives who championed AOUM programs all along. As evidence documenting the failure of AOUM programs grew (and a number of states—17 to date—actually began *rejecting* the federal funds), Senator Tom Coburn (R-Oklahoma) and former Senator Rick Santorum (R-Pennsylvania) commissioned a new federal study to scrutinize the content of comprehensive sexuality education programs. Under their direction, the Administration for Children and Families of the United States Department of Health and Human Services sought to similarly discredit sexuality education, focusing primarily on the types of words that appear in the text of sexuality education curricula. The YES essay that follows is an excerpt from the report.

In response, sexual health educator Elokin CaPece criticizes the report as "irresponsible research" and critiques its research methods and findings. She criticizes the report for its clear and inappropriate bias against the subject examined, and for its unreasonable criteria to describing the "failure" of sexuality education programs.

References

H. Brückner and P. Bearman, "After the Promise: The STD Consequences of Adolescent Virginity Pledges," *Journal of Adolescent Health* (no. 36, pp. 271–278, 2005).

D. Kirby, *Emerging Answers 2007: Research Findings on Programs to Reduce Teen Pregnancy and Sexually Transmitted Diseases.* Washington, DC: National Campaign to Prevent Teen and Unplanned Pregnancy, accessed at http://www .thenc.org./ea2007, (2007).

YES  The Administration for Children and Families (ACF), Department of Health and Human Services (HHS)

Review of Comprehensive Sex Education Curricula

Introduction

"Comprehensive Sex Education" curricula for adolescents have been endorsed by various governmental agencies, educational organizations, and teenage advocacy groups as the most effective educational method for reducing teenage pregnancy and helping prevent the spread of sexually transmitted diseases (STDs) among America's youth. The National Institutes of Health (NIH) defines Comprehensive Sex Education (CSE) as "teaching both abstinence and the use of protective methods for sexually active youth"; NIH states that CSE curricula have been "shown to delay sexual activity among teens." Non-governmental groups that support CSE have also made statements linking CSE curricula to abstinence as well as reduction of pregnancy and sexually transmitted infections (STIs).

The Administration for Children and Families, within the Department of Health and Human Services undertook an examination of some of the most common CSE curricula currently in use. The purpose of this examination was to inform federal policymakers of the content, medical accuracy, and effectiveness of CSE curricula currently in use.

Background

In 2005, Senators Santorum and Coburn requested that the Administration for Children and Families (ACF) review and evaluate comprehensive sex education programs supported with federal dollars. The Senators wrote to the Assistant Secretary for Children and Families,

> In particular, we would appreciate a review that explores the effectiveness of these programs in reducing teen pregnancy rates and the transmission of sexually transmitted diseases. In addition, please assess the effectiveness of these programs in advancing the greater goal of encouraging teens to make the healthy decision to delay sexual activity. Please also include an evaluation of the scientific accuracy of the content of these programs. Finally, we would appreciate an assessment of how the actual content of these programs compares to their stated goals.

From a report published by Administration for Children & Families (ACF)/United States Dept. of Health and Human Services. May 2007, pp. 3–12. http://www.acf.hhs.gov/programs/fysb/content/docs/comprehensive.pdf

In response, ACF contracted with the Sagamore Institute for Policy Research to review some of the most common CSE curricula currently in use. ACF also requested and received comments on these reviews from the Medical Institute for Sexual Health (MISH).

Research Questions and Methodology

In response to the request from Senators Santorum and Coburn, the curriculum reviews evaluated four questions:

1. Does the content of the comprehensive sex education curricula mirror the stated purposes?
2. What is the content of comprehensive sex education curricula?
3. Do comprehensive sex education curricula contain medically inaccurate statements?
4. Do evaluations of these curricula show them to be effective at (a) delaying sexual debut and (b) reducing sex without condoms?

The initial charge of this project was to evaluate the content and effectiveness of the "most frequently used" CSE curricula. After a thorough search, which included contacting publishers, researchers, distributors, and advocacy groups, it was determined that a list ranked by "frequency of use" or "number of copies purchased" was not in existence nor could one be produced.

Instead, curricula were chosen for this study based on the frequency and strength of endorsement received from leading and recognized sexuality information organizations and resources. A curriculum was considered to be "endorsed" if a source recommended it or promoted it as a "program that works." The curricula mentioned most frequently were chosen for this study if they were school-based (i.e., not solely for community organizations), widely available, and described by at least one source as "comprehensive" or "abstinence-plus." Additional weight was given to curricula described as evidence-based or as a "program that works."

It should be noted that some of the curricula reviewed do not state in their materials that they have an abstinence focus—i.e., that they are "comprehensive sex education," "abstinence plus," or in some other way focused on abstinence. However, if a curriculum were endorsed as "comprehensive" or "abstinence plus" by a leading sexuality information organization and resources, it was assumed that the curriculum would be purchased and used for the purpose of providing comprehensive sex education. Additionally of note, some of the curricula have recently published revisions with added abstinence components. In every case, the most recent version of the curricula available was studied.

Nine curricula met the criteria for this study and were subsequently reviewed:

1. *Reducing the Risk: Building Skills to Prevent Pregnancy, STD & HIV (4th Edition),* by R. Barth, 2004.
2. *Be Proud! Be Responsible!,* L. Jemmott, J. Jemmott, K. McCaffree, published by Select Media, Inc. 2003.

3. *Safer Choices: Preventing HIV, Other STD and Pregnancy (Level 1)*, by J. Fetro, R. Barth, K. Coyle, published by ETR Associates, 1998; and *Safer Choices: Preventing HIV, Other STD and Pregnancy (Level 2)*, by K. Coyle and J. Fetro, published by ETR Associates, 1998.

4. *AIDS Prevention for Adolescents in School*, by S. Kasen and I. Tropp, distributed by the Program Archive on Sexuality, Health, and Adolescence (PASHA), 2003.

5. *BART=Becoming a Responsible Teen (Revised Edition)*, by J. Lawrence, published by ETR (Education, Training, Research) Associates, 2005.

6. *Teen Talk: An Adolescent Pregnancy Prevention Program*, by M. Eisen, A. McAlister, G. Zellman, distributed by PASHA, 2003.

7. *Reach for Health, Curriculum, Grade 8*, by L. O'Donnell, et al., by Education Development Center, Inc., 2003.

8. *Making Proud Choices*. L. Jemmott, J. Jemmott, K. McCaffree, published by Select Media, Inc., 2001, 2002.

9. *Positive Images: Teaching Abstinence, Contraception, and Sexual Healthy*, by P. Brick and B. Taverner, published by Planned Parenthood of Greater Northern New Jersey, Inc., 2001.

The curriculum review consisted of four components. First, each curriculum underwent an extensive content analysis, i.e., a word-by-word count of instances in which certain words or themes (e.g., condoms, abstinence) are mentioned. Content analyses offer insight into the weight respective curricula give to key themes. Appendix A contains the complete content analysis for each curriculum reviewed.

Second, the stated purposes of the curricula were compared to the actual emphases of the curricula, as demonstrated by the content analysis.

Third, curriculum content was evaluated for medical accuracy, primarily the accuracy of statements about condoms (including statements on a common spermicide, nonoxynol-9, that was previously recommended to be added to condoms).

Lastly, evaluations of each curriculum—which offer insights into curriculum effectiveness at delaying sexual debut and increasing condom use—were located and summarized.

Appendix B contains a curriculum-by-curriculum review of the each curriculum's content, medical accuracy, and evaluations of each curriculum.

Findings

The curriculum reviews yielded the following findings:

- **Does the content of the curricula mirror their stated purposes?** While the content of the curricula reviewed adheres to their stated purposes for the most part, these curricula often do not spend as much time discussing abstinence as they do discussing contraception and ways to lessen risks of sexual activity. Of the curricula reviewed, the curriculum with the most balanced discussion of abstinence and safer-sex still discussed condoms and contraception nearly seven times more than abstinence. Three of the nine curricula reviewed did not have a stated purpose of promoting abstinence; however, two of these three curricula still discussed abstinence as an option (although, again, discussion of condoms and safer sex predominated). As a last note, it is important to recognize that, although some of the curricula do not include abstinence as a stated purpose, some sexuality information organizations and resources recommend these curricula as comprehensive sex education.

- **What is the content of comprehensive sex education curricula?** As mentioned in the previous paragraph, these curricula focus on contraception and ways to lessen risks of sexual activity, although abstinence is at times a non-trivial component. Curriculum approaches to discussing contraception and ways to lessen risks of sexual activity can be grouped in three broad areas: (1) how to obtain protective devices (e.g., condoms), (2) how to broach a discussion on introducing these devices in a relationship, and (3) how to correctly use the devices. Below are a few excerpts from the curricula in these three areas.

  - **How to obtain protective devices:** "How can you minimize your embarrassment when buying condoms? . . . Take a friend along; find stores where you don't have to ask for condoms (e.g., stocked on open counter or shelf); wear shades or a disguise so no one will recognize you; have a friend or sibling who isn't embarrassed buy them for you; make up a condom request card that you can hand to the store clerk (Show example)" (*AIDS Prevention for Adolescents in School,* p. 63).
  - **How to broach a discussion on introducing these devices in a relationship:** "Teacher states: "Pretend I am your sexual partner. I am going to read more excuses (for not using condoms) and I want you to convince me to use a condom" (*Making Proud Choices,* p. 157).
  - **How to correctly use the devices:** "Have volunteers come to the front of the room (preferably an equal number of males and females). Distribute one card to each. Give them a few minutes to arrange themselves in the proper order so their cards illustrate effective condom use from start to finish. Non-participants observe how the group completes this task and review the final order. When the order is correct, post the cards in the front of the room. CORRECT ORDER: (Sexual Arousal, Erection, Leave Room at the Tip, Roll Condom On, Intercourse, Orgasm/Ejaculation, Hold Onto Rim, Withdraw the Penis, Loss of Erection, Relaxation). Ask a volunteer to describe each step in condom use, using the index and middle finger or a model of a penis" (*Positive Images,* p. 102).

- **Do the curricula contain medically inaccurate statements?** Most comprehensive sex education curricula reviewed contain some level of medical inaccuracy. Of the nine curricula reviewed, three had no medically inaccurate statements. The most common type of medical inaccuracy involved promotion of nonoxynol-9, a common spermicide; three curricula had medical inaccuracies involving nonoxynol-9. While condoms with nonoxynol-9 (N-9) had previously been recommended for reducing the risk of HIV and other STD in the 1990s, research over the last decade has demonstrated that nonoxynol-9 is at best ineffective against STDs and HIV, and at worse increases risk.

Other inaccuracies included: (a) one curriculum that used the term "dental dam" instead of the FDA-approved "rubber dam"; (b) one curriculum that quoted first year condom failure rates for pregnancy at 12%, when the correct statistic is 15%; and (c) one curriculum that stated that all condoms marketed in the United States "meet federal assurance standards" (which is not true).

In terms of inaccurate statistics related to condom effectiveness, eight of the nine curricula did not have any inaccuracies. The one curriculum which did have inaccuracies, *Making Proud Choices,* had three erroneous statements.

Although there were few inaccurate statements regarding condom effectiveness, the curricula do not state the risks of condom failure as extensively as is done in some abstinence-until-marriage curricula, nor do they discuss condom failure rates in context. Indeed, there were misleading statements in every curriculum reviewed. For example, one curriculum states, "When used correctly, latex condoms prevent pregnancy 97% of the time." While this statement is technically true, 15% percent of women using condoms for contraception experience an unintended pregnancy during the first year of "typical use," and 20% of adolescents under the age of 18 using condoms for contraception get pregnant within one year.

For perspective, it may be helpful to compare the error rate reported here with statistics cited in the December 2004 report entitled "The Content of Federally Funded Abstinence Education Programs," which is typically called the Waxman Report. This report found that, of thirteen abstinence-until-marriage curricula reviewed, eleven contained medically inaccurate statements; in all thirteen curricula (nearly 5,000 pages of information), there were 49 instances of questionable information. It could easily be argued that the comprehensive sex education curricula reviewed for this report have a similar rate of error compared with abstinence-until-marriage curricula.

- **Do evaluations of these curricula show them to be effective at (a) delaying sexual debut and (b) reducing sex without condoms?** According to the evaluations reviewed, these curricula show some small positive impacts on (b) reducing sex without condoms, and to a lesser extent (a) delaying sexual debut. Specifically, there were evaluations for eight of the nine curricula reviewed. Of those eight curricula, seven showed at least some positive impacts on condom use; two showed some positive impacts on delay of sexual initiation. One curriculum (*Teen Talk*) showed the only negative impact: for sexually inexperienced females, there was a negative impact on first intercourse and on consistent use of contraceptives. Often the impacts observed in evaluations are small, and most often the impacts do not extend three or six months after a curriculum has been used. It is important to note that evaluations of the curricula do have limitations. All curricula were evaluated by the curriculum authors themselves (although all evaluations were peer-reviewed and published in established journals). Also, the sample sizes are small in some of the evaluations, and research design issues decrease the ability to draw conclusions from some of the evaluations. Appendix B contains details on the evaluations of these curricula.

Conclusion

Research on the effectiveness of nine commonly used comprehensive sex education curricula demonstrates that, while such curricula show small positive impacts on increasing condom use among youth, only a couple of curricula show impacts on delaying sexual debut; moreover, effects most often disappear over time. The fact that both the stated purposes and the actual content of these curricula emphasize ways to lessen risks associated with sexual activity—and not necessarily avoiding sexual activity—may explain why research shows them to be more effective at increasing condom use than at delaying sexual debut. Lastly, although the medical accuracy of comprehensive sex education curricula is nearly 100%—similar to that of abstinence-until-marriage curricula—efforts could be made to more extensively detail condom failure rates in context.

Appendix A: Content Analysis

Provided below is a word-by-word count of the number of times specific words or themes appears in each of the reviewed curricula.

RTR = Reducing the Risk
Be Proud = Be Proud, Be Responsible
SC1 = Safer Choices 1
SC2 = Safer Choices 2
AIDS = AIDS Prevention for Adolescents in School
BART = Becoming A Responsible Teen
Teen Talk
Reach = Reach for Health
MPC = Making Proud Choices
PI = Positive Images

	RTR	Be Proud	SC 1	SC 2	AIDS	BART	Teen Talk	Reach	MPC	PI
100% safe/effective	4	22	7	1	4	0	5	12	1	7
abortion/termination/ interruption	1	0	0	1	0	0	8	0	0	18
abstinence/abstain	90	50	5	5	0	19	32	15	18	87
alcohol	3	14	2	3	5	12	2	0	18	21
alternatives to sexual intercourse	45	10	64	40	1	7	0	5	12	16
anal sex	11	33	10	2	4	16	0	1	57	8
avoid/avoiding (behaviors/consequences)	20	9	24	1	0	14	11	9	42	18
birth control	27	5	25	25	9	5	58	10	37	37
boyfriend (s)	24	13	1	3	11	8	2	11	23	7

(continued)

	RTR	Be Proud	SC 1	SC 2	AIDS	BART	Teen Talk	Reach	MPC	PI
casual sex	0	0	0	0	0	0	0	0	0	0
cervical cap	0	0	1	0	0	0	8	0	5	15
chlamydia	5	0	16	7	1	0	5	2	6	1
committed relationship	0	2	0	0	0	1	0	1	0	1
condom/contraceptive failure	1	3	5	5	0	0	0	0	2	7
condom/condoms	183	495	383	389	136	262	22	8	650	235
contraception/contraceptive	18	3	31	38	2	0	131	3	39	381
diaphragm	0	0	3	2	0	0	31	0	7	26
douche/douching	8	0	11	10	0	0	14	5	10	2
Drug/drugs	32	58	20	8	36	45	2	2	81	75
ejaculate (tion, s, ed, "cum")	6	14	10	11	0	5	9	18	24	12
emotional (consequences)	2	0	0	0	0	0	1	2	1	0
erection (erect)	1	12	9	9	3	0	8	7	15	19
fantasy (ies, ize)	0	3	0	0	0	0	2	9	5	0
French kissing	2	1	1	0	0	0	0	0	1	1
fun (of sex)	0	24	0	1	0	0	0	0	19	0
genital warts/warts	1	0	8	4	0	0	6	1	11	1
girlfriend	31	13	3	3	6	8	3	6	24	3
gonorrhea	5	1	16	7	2	0	12	3	20	2
health/healthy	27	39	58	60	16	72	77	54	35	180
healthier/healthiest	2	2	0	0	0	1	0	1	3	1
Herpes	4	1	15	6	0	0	20	5	18	1
HIV/AIDS	451	477	369	253	28	473	20	7	210	48
IUD	0	0	4	6	0	0	0	0	0	5
kiss, kissing, kissed, kisses	29	30	15	14	2	8	0	4	33	6
love, loved, loves	51	9	35	19	6	16	0	14	22	14
lovers	1	1	0	0	0	0	0	0	1	1
making love (love making)	0	0	1	1	0	0	0	0	1	1
marriage	3	0	4	1	0	0	0	1	0	9
marry, married	3	0	0	5	1	0	4	0	0	4
masturbation, masturbate	4	5	0	0	0	3	8	2	9	13
masturbation: mutual/ partner	1	2	0	0	0	0	1	0	3	0
maximum protection	0	1	0	0	0	0	0	0	0	0
morning after pill (emergency contraception)	0	0	6	12	0	0	1	0	0	24
negative, negatively, (ism)	2	18	12	27	6	10	4	22	14	18

	RTR	Be Proud	SC 1	SC 2	AIDS	BART	Teen Talk	Reach	MPC	PI
negotiation (to use condoms)	1	37	4	1	14	35	1	0	52	1
no risk	0	0	0	0	0	2	0	0	3	1
not having sex	8	0	7	7	7	1	2	3	0	0
oral sex	10	36	9	2	3	13	0	2	73	4
orgasm	1	15	0	0	0	0	6	1	8	11
outercourse	0	2	0	0	0	0	0	0	0	13
parents/parenthood	104	0	97	118	5	34	11	13	13	65
pill (contraceptive)	45	13	37	35	7	4	27	3	31	59
pleasure, able, ing (re: sex)	0	31	2	1	1	0	3	3	8	8
practice (s, ed, ing) (techniques, skills, using condoms)	2	5	13	14	0	6	19	47	70	20
pregnant, pregnancy	348	30	167	242	3	8	155	113	184	241
prophylactics	1	0	1	1	0	0	2	0	0	0
protect (s, ed), protection	254	25	314	145	7	24	7	20	82	80
protective (products)	1	10	6	0	0	0	0	0	0	1
purchasing (buying) condoms	2	6	11	12	8	10	4	0	12	5
rape	0	1	0	0	0	0	0	0	2	3
rape: date	0	0	0	0	0	0	0	0	2	1
refuse, refusal (skills)/ delaying sex tactics	110	11	84	76	1	13	2	48	46	0
reproductive, reproduction	0	0	5	4	0	0	33	18	2	80
risk reduction	0	0	0	1	0	2	0	0	3	0
risk (high)	4	4	0	0	4	5	4	0	5	3
risk (low, lower)	1	0	0	0	0	1	1	0	1	2
risk, risks, risking	273	166	133	112	32	149	31	38	118	140
riskier	0	0	0	0	0	2	0	0	0	0
risky	8	25	9	5	21	42	2	2	18	2
rubber (s)	8	3	2	2	0	5	24	0	4	4
safe, safely	11	41	8	7	3	67	8	4	40	12
safer	0	74	297	345	2	55	0	0	61	38
safest	6	1	45	26	2	0	1	0	1	0
sex	290	334	442	287	64	168	91	168	440	83
sexual	71	152	106	81	101	94	78	116	146	232
intercourse (sexual)	46	47	81	46	77	23	22	28	58	237

(continued)

	RTR	Be Proud	SC 1	SC 2	AIDS	BART	Teen Talk	Reach	MPC	PI
sexual orientation (gay, lesbian, homosexual, same sex)	5	19	7	2	0	6	1	2	9	13
sexuality	18	0	17	19	1	3	32	115	1	98
sexually	47	46	18	23	11	33	38	49	60	85
sexy	2	1	0	1	1	0	0	4	2	0
spermicide (s, dal)	14	11	35	19	4	15	25	4	43	23
sponge	0	0	0	0	0	0	4	0	0	28
STD (s)	230	44	221	178	2	8	47	77	281	2
STI	0	0	0	0	0	0	0	0	0	64
syphilis	0	2	15	4	2	0	12	0	17	1
unprotected sex/intercourse	54	26	43	0	0	23	13	8	30	5
contraceptive film	3	0	6	5	0	0	0	0	6	4
venereal disease (VD)	0	0	0	0	0	0	3	0	0	0
withdrawal (withdraws, pull out)	10	3	12	0	0	6	9	4	13	17

Elokin CaPece  **NO**

Commentary on the *Review of Comprehensive Sex Education Curricula* (2007)

In the last several years research on the effectiveness of sex education programs that target preteens and teens has evolved into a very sophisticated and professional discourse. In 2002, a review of 73 studies of programs (including but not limited to comprehensive sex education programs) pulled out a set of characteristics that were found in programs that reduced sexual risk-taking, promoted condom use, and/or delayed sexual onset. These programs focused on behaviors that prevented unintended pregnancy or sexually transmitted infection (including HIV), utilized already-established practices for reducing risk-taking behaviors, gave a clear message that emphasized the prevention behaviors and frequently reinforced that message, provided basic and accurate information, included modeling, role-playing, and refusal skills practice, employed a high degree of student participation in a wide range of educational styles, were tailored to the age, culture, and sexual experience of their audience, lasted a sufficient length of time, and were taught by facilitators who had adequate training and believed in the program's effectiveness. This same review attempted to include abstinence-only program studies in its analysis but found that only three published studies met the criteria for his review and two of these had "important methodological limitations." The article did not make any claims about the effectiveness or ineffectiveness of such programs (due to the lack of reliable research and the wide variance in program formats), but concluded that the characteristics found common in effective comprehensive sex education programs should be considered best practices for abstinence-only programs of comparable design as well (Kirby, 2002, 51–54).

In 2004 a federally funded and commissioned review of 13 abstinence-only curricula (representing two-thirds of the programs funded by abstinence-only federal money at the time of the review), commonly known as the Waxman Report, found that 80% of the curricular material reviewed contained "false, misleading, or distorted information about reproductive health (United States House of Representatives Committee on Government Reform [United States Committee on Govt. Reform], 2004, i)." The most common inaccuracies were an exaggeration of contraceptive failure rates, inaccurate information

From *American Journal of Sexuality Education*, by Elokin CaPece, vol. 3, no. 3, September 2008, pp. 295–312. Copyright © 2008 by Routledge/Taylor & Francis Group. Reprinted by permission.

about the risks of abortion, the stating of religious belief as scientific fact, the treatment of gender role stereotypes as scientific fact, and general scientific errors (United States Committee on Govt. Reform, 2004, i–ii).

In 2007 Mathematica Policy, Inc. released a study of four federally funded abstinence-only programs. These programs were chosen because they represented the wide range of types of educational programming that fell under the banner of abstinence-only and because they served rural and urban communities in every region of the United States The report found that these programs had just as much of an impact on teens as no sex education programming at all had. Teens in the abstinence-only programs behaved in statistically similar ways to teens in the control group (who were receiving no sex education programming) (Mathematica Policy Research, 2007, 59–60).

These reviews represent the macro-level of sex education research. On the micro-level there are individual program evaluations, the quality of which has been transformed in the last ten years. In 1997 SIECUS published a manual written by researchers critiquing the research done on sex education programs as poorly designed, weakly implemented, and not well funded (Haffner & Goldfarb, 1997, 4). In 2002 Doug Kirby noted that while very few program evaluations had experimental or quasi-experimental designs and rarely were evaluations replicated in the late 1990s, by 2000 he had enough well-researched material to examine comprehensive sex education programs, reproductive health clinic services, service learning programs, and Children's Aid Society Carrera programs (Kirby, 2002). Today, the research standards put forth by SIECUS influence how many sex education programs are designed, implemented, and evaluated.

Background Information on the 2007 Comprehensive Sex Education Review

The 2007 *Review of Comprehensive Sex Education Curricula* was commissioned by Rick Santorum, former United States senator from Pennsylvania and Tom Coburn, United States senator from Oklahoma and conducted by The Administration for Children and Families (ACF) and The Department of Health and Human Services (HHS). Like the 2003 Waxman Report (commissioned by Representative Henry Waxman from California), the new report was commissioned with the intention of helping political leaders make informed decisions about sex education funding. Nine curricula were reviewed, and they were chosen by the "frequency and strength of endorsement" by sexuality and sexual health organizations (The Administration for Children and Families [ACF] & The Department of Health and Human Services [HHS], 2007, 4). These curricula were evaluated for four criteria: whether the content mirrored the curricula's stated purpose, the content itself, whether the content was medically accurate, and whether evaluations of these curricula demonstrated that they were effective at delaying sexual onset and reducing sex without condoms (ACF & HHS, 2007, 4). [See Table 1 at the end of this section for a list of the reviewed curricula.]

The remaining sections of this article will focus on the content of the review (and its appendices), specifically looking at instances of clear and interfering bias, the use of research methodologies that are not in line with presented findings, inappropriately critical benchmarks for failure, and inaccurate referencing of outside works.

Table 1

Curricula Reviewed in the 2007 Review

Title	Author	Year
Reducing the Risk: Building Skills to Prevent Pregnancy, STD, & HIV (4th Edition)	R. Barth	2004
Be Proud! Be Responsible!	L. S. Jemmott & J. B. Jemmott	2003
Safer Choices: Preventing HIV, Other STD and Pregnancy (Level 1 & Level 2)	J. Fetro, R. Barth, K. Coyle	1998
AIDS Prevention for Adolescents in School	S. Kasen & I. Troop	2003
BART = Becoming a Responsible Teen (Revised Edition)	J. Lawrence	2005
Teen Talk: An Adolescent Pregnancy Prevention Program	M. Eisen, A. McAlister, G. Zellman	2003
Reach for Health Curriculum, Grade 8	L. O'Donnell, et al.	2003
Making Proud Choices	L. Jemmott, J. Jemmott, K. McCaffree	2002
Positive Images: Teaching Abstinence, Contraception, and Sexual Health	P. Brick & B. Taverner	2001

Clear and Interfering Bias

The first criterion used to evaluate the selected comprehensive sex education curricula highlighted whether or not these curricula do what they say they will. The content of each of the curricula was compared to that curriculum's stated objectives. In several places the authors express dissatisfaction with their own measure primarily because that measure privileges ideologies they hold a bias against. Right off the bat the authors issue a warning that most of the curricula do not claim to be abstinence-based or to exclusively privilege abstinence over other safe sex practices (ACF & HHS, 2007, 4). This does not stop them from later critiquing the examined curricula for just that. They gloss over their stated measure (whether the curricula content mirrors its purpose) in favor of discussing an underlying measure:

> While the content of the curricula reviewed adheres to their stated purposes for the most part, these curricula do not spend as much time discussing abstinence as they do discussing contraception and ways to

lessen sexual activity . . . As a last note, it is important to realize that, although some of the curricula do not include abstinence as a stated purpose, some sexuality information organizations and resources recommend these curricula as comprehensive sex education (ACF & HHS, 2007, 6).

This is one place where the clear bias of the authors (toward curricula that privilege abstinence exclusively over other forms of contraception) interfered with their stated goals. If you set out to measure whether a curriculum stuck to its stated purposes, and it did, then that's a passing measurement.

A second place where clear and interfering bias presented itself was in the content section of the review. Incredibly, the content analysis for all nine curricula could be summed up in four paragraphs, all of which were related to condom use. In the section that is supposed to describe the content of the curricula, there is no discussion of abstinence, other forms of contraception, STIs, HIV, or healthy relationship programming. Instead, the authors explain that "these curricula focus on contraception and ways to lessen risks of sexual activity," then that is boiled down to three main foci: how to get condoms, how to integrate condom use into a relationship, and how to use condoms. The three subsequent paragraphs are excerpts from curricula in these three main areas. All in all, the section succeeded in likening the promotion of condom use with the marketing of cigarettes to children (ACF & HHS, 2007, 6–7).

A third place where bias creeps into the review is in the section on medical inaccuracy. In the section on condom failure rates a curriculum that uses a correct statistic on the failure rate of a condom with perfect use is considered "misleading":

> Indeed, there were misleading statements in every curriculum reviewed. For example, one curriculum states, "When used correctly, latex condoms prevent pregnancy 97% of the time." While this statement is technically true, 15% percent [sic] of women using condoms for contraception experience an unintended pregnancy during the first year of "typical use" and 20% of adolescents under the age of 18 using condoms for contraception get pregnant within one year. (ACF & HHS, 2007, 7–8)

The curriculum excerpt they chose for this part of the medical inaccuracy section is . . . accurate. According to *The Essentials of Contraceptive Technology,* 1997 [which they would have been using for their failure rates in *Safer Choices* (1998)] condoms do have a 3% failure rate with perfect use (Hatcher, 1997, 4–19). In addition, they quote *Contraceptive Technology* (2005)'s rate for "typical use" (which is clearly different from perfect use) and then throw in a statistic from a longitudinal study from 1986 (ACF & HHS, 2007, 7–8). While a longitudinal study is a great place to see a "typical use" rate in action, the authors are clearly comparing apples to oranges in a biased fishing expedition to find medical inaccuracies.

Use of Research Methodologies That Do Not Match Their Findings

The first two research questions use evidence from a keyword content analysis. The keywords used in the content analysis and how often they were found in each of the curricula are provided for the reader (ACF & HHS, 2007, 10–12). The content analysis is a valid methodology in sociology, provided it is done properly and that it only generates findings that are within its limits. According to Bernard Berelson, content analysis can be used to compare the content of communication to specific objectives, construct and apply communication standards, make assumptions about the intentions and/or beliefs of the communicators, and to reveal the focus of attention in a communication (Krippendorff, 2003, 44–47). That said, it is easy to see the difference between a methodologically sound content analysis and the content analysis in the 2007 Review.

The 2007 review was chiefly concerned with the treatment of abstinence in sex education curricula and, specifically, whether it got more time and was privileged over other sex risk-reduction strategies:

> While the content of the curricula reviewed adheres to their stated purposes for the most part, these curricula do not spend as much time discussing abstinence as they do discussing contraception and ways to lessen sexual activity (ACF & HHS, 2007, 6).

This assertion, that the studied curricula do not contain as much information about abstinence as they do about contraception is supported by the key word content analysis:

> The content analysis counted words used in each curriculum. Of the words counted, variations on the word "condom" occurred 235 times and variations on the word "contraception" occurred 381 times, while variations on the word "abstinence" occurred 87 times (ACF & HHS, 2007, 6, in footnote).

While content analysis can be used to highlight the focus of a communication, the construction of the analytical tool is critical for usable results. The 2007 review content analysis tool was designed in such a way that it could not help but indicate that condoms/contraceptives were more discussed than abstinence. A breakdown of the keywords used with attention placed on what would count as an "abstinence reference" versus a "condom/contraceptive reference" reveals:

- 21 keywords explicitly related to condoms/contraceptives
- 2 keywords explicitly related to abstinence
- 8 keywords were ambiguous but could have been tied to one or the other
- 3 keywords were conversation descriptors were condoms were designated as the subject (for example: "negotiation (to use condoms)"
- 0 keywords had abstinence designated as the subject (ACF & HHS, 2007, 10–12)

The keywords notably did their own injustice to abstinence by not looking for it in as many ways as they looked for condoms. There was the keyword
"negotiation (to use condoms)" but not "negotiation (to abstain from sex)",
and similarly "practice (s, ed, ing) (techniques, skills, using condoms)" but no
"practice (s, ed, ing) (techniques and skills for abstaining)".

That said, even if the keyword search had been carefully designed to
balance abstinence and condom terminology, it still would not have been an
appropriate assessment tool for curricula. When looking at teaching tools, it
is important to remember that often the themes and "take home" messages in
a lesson are not completely spelled out. One example of this can be found in
Positive Images, one of the reviewed curricula. In a lesson titled "Choices and
Consequences", this scenario is described:

> Jerome's family has strong values, including the belief that intercourse
> should be saved for marriage. Jerome respects both his parents and his
> religion (Brick & Taverner, 2001, 51–56).

This scenario is part of an activity where students are urged to advise
Jerome on the contraceptive option best for him where the best answer is
clearly abstinence. Activities like this get no acknowledgement as abstinence-
promoting lessons when content analysis is used. Often in educational tools the
use of a word in a lesson plan is not nearly as effective as the use of a theme.
The measurement tool did not take into account the language and treatment
of abstinence in comprehensive sex education before trying to measure it.
With this measuring tool, there was no way abstinence would have come out
ahead.

Inappropriately Critical Benchmarks For Failure

It is obvious from the tone of the review that the authors were looking
for their chosen curricula to fail. Frequently in an effort to achieve that
goal the article contains inappropriately critical benchmarks for failure.
The main place this occurs is in the section on medical inaccuracies. This
section starts out with the sentence, "Most comprehensive sex education
curricula reviewed contain some level of medical inaccuracy (ACF & HHS,
2007, 7)." From there they break down exactly which curricula contained
what inaccuracies:

- One-third of the curricula contained no medical inaccuracies.
- One-third of the curricula had errors in their discussion of nonoxyl-9
  (N-9).
- One of the curricula called a "rubber dam" a "dental dam". This curriculum was one of the three with an N-9 error.
- In the last one-third (the 3 that had "medical inaccuracies", but none
  related to N-9), one was a 1998 curriculum whose condom failure rate
  did not match the rate quoted in *Contraceptive Technology* 2006, and
  the other (which they footnoted as *Positive Choices* but which they
  corrected in their appendix as *Positive Images*) was quoted as saying

that all condoms marketed in the United States today meet federal quality standards.
- Eight out of the 9 curricula did not contain incorrect condom failure rates. The one that the reviewers cited as having an incorrect rate was a 1998 curriculum compared to a 2006 failure rate (ACF & HHS, 2007, 7–8).

Some of these "medical inaccuracies" are themselves inaccurate. "Dental dam" is an acceptable name for a "rubber dam" and is used by both health educators and contraceptive suppliers. One of the most popular "rubber dam" products in the United States, the Trustex/LIXX Dental Dam, has "dental dam" on the box (Total Access Group, 2005–2006, 1, 9). Another "medical inaccuracy" that can be dismissed is the erroneous condom failure rate in *Safer Choices* (1998). A curriculum can only be expected to be accurate according to the information available at least a year before its release, so *Safer Choices* statistics should only be compared with the condom statistics available in 1997 or before. In *The Essentials of Contraceptive Technology* (1997), which is the correct reference for this curriculum, the statistic is 14%, so *Safer Choices* was off by one, but so was the Review (Hatcher, 1997, 4–19).

When these are dismissed, 4 out of 9 of the curricula have one medical inaccuracy each. Those involving nonoxynol-9 are serious, but as they involve developing research on the subject that was not confirmed by the CDC until 2002 (and even then this confirmation only led to a recommendation to no longer purchase N-9 products) this does not constitute what the authors cite as a "serious medical error" (Centers for Disease Control and Prevention [CDC], 2002, 3–4; ACF & HHS, 2007, 18). This also does not take into account the live teaching of these curricula by trained professionals. It is reasonable to assume that, when reproductive health care clinics were advised to use up their stores of N-9 condoms and then stop purchasing more, that reproductive health educators would either omit or modify the N-9 phrase in their curricula to the new guidelines (CDC, 2002, 3–4). This leaves *Positive Images,* which states that all condoms marketed in the United States are federally approved. Though there are products marketed as condoms that are not federally approved for pregnancy and disease prevention (e.g. condoms made of lambskin), the majority of condoms readily available to the general public, even those with novelty enhancements, do follow FDA guidelines for pregnancy and disease prevention. Again, this is another instance where it can be assumed a trained curriculum implementer would elaborate based on knowledge and experience. That said, it is uncertain whether condom product sales can even count as "medical inaccuracy."

When critically examined, 5 out of the 9 curricula had no reasonable medical inaccuracies, and 4 of the 9 had one to two sentences of technical inaccuracy, medical or otherwise, in their entire content. Compared to textbooks on other subjects geared towards middle and high school age American children, this is an amazing level of accuracy (for common inaccuracies in middle and high school textbooks see Beaty, 2007; Loewen, 1996).

Medical inaccuracies were addressed in the appendices as well, and there "inaccuracy" was expanded to include content excerpts that did not make it into the executive summary findings. The appendix entry for *Reducing the Risk* was an excellent example of this. It had three quotes from the curriculum on condom failure rates. Two of the three stated that when condoms were used "correctly and consistently" or "correctly . . . every time a couple has sex" they "provide good protection" or "work almost all of the time" (ACF & HHS, 2007, 14–15). The authors followed the quotes with the statement that, "'Good', 'almost all the time', and 'very effective' are subjective terms (ACF & HHS, 2007, 15)." Even with an explicit reference to perfect use and admittance that condoms were not 100% safe or effective, these descriptors were still picked out for failure. The third quote stated that condoms were "very effective" at preventing STI transmission, including "gonorrhea, Chlamydia and trichomoniasis", but they added that "further studies are being done in this area (ACF & HHS, 2007, 14)." Even after the caveat, the authors criticized this quote for not acknowledging a specific 2001 study that did not find enough evidence to claim that condoms reduced trichomoniasis risk (ACF & HHS, 2007, 15). All of this fell under a statement claiming that these quotes "did not provide explicit details of condom failure rates". When reading a review, one assumes that quotes pulled from the text are the best representation in that text of the subject under discussion. However, someone reading this who was unfamiliar with *Reducing the Risk* would have no idea that the curriculum has a whole appendix dedicated to the subject of "Condom Use Effectiveness" (Barth, 2004, 23–24). These extremely critical benchmarks appear in every curriculum entry in the appendix. In *Reach for Health* (2003), a quote giving an incidence rate for HPV was deemed inaccurate because it did not match a report that came out in 2004, a *year after it* (ACF & HHS, 2007, 32).

Inappropriately critical benchmarks for failure went beyond the medical inaccuracies sections. The first two research questions, 1) comparing curriculum content to its stated purpose and 2) examining the content on its own, both contained failure language because the curricula did not place enough of an emphasis on abstinence. From the language, "enough of an emphasis" for the authors was at least more content on abstinence than on contraceptive methods. As discussed in the section on methodology, it is inappropriate to consider the content of these curricula as inadequate solely from the results of the keyword content analysis.

The final research question, whether evaluations of the curricula demonstrated that they were effective at delaying sexual onset and increasing condom use, also suffered from inappropriately critical analysis. This section also only merited one paragraph, which started with a summary of the research findings:

> According to the evaluations reviewed, these curricula show some small positive impacts on (b) reducing sex without condoms and to a lesser extent (a) delaying sexual debut (ACF & HHS, 2007, 8).

According to their appendices, here is a breakdown of the reviewed research results for the 8 curricula that had research:

- 6 out of the 8 had positive impacts at their first review
- 4 out of 8 had one or more subsequent reviews

- 4 out of the 4 with subsequently reviews still had positive impacts (though 2 of the 4 had greatly diminished impacts at the time of second review)
- 2 of the 8 had positive impacts on delaying sexual initiation
- 6 of the 8 had positive impacts on condom use (ACF & HHS, 2007, 10–40)

Left out of this analysis was the range of other risky behaviors that many of these curricula were shown to reduce, including number of sexual partners, frequency of sex, and increased knowledge about contraceptives and HIV (ACF & HHS, 2007, 13–40). The authors summarized these impacts as "often . . . small, and most often the impacts do not extend three or sex months after a curriculum has been used," though they immediately footnoted that with examples of 2 curricula that had demonstrated positive impacts after three months (of which there were four) and neglected to note that only 4 of the curricula studied had subsequent studies (which means that it is impossible to say that the remaining 5 out of 9 did not have enduring impacts) (ACF & HHS, 2007, 8). They followed up with a comment on the limitations of the research, specifically that "all curricula were evaluated by the authors themselves (ACF & HHS, 2007, 8)." This makes it sound like all of the evaluations were done only by the authors, when the reality was much more complex:

- 4 out of 8 only had research that was solely conducted by one or more of the authors
- 3 out of 8 had research that was conducted by one or more of the authors plus one or more independent researchers
- 2 out of 8 had at least one published research study conducted solely by independent researchers
- 4 out of 8 had research where independent researchers were represented either in a study collaborating with one or more of the authors or in a study without an author on the research team (ACF & HHS, 2007, 10–40)

A detailed look at their appendices revealed that at least half of the curricula had some sort of outside input in the research, and one-fourth had at least one study conducted by a completely unaffiliated research team (with "affiliated" meaning they were not a part of the curriculum's design). To represent this with the phrase "conducted by the curriculum's author", which appears in some permutation in every appendix with a research section, is inappropriately critical, not to mention misleading and technically inaccurate. Furthermore, it is important to note that having a curriculum designer on its research team, or having a researcher on a curriculum design team, is not necessarily a bad thing. Sex education curricula benefit when researchers are on board in the design phase to make sure they reflect current best practices, and research on sex education benefits when curriculum designers work with researchers to ensure that all of the curriculum's target behavior goals are measured.

All-in-all, every section of the review contained some example of inappropriately critical benchmarks for failure. But while the reviewers apparently went through selected portions of each curriculum with a fine tooth comb, their reading of outside sources was not as detailed.

Inaccurate Referencing of Outside Works

Often in the 2007 Review outside sources were brought in to prove the inaccuracy of the studied curricula. The bringing in of outside sources also went hand-in-hand with inaccurate referencing. Take this excerpt from the section on medical inaccuracy:

> For example, once curriculum states, "When used correctly, latex condoms prevent pregnancy 97% of the time." While this statement is technically true, 15% of women using condoms for contraception experience an unintended pregnancy during the first year of "typical use" and about 20% of adolescents under the age of 18 using condoms for contraception get pregnant within one year (ACF & HHS, 2007, 7–8).

Contraceptive technology has always used two measures to capture how effective contraceptive methods are in real-life situations: "perfect" and "typical". "Perfect" refers to how effective a particular method is when that method is employed consistently and correctly. "Typical" refers to how effective that method is when it is employed inconsistently or when user-error is taken into account (Hatcher, 2004, 225–228). "When used correctly" or "When used correctly and consistently" are reasonably clear and accurate ways to explain "perfect use" statistics to preteens and teens according to the Centers for Disease Control (CDC, 2003, 2). Proving a "perfect use" statistic wrong with a "typical use" statistic, especially in a context when the potential condom users are being taught how to use condoms correctly and how to obtain them consistently (and thus prepared to be "perfect" users) is both an instance of inaccurate referencing and an inappropriately critical benchmark for failure.

A second instance of inaccurate referencing compared the "medical inaccuracies" of selected comprehensive sex education curricula found in the 2007 Review with those found in selected abstinence-only curricula in the 2004 Waxman Report:

> For perspective, it may be helpful to compare the error rate reported here with statistics cited in the December 2004 report entitled "The Content of Federally Funded Abstinence Education Programs," which is typically called the Waxman Report. This report found that, of the thirteen abstinence-until-marriage curricula reviewed, eleven contained medically inaccurate statements; in all thirteen curricula, (nearly 5,000 pages of information), there were 49 instances of questionable information. It could easily be argued that the comprehensive sex education curricula reviewed for this report have a similar rate of error compared with abstinence-until-marriage curricula (ACF & HHS, 2007, 8).

This reference to the 2004 Waxman Report is brought up again in the conclusion:

> Lastly, although the medical accuracy of comprehensive sex education curricula is nearly 100%—similar to that of abstinence-until-marriage curricula—efforts could be made to more extensively detail condom failure rates in context (ACF & HHS, 2007, 9).

At the beginning of this article, the 2004 Waxman Report itself was quoted stating that 80% of the curricular material reviewed contained "false, misleading, or distorted information about reproductive health (United States House of Representatives Committee on Govt. Reform, 2004, i). These quotes ignore the fundamental differences in the quality and quantity of errors found in the Waxman Report versus the 2007 Review. These quality and quantity differences can be broken down into several categories:

- **Quantity:** The inaccuracies cited in the 2007 Review curricula were one to two sentences at most, while the inaccuracies cited in the Waxman Report were often whole blocks of text or reoccurring themes in the text (ACF & HHS, 2007, 7–8; United States House of Representatives Committee on Govt. Reform, 2004, 8–22).
- **Reference Use:** In the 2007 Review curricula, inaccuracies in the curricula were either instances where the reviewers were not satisfied with specific phrasing or where statistics and details did not match current research either because the research was published right at or after the curriculum, or because the body of research had still not come to a satisfactory consensus. In the Waxman Report, inaccuracies were consistently defended with research that was either extremely outdated or rejected by federal bodies at large (ACF & HHS, 2007, 7–8; United States House of Representatives Committee on Govt. Reform, 2004, 8–22).
- **Ability of Implementer to Circumvent:** The inaccuracies in the 2007 Review curricula were the types of errors that could be corrected by a trained professional implementer (for example: when studies consistently showed that N-9 was ineffective, a trained implementer could easily leave out N-9 info or give updated, correct information for N-9). While some of the inaccuracies of the Waxman Report were of that type, most were thematic, making them impossible for a trained implementer to completely eliminate (for example, repeated emphasis on exaggerated condom failure rates throughout curricular materials in statistics, phrasing, and activities) (ACF & HHS, 2007, 7–8; United States House of Representatives Committee on Govt. Reform, 2004, 8–22).

Any assumption of similarity between the reviewed abstinence-only curricula and the reviewed comprehensive sex education curricula is, at best, wishful thinking on behalf of those who wish to debunk comprehensive sex education. Of the six inaccuracies cited in the 2007 Review's executive summary, three were N-9 statements (one to two sentences) that reflected the research at the time of publication (where the curricula was a few years old or N-9 statements were still not conclusive across the body of research), one was the use of manufacturer and layman terminology instead of FDA terminology, one was a condom failure rate that was correct when compared with a referent published before the curriculum, and one was a condom accessibility statement that could easily be corrected by the implementer. In addition, there were several instances of phrasing and statistic use around condom failure rates that were technically correct and used CDC-approved language about condom effectiveness, but that the authors took issue with.

The errors found by the Waxman Report for abstinence-only curricula were fundamentally different. The treatment of condom use is an excellent example of this fundamental difference. Studied abstinence-only curricula consistently used a 1993 study (commonly referred to as the Weller Study) which was rejected by the Department of Health and Human Services in 1997. Of the studied curricula, only one was put out at a time where use of the Weller Study might have been acceptable (*Sex Can Wait,* published in 1997). Even so, the Weller Study was a poor reference for condom failure rates when compared with the primarily used and endorsed *Contraceptive Technology,* which was available before 1997. Several abstinence-only curricula had activities which explicitly taught students that condoms did not work and had holes big enough for STIs to pass through. Many included erroneous research that STI rates have not fallen as condom use rates rose. STI risks were exaggerated in many curricula alongside exaggerated condom failure rates (United States House of Representatives Committee on Govt. Reform, 2004, 8–11, 21). For pregnancy prevention, curricula confused "perfect" and "typical" use and had activities designed to convince preteens and teens that condoms do not work to prevent pregnancy. Some have gender role lessons that imply that contraceptive use is a man's decision and that if women make demands in relationships (contraceptive demands included) that they will lose their partners (United States House of Representatives Committee on Govt. Reform, 2004, 11–12, 17–18). These types of errors were designed to scare teens to abstinence, but as a consequence create a dangerous false consciousness about condoms and contraceptive use in relationships that is too pervasive for an implementer to single-handedly correct.

In light of a careful reading of the 2007 Review and the 2004 Waxman Report, any comparison between the results of the two is both inaccurate and misleading. Abstinence-only programs benefit from their counterparts' exceptional performance in terms of medical accuracy. Comprehensive sex education programs are pulled down by the assumption that they are "similar to that of 'abstinence-until-marriage curricula'" (ACF & HHS, 2007, 9).

Conclusion

The 2007 *Review of Comprehensive Sex Education Curricula* was a timely addition to the current sex education discourse. As such, the Review garnered press attention and its conclusions were put out to the public at large. But the real impact of this study was not the attention it received from the press, but the ability it gave to supporters of abstinence-only education to say that comprehensive sex education did not work. One example of this comes from Project

Reality, a publishing company that puts out two abstinence-only curricula, *A.C. Green's Game Play* and *Navigator,* both products which received negative reviews in the Waxman Report. Project Reality covered the 2007 Review's release, and has a handy fact sheet to help people browsing its website understand the findings of the Review. Its summary of the "overall findings of interest" included:

> Of the curricula reviewed, the curriculum with the most balanced discussion of abstinence and safer sex still discussed condoms and contraception nearly **seven times more than abstinence.** (their emphasis)
>
> Every curricula reviewed contained misleading statements about condom effectiveness—leading teens to believe condoms are more effective than they actually are.
>
> All curricula were evaluated by the program authors themselves.
>
> **Seven of the nine curricula reviewed instructed and encouraged teens to shop for condoms themselves.** (their emphasis)
>
> **THERE WAS NO REFERENCE IN ANY OF THESE COMPREHENSIVE SEX ED CURRICULA TO THE EMOTIONAL RISKS ASSOCIATED WITH SEXUAL ACTIVITY.** (their emphasis) (Project Reality, 2007)

Irresponsible research on the federal level affects how people on the local level chose what sex education is appropriate for their youth. The 2007 *Review of Comprehensive Sex Education Curricula* is not responsible research for all the reasons stated. The sooner it can be removed from the discourse and replaced with research that is less biased, uses reasonable benchmarks for success and failure, and which appropriately references other works, the better.

POSTSCRIPT

Is There Something Wrong with the Content of Comprehensive Sex Education Curricula?

Organizations supporting abstinence-only-until-marriage (AOUM) programs lauded the government's report and seized on the opportunity to criticize sexuality education. One AOUM-promoting organization, Operation Keepsake, based in Twinsburg, Ohio, complained that the word "abstinence" or "abstain" was mentioned only 321 times in sexuality education curricula, compared to 928 mentions of the word "protection." The conservative group Concerned Women for America responded to the report by calling sex education "Rated X." Most conservative organizations expressed alarm that the words "condoms" and "contraceptives" were mentioned most frequently than abstinence. Several organizations, including the National Abstinence Education Association, responded to the report by taking aim at *Making Sense of Abstinence*, a manual that was not even among those curricula examined. In the spirit of full disclosure, *Making Sense of Abstinence* was coauthored by William J. Taverner, one of the editors of this *Taking Sides* book. (His explanation of his innovative approach to abstinence education is explored in another issue in this book.) A principal objection of *Making Sense of Abstinence* was its discussion of outercourse—kissing and touching behaviors that do not involve the genitals. Taverner is also the coauthor of one of the "curricula" that was examined in the report, *Positive Images: Teaching about Abstinence, Contraception, and Sexual Health*, which is a collection of lessons but not a curriculum at all.

Meanwhile, organizations supporting sexuality education rose to the defense of these programs. The Guttmacher Institute, which publishes the peer-reviewed journal *Perspectives on Sexual and Reproductive Health*, said, "The analysis was poorly conducted and would never pass peer review by an established journal. Its findings should not be viewed or described as a credible or unbiased assessment of the content of sexuality education curricula."

What's your opinion of the content of the sexuality education curricula examined? Did the federal government use appropriate research methods? Which words or concepts, if any, do you think should be excluded from a teenager's sexuality education?

What insights might be gained from examining the words that appear in a curriculum? Is such an examination a reasonable barometer for programs' contents? "HIV" and "AIDS" are words that appeared most frequently in the content analysis, yet the government's report did not comment on this, choosing instead to emphasize the number of times phrases such as "100%

safe" were mentioned compared to "condoms" or "contraceptives." Other frequently cited words that received little attention in the government's descriptive summary were "pregnant" and "pregnancy"; "sex," "sexual," and "sexual intercourse"; and STDs. Why did the report elect not to comment on these frequently mentioned words?

What do you think of the report's description of "medical inaccuracies" contained within sexuality education curricula? Were these legitimate concerns? Was CaPece's critique of the government's critique fair or biased? Were her explanations of the "medical inaccuracies" valid? How might you critique her analysis?

Suggested Readings

T. Coburn, "Study: More 'Condoms' Than 'Abstinence' in Sex Ed," *Washington Times* (June 13, 2007).

J.B. Jemmott et al., "Efficacy of a Theory-Based Abstinence-Only Intervention Over 24 Months: A Randomized Controlled Trial with Young Adolescents," *Archives of Pediatrics & Adolescent Medicine* (vol. 164, no. 2, pp. 152–159, 2010).

D. Kirby, *Emerging Answers 2007: Research Findings on Programs to Reduce Teen Pregnancy and Sexually Transmitted Diseases* (Washington, DC: National Campaign to Prevent Teen and Unplanned Pregnancy, 2007), accessed at http://www.thenc.org./ea2007.

C. Lee, "HHS Counters with Its Own Sex Ed Critique," *Washington Post* (June 21, 2007).

Mathematica Policy Research, Inc., *Impacts of Four Title V, Section 510 Abstinence Education Programs* (Princeton, NJ: Trenholm, 2007).

National Abstinence Education Association, *Straight from the Source: What So-Called Comprehensive Sex Education Teaches to America's Youth* (Washington, D.C.: National Abstinence Education Association, 2007).

E. Schroeder and J. Kuriansky, *Sexuality Education: Past, Present, & Future Issues* (Westport, CT: Greenwood Press, 2009).

B. Taverner and S. Montfort, *Making Sense of Abstinence: Lessons for Comprehensive Sex Education* (Morristown, NJ: Planned Parenthood of Greater Northern New Jersey, 2005).

ISSUE 10

Is There Academic Merit to Students Viewing Live Sexual Acts in College Courses?

YES: **A.M. Rosenthal**, from "Toying with Academic Freedom," an original essay written for this volume (2011)

No: **Cory Silverberg**, from "Thoughts on a Campus Dildo Controversy: Sexuality, Power, and Privilege," http://sexuality.about.com/ (2011)

ISSUE SUMMARY

Yes: A.M. Rosenthal, a doctoral student in clinical psychology, argues for academic freedom and suggests there can be academic merit in viewing live sexual acts in the classroom, provided harm is avoided and the demonstration fulfills course goals.

No: Cory Silverberg, a columnist who writes about sexual topics for About.com, argues that the problems surrounding such live sex demonstrations in the classroom are rooted in issues of sexuality, power, and privilege.

Introduction

The use of sexually explicit materials (SEMs), such as film, videos, images displayed on PowerPoint, explicit passages in literature, etc., is commonplace among professors who teach college and university courses in human sexuality. For example, consider this often-used passage used to teach students the significance of touching:

> It was dusk. The apartment was empty save for the two of them. As they lay entwined in warm embrace, this room, this bed, was the universe. Aside from the faint sound of their tranquil breathing, they were silent. She stroked the nape of his neck. He nuzzled her erect nipple, first gently with his nose, then licked it, tasted, smelled and absorbed her body odor. It was a hot and humid August day, and they had been perspiring. Slowly he caressed her one breast as he softly rolled his face over the contour of the other. He pressed his body close against her, sighed, and fully spent, closed his eyes and soon fell into a deep satisfying sleep. Ever so slowly she slipped herself out from under him lest she disturb him, cradled him in her arms, and moved him to his crib. Having completed

his six o'clock feeding, the four-month-old had also experienced one more minute contribution to his further sexual development.[1]

A professor might read this passage to elicit a response from students, knowing that they might initially imagine the characters in the story differently. The pedagogical purpose of reading such a passage would be to use students' surprise to help them recognize the importance of touch throughout the life.

Professors may use sexually explicit film, videos, and images as educational triggers to achieve a variety of pedagogical goals. A professor might, for instance, display pictures with varying degrees of nudity or sexual activity in order to help students understand the subjective nature of "pornography" and "erotica." Or, instructors may carefully select films that depict a couple taking their time during sexual response, which can help students understand that sex need not be rushed. Films that show older adults engaged in sexual activity can help students recognize that sex isn't only for the young, while also demonstrating how sexual activity may be experienced differently as one grows older. A video showing a *real* lesbian couple can be contrasted with lesbian porn that is made for the entertainment of heterosexual male viewers. Some films and videos show people who are usually not portrayed in sexual films (such as persons with disabilities) or behaviors that are not well understood (such as BDSM).

SEMs have been used in college courses for decades, with a number of films made specifically for sexuality education, such as those produced by Focus International, the Sinclair Institute, and a library of sexual films used in academia housed at http://www.sexsmartfilms.com. In all cases, it is incumbent upon the instructor to have a specific education purpose for using the SEM.

In early 2011, J. Michael Bailey, a professor of human sexuality at Northwestern University, came under fire after students in his class observed a live demonstration of a sex toy. In front of the class, two people used a "fucksaw," which was more euphemistically referred to as a "reciprocating saw" in the national media attention that immediately followed. The toy used is a dildo attached to a drill-like device, which results in rapid and intense stimulation of the person penetrated.

In the following essays, A.M. Rosenthal, a doctoral student whose advisor is Dr. Bailey, gives a firsthand account of the events that unfolded and argues for academic freedom, as well as the academic merit of this particular demonstration. Rosenthal explains how the class was prepared, and was also invited to opt out of viewing the demonstration.

Cory Silverberg, a columnist who writes about sexual topics for About.com, argues that the problem with the sexual demonstration is rooted in issues of power and privilege held by professors. Silverberg argues that a warning notice sent to students ahead of time and invitations to leave the class were insufficient for obtaining their true informed consent to observe the demonstration.

As you read the essays and examine the events and analyses of the demonstration at Northwestern University, consider what you think not only about this one particular event but also about the use of SEM in general, live or otherwise.

---

[1] From A. Montagu, *Touching: The Human Significance of the Skin*. (New York: Harper & Row, 1986).

YES

A.M. Rosenthal

Toying with Academic Freedom

Every spring, Northwestern University Professor J. Michael Bailey teaches the largest class on campus, "Human Sexuality," a psychology course so well attended that it fills a 650-seat auditorium to capacity. The student newspaper named it one of the five courses that students should make sure to take before graduating. Despite its popularity, however, the course is not a cakewalk nor is it a how-to course for students interested in having better sex. Rather, course material addresses the *science* of sexuality. Prof. Bailey presents the results of sexuality research and encourages his students to critically examine many of their commonly held assumptions about sex. Many days after class, optional events such as films and speakers are offered to enhance students' learning by providing exposure to people who embody the more interesting aspects of that day's lecture. At one of these events, following a lecture on—among other things—"kinky" sexuality and female ejaculation, Prof. Bailey famously permitted a live sex toy demonstration by some of the panelists (Bailey, 2011a). Prior to the demonstration, the students were informed several times about its explicit nature and were given the opportunity to leave the auditorium. The 5-minute demonstration included a man vaginally penetrating his fiancé with a modified hand-tool designed to simulate rapid penile thrusting. An additional purpose of the demonstration—besides the obvious exposure to kinkiness through exhibitionism and sex toy usage—was to (potentially) demonstrate female ejaculation (a topic about which there is much debate in the scientific literature on female sexuality).

Academic Merit

Prof. Bailey does not claim the demonstration was an essential part of students' education, nor does he describe kinkiness as an essential part of sex (Bailey, 2011a). Considering this, did the demonstration have any tangible academic merit? To be sure, the demonstration was related to the lecture and fulfilled the goal of providing students with "real life" exposure to course topics. However, I argue that the academic merit of any pedagogical exercise can only be measured by the extent to which it fulfills a course objective. "Academic merit" is an ill-defined term about which there will always be reasonable disagreements. However, I propose that evaluating the academic merit of any event/topic can only occur when considering that event/topic within the context of a given course. This is important, because the heated commentary in the weeks after the demonstration dealt mostly with the ethical and moral implications of the demonstration rather than its relevance to the course material or learning objectives.

Given the amorphous nature of academic merit, one might consider other questions to ask when determining the value of a pedagogical technique. The first question might be: Does this technique cause harm? When a pedagogical technique is unlawful or causes physical injury or intense, lasting, or debilitating psychological distress, its value is outweighed by its cost. Under this definition, watching adults engage in consensual, non-injurious sexual activity is not *intrinsically* harmful. Nevertheless, it may be distressing to individuals who believe public exhibitions of sexuality are morally wrong. Had the demonstration been sprung on the students without their consent, it may have harmed some of those who were present. But this was not the case. To date, there has been no indication that those present experienced distress either during or after the demonstration (Bailey, 2011a). This may be due to the fact that those who would have been seriously distressed chose to leave prior to the demonstration. The fact that it may have made some students uncomfortable does not justify banning the demonstration, however. College students are exposed to ideas and phenomena with which they (or the public) may disagree on moral or intellectual grounds. This may make them uncomfortable, but this may also be a valuable part of the educational experience.

We have thus far established that the demonstration was consistent with a goal of the course and did not appear to harm those who were present. Why the public outcry? There are at least three reasons for this. First, sensational journalism popularized a story that easily lent itself to the generation of many lascivious, eye-catching headlines. Second, the demonstration roused American's tendency to be uncomfortable with nudity and sexuality. Third, the demonstration violated the widespread modern belief that young people are pure and innocent. If an 18-year-old "child" knowingly chooses to attend a live sex toy demonstration, they are no longer innocent. That disconcerting realization can be averted, however, by the convenient belief that a corruptor had coerced them. Does condoning displays of sexuality in the classroom amount to academic debauchery, or rather, does it fall within the purview of academic freedom? That is, does a professor have the right to condone live sex demonstrations in a course on human sexuality without fear of reprisal from university officials or other authorities?

Academic Freedom

During the media firestorm in the weeks following the demonstration, the majority of academicians and sex educators who contributed to the public discourse defended Prof. Bailey's actions. However, a small contingent voiced negative, unsupportive reactions. Sexuality writer Robin Mathy, a long-time detractor of Prof. Bailey's research (e.g., Gsovski, 2008), alleged that the demonstration constituted a "gross violation" of professional ethics, although she failed to clarify what ethical principle was violated (Svitek, 2011b, para. 1). A more moderate criticism suggested that the controversy might lead conservative parents to oppose non-abstinence sex education for elementary and secondary school students (Joannides, 2011). Broader questions asked whether the value of the demonstration outweighed its potential harm and the intense negative reaction that it elicited from some members of the public. The latter—although a retrospectively interesting question—wrongly assumes that Prof. Bailey foresaw a public reaction of any kind (Bailey, 2011b). Perhaps this constitutes a failure in judgment on Prof. Bailey's part, but to the extent that this demonstration reignited the public debate about sexuality norms and academic freedom (in addition to fulfilling its original pedagogical intention), I argue that it outweighs the negative reaction of a minority of Americans. Finally, there were the contradictory statements released by Northwestern University, first in support of "the efforts of its faculty to further the advancement of knowledge" (Cubbage, 2011, as quoted in Svitek, 2011a, para. 1), and, a day later, "troubled and disappointed" by the demonstration to the point of launching an investigation (Schapiro, 2011, para. 1). As a point of contrast, during a different controversy at the same university, emeritus Northwestern president, Henry S. Bienen, opprobriously spoke out against the actions of Holocaust denier and Northwestern professor Arthur Butz, but concluded, "We cannot take action . . . without undermining the vital principle of intellectual freedom that all academic institutions serve to protect" (2006, para. 3).

None of the negative reactions truly consider the import of this controversy to the issue of academic freedom. This is surprising, considering that the purpose of academic freedom is to provide scholars with the license to study and profess ideas *without intervention or sanctions* from administrators or authorities, even when those ideas are politically incorrect, controversial, or otherwise upset the status quo. Of course, a live sex toy demonstration is more than an idea. It is the expression of an unorthodox idea. Specifically, that something educational can be gained by having exposure to unusual displays of sexuality, even when those displays violate traditional norms. It is noteworthy that Northwestern administrators have never attempted to stifle any of the ideas that Prof. Bailey has taught. However, it is almost certain that serious sanctions would follow a similar demonstration in the future. To the extent that such a demonstration is the embodiment of an idea, academic freedom would be attenuated. Academic freedom is not only essential to the expansion of scientific knowledge, it is also a "canary in coal mine" for the infringement on free speech. When academic freedom is vehemently challenged, so too is the maintenance of free speech. Indeed, nearly every totalitarian regime of the twentieth century suppressed the free expression and study of ideas in academia prior to more sweeping suppression of free press (Metzger, 1977).

Academic freedom is built upon the realization that current mores often differ dramatically from those of previous eras, and are thus somewhat morally relative. For example, prior to the mid-1960s, most social scientists regarded homosexuality as a pathological condition; presently, that position is held by a small minority. This raises the question: what mores of the current age will be depopularized or denounced by future generations? As unimaginable as it sounds, might some of them involve our attitudes about nudity and sexuality in general? This does not mean that we are free to violate today's mores and offend with impunity, just because what we do now may not be considered offensive in twenty or thirty years. However, intellectual inquiry, expression, and experimentation may be especially useful in challenging mores that are unreasonable or morally unjust in any time. If social scientists had never entertained the possibility that homosexuality was not a disease, it is unlikely that the subsequent change in public attitudes toward homosexuality would have occurred as rapidly.

Despite its importance, academic freedom is vulnerable. It is weakened by the fact that its precepts have not been codified in a formally recognized manner. There is not a body that oversees disputes pertaining to academic freedom (although many groups may weigh in on the matter). Further, academic freedom only protects against the most egregious acts of retaliation (e.g., termination). Thus, the scope of its protections may be too superficial to protect scholars from the actual, insidious effects of such controversies: political fallout within academia and a weakened ability to publish and obtain research funding. At this point, it is too early to say whether any of these effects will happen to Prof. Bailey, but the fact that they are even possibilities suggests that some ideas and acts, however intrinsically harmless, are still dangerous things to teach.

References

Bailey, J. M. (2011a). The February 21st demonstration: Bailey's account. Retrieved from http://www.faculty.wcas.northwestern.edu/JMichael-Bailey/articles/Baileystatement.pdf

Bailey, J. M. (2011b). Untitled statement. Retrieved from http://www.faculty.wcas.northwestern.edu/JMichael-Bailey/articles/BaileyStatement2.pdf

Bienen, H. S. (2006). Statement by Northwestern University president Henry S. Bienen regarding associate professor Arthur Butz. Retrieved from http://www.northwestern.edu/newscenter/stories/2006/02/bienen.html

Gsovski, M. (March 19, 2008). Debate resumes on methods of psych professor's research. *Daily Northwestern*.

Joannides, P. (2011, March 6). Beyond Alice's new blog entry. Message posted to Northwestern University SEXNET listserv.

Metzger, W. (Ed.) (1977). American concept of academic freedom information: A collection of essays and reports and original anthology. Manchester, NH: Ayer Company Publishers.

Schapiro, M. (2011). Statement by Northwestern President Morton Schapiro. Retrieved from http://www.northwestern.edu/newscenter/stories/2011/03/statement-president.html

Svitek, P. (2011a, March 1). Class sex toy demonstration causes controversy. *Daily Northwestern*.

Svitek, P. (2011b, March 4). Updated: Northwestern copes with fallout, attention from sex toy demo. *Daily Northwestern*.

 **NO**

Thoughts on a Campus Dildo Controversy: Sexuality, Power, and Privilege

Northwestern University professor John Michael Bailey is worried about what people will say about his *on campus sex toy demonstration* where two people used a sex toy (called a "fucksaw") as part of the after-class lecture series he curates. He's worried despite the fact that there didn't appear to be any official complaints or protests following the demonstration.

So what's the problem?

The particular reasons Bailey is worried expose his deeply problematic understanding of sexuality, power, and privilege. It isn't the first time Bailey has demonstrated a lack of understanding of these issues, and the impact they have on the lives of others (see *Madeline Wyndzen's critique* of Bailey's ill-conceived and poorly researched book, and *Alice Dreger's extensive and fascinating account of the controversy* which followed its publication).

This time, let's start with *the statement* that Bailey sent to the 600 students in his human sexuality class and read out loud during a class.

In it, Bailey described his own experience of being "silenced" because of his research, and suggested that he let the dildo demonstration happen because to do otherwise would have meant giving in to "sex negativity." In response to his imagined critics who (if they were speaking up) might presumably say this kind of demonstration is harmful, he said this:

"Sticks and stones may break your bones, but watching naked people on stage doing pleasurable things will never hurt you."

How could he, or anyone, say something like this? Well, being an essentialist helps. But if you live in this world and you care about other people and their experience then you know that context matters.

There is NOTHING that you can say will never hurt someone. This statement is making a universal claim about sex, pleasure, and experience. You can't do that because experience is always particular, always belongs to a person, a place, and a time.

Our experience of something like watching two people on stage having sex is situated in other experiences of things like race, class, gender, and embodiment, to name just a few. I can think of lots of people who would experience what happened on stage as not only painful, but maybe even assaultive (it is worth noting that the "fucksaw" is actually a dildo attached to a reciprocating saw). Watching this demonstration might hurt someone. To suggest otherwise is to engage in a denial of others lived experience on an epic scale. Perhaps it's true that Professor Bailey would never experience this as harmful. But the world is not actually made up of billions of Professor Baileys.

This isn't a reason to ban such demonstrations on college campuses. I'm not suggesting that should be the response to Bailey's ridiculous statement. Nor am I suggesting that in this particular case anyone was harmed. I have no idea of knowing this (and, more to the point, neither does Bailey).

And I acknowledge that people might have chosen to leave the room before the demonstration had they thought it would be bad, dangerous, or unsafe for them to stay. But the idea that giving a warning means that everyone who stays has expressed their free and informed consent to be part of whatever comes next is a gross oversimplification of the very nature of consent and choice and, again, obliterates the context, in this case the subtle power dynamics of a college campus, not only as they relate to sex (in public and private) but also between professors and students.

I'm not saying that on the one hand you've got consent and on the other coercion. Nor am I suggesting that professors (whoever they are) have "the power" and students (whoever they are) have none. What I'm suggesting is that if Bailey had a more complicated understanding of power, privilege, and sexuality these kinds of events could be more thoughtful, educational, and safer for everyone.

In perfect PR fashion, Bailey tried to "get out in front" of the controversy he anticipated by setting the terms of the debate, suggesting that he is sex positive and his detractors are motivated by only one thing: sex negativity.

Here he is suggesting that since it was pleasure on stage, everything must be okay, and anyone who argues otherwise is engaging in censorship. Here again, Bailey exposes his tragically narrow understanding of the material we are told is his area of expertise. Being sex positive doesn't mean everything is okay all the time. Being sex positive, in part, includes acknowledging that sexuality is a site of both tremendous pleasure but also pain, which is something that becomes apparent when you pay attention to *experiences and their contexts*.

Sure being sex positive means supporting the inclusion of more voices into public and private discussions of sexuality. But giving those voices a stage is not enough: a million diverse voices on a stage isn't a discussion—it's a spectacle.

So being sex positive also means *listening* and having inclusive *conversations* (that other meaning of the word "intercourse") By casting any opposition to his events as sex negative, Bailey is preempting a conversation and is certainly not listening to students who might disagree with his particular constructions of sexuality, sexual pleasure, and the most productive modes for thinking about them.

Which brings me to the last point I want to make. In his statement (and, one presumes, in his everyday teaching) Bailey is not only silencing his students or anyone who would critique his way of thinking, he is engaging in an erasure of modes of pleasure, the opposite of what one would hope from a human sexuality professor. How is he doing this?

Let's remember the context.

Bailey, we're told, has won a lot of teaching awards. His class, we're told, is very popular. Aside from the general power and privilege he experiences as someone read as white and male, he's someone with particular power around discourses of sexuality on the Northwestern campus. And he's inviting us lowly undergraduates to a special after class lecture where "real people" tell us about what's really happening with sex. He claims that he does this so students can see what sexual pleasure looks like. But what he's actually doing is carefully curating a kind of token sexual identity freak show.

Here's the sex offender (this is what a sex offender looks like!). Here's a swinger (see the swingers swing!). I don't mean to sound facetious but it's a kind of dated and lazy understanding of sexuality and sexual pleasure which really has no place in human sexuality courses. There are other ways of talking about sexual pleasure and engaging students (who let's not forget are "real people" themselves, perhaps with their own diverse experiences of sexual pleasure). Trotting out the panel of people to essentially be gawked at (as *Eli Clare* reminds us, gawking doesn't only take place at a zoo or a formal freak show, it happens in everyday life) may be something that's still commonly practiced among sex educators. But that doesn't make it educational, useful, or right.

POSTSCRIPT

Is There Academic Merit to Students Viewing Live Sexual Acts in College Courses?

The two editors of this book happened to be at a conference of the Society for the Scientific Study of Sexuality, the nation's oldest network of sexologists, when the news broke, and we had a chance to listen to the reactions of various people in the field. Many fiercely and vocally defended Bailey's academic freedom, and the freedom due all professors to determine what is appropriate to be taught in their classes. During his award acceptance speech, Mickey Diamond, a well-accomplished sexologist, proclaimed, "This is our Wisconsin moment!" drawing an analogy between the risks of stripping academic freedom to the labor rights that had recently been stripped of Wisconsin state employees. Listserv messages for sexologists echoed the idea that academic freedom is tantamount.

A number of quieter conversations—both at the conference and in offline e-mail discussions—were questioning Bailey's judgment and pondering the larger impact on the fields of sex research and sexuality education, which were already under frequent attack. Colleagues worried that the live demonstration of a sex toy at a university would be likened to puberty education for fourth graders, in the same way as President Barack Obama's support for K-12 sex education, which was misconstrued by some meaning that he wanted condoms handed out to kindergartners.

In his article, "Ethical Considerations in the Use of Sexually Explicit Visuals as an Instructional Methodology," Chuck Rhoades recommends that instructors adhere to the American Psychological Association (APA's) Ethics Code when using sexually explicit materials (SEMs) in their courses. The code includes five main ideals:

- *Beneficence and Nonmaleficence*—that SEM should first and foremost "do no harm."
- *Fidelity and Responsibility*—that instructors must establish trust with their students, including being clear on the content, as well as the processes under which explicit materials are used.
- *Integrity*—that educators should use materials that accurately represent the content being studied.
- *Justice*—that educators should recognize that some students may not be able to benefit from SEM, and that alternate means of learning should be available to them.

- *Respect for People's Rights and Dignity*—that educators must acknowledge the various perspectives that students bring to class, in terms of gender, sexual orientation, religious beliefs, cultural traditions, etc., and how these perspectives may affect their experiences with explicit materials, including their readiness.

In terms of informed consent, Rhoades also recommends that professors fully inform their students on the course syllabus of the intention to use SEM, delineating the purpose, the potential benefits, and the potential problems. Based on Rosenthal's and Silverberg's accounts of the use of SEM at Northwestern University, how well do you think Bailey met the standards recommended by Rhoades?

Moving away from the particulars of the demonstration at Northwestern University, what are your thoughts about the use of sexually explicit materials in college courses? What has been your experience? Does your instructor use sexually explicit films, literature, or other materials? What do you think are the educational purposes of such materials? How does your professor prepare you (or how would you want to be prepared) for the use of such materials? What essential steps do you think an instructor would need to take to ensure that you or a classmate truly had the option to not participate in a class in which sexually explicit materials were used?

Suggested Readings

J.S. Cohen, "Sex Toy Demonstration: Controversial Northwestern Class Won't be Offered Next Year," *Chicago Tribune* (May 9, 2011).

J.B. Kelleher, "Northwestern University Cancels Controversial Sex Ed Class," *Reuters* (May 9, 2011).

C. Rhoades, "Ethical Considerations in the Use of Sexually Explicit Visuals as an Instructional Methodology," *American Journal of Sexuality Education* (vol. 2, no. 4, pp. 5–23, 2007).

K. Wallace, "University Cancels Course After Live Sex-Toy Demonstration," *Toronto Star* (May 11, 2011).

ISSUE 11

Should Libraries and Other Places That Provide Public Wi-Fi Restrict the Sexual Content?

YES: American Family Association, from "Library Internet Filtering: Internet Porn in Public Libraries and Schools," http://www.afa.net/lif/schools.asp (2007)

NO: Donald Dyson and Brent Satterly, from "Hey, Uncle Sam. Let My Wi-Fi Go!" an original essay written for this volume (2009)

ISSUE SUMMARY

YES: The American Family Association, an organization that advocates for "traditional family values," argues that library filtering software is essential to protect children from harm.

NO: Donald Dyson and Brent Satterly, professors at Widener University, argue that filtering software limits free access to information and state that Wi-Fi should be unrestricted in all settings, including libraries.

Wi-Fi is a term often used to describe wireless local area networks (WLAN). Wi-Fi transmits and receives high-frequency radio signals over distances of a few hundred feet. Free Wi-Fi seems to be available everywhere nowadays, and wireless capability has become a standard feature in new computers. It enables people to log onto the Internet using their laptop computers in local and university libraries (and often throughout campuses), and in many other public buildings. Free Wi-Fi is also offered in many private and corporate institutions. A colleague of ours reported once walking into a hotel and being dissatisfied with the rate he was quoted at the desk. Realizing he could get a better rate online, he went back to his car in the hotel parking lot, took out his laptop, and used the hotel's own free Wi-Fi to book a better rate!

Wi-Fi has become a ubiquitous source of Internet use. Large parts of this book were researched and written in coffee shops, restaurants, airports, and hotels that provide free Wi-Fi. Some institutions—both public and private—have taken steps to restrict access to sexual content in the Wi-Fi services their patrons receive. In Panera Bread restaurants, for instance, filters on the Wi-Fi service prevent diners from viewing erotic or sexual material online. Intentionally or not, the Panera Bread filters also restrict access to nonerotic material. For example, members of the American Association of Sexuality Educators, Counselors, and Therapists are blocked when they try to view the program for an academic conference housed at http://www.aasect.org/. Employees of Planned Parenthood cannot check their e-mail because reproductive choice content is likewise blocked at these restaurants. And teenagers cannot read articles written by other teenage editors at the educational portal http://www.sexetc.org/. In fact, the development of parts of this book was delayed when filters at certain establishments providing Wi-Fi prevented the editors from finding biographies of some contributing authors who are sex educators, sex researchers, or sex therapists.

What is the purpose of restricting Wi-Fi? Dennis Sarich, customer-comment coordinator for Panera Bread, explained that some content is restricted to "maintain the community tone and standards that Panera Bread is known for." Many would find it quite reasonable to restrict sexual imagery in establishments that serve many people with many different sets of values. However, some hotels—such as Radisson hotels—also restrict sexual content in their overnight guest rooms. In such cases, supporters of free speech wonder why hotels would have an interest in preventing their visitors from viewing erotic material in privacy.

The American Library Association (ALA) has been an outspoken critic of attempts to restrict online access in one place where Wi-Fi is commonly used—libraries. Some patrons wish libraries would install filtering software to ensure that sexual material cannot be viewed. What exactly should be blocked—if anything—is debatable, with some wanting only sexually explicit content blocked and others wanting more aggressive filters that would also block sexuality-education-related Web sites.

In the following essays, the American Family Association (AFA), a social conservative advocacy group, describes library filtering software as essential to protecting children from harm and severely criticizes the ALA for its efforts resisting filtering software. The AFA suggests steps for taking action at your local library to ensure that sexual content cannot be accessed by patrons. Donald Dyson and Brent Satterly, professors at Widener University, argue that Wi-Fi should be unrestricted in all settings, including libraries.

YES  American Family Association

Library Internet Filtering: Internet Porn in Public Libraries and Schools

It is critically important for our children and communities that we free our local libraries from the grip of the American Library Association and make our libraries safe for our children! Make no mistake, the danger to our children is real!

Consider these sobering facts:

- A teenager molested a little boy in a library restroom after viewing Internet porn on the library's computer.
- Smut dealers used their local library to run a child pornography ring.
- A report entitled "Dangerous Access 2000," published by the Family Research Council, documents hundreds of incidents of library patrons accessing pornography in public libraries, including many involving children.

ALA Refuses to Keep Porn from Kids

But when begged for help to protect children, not only did the American Library Association turn a blind eye and a deaf ear, the organization further demanded that every library in the country provide children with totally unrestricted access to Internet porn!

For example, when asked about "blocking software" for library computers so children couldn't access Internet porn, Judith Krug, director of the ALA Office of Intellectual Freedom, said, "Blocking material leads to censorship. That goes for pornography and bestiality too. If you don't like it, don't look at it."

Another ALA spokesman, Richard Matthews, echoed Krug saying, "We recognize that minors have First Amendment rights, and any attempt to treat them differently from adults really infringes on those rights."

ALA Influence Felt Far and Wide

And to make things worse, the American Library Association wields significant power in our local libraries, giving it great influence over:

- The universities that train librarians.
- Job market requirements for most librarians.

- Sizable portions of state monies for local libraries.
- Major book awards (especially children's). NOTE: The ALA awards both the Newbery and Caldecott Medals for excellence in children's books.
- Training of local library board trustees.
- Lobbying at both state and federal levels on legislation relevant to the ALA's agenda.

ALA Works to Undermine Protection of Kids

Based on their statements and policies about Internet filtering, it's clear that protecting children from harmful material is not part of the ALA's agenda. The sad truth is that unsupervised, curious eyes will seek out the forbidden. That's what children do. And that's why God calls on us, their parents and concerned adults, to protect them. A brief look at the ALA's record is proof:

- The ALA played a major role in convincing the Supreme Court to overturn the Communications Decency Act, which Congress passed to protect children from Internet pornography.
- The ALA sued to stop the enforcement of a federal law that would withhold federal funds from any library or school that does NOT filter Internet pornography from children.
- Not only does the pornography industry help fund the ALA, but ALA president Ann Symons has served on the Playboy Foundation's awards committee.
- Playboy executive Christie Hefner was a forum panelist at an ALA convention.
- The bottom line always comes down to this official policy statement of the American Library Association: "Libraries, acting within their mission and objectives, must support access to information on all subjects that serve the needs or interest of each user, regardless of the user's age or the content of the material." (See ALA's Article V of the Library Bill of Rights. . . .)

Something Can Be Done about Reckless Endangerment of Our Children

Children do NOT have a Constitutional right to access and view Internet pornography in our local libraries! Or anywhere for that matter.

The question that must be answered is why is a private organization with no legal standing and no authority having so much influence over our libraries and the policies that protect children from harm.

Here's the good news: the ALA truly has no legal authority over what goes on in your local library. The answer lies with the citizens. YOU and your fellow taxpayers own your local library, not the ALA.

If you want the ALA and its pornographic policies out of your community and your local library, GET INFORMED, GET INVOLVED and KICK THEM OUT!

If concerned citizens are armed with solid information and commitment, our local libraries can be rescued from the ALA.

Take note: this fight will not be easy. The people who run the ALA—the Krugs, Symonses, and Matthewses—are radicals of the 1960s. They will not give up their control of your library without a tough fight.

Nevertheless, for the sake of our children and our communities, we must fight to free our local libraries from the radical, immoral agenda of the American Library Association. No sacrifice and no expense is too great when it comes to safeguarding children.

This fight is a local fight. There is no way it can be conducted from some national headquarters. YOU must fight for your own school and public libraries—you and the members of your local community.

There are already over FIVE MILLION sexually explicit adult web sites on the Internet. And thousands more are added EVERY DAY! And the American Library Association wants our children to have totally unrestricted access to every single one of them! We cannot afford to put this fight off a single day.

You Can Do It One Step at a Time

Here are some steps and information that will help you begin the process of communicating to your local librarian and directors the need to install filtering on your local library's Internet computers. By following the recommended guidelines, you will be better prepared to:

- Address the current problem of Internet porn in your library.
- Articulate your position to the library, civic leaders, and local media.
- Persuade others to join and support your goal and purpose.

Pray

Ask God to direct and guide you through the entire process. You are going to face opposition by the ALA and others. Pray for wisdom and success in your efforts.

Research

1. Read and understand as much as possible the facts surrounding Internet filtering, your library's Internet use policies, your library board members and their terms of service and authority.
2. Learn how the library administration is structured. Who are the board of directors? How are they selected? Is the library part of a regional system under authority of a central board? Do other cities contribute to the library budget?
3. Request to look at the public complaint file. Are there any "red flags" that suggest a problem, i.e., patrons viewing pornography, children accessing inappropriate material. What was the library's response to the complaints?
4. Learn state and local laws concerning legislative measures that can be taken, such as placing a ballot issue that would mandate filtering

before the people during the next election. What is the librarian's liability for allowing children to access harmful material?
5. Prepare a list of friends, families and churches that you feel will support you in this project.

Action Steps

1. Write or visit your local librarian. Share your concerns about the dangers of Internet pornography in the local library. Ask the librarian to consider placing filtering devices on library computers. However, be aware that the American Library Association has policies that instruct librarians how to respond.
2. Write or call the chairman of the library board. Request to address the board at their next scheduled meeting. A day or two before the meeting, you may wish to notify the local media that you are concerned about pornography in the library. This will help take your message to others who will agree and join with you. Invite friends and supporters to attend meetings and to voice their support of filtering.
3. Contact your city and county officials. Ask them to publicly stand with you on the issue by proclamation or resolution.
4. Write letters to the editor. Recruit others to do the same.
5. Form a local coalition in favor of safer libraries. Discuss ways to reach the community with your message. Newsletters, church bulletin inserts and flyers are excellent tools. Start a petition drive to raise public awareness and to create a database of supporters.
6. If your local library fails to implement filtering, ask an attorney who supports your efforts to begin drafting a voter initiative for your group. The attorneys at the AFA Center for Law & Policy are available to assist in this effort as well.
7. **Order the "Excess Access" video**, documenting the dangers that ALA policies can yield. Excess Access scrutinizes the ALA and uses both drama and interviews with experts who have analyzed the growing power of the group.

Donald Dyson and
Brent Satterly

 **NO**

Hey, Uncle Sam. Let My Wi-Fi Go!

In March of 2008, the Pew Research Center released a report indicating that 62% of all Americans are members of what they referred to as "a wireless mobile population" (p. 1). This population of fast, connected, mobile users crosses generational and demographic lines of all types. And, as cell phones and PDAs become more sophisticated and as laptop computers and public Internet "hotspots" become more common, these numbers are likely to increase significantly in the next few years.

Within the context of this mobile population, Pew reports that 64% of Internet users have accessed the Internet from places outside of their homes or their workplaces, likely from settings such as libraries, hotel rooms, and public "hot spots." Looking further at this report, it can be seen that although younger users access information at higher rates, the use of laptops to access the Internet crosses generational lines. In fact of all Internet users, 70% of those between the ages of 18 and 29 have used a laptop to log on wirelessly, 53% of those between 30 and 49, 39% of those between 50 and 64 and 29% of those 65 and older. It is clear that wireless Internet access is a significant and growing cultural phenomenon.

Add to this the growing list of locations from which such wireless access can found. In addition to libraries and hotels, airports [and] coffeeshops, laundromats and a host of retail outlets are adding wireless access to their list of services in attempts to meet customer demands and to attract new customers.

This proliferation of access meets a challenging intersection when considered in light of the vast array of content available on the net. Specifically, it is sexually explicit or "objectionable" content that is most often the issue of debate.

Sex Panic and the Internet

We know that the open discussion of sex and sexuality is problematic for many of us for many reasons. They may be related to our personal beliefs, our spirituality, our individual moral codes or simply our embarrassment and shame. However, there is a greater phenomenon that is occurring to further complicate these discussions.

In his book *America's War on Sex* (2006), Dr. Marty Klein identifies a cultural phenomenon that has been growing in the United States for many years. Dubbed the "Sexual Disaster Industry (SDI)," this group has been working behind the cultural scenes to create a culture of panic connected to sex and sexuality that has significantly threatened many of our freedoms. According to Klein, the SDI works through many outlets to overstate the statistics of sexual violence and sexual danger in an effort to generate fear and attention.

Consider the popularity of television shows that sensationalize the capture of sexual predators for a national audience, or the outrage of some morality groups about the abundance of pornography available on the Internet. These things and more generate a sense of fear related to sexuality and a mysterious and dangerous "sexual other."

It is precisely this sexual panic, then, that fuels the push for filters that "protect" us from this mysterious and dangerous sexual predator hiding within our laptops and threatening our children, our marriages, our families and our morality. These are the arguments for Internet filters and blocking software designed to prevent the average coffeeshop consumer from looming sexual dangers.

Internet Filters and Censorship

Internet filters are designed to complete an advanced view of the Internet content that a given user is attempting to access, search it for specific keywords or images, and prevent access to that content if the word or image is included in a list of "unacceptable" content. While most filter companies do not release the specifics of their filters, the concept is generally the same: the software package will prevent the surfer from having access to content that the software designers have deemed to be unacceptable.

This concept is not a new one in human history. Since before the printed word, censorship has played a role in human politics and interactions as some groups of people attempt to control access to content that it deems unacceptable for others. It is no surprise that this same experience, fueled by sex panic, has affected Internet access.

Consider the case of the Child Online Protection Act of 1998. Originally passed by Congress to levy criminal charges and impose civil penalties on people who put material the government deems "harmful to minors" on the Internet. Although immediately challenged by the ACLU and other organizations, and as a result never enforced, a ten-year legal battle ensued. In 2009, the Supreme Court upheld the injunction against enforcement, arguing that the law censored material that was protected by the First Amendment of the Constitution.

In a similar case involving the 2000 Children's Internet Protection Act, which required libraries receiving public funds to put filters on public computers, the Supreme Court ruled that the libraries *must* remove such filters if a patron asks that they be removed. This once again demonstrated that Internet content was protected by the first amendment.

Consider the argument so far. Wireless Internet use is growing across the nation for people of all ages. More wireless hotspots are being introduced to everyday life and technology is increasing mobile access to the World Wide Web. At the same time, the sexual disaster industry is generating increasing fear of sexual danger and the sexual other, increasing a public's panicked cry for "protection". As a result, attempts to censor Internet content arise in unconstitutional attempts to safeguard our communities. As a result, constitutionally protected content gets blocked and the freedoms Americans hold dear threatened.

What Else Is Threatened?

It is not only freedom that is being threatened. Recent reports indicate that a vast majority of Internet users are accessing health-related data through the Internet. The Pew Internet and American Life project reports that between 75 and 80% of Internet users have looked up health-related information. The popularity and ubiquity of webMD© and other health-related websites has transformed the medical landscape in many ways.

More specifically, more and more people have been accessing sexual health information through the World Wide Web as well. In 2003, it was estimated that one in ten Internet users accessed information related to sexual health. Among adolescents, estimates rise to over 25% of teens seeking information about sexual health issues such as birth control, HIV, AIDS, or STDs. In a culture that is often silent on healthy sexual expression, such access is at the very least a necessity and at times, lifesaving.

This access goes beyond the basics of health, however. For some gay, lesbian, bisexual, and transgender youth the Internet offers the only resource for accessing information about their experiences, their communities, and the specific health information that affects them.

Research has indicated that not only is access related to sexual health blocked by a vast number of Internet "safety" packages, but that information is blocked at higher rates when it relates to those individuals who identify as gay, lesbian, bisexual or transgender (GLBT) (Richardson, Hansen, Resnick, & Derry, 2002). As a result, health information is denied to individuals already dealing with societal discrimination.

Beyond the sexual health needs of the general public, such censorship also limits access to important websites for educators and other professionals. The columnist working on an article related to youth suicide is restricted from accessing websites related to GLBT youth. The therapist, seeking information on working with married couples and sexual dysfunction cannot access the websites of the American Association of Sexuality Educators, Counselors and Therapists (AASECT) or the Society for Sex Therapy and Research (SSTAR). The middle school administrator cannot gather information on gender-based bullying from the Sexuality Information and Education Council of the United States (SIECUS).

What is the Solution?

In the end, the sexual disaster industry wants Americans to believe that there is an uncontrollable avalanche of unwanted pornography in every wireless coffeeshop and a predator lurking in every laptop at every library across the nation. Aided by the sensationalism of media that seeks ratings and readership over reliability, the sexual panic grows and the fear intensifies. Even in the face of decreasing rates of online sexual solicitation (Mitchell, Wolak, & Finkelhor, 2007), the panic and push for filters increases.

The answers, however, do not lie in the increasing censorship of online content. The honest reality is that sexual predators have been problematic for generations and that pornography has been accessible to industrious and curious youth for at least that long as well. Well-meaning attempts to protect people from experiences with unwanted sexual material, in the end, silence honest discussions about sexuality and prevent the development of lifesaving skills in navigating an increasingly complex sexual world.

Instead of attempting to block sexuality from our lives, time and energy is far better spent in teaching people the critical thinking skills necessary to make sense of the myriad sexual images that bombard them everyday. Rather than generating disproportionate panic about online sexual predators, teach adolescents Internet safety skills. Take the time to educate young people about how to recognize and report unwanted and inappropriate sexual overtures. Rather than limiting the access to sexual health information, increase the dialogue about its importance to our overall well-being.

In your panic about sexuality, do not seek to over-protect the people. It only serves to weaken our ability to manage the realities of our world. Instead, seek to build critical thinking and thoughtful action that can help every American become responsible sexual citizens. Hey, Uncle Sam, let my Wi-Fi go!

POSTSCRIPT

Should Libraries and Other Places That Provide Public Wi-Fi Restrict the Sexual Content?

As with all articles in *Taking Sides,* it is important to read these articles critically, and challenge statements that are presented as facts. The American Family Association (AFA) opens its argument by describing several "sobering facts," including a boy who was said to be molested in a library after viewing porn, and "smut dealers" who ran a child pornography ring from the local library. It is important to observe that the AFA offers no sources for these allegations, and no further details that might enable the reader to verify these claims independently. The AFA also provides a set of "Action Steps" for readers to take in order to curtail the availability of pornography in libraries. Do these steps seem effective?

In their opposing article, Dyson and Satterly also present several situations, but do so as hypothetical circumstances, rather than facts. They describe a columnist who is blocked from researching GLBT suicide, a therapist who cannot access professional Web sites, and a middle school administrator who cannot access information on gender-based bullying. Do you think their depiction of the far-reaching effects of Wi-Fi restrictions is accurate? Why, or why not?

Marty Klein, author of *America's War on Sex,* tells of another related controversy that came to light late in 2008 when several airlines introduced Wi-Fi to their passengers. For a fee, passengers could access the Internet during their flights. Most airlines offering this new service placed filters, restricting access to sexual material. At first, American Airlines decided that such filters were not needed, choosing instead to rely on its passengers to exercise "good judgment." After public pressure, American Airlines changed its decision and decided to block sexual content. Much of the pressure came from the Association of Professional Flight Attendants, a union that did not want its members in the awkward position of having to ask passengers to curtail their online, in-flight viewing habits. The group said that they had received "a lot of complaints" from passengers seeing "inappropriate content" on others' computer screens, although specific examples could not be produced. Klein wonders where the line is drawn on defining what is "inappropriate." Should Web sites on breast cancer be blocked? Those that advocate gay rights? "The Daily Show"? "And what about the rest of what people do on their laptops?" (Klein, 2008).

Today, 3G and 4G networks have enhanced users' ability to access the Internet virtually anywhere. These networks are based on mobile broadband communications, largely associated with tablet computers and smartphones, allowing users to access the Internet from any location where their 3G- or 4G-capable devices can reach a network signal. These new technologies are currently beyond the reach of filtering devices in libraries and other establishments offering Wi-Fi. Thus, while one library patron's Web site access is restricted on a laptop, another patron equipped with a smartphone will be able to surf unfettered.

What do you think about this issue? Have you ever seen someone viewing (or viewed for yourself) pornographic material in a public library? Have you ever been blocked from viewing sexuality-related information in a public space? How did this make you feel? Should libraries and other public and private institutions block access to sexual content? Should some establishments filter content, but not others (i.e., should airlines restrict content because of the close proximity of patrons)? If establishments are to block sexual content, should they block other content that might be offensive, such as Web sites that provide hate speech or violent imagery? And should filters be the responsibility of the person owning the laptop or the entity providing the service?

Suggested Readings

S. Fox, *The Engaged E-Patient Population.* (Pew Internet & American Life Project, August, 2008).

M. Klein, *America's War on Sex* (Santa Barbara, CA: Praeger, 2006).

M. Klein, "Porn on Planes: Another Urban Legend Fans Hysteria," *Sexual Intelligence* (October 26, 2008).

K. Mitchell et al., "Trends in Youth Reports of Sexual Solicitations, Harassment and Unwanted Exposure to Pornography on the Internet," *Journal of Adolescent Health* (vol. 40, no. 2, pp. 116–126, 2007).

M. Schlangenstein, "American Air Attendants Urge Filters to Bar Web Porn," *Bloomberg News* (September 10, 2008).

ISSUE 12

Is Pornography Harmful?

YES: Pamela Paul, from "The Cost of Growing Up on Porn," http://www.washingtonpost.com/wp-dyn/content/article/2010/03/05/AR2010030501552.html?sid=ST2010030502871 (March 7, 2010)

NO: Megan Andelloux, from "Porn: Ensuring Domestic Tranquility of the American People," an original essay written for this volume (2011)

ISSUE SUMMARY

YES: Pamela Paul, author of *Pornified: How Pornography Is Transforming Our Lives, Our Relationships, and Our Families,* argues that studies declaring the harmlessness of pornography on men are faulty and that consequences of porn consumption can be seen in the relationships men have with women and sex.

NO: Meghn Andelloux, sexuality educator and founder of the Center for Sexual Pleasure and Health, argues that the benefits of porn on American society outweigh the questionable consequences.

Is pornography harmful? And who, if anyone, does it harm? As in-home access to the Internet has risen, so has risen the access to a seemingly unlimited supply of pornography. Although the debate over erotic and explicit material is nothing new, the widespread availability of online pornography has raised new concerns about an old issue.

Debates over pornography in the United States have largely focused on the perceived negative impact of porn versus free-speech arguments that oppose censorship of any kind. While many see this conflict as a feminist issue, even feminists can find themselves on opposing sides of the argument. In the 1970s and 1980s, an often intense academic debate (referred to as the Feminist Sex Wars) raged between "radical feminists" and a new school of feminist thinkers who labeled themselves "sex-positive." Radical feminists, such as Andrea Dworkin and Catharine MacKinnon, opposed pornography. Sex-positive feminists were weary of calls for censorship and alarmed by antiporn feminists who were now allied with the conservative movement they saw in opposition to women's liberation.

A key part of the debate hinges on the effects of the consumption of pornography. Opponents point to researchers who have found connections between porn and a decrease in compassion toward rape victims and the support of violence against women. Recently, several popular authors (including Pamela Paul, whose essay is featured in this issue) have warned against the negative impact easily accessible porn can have on relationships, masculinity, and femininity.

However, supporters of porn point to other studies that show no significant correlation between sexually explicit material and attitudes that are supportive of violence against women. Anticensorship advocates like Nadine Strossen and sex-positive feminists like Susie Bright and Violet Blue have written about the ways pornography can empower both performers and viewers. The growing market for feminist and queer erotica, featuring films produced and directed by women such as Candida Royalle, Tristan Taormino, and Jayme Waxman, suggests that women are supporting porn in increasing numbers.

Although the feminist sex wars cooled over time, the debate was never settled—thanks in large part to the ambiguous definition of porn. What, exactly, is pornography? Is there a line between art and pornography, and between pornography and obscenity? In 1964, Supreme Court Justice Potter Stewart, in an opinion stating the scope of obscenity laws should be limited, famously said of hard-core porn, "I know it when I see it." Nearly 50 years later, controversial porn producer Max Hardcore was sentenced to 46 months in prison (although the sentence was later reduced) for violating federal obscenity laws by distributing his films and promotional material via mail and over the Internet.

As you read the selections, think about how you define pornography? Does it need to be explicit to be considered pornographic? How should feminist, gay, lesbian, or queer-produced porn that portrays people of various genders and body types enjoying sex be viewed in the conversation? What about erotic romantic novels, or paintings, illustrations, and sculptures depicting nudity or sex? Should soft-core porn be treated the same way as hard-core? What about animated scenes of nudity or sexual intercourse that are often depicted in video games? Consider your own porn viewing habits, or the porn viewing habits of people you know. Do you think it has had an impact on your (or your friends') attitudes toward women, men, or sex in general? If you believe pornography is harmful, do you feel it is more damaging to women or men? Do you believe society would benefit from restricting or banning some types of sexually explicit materials? Where would you draw the line (or lines) in deciding something was illegal?

In the following selections, Pamela Paul, author of *Pornified: How Pornography Is Transforming Our Lives, Our Relationships, and Our Families,* calls into question the findings of a Canadian researcher who found in his sample that viewing pornography had no negative effects on men. Megan Andelloux, sexuality educator and founder of the Center for Sexual Pleasure and Health, argues that pornography is not only healthy but also a valuable part of the fabric of American society.

YES

Pamela Paul

The Cost of Growing Up on Porn

Guess what, guys? Turns out pornography—the much-maligned bugaboo of feminists, prigs and holy rollers—is nothing more than good, not-so-dirty fun.

The proof comes from the University of Montreal, where recent research showed that connoisseurs easily parse fantasy from reality, shudder at the idea of dating a porn star (what would Maman think?) and wholeheartedly support gender equality. "Research contradicts anti-pornography zealots," gloated a column's headline in the Calgary Sun.

So, I've been contradicted. Presumably, I'm one of the zealots in question. My anti-porn fanaticism took the form of a 2005 book, "Pornified," in which I dared to offer evidence that all is not well in the era of Internet porn. Today, 20-somethings, teenagers and even—sorry to break it to you, parents—tweens are exposed to the full monty of hard-core pornography.

Wasn't it time someone asked some obvious questions? What will happen now that the first generation of men raised on Internet porn is making its way onto the marriage market? What influence does the constant background blare of insta-porn have on their ideas about women and monogamous relationships?

The answers I found to those questions were less than cheering. In dozens of interviews with casual and habitual porn users, I heard things such as: "Real sex has lost some of its magic." "If I'm looking like eight or 10 times a day, I realize I need to do something to build my confidence back up." "My wife would probably think I was perverted and oversexed if she knew how much I looked at it every day."

In the years since I wrote the book, I have heard from dozens of readers who described the negative effects of porn. One was a student at Berkeley, who observed that "ever more deplorable acts needed to be satiated" and noted: "As a child, we are exposed to things that we may not realize have formative effects. As adults, many times we simply continue without questioning." (Women, it seems, also turn to iVillage.com, where a board devoted to "relationships damaged by pornography" contains more than 32,280 messages to date.)

Yet there's still so much we don't know. Perhaps we can learn from the scintillating news out of Montreal. Let's have a closer look at that—oops!—turns out there is no study. Simon Louis Lajeunesse, a postdoctoral student and associate professor at the university's School of Social Work, has yet to publish a report. His findings, such as they exist, were based on interviews with 20 undergraduate males who detailed their views on sex, gender and pornography in one to two lickety-split hours.

Granted, it's qualitative, not quantitative, research, but the brevity of the interviews is concerning. While reporting "Pornified," I felt the need for more than four hours with many of my 100 interviewees. Of course, my guys could talk anonymously to a disembodied voice on the phone; the poor fellows in Montreal had to sit down and look a male social worker in the eye before confessing a penchant for three-ways. Lajeunesse asked 2,000 men before he found 20 willing subjects. Most of them, he said, were referred by women in their lives. Hmm.

And just how did Lajeunesse learn that pornography hadn't affected their views of said women? Why, he asked and they said so! "My guys want to have equal relationships, equal income, equal responsibility domestically," Lajeunesse told me. Color me dubious, but I hardly think most men would own up to discriminating against women, spurred on by porn or not.

To be fair, researching the relationship between men and pornography isn't easy. My methods had flaws, too. The most methodologically sound study would involve gathering a sample of men, scheduling regular sessions to view online porn, and comparing their subsequent sexual attitudes and behaviors with those of a control group that did not use pornography. Through a series of measures—interviews, questionnaires, observations—the data would be collected and analyzed by a team of objective academics.

That's not going to happen now, though it once did. Back in 1979, Jennings Bryant, a professor of communications at the University of Alabama, conducted one of the most powerful peer-reviewed lab studies of the effects of porn viewing on men. Summary of results: not good. Men who consumed large amounts of pornography were less likely to want daughters, less likely to support women's equality and more forgiving of criminal rape. They also grossly overestimated Americans' likelihood to engage in group sex and bestiality.

Yet Bryant's research (conducted with colleague Dolf Zillmann) was carried out long before the Internet brought on-demand porn to a computer screen near you. So why no update? Other than a spate of research in the '80s and '90s that attempted to link pornography with violence (results: inconclusive), nobody has looked at the everyday impact of hard-core porn. "That's a catch-22 with most studies about media effects," Bryant told me. "If you can't demonstrate that what you're doing to research participants is ultimately beneficial and not detrimental, and you can't eradicate any harm, you're required not to do that thing again."

Every university has a review board for the protection of human subjects that determines whether a study is ethically up to snuff. "It is commonly the case that when you get studies as clear as ours, human subjects committees make it difficult to continue to do research in that area," Bryant explained. "Several graduate students at the time wanted to follow up, but couldn't get permission." In other words, the deleterious effects were so convincing, ethics boards wouldn't let researchers dip human subjects back into the muck.

No matter—people will take care of that on their own. As one young man explained, after mentioning that "porn may have destroyed my relationship with my girlfriend" in an e-mail: "I always feel that I'm over porn, but I find myself keep coming back to it. There seems to be an infinite number of porn sites with limitless variations, one never becomes bored with it. . . . It's a very difficult habit to break."

Or as one 27-year-old female lawyer noted recently: "All of my girlfriends and I expect to find histories of pornographic Web sites on our computers after our boyfriends use it. They don't bother erasing the history if you don't give them a lot of hell." The implications troubled her. "I fear we are losing something very important—a healthy sexual worldview. I think, however, that we are using old ideas of pornography to understand its function in a much more complex modern world."

Of the many stories I've heard revealing the ways in which young men struggle with porn, I offer here just one, distilled, from a self-described "25 year old recovering porn-addict" who wrote to me in October. "Marc" began looking at his father's magazines at age 11, but soon, he wrote, he "turned to the Internet to see what else I could find." This "started off as simply looking at pictures of naked women. From there, it turned into pictures of couples having sex and lesbian couples. When I got into watching videos on the Internet, my use of porn skyrocketed." At 23, he began dating a woman he called "Ashley." "However, since Ashley's last boyfriend had been a sex/porn addict, I was quick to lie about my use of porn. I told her that I never looked at it. But after 5-6 months, Ashley discovered a hidden folder on my computer containing almost a hundred porn clips. She was devastated."

Marc and Ashley broke up, got back together and spent several months traveling in India. He continued to look at porn behind her back, and on a trip to Las Vegas, he got lap dances despite promising not to. Ashley broke up with him again. "I had never thought about the adverse effects of my use of porn. . . . I want to change. I want to be a respectful human being towards all human beings, male and female. I want to be a committed and loving boyfriend to Ashley."

This is hardly solid lab research. But it is one of many signs of pornography's hidden impact. And flimsy "if only it were true!" research isn't an acceptable substitute for thorough study. An entire generation is being kept in the dark about pornography's effects because previous generations can't grapple with the new reality. Whether by approaching me (at the risk of peer scorn) after I've spoken at a university or via anonymous e-mails, young people continue to pass along an unpopular message: Growing up on porn is terrible. One 17-year-old who had given up his habit told me that reading about porn addicts "was like reading a horrifying old diary, symptoms, downward spirals, guilt, hypocrisy, lack of control, and the constant question of to what degree fantasy is really so different from reality. I felt like a criminal, or at the very least, a person who would objectively disgust me."

Let's not ignore people like him, even if it's tempting to say, as one headline did, "All men watch porn, and it is not bad for them: study."

That's just one more fantasy warping how we live our real lives.

Megan Andelloux  **NO**

Porn: Ensuring Domestic Tranquility of the American People

Pornography. Images of happy people rolling over one another, flashes of arched backs, moans that cannot be ignored, and giggles pouring from the mouths of stars. Out of the corner of the eye a flash of skin on the monitor catches our attention and draws us in. Porn has become ubiquitous on the Internet in the modern day, but its existence has graced the surface of the Earth since humans first began tracing stick figures on cave walls. One of its earliest forms comes to us from the town of Santillana del Mar, in the Cantabria region of northern Spain during the Upper Paleolithic Period.[1] Coital scenes were drawn out on cave walls 40,000 years ago depicting oral sex, voyeurism, and sex for the sake of fun! Records of these "graphic" images coming from France, Portugal, and Egypt beg the question: did rulers like the great Pharaoh Ramses have to hide his papyrus porn from the royal court? Were our ancestors riddled with angst and shame about the potential damage of gazing at naked bodies drawn on scrolls? Probably not. The danger of depicting human nudity wasn't a social concern until the middle of the 18th century, when the written word made erotica available to the common man.[2] Suddenly, politicians, clergy members, and authority figures of all types decried the erotic word and spread fear of its supposed dangerous and corrupting influence. Today, alas, we still face the same argument: Is pornography harmful?

Not all porn is created equal, but it is a form of speech that has been and must continue to be protected in our society. What may be found offensive by one citizen or group of citizens should not dictate whether or not the rest of society is to be allowed free access to it, lest tyranny of minority opinion rule the day. It's clear the American court systems agree.[3] If the US Supreme found that the Westboro Baptist Church's hate speech is to be afforded protection, how could one ever think to outlaw pornography's message of pleasure? Porn virtually embodies everything the founders envisioned when they penned "the right to life, liberty, and the pursuit of happiness!"

It's been reported that over 372 million websites are devoted to displaying images of people having sex of one sort or another.[4] There are untold thousands of magazines, flash drives, comic strips, and pornographic images that circulate around us every day. Porn is a major part of our American culture, and it could be argued that watching porn is America's real pastime. Now before I start getting hate mail for an inflammatory statement like that, let me point out that regardless of a person's religious preference or political affiliation, about 36% of the American population uses porn at least once a month.[5] One would never know it because very few people publicly claim to enjoy pornography. It's understandable why. Acknowledging that you watch pornography is tantamount to identifying yourself as a "pervert" in our society.

It is astonishing that 40 years after a conservative administration spent years and millions of dollars trying to find a correlation between violence and porn (which they were unable to do), and show that porn has damaging effects on individuals and their personal relationships (which they have not), Americans are still shamed when they enjoy such a basic, ancient part of our humanity.

So, when we have hard, reputable data that tens of millions of Americans have watched porn in the past month, that our crime rates are lower when we have access to it,[6] that the most prevalent images *by far* are of adults having sex,[7] and that the performers in the field like the work they do,[8] why then is porn still vilified? It's because a group of highly motivated, yet select few people yell hard, long, and loud. They shame both people who watch and the actors who perform in porn. They portray those who stand up for porn as being misguided, or as duped by the industry itself, and browbeat people with their opinion that looking at images of people having sex is somehow immoral. We rarely hear that using porn is beneficial, empowering and a healthy choice in sexual development, exploration and expression.

Let's look at why pornography is indeed, good for society and individuals.

Pornography Shows Human Beings as Being Sexual Creatures

Pornography exposes sexual desire, and it is unashamed of what it produces. It shows the lust, the yearning, and the appreciation of other human bodies and their sexual energy. Pornography rejoices in the very things society works so hard to suppress.

Whether stumbled upon or sought out intentionally, porn is a part of society because we enjoy it. People derive pleasure seeing other people be sexual. Porn helps individuals explore behaviors they may feel alone in experiencing, such as fetishes, non-heterosexuality, or even simple masturbation. The anti-porn folks are right in at least one thing: We do learn from the images. Although, the moral crusaders will then go on to argue that we in the audience are without free will and are forced to mimic the most degrading images we see in pornographic films. But just as I will continue to come to a full stop at the next red light I see despite having enjoyed *The French Connection* last night, free will gives us the option to imitate movie scenes or not at will. Nearly everyone is sexual. Porn helps us to share in our sexuality without overriding or sublimating it.

"Old, young, black, white, male, female, trans, pretty, ugly, tall, short, big, little, all types are represented on screen. A wider variety of body types are welcome on the porn screen as opposed to mainstream media representations of love, sex and romance. We may not look like Angelina Jolie, but we can find someone on a porn screen who looks a lot like we do, having a fun time and living to tell the tale. That's no small thing."

Nina Hartley
Porn Performer, Sex Educator

Pornography Shows the Wide Variety of Human Sexual Desires and Actions

Porn gives hope to those who feel alone and/or sexually isolated. Queers, women, the elderly, or any marginalized group can see, with full representation, that there may be others out there, sexual like they are.

"I started performing in pornography so that I could participate in what I felt is much needed visibility of queer sexuality, gender expressions, and sex-positive behaviors and culture. My work reflects the minority/marginalized communities that I am a part of, while allowing me to connect with a universal audience who can all appreciate great sex."

Jiz Lee, Feminist Porn Award's Boundary Breaker
and AVN Nominated Best New Web Star

And now with amateur porn being the highest accessed sexually explicit material,[9] we have more evidence of the sex-lives of average Americans! We have proof that it's not just the "evil" porn industry that wants ejaculation scenes or spankings. We see normal bodies on film, flaws and all, having the best most creative sex.

And rather than a for-profit corporation behind the production, amateur porn has become the sexual art of folk. It's Bob and Jane playing here, or Jane and Jane, or Bob and Bob—beer belly, thick legs, short hair and . . . all frolicking around in sexual bliss.

"Porn has afforded me the ability to feel out my sexuality without the fear of rejection or humiliation."

Mark Farlow

Ethically made pornography is a sub-genre of porn comprised of actors who are paid living wages for depiction of realistic sex. Ethically made pornography allows a performer to participate as more than just an actor in the sexual act being depicted. Ethical porn is an emerging powerful field within the adult market. The individuals and companies behind this movement seek out participants who DON'T look like the typical porn-stars. The ultimate goal seems to be to bring real sex to the masses. Some notable companies in this field include:

- Comstock Films
- Pink and White Productions
- Good Releasing
- Fatale Media
- Reel Queer Productions
- Sir Video
- Tristan Taormino's Expert Guide Series
- Nina Hartley's Guide Series

"Independent and feminist porn especially can be an incredible validation for those who don't see their own desires reflected in mainstream media."

Alison Lee, Good For Her Feminist Porn Awards

Pornography Is a Risk Reduction Method. It Is the Safest of Safe Sex.

Watching porn is one of the safest ways to explore sexuality. There is no risk of STI transmissions, no risk of an unwanted pregnancy, no risk of feeling disappointed by the way our body performed, no risk of cheating, and no risk of violence. Human beings fantasize about forbidden fruit. We often wonder what it would be like to be with someone of the same gender, experience a threesome, engage in anal play, explore power dynamics, or talk dirty to our lover. Porn lets us find out, risk-free.

"Pornography can be a great way for people to explore their sexuality and fantasies without affecting others in society. Through pornography, they are able to jump their pizza delivery person or proposition their car dealer without actually disturbing others."

Shanna Katz, Sexologist

Pornography Gives Access to Sex Information to All

While pornography isn't the best way to educate individuals on how to have sex, it does grant access to sexual information. It allows a great number of people to see what it means to have oral sex, pull-my-hair-play, or cis-gendered experiences. They say a picture is worth a thousand words. There is a clear difference between reading about it in a book and seeing it live in front of you, where you can watch the emotions, see the actual behaviors that take place, and process that information in a different way.

A person may feel titillated or disgusted, intrigued or off put, but all of these feelings are important parts of the learning process. What better starting point could one have when making decisions about the type of sexual behavior one wants to engage in?

I'm not arguing that pornography pretends to be educational. But it does purport to be experiential. Not everyone goes to college, nor do they have access to a sex educator, nor sex education programs, nor even a well stocked sex-ed self-help bookshelf. Accessing pornography can often be the first guidepost pointing the way to what one may want to do (or not do) in bed. The experience that porn brings, surrogate to real life as it may be, helps create a more informed decision making process.

> "We know that many people turn to porn for sex information because there is a dearth of sex ed media. So even if we're making a movie that is in no way intended to be primarily educational, (that is, porn) we want to show sex as people actually have it."
>
> *Carol Queen, Good Releasing Films*

Pornography Encourages Conversations to Take Place about Sex

Hate it or love it, pornography is part of America.

Whether you call the risqué PETA commercial banned from prime-time porn, or find Charlie Sheen's latest sexual adventures pornographic, porn can start a conversation. We can turn to our neighbor or friend and ask, with all good intentions and proper decorum, "What do you think about Sasha Grey going into mainstream movies? Do you think she's going to make it? Why?" These probing questions serve a vital public service of allowing us to learn the sexual attitudes of our neighbors and friends.

American culture doesn't speak openly about sexuality yet harbors a judgmental attitude. Knowing the sexual mores of our peers can be vital for our social well-being. With the pornography industry putting "sexy time" out there for everyone to see and critique, seize the opportunity and talk about it!

> "Viewing porn was helpful to convey what turned me on (and off) to my partner, ultimately making the sex and relationship stronger."
>
> *Kim Chanza*

Myth-Busting

In cultures that have access to pornography, violent crimes rates decreased. Yes, decreased. The US Government shows there is no correlation between violence and having access to and watching pornography.

The media routinely blares headlines bearing shocking titles such as "Porn made him sodomize his child!" Therefore, one would think that porn contributes to all manner of bad outcomes. The facts show, however, that pornography has been established not to increase rates of sexual violence. In 1970, the President's Commission on Obscenity and Pornography (also known as The Lockhart Report) found no link between pornography and delinquent or criminal behavior among youth and adults.[10] William B. Lockhart, Dean of the University of Minnesota Law School and chairman of the commission, famously said that before his work with the commission he had favored control of obscenity for both children and adults, but had changed his mind as a result of scientific studies done by commission researchers.

Similarly, in 1984 the Metro Toronto Task Force on Public Violence against Women and Children failed to demonstrate a link between pornography and sex crimes,[11] as did the 1994 US National Research Council Panel on Understanding and Preventing Violence.[12] Even the Meese Report, a famously biased hand-picked group of anti-pornography advocates hired by Ronald Regan to prove the damaging effects of pornography failed to show any hard evidence. In fact, they got more than they bargained for when they hired Canadian sociologist Edna F. Einsiedel to summarize the current scientific studies linking pornography and violence. Her conclusion was that "No evidence currently exists that actually links fantasies with specific sexual offenses; the relationship at this point remains an inference.[13]"

Those talking heads who cling to the canard that porn leads to violence, rape, sexual assault, or child molestation are preaching from emotion, not facts. They fear what horrors "might" come to pass, and their fear is contagious. Terrifying tales without background or prelude are woven in the media to provoke a base response in their audience. Unfortunately, American history is littered with examples of just such emotional arguments being more powerful than well-reasoned counterparts. Witness the Salem witch trials, Japanese internment camps during WWII, or the sordid history of The House Un-American Activities Committee.

The anti-porn community (be it conservative religious or liberal feminist) stuffs the news media with anecdotal evidence of the danger posed by porn. Anecdotal evidence is of course the least reliable type of scientific data; one person, with a pretty face and a sob-story, can be more convincing than stacks of peer-reviewed journal articles. Though it can be moving to hear stories such as "Porn made me masturbate all day," or, "Porn made me see people as if they were naked," porn has not been actually shown to cause any such behavior.

Porn is an easy target for attack, but here is the thing: Humans have free will. We can choose to act one way or another, but pornography does not force us to do evil.

In all seriousness, rape and sexual assault are caused by violent antisocial tendencies, complete disregard for another's rights, and pure self-interest. To pin it on porn relieves the rapist of the guilt and blame.

One may not like certain aspects of pornography, but that discomfort should not restrict other's access to it. A society that produces legal pornography, a people that have access to pornography, is a sexually healthy nation. Pornography, a blessing of liberty, creates for us a more perfect union.

Resources

- Feminists for Free Expression
- ACLU
- Woodhull Freedom Foundation
- National Coalition for Sexual Freedom
- Free Speech Network
- Society for the Scientific Study of Sexuality
- America's War on Sex, Marty Klein
- Planned Parenthood of Western Washington, Pornography: Discussing Sexually Explicit Images, Irene Peters, Ph.D.

References

1. Cave paintings show aspects of sex beyond the reproductive. (2006, May 2). *Dominican Today,* Retrieved from http://www.dominicantoday.com/dr/people/2006/5/2/12982/Cave-paintings-show-aspects-of-sex-beyond-the-reproductive.

2. Carroll, J.L. (2007). *Sexuality now.* Belmont, CA: Wadsworth.

3. Corry v. Stanford University, Case No. 740309 (Cal. Super. Ct. 1995); Dambrot v. Central Michigan University, 839 F. Supp. 477 (E.D. Mich. 1993); Doe v. University of Michigan, 721 F. Supp. 852 (E.D. Mich. 1989).

4. Joseph, M. (Producer). (2007). *Internet porn* [Web]. Available from http://www.good.is/post/internet-Porn.

5. Media Metrix Demographic Profile – Adult. (2008, June). comScore

6. Kendall, T.D. (2006). Pornography, rape, and the internet. *Proceedings of the law and economics seminar* Stanford, CA: http://www.law.stanford.edu/display/images/dynamic/events_media/Kendall%20cover%20+%20paper.pdf.

7. Diamond, M. (2009). Pornography, public acceptance, and sex related crime: a review. *International Journal of Law and Psychiatry* 32 (2009) 304–314; corrected with Corrigendum IJLP 33 (2010) 197–199.

8. Paulie & Pauline. (2010). *Off the set: porn stars and their partners.* Glen Rock, NJ: Aural Pink Press.

9. Klein, M. (2006). *America's war on sex: the attack on law, lust, and liberty.* Santa Barbara, CA: Praeger.

10. The Commission on Obscenity and Pornography, (1970). *President's commission on obscenity and pornography.* Washington, DC: U.S. Government Printing Office.

11. Task Force on Public Violence against Women and Children, Final Report (1984). *Metro Toronto.* Toronto, Canada.

12. Reiss, A.J., & Roth, A.J. National Research Council, (1993). *Understanding and preventing violence.* Washington, DC: National Academy Press.

13. United States Attorney General, Commission on Pornography. (1986). *Attorney general's commission on pornography.* Washington, DC.

POSTSCRIPT

Is Pornography Harmful?

The issue of pornography and its potential harms, particularly in reinforcing the subjugation and humiliation of females, is a perplexing one. Efforts to censor speech, writing, and pictorial material (including classical art) have been continuous throughout the American history. The success of censorship efforts depends mainly on the dominating views in the particular era in which the efforts are made, and on whether conservative or liberal views dominate during that period. In the conservative Victorian era, moral crusader Anthony Comstock persuaded Congress to adopt a broadly worded law banning "any book, painting, photograph, or other material design, adapted, or intended to explain human sexual functions, prevent conception, or produce abortion." That 1873 law was in effect for almost a hundred years, until the United. State. Supreme Court declared its last remnants unconstitutional by allowing the sale of contraceptives to married women in 1963 and to single women in 1972.

In 1986, a pornography commission headed by then attorney general Edwin Meese maintained that the "totality of evidence" clearly documented the social dangers of pornography and justified severe penalties and efforts to restrict and eliminate it. At the same time, then surgeon general C. Everett Koop arrived at conclusions that opposed those of the Meese Commission. Koop stated, "Much research is still needed in order to demonstrate that the present knowledge [of laboratory studies] has significant real-world implications for predicting [sexual] behavior."

It is doubtful that Justice Stewart, the feminists of the 1970s, or the Meese Commission could have foreseen the impact of the Internet and "smart phones" (such as iPhones, Androids, and Blackberries) on the availability and distribution of porn. The seemingly unlimited availability of free hard-core porn at our fingertips has been cited by many as a need for further restrictions. However, the implications of porn consumption are still hotly debated. Although accurate statistics are difficult to come by, there is no debating porn's popularity or billion dollar revenues.

Suggested Readings

F. Attwood, "What Do People Do with Porn? Qualitative Research into the Consumption, Use, and Experience of Pornography and Other Sexually Explicit Media," *Sexuality and Culture* (vol. 9, no. 2, pp. 65–86, 2005).

V. Blue, *The Smart Girl's Guide to Porn* (Cleis Press, 2006).

A. Levy, *Female Chauvinist Pigs: Women and the Rise of Raunch Culture* (Free Press, 2006).

P. Paul, *Pornified: How Pornography Is Transforming Our Lives, Our Relationships, and Our Families* (Holt, 2006).

C. Sarracino and K.M. Scott, *The Porning of America: The Rise of Porn Culture, What It Means, and Where We Go from Here* (Beacon Press, 2009).

N. Strossen, *Defending Pornography: Free Speech, Sex and the Fight for Women's Rights* (NYU Press, 2000).

ISSUE 13

Should Prostitution Be Legalized?

YES: Susan A. Milstein, from "Want a Safer Community? Legalize Prostitution," an original essay written for this volume (2009)

NO: Donna M. Hughes, from "The Demand: Where Sex Trafficking Begins," text of a speech given at the conference *A Call to Action: Joining the Fight Against Trafficking in Persons*, Rome, Italy (2004)

ISSUE SUMMARY

YES: Susan Milstein, associate professor in the Health Department at Montgomery College and advisory board member for Men's Health Network, argues that while the legalization of prostitution will not stop all of the social problems associated with the institution, the benefits of legalization make it the best option.

NO: Donna Hughes, professor at the University of Rhode Island and leading international researcher on trafficking of women and children, counters that the criminalization of prostitution not only reduces demand, but also slows the spread of international sex trafficking.

P rostitution is often referred to as the "oldest profession in the world." Despite the fact that prostitution is illegal in many places of the world, both female and male prostitutes can be found in every city of every country of the world. Prostitution, often referred to as "sex work," ranges from solicitation in outdoor settings like parks or the street to brothels and high-end escort services to the trafficking of unwilling individuals. There exists an ongoing debate about whether prostitution should be criminalized, decriminalized, or legalized.

It may be helpful when examining this issue to gain clarity about the distinction among criminalization, decriminalization, and legalization. Those who seek to end the practice through the criminalization of prostitution would take an abolitionist perspective, meaning that all aspects of prostitution would be illegal and punishable by law. The decriminalization of prostitution would remove any criminal penalties associated with the trade and allow prostitutes to operate in a manner similar to independent contractors or other independently licensed businesses. The third option, the legalization of prostitution, would call for state licensing and regulations, including the possibility of mandated testing for sexually transmitted infections (STIs) (Brents and Hausbeck, 2001). According to the United States Department of State Bureau of Democracy, Human Rights, and Labor (2008), the legality of prostitution varies across the world with it being illegal in many countries, legalized and regulated in others, while in some parts of the world, the act of prostitution itself is legal, although other activities related to it are illegal, such as soliciting sex in a public place.

In the United States, prostitution is legal in two states: Nevada and Rhode Island. Although prostitution (the act of engaging in sexual activity in exchange of money) is technically legal in Rhode Island, operating a brothel and street prostitution (referred to as loitering for indecent purposes) are illegal before the Rhode Island law. On the other hand, Nevada, which legalized prostitution in 1971, has 25 legal brothels and about 225 licensed female prostitutes (*NY Times*, 2009). Brothels in Nevada are allowed in counties that have fewer than 400,000 residents, which excludes the county where Las Vegas is located. However, research indicates that 90% of prostitution in Nevada takes place in Las Vegas and Reno, where it is in fact illegal (Farley, 2007). Legalized brothels are highly regulated and state law requires that brothel prostitutes receive weekly tests for chlamydia and gonorrhea and monthly tests for HIV and syphilis (Nevada Law). Condom use is also required. In fact, research shows that condom use is higher during sexual activity between a prostitute and a client, compared to sexual activity between a prostitute and a nonpaying sex partner (lover) (Albert et al., 1998). Such regulations exist as a public health measure, to reduce the rates of STIs, and they seem to be working. Among prostitutes affiliated with Nevada brothels studied, there have been no cases of HIV infection and the positive gonorrhea rate is about 1 percent (Reade et al., 1990). A 1998 study found that the prevalence of STIs among illegal street prostitutes in Australia, working outside of the legalized and regulated system, was drastically higher (80 times greater) than that of their brothel counterparts (cited in Loff et al., 2000).

The views expressed by many about prostitution may depend on the context in which it takes place. Organizations such as the Coalition Against Trafficking in Women (CATW) consider prostitution to be sexual exploitation and focus on abolishing sex trafficking of women and girls. According to the United States Department of State (2004), "Where prostitution is legalized or tolerated, there is a greater demand for human trafficking victims and nearly always an increase in the number of women and children trafficked into commercial sex slavery. Of the estimated 600,000 to 800,000 people trafficked across international borders annually, 80 percent of victims are female, and up to 50 percent are minors. Hundreds of thousands of these women and children are used in prostitution each year."

Some sex worker activist organizations such as Call Off Your Old Tired Ethics (COYOTE) and the North American Task Force on Prostitution view prostitution as a choice and support the decriminalization of prostitution, but oppose the regulations that come with legalization such as in Nevada.

In the following essays, Susan Milstein presents a rationale for legalizing prostitution, outlining the benefits of doing so, including financial and public health benefits, while Donna M. Hughes asserts that prostitution is a violation of human rights, leads to the dehumanization of women and children, and should not be legalized.

YES

Susan A. Milstein

Want a Safer Community?
Legalize Prostitution

Prostitution is a reality in the United States, regardless of its legal status. If it becomes legal, then outreach services, like drug and mental health counseling, can be provided. This will not only improve the prostitute's quality of life, it may encourage them to leave the profession. Legalization means that measures could be taken to protect prostitutes from becoming victims of rape and other forms of violence, while mandatory condom use, and STI and HIV testing, will help decrease disease transmission. There is also the benefit of the government being able to make money by imposing taxes. It's in society's best interest to make prostitution as safe as possible, which can be accomplished through legalization.

Legalize it, decriminalize it, or keep it illegal, the fact remains that prostitution is going to happen regardless of what the law says. Once we come to accept that as fact, the question then becomes, what is the best way to approach it?

So What Is Prostitution?

When you say "prostitute" people automatically get an image in their head. That image may be of a streetwalker, a call girl or a male escort. It may be of Heidi Fleiss or Deborah Jeane Palfrey, the DC Madam. It may even be of Elliott Spitzer. But what is prostitution? It's the exchange of sex for money. With this definition in mind, let's change how we look at prostitution. Instead of thinking of a streetwalker and pimp, imagine a woman who sleeps with a man in exchange for rent money and gifts. Is this prostitution? Some might say no, others might say yes.

Change the scenario again. Imagine a woman who is engaging in a specific behavior in exchange for money. Is that prostitution, or is it a job? It may be difficult to think of prostitution as just another job, but why? Is it because prostitution is seen as demeaning and degrading? What's the difference between working as a prostitute, and being locked into a Wal-Mart overnight and being forced to clean (Greenhouse, 2005)? It may be difficult to separate prostitution out from what may seem like other degrading and dehumanizing jobs simply because it involves sex. But if we can look past the sexual aspect, if we can stop looking at prostitution as being inherently immoral or unacceptable, if we can start to look at it as an industry, then we can start to see the benefits of legalizing it.

Benefits of Legalizing Prostitution

There are multiple benefits to legalizing prostitution, the first of which is improving the health of the prostitute. If the United Sates were to legalize prostitution then there could be legislation that would mandate regular STI and HIV testing. This is currently how it works in Nevada, the only state in the United States that has legalized prostitution. In addition to STI and HIV testing, using condoms for every sex act could also be made mandatory. Both of these types of mandates would help to prevent disease transmission among the prostitutes, their clients, and their clients' other sexual partners. But decreasing the risk of disease transmission, while important, is not the only health benefit of legalizing prostitution.

A study done in New York City found that the majority of prostitutes were addicted to drugs. Many continue to work as prostitutes as a way of making money so that they can feed their addiction. If prostitution were legalized, it would be easier to do drug outreach and education for the prostitutes. This might decrease the amount of drug use that is seen amongst prostitutes, and it may also help to decrease the number of people who are engaging in sex for money. Once sober, they may look to other professions for a steady source of income.

In addition to drug use, another problem facing many prostitutes is that of violence. Many prostitutes are raped by their clients. One study found that 80% of prostitutes had either been threatened with violence, or had been victims of violence. Violence, and threats of, may come from clients, pimps or the police. Currently, if a prostitute is raped or otherwise victimized, he or she has little to no legal recourse. But if prostitution were to be legalized, a sex worker who is raped would have the ability to go to the police and report it without fear of being arrested.

Legalizing prostitution may also make the work safer in that precautions can be put into place ahead of time to try and prevent violence from occurring. Many of these types of strategies have already been implemented in Nevada, where prostitution is legal in selected counties. Installing panic buttons in rooms may help to save a prostitute from harm if a client does get violent. Additionally, if violence occurs, the brothel owners can call the police without fear of being arrested.

A safer working environment, counseling services to help deal with drug use and being victims of violence, and reducing the disease transmission rates all create a safer environment for the prostitutes and their customers, but what about the community?

Benefits to the Community

What kind of community are we creating if we legalize prostitution? Perhaps we can create a safer one. If we pass legislation mandating STI and HIV testing, and condom use during each sex act, we can also pass legislation that restricts where prostitutes can work. Since men and women won't be out be on the street trying to attract customers, the streets will see fewer streetwalkers, and fewer people trolling for prostitutes. Combine this with a decrease in the amount of violence and drugs that surround the profession, and all of this is a benefit to the community. There is also the financial benefit.

If we require a prostitute to register so that we can monitor his or her STI and HIV testing, then that will create jobs. There will be a need for more people to work in the labs that will be doing the testing, as well as a need to staff an office that deals with regulation and record maintenance. Increases in social service programs, like crisis counseling and drug programs, will provide even more jobs. And if it's legalized, it can be taxed.

Sin taxes are taxes that are imposed on activities that are considered immoral, yet are still legal. These taxes may be imposed on drugs, like nicotine and alcohol, or on specific activities like gambling. With this kind of precedent, there is no reason why prostitution couldn't be legalized, and then taxed. The revenue generated by a prostitution tax could be used to help benefit a myriad of different government programs. This could in turn lead to an increase in the quality of life for thousands of United States citizens.

Rethinking Prostitution in the United States

Some may wonder why it is that Americans say they live in a free society, yet an individual does not have the right to decide to have consensual sex for money. If the country, outside of Nevada, is so anti-prostitution, why do we punish the sex worker, and not the person who is paying for sex? The majority of laws in the United States actually trap a person in a life of prostitution. It may be that one way to decrease the number of people who work as prostitutes, is to legalize it.

When someone gets arrested for prostitution, they have a criminal record that will follow him or her. What jobs are available to someone who has been arrested for prostitution? If we don't make it a crime, a prostitute may be able to get the job training, health care, and mental and legal counseling that would enable them to leave the world of prostitution. Perhaps the answer is to change the way we deal with prostitution and arrest the people who are paying for sex, which is the law in Sweden. Or perhaps the United States can do what many other countries are doing, and either decriminalize or legalize prostitution.

The fact is that the United States has already taken a step towards legalization. Depending on the population of the county, prostitution is legal in Nevada. Prostitutes must register to work, must use condoms for all sex acts, and must be tested for STIs and HIV on a regular basis. Some countries have chosen to decriminalize prostitution. Since changing the law in 2003, New Zealand has found no major increase in the number of prostitutes in the country, and there has been a positive change in the lives of many sex workers. Other countries, including England, Argentina, Canada, Germany, Greece, Scotland, and more than twenty others, have chosen to legalize prostitution (Procorn.org, 2008).

Bottom Line. . . . Prostitution Happens

Legalizing prostitution will not make the industry perfectly safe. False negatives can occur on STI and HIV tests, and condoms can break, which means disease transmission is always a possibility. Panic buttons and good working relationships with police won't guarantee a prostitute's safety. Make eighteen the minimum working age for a prostitute, and you will find people younger than that selling their bodies for sex, and others who are more than willing to pay for it. Legalization is not a cure for all the issues surrounding sex work in the United States.

The bottom line is that regardless of the law, prostitution is going to happen. By legalizing it we can make it safer, for the prostitutes, the clients, their significant others, and society at large.

Donna M. Hughes

The Demand: Where Sex Trafficking Begins

In light of shared moral responsibility to help the millions of people who are bought, sold, transported and held against their will in slave-like condition, a conference entitled "A Call to Action: Joining the Fight Against Trafficking in Persons" was held at the Pontifical Gregorian University in Rome on June 17, 2004. The event was part of the 20th anniversary celebration of full diplomatic relations between the United States and the Holy See, and their shared work to promote human dignity, liberty, justice, and peace. The following is the text of my speech.

The Trafficking Process: The Dynamics of Supply and Demand

The transnational sex trafficking of women and children is based on a balance between the supply of victims from sending countries and the demand for victims in receiving countries. Sending countries are those from which victims can be relatively easily recruited, usually with false promises of jobs. Receiving or destination countries are those with sex industries that create the demand for victims. Where prostitution is flourishing, pimps cannot recruit enough local women to fill up the brothels, so they have to bring in victims from other places.

Until recently, the supply side of trafficking and the conditions in sending countries have received most of the attention of researchers, NGOs, and policy makers, and little attention was paid to the demand side of trafficking.

The trafficking process begins with the demand for women to be used in prostitution. It begins when pimps place orders for women. Interviews I have done with pimps and police from organized crime units say that when pimps need new women and girls, they contact someone who can deliver them. This is what initiates the chain of events of sex trafficking.

The crucial factor in determining where trafficking will occur is the presence and activity of traffickers, pimps, and collaborating officials running criminal operations. Poverty, unemployment, and lack of opportunities are compelling factors that facilitate the ease with which traffickers recruit women, but they are not the cause of trafficking. Many regions of the world are poor and chaotic, but not every region becomes a center for the recruitment or exploitation of women and children. Trafficking occurs because criminals take advantage of poverty, unemployment, and a desire for better opportunities.

Corruption of government officials and police is necessary for trafficking and exploitation of large numbers of women and children. In sending countries, large-scale operations require the collaboration of officials to obtain travel documents and facilitate the exit of women from the country.

In destination countries, corruption is an enabler for prostitution and trafficking. The operation of brothels requires the collaboration of officials and police, who must be willing to ignore or work with pimps and traffickers. Prostitution operations depend on attracting men. Pimps and brothel owners have to advertise to men that women and children are available for commercial sex acts. Officials have to ignore this blatant advertising.

Components of the Demand

There are four components that make-up the demand: 1) the men who buy commercial sex acts, 2) the exploiters who make up the sex industry, 3) the states that are destination countries, and 4) the culture that tolerates or promotes sexual exploitation.

The Men

The men, the buyers of commercial sex acts, are the ultimate consumers of trafficked and prostituted women and children. They use them for entertainment, sexual gratification, and acts of violence. It is men who create the demand, and women and children who are the supply.

I recently completed a report for the TIP Office, United States Department of State on the demand side of sex trafficking that focuses on the men who purchase sex acts. Typically, when prostitution and sex trafficking are discussed, the focus is on the women. The men who purchase the sex acts are faceless and nameless.

Research on men who purchase sex acts has found that many of the assumptions we make about them are myths. Seldom are the men lonely or have sexually unsatisfying relationships. In fact, men who purchase sex acts are more likely to have more sexual partners than those who do not purchase sex acts. They often report that they are satisfied with their wives or partners. They say that they are searching for more—sex acts that their wives will not do or excitement that comes with the hunt for a woman they can buy for a short time. They are seeking sex without relationship responsibilities. A significant number of men say that the sex and interaction with the prostitute were unrewarding and they did not get what they were seeking; yet they compulsively repeat the act of buying sex. Researchers conclude that men are purchasing sex acts to meet emotional needs, not physical needs.

Men who purchase sex acts do not respect women, nor do they want to respect women. They are seeking control and sex in contexts in which they are not required to be polite or nice, and where they can humiliate, degrade, and hurt the woman or child, if they want.

The Exploiters

The exploiters, including traffickers, pimps, brothel owners, organized crime members, and corrupt officials make-up what is known as the sex industry. They make money from the sale of sex as a commodity. Traffickers and organized crime groups are the perpetrators that have received most of the attention in discussions about the sex trafficking.

The State

By tolerating or legalizing prostitution, the state, at least passively, is contributing to the demand for victims. The more states regulate prostitution and derive tax revenue from it, the more actively they become part of the demand for victims.

If we consider that the demand is the driving force of trafficking, then it is important to analyze the destination countries' laws and policies. Officials in destination countries do not want to admit responsibility for the problem of sex trafficking or be held accountable for creating the demand. At this point to a great extent, the wealthier destination countries control the debate on how trafficking and prostitution will be addressed. Sending countries are usually poorer, less powerful, and more likely to be influenced by corrupt officials and/ or organized crime groups. They lack the power and the political will to insist that destination countries stop their demand for women for prostitution.

In destination countries, strategies are devised to protect the sex industries that generate hundreds of millions of dollars per year for the state where prostitution is legal, or for organized crime groups and corrupt officials where the sex industry is illegal.

In the destination countries, exploiters exert pressure on the lawmakers and officials to create conditions that allow them to operate. They use power and influence to shape laws and polices that maintain the flow of women to their sex industries. They do this through the normalization of prostitution and the corruption of civil society.

There has been a global movement to normalize and legalize the flow of foreign women into sex industries. It involves a shift from opposing the exploitation of women in prostitution to only opposing the worst violence and criminality. It involves redefining prostitution as "sex work," a form of labor for poor women, and redefining the transnational movement of women for prostitution as labor migration, called "migrant sex work." It involves legalizing prostitution, and changing the migration laws to allow a flow of women for prostitution from sending regions to sex industry centers. The normalization of prostitution is often recommended as a way to solve the problem of trafficking.

States protect their sex industries by preventing resistance to the flow of women to destination countries by silencing the voice of civil society. In many sending countries, civil society is weak and undeveloped. Governments of destination countries fund non-governmental organizations (NGOs) in sending countries to promote the destination country's views on prostitution and trafficking. Authentic voices of citizens who do not want their daughters and sisters to become "sex workers" in other countries are replaced by the voice of the destination country, which says that prostitution is good work for women. The result is a corruption of civil society.

In a number of countries, the largest anti-trafficking organizations are funded by states that have legalized prostitution. These funded NGOs often support legalized prostitution. They only speak about "forced prostitution" and movement of women by force, fraud, or coercion. They remain silence as thousands of victims leave their communities for "sex work" in destination countries. Effectively, these NGOs have abandoned the women and girls to the pimps and men who purchase sex acts.

When prostitution is illegal, but thriving, government officials often look jealously at the money being made by criminals, and think they are not getting their share. In countries that are considering the legalization of prostitution, the estimated amount of the future tax revenue is often used to argue for legalization.

Germany legalized brothels and prostitution in 2002. German lawmakers thought they were going to get hundreds of millions of euros in tax revenue. But the newly redefined "business owners" and "freelance staff" in brothels have not been turned into taxpayers. The Federal Audit Office estimates that the government has lost hundreds of millions of euros in unpaid tax revenue from the sex industry. Recently, lawmakers started to look for ways to increase collection of taxes from prostitutes. The state seems to be taking on the role of pimp by harassing prostitutes for not giving them enough money.

Although legalization has resulted in big legal profits for a few, other expected benefits have not materialized. Organized crime groups continue to traffic women and children and run illegal prostitution operations along side the legal businesses. Legalization has not reduced prostitution or trafficking; in fact, both activities increase as a result of men being able to legally buy sex acts and cities attracting foreign male sex tourists.

The promised benefits of legalization for women have not materialized in Germany or the Netherlands. In Germany, legalization was supposed to enable women to get health insurance and retirement benefits, and enable them to join unions, but few women have signed up for benefits or for unions. The reason has to do with the basic nature of prostitution. It is not work; it is not a job like any other. It is abuse and exploitation that women only engage in if forced to or when they have no other options. Even where prostitution is legal, a significant proportion of the women in brothels is trafficked. Women and children controlled by criminals cannot register with an authority or join a union. Women who are making a more or less free choice to be in prostitution do so out of immediate necessity—debt, unemployment, and poverty. They consider resorting to prostitution as a temporary means of making money, and assume as soon as a debt is paid or a certain sum of money is earned for poverty-stricken families, they will go home. They seldom tell friends or relatives how they earn money. They do not want to register with authorities and create a permanent record of being a prostitute.

The Culture

The culture, particular mass media, is playing a large role in normalizing prostitution by portraying prostitution as glamorous or a way to quickly make a lot of money. Within academia, "sex workers" are represented as being empowered, independent, liberated women.

To counter these harmful messages, there is an important role for churches to play in describing the harm of prostitution to women, children, families, and communities. In the United States, the Evangelical Christian churches are increasingly involved in the human rights struggle against sex trafficking and exploitation.

Unfortunately, in the battle against the global sex trade, the voice of moral authority that condemns all forms of sexual exploitation and abuse is being lost. Some churches are compromising on their mission and their vision. For example, in the Czech Republic, there is a government proposal to legalize and regulate prostitution, as a way to combat trafficking. Catholic Bishop Vaclav Maly, the Auxiliary Bishop of Prague, has made a statement in favor of legalization of prostitution. According to a *Radio Praha* report in April 2002, he has given up the moral battle saying, "The chances of eliminating it are practically nil. . . . Under those circumstances, it is better to keep it in check and under control by giving it a legal framework. This is not to say that I approve of brothels—but it seems to me that it would be better to have prostitution take place there—with medical checks-ups and prostitutes paying taxes. It would be the lesser of two evils."

More recently, Bishop Maly has been silent in the legalization debate in Czech Republic, but his original statement is posted on web sites supporting legalization, which gives the impression that the Catholic Church supports legalization. A voice of moral authority in support of human dignity and against the sexual exploitation and abuse of victims of prostitution and trafficking is needed in the Czech Republic. Bishop Maly could be this voice. He has a long history of supporting human rights. He was an original signer and spokesman for Charter 77, the petition calling for the communist government of Czechoslovakia to comply with international human rights agreements they had signed. He knows the importance of resisting abusive power and laws that enslave people instead of freeing them.

Faith communities, from the grassroots to the leadership, need to use their voice of authority to combat the increasing sexual exploitation of victims and its normalization.

Abolitionist Movement

There is a growing abolitionist movement around the world that seeks to provide assistance to victims and hold perpetrators accountable.

In Sweden, beginning in 1999, the purchasing of sexual services became a crime. The new law was passed as part of a new violence against women act that broadened the activities that qualified as criminal acts of violence. With this new approach, prostitution is considered to be one of the most serious expressions of the oppression of and discrimination against women." The focus of the law is on "the demand" or the behavior of the purchasers of sex acts not the women.

The United States government has adopted an abolitionist approach at the federal level. In 2003, President George W. Bush issued a National Security Presidential Directive. It was the first United States opinion on the link between prostitution and trafficking: "Prostitution and related activities, which are inherently harmful and dehumanizing, contribute to the phenomenon of trafficking in persons . . . " This policy statement is important because it connects trafficking to prostitution and states that prostitution is harmful. This policy goes against attempts to delink prostitution and trafficking and redefine prostitution as a form of work for women.

As a result of this abolitionist approach, more attention is being focused on the demand side of sex trafficking. Destination countries, particularly those that legalize prostitution, are coming under new scrutiny.

Conclusion

I believe that only by going to the root causes, which are corruption and the demand in destination countries, will we end the trafficking of women and children.

We need to urge all governments, NGOs, and faith communities to focus on reducing the demand for victims of sex trafficking and prostitution. All the components of the demand need to be penalized—the men who purchase sex acts, the traffickers, the pimps, and others who profit, states that fund deceptive messages and act as pimp, and the culture that lies about the nature of prostitution.

We could greatly reduce the number of victims, if the demand for them was penalized. If there were no men seeking to buy sex acts, no women and children would be bought and sold. If there were no brothels waiting for victims, no victims would be recruited. If there were no states that profited from the sex trade, there would be no regulations that facilitated the flow of women from poor towns to wealthier sex industry centers. If there were no false messages about prostitution, no women or girls would be deceived into thinking prostitution is a glamorous or legitimate job.

POSTSCRIPT

Should Prostitution Be Legalized?

The "oldest profession in the world" exists in most places of the world. What differs are the ways with which it is dealt in the communities where it occurs. These communities consider a variety of issues when trying to determine the legal state of prostitution.

In the last few years, prostitution and sex work have also found their place on the Internet, where prostitutes and clients arrange meetings on Web sites such as Craigslist, even though such Web sites don't condone the behavior. Web sites have also cropped up offering other Internet-based sex work, such as adult Web camera video chat hosting, or "chat hosts." Chat hosts use their cameras to broadcast erotic acts live to viewers, often in private chat rooms, where a viewer may communicate with a chat host via text-based chat, audio, or audio-visual chat, depending on preferences and the capabilities of the Web site. Another notable example of virtual sex work can be found in the game, Second Life, a three-dimensional online virtual world where users log on to learn, explore, and shop for virtual items, and conduct business, including virtual prostitution, all carried out by customizable avatars.

Susan Milstein posits that if we are able to move beyond viewing prostitution as immoral or unacceptable and begin seeing it as an industry, it is easier to understand the benefits of legalizing it. Milstein outlines the benefits of legalization, to both prostitutes and the society. Legalization would lead to mandated STI and HIV testing, and condom use for all sex acts, dramatically reducing the spread of STIs between prostitutes and their nonpaying partners, as well as between clients and their partners. She also highlights other health benefits of legalized prostitution, namely, the reduction of drug abuse and violence against prostitutes. Violence against prostitutes, such as rape, typically comes from their clients, pimps, or the police, and the criminal penalties associated with prostitution often leave the prostitute with no ability to report the violence or take legal recourse against it. Milstein suggests that legalization, as in Nevada, would decrease violence against prostitutes through the installation of panic buttons in rooms and the ability to report violence without fear of arrest. Milstein also suggests that legalizing prostitution would facilitate more drug outreach and education for the prostitutes. Do you think that legalized prostitution would reduce violence against prostitutes and drug addiction among them? How would these protections work if prostitution were to occur outside the confines of a brothel? How would a street prostitute be safe from violence or access drug education and outreach? Are there ways to reduce violence and increase drug outreach and education to prostitutes without legalization?

Milstein also outlines the financial benefit of legalized prostitution, including taxation and job creation at STI testing labs. What do you think about this? Is it appropriate for communities to reap the financial benefits resulting from prostitution? Perhaps this question lends itself to the morality of prostitution. Donna M. Hughes disagrees with proponents of legalized prostitution who argue that prostitution is a sexual choice and people have the right to choose what they do with their bodies. Hughes argues that prostitution is demoralizing and prostitutes, the majority of whom are women, are not exerting personal choice, but are rather being subjected to criminal assault and kidnapping that arise from the exploitation of people from communities devastated by economic strife. Who do you think is in control in these types of relationships? Are women (and men) simply choosing to express their sexuality in this manner? Are the clients seeking their services exploiting or dehumanizing prostitutes in any way? Do the social, economic, and policy imbalances between men and women in our society influence the context in which the women's choices are being made? Do you think there is a distinction between women who knowingly enter prostitution and those who are forced into it through human trafficking? Do the women who choose to enter prostitution really have a choice? Hughes also posits that women may be coerced into prostitution because they find they have no other options for employment. Does this also stem from societal imbalances? Should we simply accept the lack of other viable jobs for women as an argument for legalized prostitution, or should we strive to create additional opportunities for women and a society where there are less structural imbalances based on sex and gender?

It is evident that the arguments for and against the legalization of prostitution are varied. Where do you stand on the issue? Will legalizing prostitution reduce rates of STIs? Will it lower violence toward prostitutes? Will it financially benefit our communities? Does it represent a core human right to be able to choose how to express one's sexuality? Does prostitution as it exists around the world today represent free choice or coercion? Does it support a patriarchal society?

Suggested Readings

P.R. Abramson et al., *Sexual Rights in America: The Ninth Amendment and the Pursuit of Happiness* (New York: New York University Press, 2003).

B.G. Brents and K. Hausbeck, "Violence and Legalized Brothel Prostitution in Nevada: Examining Safety, Risk and Prostitution Policy," *Journal of Interpersonal Violence* (vol. 20, no. 3, pp. 270–295, 2005).

S. Church et al., "Violence by Clients towards Female Prostitutes in Different Work Settings: Questionnaire Survey," *British Medical Journal* (vol. 322, pp. 524–525, 2001).

"Craigslist Can't Stop Online Prostitution," *CBS News* (Associated Press, September 6, 2010).

M. Farley, *Prostitution and Trafficking in Nevada: Making the Connections* (San Francisco: Prostitution Research and Education, 2007).

S. Friess, "Brothels Ask to Be Taxed, but Official Sees a Catch," *The New York Times* (January 26, 2009).

ISSUE 14

Is Female Circumcision/FGM an Acceptable Practice?

YES: Fuambai S. Ahmadu, from "Disputing the Myth of the Sexual Dysfunction of Circumcised Women," an interview by Richard A. Shweder, *Anthropology Today* (vol. 25, no. 6, December 2009)

NO: World Health Organization, from "Female Genital Mutilation," http://www.who.int/mediacentre/factsheets/fs241/en (February 2010)

ISSUE SUMMARY

YES: Fuambai S. Ahmadu, associate professor at the University of Chicago, in an interview with Richard A. Shweder, argues that studies reporting traumatic effects of female circumcision have been greatly exaggerated and that opposition to the practice represents an ethnocentric bias among researchers and policy makers.

NO: The World Health Organization, the directing and coordinating authority for health within the United Nations system, details the common procedures and reasons for the practice of FGM, while arguing that the health risks and social implications deem the practice a violation of basic human rights.

Around the world, an estimated 100 to 140 million women and girls have had parts of their genitals surgically removed in ceremonies intended to honor and welcome girls into their womanhood or their communities. The ritual is said by many of its supporters to promote chastity, religion, group identity, cleanliness, health, family values, and marriage goals. Female circumcision (FC) is deeply embedded into the cultures of many countries including Ethiopia, Sudan, Somalia, Sierra Leone, Kenya, Tanzania, Chad, Gambia, Liberia, Mali, Senegal, Eritrea, Ivory Coast, Nigeria, and Egypt.

Opponents of FC refer to the practice as female genital mutilation (FGM) because the usual ways of performing the procedure have been reported to cause serious health problems, such as hemorrhaging, urinary and pelvic infection, painful intercourse, infertility, delivery complications, and even death. Besides denying women orgasm, opponents argue, the consequences of FGM also strain the overburdened health care systems in the developing nations in which it is practiced.

Many people are not aware that there are different types of this practice. In Type 1, the simplest form, the clitoral hood is pricked or removed. Type 1 should not preclude orgasms later in life, but it can when performed on the tiny genitals of infants with pins, scissors, and knives that traditional practitioners commonly use. In Type 2, the clitoris and most or all of the labia minora are removed. In Type 3, known as pharonic circumcision, or infibulation, the clitoris, labia minora, and parts of the labia majora are removed. The vulval wound is stitched closed, leaving only a small opening for passage of urine and menstrual flow. Traditional practitioners often use sharpened or hot stones or unsterilized razors or knives, frequently without anesthesia or antibiotics. Healing can take a month or more.

Cultural clashes can occur when families migrate from countries where FC/FGM is customary to parts of the world where it is not practiced. In their new countries, traditional practitioners or local health professionals are sometimes asked to perform the circumcision. Some doctors and nurses charge large fees; others do it because they are concerned about the unhygienic techniques of traditional practitioners. In the United Kingdom, thousands of girls undergo FC/FGM each year, even though it is legally considered child abuse. In 2006, Khalid Adem became the first person prosecuted and convicted for FGM in the United States (although the practice was carried out by anti-masturbation advocates in the United States around the turn of the twentieth century).

Researcher Carla Obermeyer caused great controversy when she published a review of the empirical data on FC/FGM. Her findings indicated that while there were some health issues that had been reported, there was no statistically significant correlation between the practice and a number of health conditions thought to be directly linked. The question discussed here is whether or not the traditional practice of FC/FGM is acceptable around the world. Accepting the practice would allow thousands of immigrants to maintain the essence of their ancient, traditional rites of passage for young girls. Some argue that Types 2 and 3 should be prohibited for health reasons, but some symbolic ritual nicking of the clitoral hood should be allowed as a symbolic element in the extensive ceremonies and educational rites of passage that surround a girl's birth into her family and community, or her passage into womanhood in these cultures.

In the following selections, Fuambai Ahmadu, associate professor at the University of Chicago, in an interview with Richard A. Shweder, argues that studies reporting traumatic effects of female circumcision have been greatly exaggerated and that opposition to the practice represents an ethnocentric bias among researchers and policymakers. The World Health Organization, the directing and coordinating authority for health within the United Nations system, argues that the health risks and social implications deem the practice a violation of basic human rights and expresses concern for the increased procedures being performed by medical professionals.

YES

Fuambai S. Ahmadu

Disputing the Myth of the Sexual Dysfunction of Circumcised Women: An Interview with Fuambai S. Ahmadu by Richard A. Shweder

Richard Shweder: The voices of the many East and West African women who value the practice of genital modification for both girls and boys have not been audible in North American and European media accounts of the practice. How do you address the subject when you lecture on this topic?

Fuambai Ahmadu: I opened my talk at Regina with a short documentary film produced by my younger sister, Sunju Ahmadu, which depicted parts of the public celebrations of our own initiation/excision ceremony nearly two decades ago. The audience thoroughly engaged with the film and in the discussion that followed. I first talked about the film, addressing what I felt was the most obvious question in their minds: how could it be that the African women in the documentary spoke so positively about female initiation and excision (both referred to as bondo among the Kono and other ethnic groups in Sierra Leone)?

The Kono are a minority population who reside in the eastern part of Sierra Leone. This area became known throughout the world as a result of the publicity surrounding the CNN documentary *Cry Freetown* and the Hollywood feature film *Blood Diamond* that followed, which depicted the gruesome, protracted war in the country and its effect on Kono in particular because of the region's high concentration of diamond deposits. The Kono, who are descendents of the Mande from what is now the area of Mali, practise female and male initiation and excision/circumcision as complementary and parallel cultural and symbolic processes celebrating the transition from boyhood to manhood and girlhood to womanhood respectively.

Among many Kono, like perhaps most other Mande groups, there is a view of children as being part of nature, undefined and possessing both male and female elements. In male initiation rituals, the prepuce or foreskin of the penis symbolizes femininity and is associated with female sexual organs, thus removal of the foreskin represents the masculinization of the boy. In

From *Anthropology Today*, vol. 25, no. 6, December 2009, pp. 14–17. Copyright © 2009 by the Royal Anthropological Institute. Reprinted by permission of Wiley/Blackwell via Rightslink.

parallel and complementary form the exposed clitoris represents the male sexual organ or penis and thus its removal symbolizes the feminization of the girl child and marks her adult sexual status. In men's ceremonies, men identify and celebrate their differences from women; similarly women's ceremonies elaborate, exaggerate and celebrate their differences from men, often ridiculing and belittling male sexuality and supposed social and sexual superiority.

In Sierra Leone, women's initiation is highly organized and hierarchical: the institution itself is synonymous with women's power, their political, economic, reproductive and ritual spheres of influence. Excision, or removal of the external clitoral glans and labia minora, in initiation is a symbolic representation of matriarchal power. How can this be so? Removal of the external glans and hood is said to activate women's 'penis' *within* the vagina (the clitoral 'shaft' and 'g-spot' that are subcutaneous). During vaginal intercourse, women say they dominate the male procreative tool (penis) and substance (semen) for sexual pleasure and reproductive purpose, but in ritual they claim to possess the phallus autonomously. Excision also symbolizes the 'separation' of mother and son or of matriarchy and patriarchy (in Mande mythology matriarchy is portrayed as prior to and giving birth to patriarchy). Female elders say that initiation and the act of excision is a potent emotional and psychological reminder to men that it is women who give birth to them and mothers who, after God, are the natural origins or raw elements from which all human creation, culture and society are derived. This concept of a primordial, supreme and all-powerful Mother is at the core of Mande creation mythology and ritual practices that are prevalent even today.

Male circumcision reflects the other side of this duality, the separation of son from mother, phallus from owner, male from female. In men's initiation it is not the phallus that is the dominant symbol of power, as in women's rituals. It is the vagina itself and the obscurity of the womb that we see reflected in the secret ritual masks of the Mande male initiatory societies, as anthropologist Sara Brett-Smith (1997) aptly pointed out. It is through these symbolic means that Mande male ancestors learned the secrets and obtained ritual medicines that prepared them for warfare and hunting in the deep forests of the past. The dominant female substance that associates men with death is blood, and both menstrual and parturition blood in particular are imbued with awesome destructive powers.

So, contrary to much of the rhetoric of the anti-FGM campaigns, the female sex and female sexuality are not oppressed in, through or by these ritual practices. On the contrary, female sexuality and reproductive powers are celebrated and reified in the masquerades, as the origins of creation, of nature and of culture, and feared as potent weapons of death and destruction. This cultural and symbolic context of female initiation and excision explains how it could be that Kono girls and women in the film were speaking in positive, almost reverential terms, about the practice, their bodies and the experience of womanhood. There are different types of female genital cutting practices that are performed for many different reasons, and these practices prevail in diverse socio-cultural contexts, so not all women who are affected necessarily support these practices or view them as empowering to girls and women.

RS: What is your general view of the relationships between informed anthropological and medical research on this topic and representations in the advocacy literature which describe the practice as 'female genital mutilation'?

FA: The anthropological literature on this topic (prior to the nearly universal acceptance of the term FGM in the mid-1990s) was more nuanced and contextualized within the dominant socio-cultural frameworks of affected women. But what about the health risks? How could even well-meaning anthropologists justify the medical hazards of this practice and the sexual oppression of women as represented by advocacy groups who see culture in this instance as an excuse for male barbarism and domination? The problem with the representation of various forms of female circumcision as 'mutilation' is that the term, among other things, presupposes some irreversible and serious harm. This is not supported by current medical research on female circumcision.

Carla Obermeyer (1999, 2003), who was a consultant for WHO, published two comprehensive and critical reviews. The first looked at the available literature on female circumcision up to 1996, the second from 1997 to 2002. Her conclusion is as follows: 'On the basis of the vast literature on the harmful effects of genital surgeries, one might have anticipated finding a wealth of studies that documents considerable increases in mortality and morbidity. This review could find no incontrovertible evidence on mortality, and the rate of medical complications suggests that they are the exception rather than the rule' (Obermeyer 1999: 92).

Another major source, which contradicts received notions about the health hazards of excision in particular, is a study by Linda Morison et al. (2001) at the UK's Medical Research Council Laboratories located in Fajara, The Gambia. Widely cited as authoritative in the literature, this research is the most systematic, comprehensive and controlled investigation of the health consequences of female circumcision yet to be conducted. In summary, the study found that the supposed morbidities often cited as common problems associated with excision (such as infertility, painful sex, vulval tumours, menstrual problems, incontinence and most endogenous infections) did not distinguish women who had the surgery from those who did not. The rate of infertility was exactly the same for both groups – 10%. The authors noted additionally that women expressed high levels of support for the practice.

However, neither Obermeyer's reviews nor the Morison et al. study have been mentioned in any major Western press, despite their startling and counterintuitive findings on female circumcision and health. This is in contrast to the highly publicized *Lancet* report by the WHO Study Group on FGM, released in June 2006, which received widespread, immediate and sensationalized press coverage highlighting claims about infant and maternal mortality during hospital birth. As Bettina Shell-Duncan (2008) pointed out, the *New York Times* unquestioningly sensationalized this group's findings under the heading: 'Genital cutting raises by 50% likelihood that mothers or their newborns will die, study finds' (Rosenthal 2006). Shell-Duncan notes that what this shocking headline failed to mention is the modest magnitude of risk. Another observer noted that, in comparing risk factors in pregnancy, this places female circumcision somewhere behind maternal smoking.

I would note that in the extended *New York Times* Tierneylab blog discussion of this topic you [Shweder] also questioned the findings of the WHO *Lancet* study and its purported evidence of increased 'harm' for circumcised women. You noted that the study collected data on women across six nations but never displayed the results for individual nations to see if they could be replicated; there was no direct control for the quality of health care available for 'circumcised' versus 'uncircumcised' women; the sample was unrepresentative of the whole population; and even given the evidence presented, any risk of genital surgery was astonishingly small and hardly a mandate for an eradication rather than a public health programme.

Sweden-based studies conducted by Birgitta Essen, an obstetrician, and by Sara Johnsdotter, a medical anthropologist, are worthy of mention (Johnsdotter and Essen 2004, Birgitta Essen et al. 2002, 2005). In Essen et al. 2002 no evidence was found of causal connection between genital surgeries and obstructed or prolonged labour. Essen et al. (2005) concluded, surprisingly, that circumcised women were at a lower risk of prolonged labour as compared with uncircumcised Swedish women.

Another obstetrician/gynaecologist, Crista Johnson (2008), who attends to a large number of Somali immigrant patients, has pointed out that the risk of still births may be particularly increased for circumcised women who delay prenatal care and getting to hospitals when they are experiencing complications because they fear being stigmatized by healthcare workers, and because these workers lack specialized knowledge of these women's bodies. In other words, could it be the low standard of care circumcised women are receiving, and fears on the part of both affected women and healthcare providers in zero-tolerance and anti-FGM environments, that contribute to small differences in infant mortality rates in the *Lancet* study?

So, even if the purported negative health outcomes have been exaggerated and circumcised women rightly have their own fears about the risks of being uncircumcised, how can they justify excision of the very sensitive tissue that makes up the clitoris? As some concerned students have asked me, isn't this tantamount to castration?

It has somehow become ubiquitous and obvious knowledge that female circumcision is intended to and actually does inhibit female sexual desire and feeling and that it is like cutting off the male penis, an analogy I never quite understood. But what is the research evidence on female circumcision and sexual pleasure? Obermeyer (1999:55) stated in her review that: 'studies that systematically investigate the sexual feelings of women and men in societies where genital surgeries are found are rare, and the scant information available calls into question the assertion that female genital surgeries are fundamentally antithetical to women's sexuality and incompatible with sexual enjoyment.'

In addition to my own research in the Gambia (Ahmadu 2007), there are several important texts on this issue. The first paper was published by an ardent and vocal anti-FGM activist, Hanny Lightfoot-Klein, the author of *Prisoners of Ritual*, a seminal work for anti-FGM advocates. In her article, Lightfoot-Klein (1989) challenges whether infibulation, the most extreme form of female circumcision, is inimical to women's enjoyment of sex and experience of orgasm. According to her five-year research, 94% of circumcised women reported sexual satisfaction and orgasm and many said they had sex three or four times a week. So what was the problem for Lightfoot-Klein? Sudanese women, in her view, are completely subjugated by their husbands and have no authority whatsoever or agency over their own bodies. But I see a disturbing problem with the implications of this picture: how is that so-called mutilated African women are at one and the same time subjugated by their husbands and also enjoying sex with these patriarchal oppressors and reaching orgasm several times per week?

Is it that African women are masochistic and disturbingly enjoy their own sexual subjugation? Or might this suggest that some Westerners and feminists have it wrong about the nature of African marriages, social systems and male-female interactions and intimacies? If the experiences of these Sudanese women are anything like my own and those of the community of women I was raised among, then I doubt very much that they are somehow sexually deviant masochists who are ignorant of and enjoy their own oppression.

Of particular interest is a recent publication by Lucrezia Catania (Catania et al. 2007), an Italian obstetrician and gynaecologist who runs a clinic with her Somali husband in Italy that is frequented by mainly Somali immigrants. According to the study, the findings 'suggest, without doubt, that healthy "mutilated/circumcised" women who did not suffer grave long-term complications and who have a good and fulfilling relationship may enjoy sex and have no negative impact on psychosexual life (fantasies, desire and pleasure, ability to experience orgasm)'. Catania's findings were also interesting in that, in comparison with her Italian control group, infibulated Somali women reported greater frequency of orgasms. These findings are very much in line with those of Lightfoot-Klein in her fieldwork with Sudanese women.

Kirsten Bell (2005) provides an interesting context for this debate by looking at changes in Western discourses on genital cutting and sexuality. In particular, she questions the current unspoken assumption that the male body provides the basis of understanding the female body. This is the assumption, Bell argues, that makes sense of how people readily, but in my view mistakenly, equate female circumcision with male castration.

In my own research in the Gambia and Sierra Leone (Ahmadu 2000, 2007), I have tried to point out the cultural and symbolic importance of gender complementarity and interdependence and the construction of heterosexual marriage and intercourse in understanding female and male initiation and excision/circumcision. For circumcised African women brought up in dual-sex (as opposed to male-dominated) cultures that celebrate male and female powers, heterosexual intercourse (rather than the presence of an external clitoris) is seen as key to women's most intense, vaginally induced orgasms. Same-sex sexual interactions and relationships and 'auto-sexuality' exist and were largely ignored in the past as part of the realm of nature or childhood. *Bondo* women elders believe and teach that excision improves sexual pleasure by emphasizing orgasms reached through stimulation of the g-spot, which is said to be more intense and satisfying for an experienced woman. Excision of the protruding clitoris is said to aesthetically and physiologically enhance the appearance of the vulva and facilitate male/female coitus by removing any barrier to complete, full and deep penetration.

According to the women I interviewed, sexual foreplay is complex and requires more than immediate physical touch: emphasis is on learning erotic songs and sexually suggestive dance movements; cooking, feeding and feigned submission, as powerful aphrodisiacs, and the skills of aural sex (more than oral sex), are said to heighten sexual desire and anticipation. Orgasms experienced during vaginal intercourse, these female elders say, must be taught and trained, requiring both skill and experience on the part of both partners (male initiation ceremonies used to teach men sexual skills on how to 'hit the spot' in women – emphasizing body movement and rhythm in intercourse, and importantly, verbal innuendoes that titillate a woman's senses). Thus, from the viewpoint of these women elders vaginal intercourse is associated with womanhood and adult female sexuality. In Mande cultures the emphasis is on the vagina as the source and symbol of womanhood or – to refer to Alice Walker's popular anti-FGM novel – the hidden g-spot, rather than the visible protruding clitoris, is the 'secret' 'joy' adult women 'possess'.

And it is the vagina that is the object of awe and deference in male initiation ceremonies. Male initiates (at least in the past) learn not to fear this powerful female sexual organ but rather how to manipulate it for their own and their partners' pleasure and reproduction, as well as to obtain other secret powers of protection in hunting and warfare. Likewise female initiates are taught not to fear the male phallus but to dominate the penis for pleasure and semen in reproduction as well as in certain medicinal uses. Both male and female initiates, especially in the past, learn that sexual pleasure is not only an innate capacity in women but a right of all women in marriage. That a woman can be physiologically or psychologically *incapable* of sexual enjoyment and desire seems foreign to the accounts of most of my older female informants.

RS: You recently engaged in a debate in New York City about the practice at a meeting of a foundation concerned with the welfare of African women, which was reviewed in *The American Prospect* (Goldberg 2009a). Could you describe the context of the debate, and reflect on the way it was represented in that article as 'rites v rights'?

FA: Sauti Yetu, which is a grassroots African women's organization that is dedicated in part to addressing issues of violence as well as other injustices in our communities and larger society, hosted an amicable debate in New York between me and a Kenyan woman, also circumcised, to discuss our experiences of initiation and views about the practice. This was organized as a reflection upon the fourth annual International Day of Zero Tolerance of Female Genital Mutilation, an occasion for events across the globe dedicated to abolishing the practice. Michelle Goldberg was there to research the event for her new book on the politics of women's reproduction worldwide (published as Goldberg 2009b). In her review of the event, Goldberg (2009a) made reference to this debate and acknowledged the need to consider other voices such as my own on this topic. On the one hand I thought her review went a long way to dispel myths about circumcised women (as being traditional, culturebound, uneducated and necessarily coerced into 'mutilation'); however, on the other hand, I thought the article continued to reproduce stereotypes of the practice as being medically harmful and extremely traumatic for most women.

Goldberg conveniently ignored the lack of medical evidence to support her assertion about the 'thousands' of women who suffer from female circumcision and continued to carry the message that eradication is the only moral and appropriately feminist response to this 'human rights abuse' against African women. Underlying her assertion is the uncritical assumption of a universal category of woman, whose 'intact' external clitoral glans and hood is somehow essential to her identity, sexual pleasure and experience of wholeness. Circumcised African women, according to this view, are in a permanent condition of 'pain' and 'suffering' from which, Goldberg would argue, only other enlightened African women (with the indirect but certain guidance of Western women) can provide escape. Of course, I find this view patronizing and infantilizing of adult African women who, like Western women who opt for cosmetic genital surgeries, should be free to decide for themselves what to do with their own bodies.

Another point I made that Goldberg overlooked is that supporters of female circumcision justify the practice on much of the same grounds that they support male circumcision. The uncircumcised clitoris and penis are considered homologous aesthetically and hygienically. Just as the male foreskin covers the head of the penis, the female foreskin covers the clitoral glans. Both, they argue, lead to build-up of smegma and bacteria in the layers of skin between the hood and glans. This accumulation is thought of as odorous, susceptible to infection and a nuisance to keep clean on a daily basis. Further, circumcised women point to the risks of painful clitoral adhesions that occur in girls and women who do not cleanse properly, and to the requirement of excision as a treatment for these extreme cases. Supporters of female circumcision also point to the risk of clitoral hypertrophy or an enlarged clitoris that resembles a small penis. For these reasons many circumcised women view the decision to circumcise their daughters as something as obvious as the decision to circumcise sons: why, one woman asked, would any reasonable mother want to burden her daughter with excess clitoral and labial tissue that is unhygienic, unsightly and interferes with sexual penetration, especially if the same mother would choose circumcision to ensure healthy and aesthetically appealing genitalia for her son?

I write and teach about different cultural perspectives on female circumcision with regard to pleasure, hygiene and genital aesthetics, not to insist that uncircumcised Western women opponents have it wrong and circumcised African women proponents are right (such stereotypical categorizations are never quite so neat anyway) but to point out that there are different and contested views and experiences and that no one is more right than the other. So it is my opinion that we need to remove the stigma of mutilation and let all girls know they are beautiful and accepted, no matter what the appearance of their genitalia or their cultural background, lest the myth of sexual dysfunction in circumcised women become a true self-fulfilling prophecy, as Catania and others are increasingly witnessing in their care of circumcised African girls and women.

Female Genital Mutilation

Key Facts

- Female genital mutilation (FGM) includes procedures that intention-ally alter or injure female genital organs for non-medical reasons.
- The procedure has no health benefits for girls and women.
- Procedures can cause severe bleeding and problems urinating, and later, potential childbirth complications and newborn deaths.
- An estimated 100 to 140 million girls and women worldwide are cur-rently living with the consequences of FGM.
- It is mostly carried out on young girls sometime between infancy and age 15 years.
- In Africa an estimated 92 million girls from 10 years of age and above have undergone FGM.
- FGM is internationally recognized as a violation of the human rights of girls and women.

Female genital mutilation (FGM) comprises all procedures that involve partial or total removal of the external female genitalia, or other injury to the female genital organs for non-medical reasons.

The practice is mostly carried out by traditional circumcisers, who often play other central roles in communities, such as attending childbirths. Increas-ingly, however, FGM is being performed by health care providers.

FGM is recognized internationally as a violation of the human rights of girls and women. It reflects deep-rooted inequality between the sexes, and constitutes an extreme form of discrimination against women. It is nearly always carried out on minors and is a violation of the rights of children. The practice also violates a person's rights to health, security and physical integrity, the right to be free from torture and cruel, inhuman or degrading treatment, and the right to life when the procedure results in death.

Procedures

Female genital mutilation is classified into four major types.

1. Clitoridectomy: partial or total removal of the clitoris (a small, sensi-tive and erectile part of the female genitals) and, in very rare cases, only the prepuce (the fold of skin surrounding the clitoris).

2. Excision: partial or total removal of the clitoris and the labia minora, with or without excision of the labia majora (the labia are "the lips" that surround the vagina).
3. Infibulation: narrowing of the vaginal opening through the creation of a covering seal. The seal is formed by cutting and repositioning the inner, or outer, labia, with or without removal of the clitoris.
4. Other: all other harmful procedures to the female genitalia for non-medical purposes, e.g. pricking, piercing, incising, scraping and cauterizing the genital area.

No Health Benefits, Only Harm

FGM has no health benefits, and it harms girls and women in many ways. It involves removing and damaging healthy and normal female genital tissue, and interferes with the natural functions of girls' and women's bodies.

Immediate complications can include severe pain, shock, haemorrhage (bleeding), tetanus or sepsis (bacterial infection), urine retention, open sores in the genital region and injury to nearby genital tissue.

Long-term consequences can include:

- recurrent bladder and urinary tract infections;
- cysts;
- infertility;
- an increased risk of childbirth complications and newborn deaths;
- the need for later surgeries. For example, the FGM procedure that seals or narrows a vaginal opening (type 3 above) needs to be cut open later to allow for sexual intercourse and childbirth. Sometimes it is stitched again several times, including after childbirth, hence the woman goes through repeated opening and closing procedures, further increasing and repeated both immediate and long-term risks.

Who Is at Risk?

Procedures are mostly carried out on young girls sometime between infancy and age 15, and occasionally on adult women. In Africa, about three million girls are at risk for FGM annually.

Between 100 to 140 million girls and women worldwide are living with the consequences of FGM. In Africa, about 92 million girls age 10 years and above are estimated to have undergone FGM.

The practice is most common in the western, eastern, and north-eastern regions of Africa, in some countries in Asia and the Middle East, and among certain immigrant communities in North America and Europe.

Cultural, Religious and Social Causes

The causes of female genital mutilation include a mix of cultural, religious and social factors within families and communities.

- Where FGM is a social convention, the social pressure to conform to what others do and have been doing is a strong motivation to perpetuate the practice.
- FGM is often considered a necessary part of raising a girl properly, and a way to prepare her for adulthood and marriage.
- FGM is often motivated by beliefs about what is considered proper sexual behaviour, linking procedures to premarital virginity and marital fidelity. FGM is in many communities believed to reduce a woman's libido, and thereby is further believed to help her resist "illicit" sexual acts. When a vaginal opening is covered or narrowed (type 3 above), the fear of pain of opening it, and the fear that this will be found out, is expected to further discourage "illicit" sexual intercourse among women with this type of FGM.
- FGM is associated with cultural ideals of femininity and modesty, which include the notion that girls are "clean" and "beautiful" after removal of body parts that are considered "male" or "unclean".
- Though no religious scripts prescribe the practice, practitioners often believe the practice has religious support.
- Religious leaders take varying positions with regard to FGM: some promote it, some consider it irrelevant to religion, and others contribute to its elimination.
- Local structures of power and authority, such as community leaders, religious leaders, circumcisers, and even some medical personnel can contribute to upholding the practice.
- In most societies, FGM is considered a cultural tradition, which is often used as an argument for its continuation.
- In some societies, recent adoption of the practice is linked to copying the traditions of neighbouring groups. Sometimes it has started as part of a wider religious or traditional revival movement.
- In some societies, FGM is being practised by new groups when they move into areas where the local population practice FGM.

International Response

In 1997, the World Health Organization (WHO) issued a joint statement with the United Nations Children's Fund (UNICEF) and the United Nations Population Fund (UNFPA) against the practice of FGM. A new statement, with wider United Nations support, was then issued in February 2008 to support increased advocacy for the abandonment of FGM.

The 2008 statement documents new evidence collected over the past decade about the practice. It highlights the increased recognition of the human rights and legal dimensions of the problem and provides current data on the frequency and scope of FGM. It also summarizes research about why FGM continues, how to stop it, and its damaging effects on the health of women, girls and newborn babies.

Since 1997, great efforts have been made to counteract FGM, through research, work within communities, and changes in public policy. Progress at both international and local levels includes:

- wider international involvement to stop FGM;
- the development of international monitoring bodies and resolutions that condemn the practice;
- revised legal frameworks and growing political support to end FGM; and
- in some countries, decreasing practice of FGM, and an increasing number of women and men in practising communities who declare their support to end it.

Research shows that, if practising communities themselves decide to abandon FGM, the practice can be eliminated very rapidly.

WHO Response

In 2008, the World Health Assembly passed a resolution (WHA61.16) on the elimination of FGM, emphasizing the need for concerted action in all sectors —health, education, finance, justice and women's affairs.

WHO efforts to eliminate female genital mutilation focus on:

- advocacy: developing publications and advocacy tools for international, regional and local efforts to end FGM within a generation;
- research: generating knowledge about the causes and consequences of the practice, how to eliminate it, and how to care for those who have experienced FGM;
- guidance for health systems: developing training materials and guidelines for health professionals to help them treat and counsel women who have undergone procedures.

WHO is particularly concerned about the increasing trend for medically trained personnel to perform FGM. WHO strongly urges health professionals not to perform such procedures.

POSTSCRIPT

Is Female Circumcision/FGM an Acceptable Practice?

"**C**ultural relativism" is the idea that in order to understand a person's beliefs, we must understand the cultural norms in which the person has been socialized. Thus, in order to understand the practice of FC/FGM, we must understand the value it has within a particular culture. Proponents of FC/FGM argue that the tradition has great value to the people who practice it, and that outsiders cannot understand the meaning and importance. Opponents argue that, tradition or not, the practice does real physical and social harm to women. Attempts at compromise have been suggested, including simply "nicking" the clitoris or clitoral hood, or having trained medical staff perform the procedures (which is advised against by the WHO). In Kenya, a practice known as *Ntanira na Mugambo,* or "Circumcision Through Words" has become a growing trend. Developed by several Kenyan and international nongovernmental agencies, "Circumcision Through Words" brings young girls together for a week of seclusion during which they learn traditional teachings about their coming roles as women, parents, and adults in the community, as well as more modern messages about personal health, reproductive issues, hygiene, communication skills, self-esteem, and dealing with peer pressure. A community celebration of song, dance, and feasting affirms the girls and their new place in the community. But is the move away from FC/FGM to an end or compromise an ethnocentric one? Ethnocentrism is, in brief, judging all other cultures against what you feel are the standard beliefs and practices of your own. Are attempts to ban or modify FC/FGM practices an imposition of outsiders' cultural values? Are international health agencies and activists right to challenge the practice? Should laws, which are already on the books in many countries, be implemented everywhere to stop the practice? Or should the practice be allowed to stand as an important cultural tradition in parts of the world? Is there a middle ground that would appease both sides?

At the time of this writing, a ballot initiative banning circumcision for male under the age of 18 was scheduled for a vote in San Francisco's November 2011 elections. The measure is controversial, pitting many religious and cultural leaders against anti-circumcision advocates. The arguments over this proposed law sound incredibly similar to the calls to ban the practice around the world. While comparisons of male circumcision to FGM often draw stern reminders of the invasiveness of Types 2 and 3, the underlying arguments of tradition and culture versus health risks and bodily autonomy are comparable. Do you feel that this ballot initiative has merit? Or should it be upheld as an honored tradition? What about labiaplasty or cosmetic surgeries performed on women's vulvas. Such surgeries have become more popular in recent years as women (and surgeons) have sought the "perfect" vulva. Should labiaplasty be banned? Does a challenge to the practice of male circumcision or the availability of labiaplasty change or influence your stance on the practice of FC/FGM? Why or why not?

Suggested Readings

"Abandon the Knife," *Al Jazeera* (May 26, 2011).

A. Cohen, "Sexual Cosmetic Surgery: Should Cosmetic Surgery on Your Lady Parts Be Banned?" *Marie Claire* (November 8, 2008).

E. Dorkenoo, *Cutting the Rose: Female Genital Mutilation—The Practice and Its Prevention* (Minority Rights Group, 1994).

R. Jaslow, "Circumcision on Ballot in San Francisco: Will Voters Okay Ban?" *CBS News* (May 19, 2011).

N. Kristof, "A Rite of Torture for Girls," *The New York Times* (May 11, 2011).

N. Lakhani, "UK Fails to Halt Female Genital Mutilation," *The Independent* (December 20, 2009).

C. Obermeyer, "The Health Consequences of Female Circumcision: Science, Advocacy, and Standards of Evidence," *Medical Anthropology Quarterly* (vol. 17, no. 3, pp. 394–412, 2003).

V. Rubadiri, "School Provides Refuge from FGM," *Capital FM Kenya* (May 27, 2011).

ISSUE 15

Should Same-Sex Marriage Be Legal?

YES: Human Rights Campaign, from *Answers to Questions About Marriage Equality* (Human Rights Campaign, 2011)

NO: Timothy J. Dailey, from *Ten Facts About Counterfeit Marriage* (Family Research Council, 2008)

ISSUE SUMMARY

YES: The Human Rights Campaign (HRC), America's largest gay and lesbian organization, explains why same-sex couples should be afforded the same legal right to marry as heterosexual couples.

NO: Timothy J. Dailey, senior fellow for policy at the Family Research Council, argues that allowing same-sex marriage would go against thousands of years of human social norms and would be a "counterfeit" version of traditional, other-sex marriage.

On May 17, 2004, Massachusetts became the first state in the United States to grant marriage licenses to same-sex couples. The state acted under the direction of its supreme court, which had found that withholding marriage licenses from lesbian and gay couples violated the state constitution. More than 600 same-sex couples applied for marriage licenses that first day alone. The first same-sex couple to be issued marriage licenses were Marcia Kadish and Tanya McCloskey. That couple had waited over 18 years for the day to arrive.

After the Massachusetts ruling, gay and lesbian couples across the country sought marriage licenses from their municipalities. Many were denied, while others found loopholes in laws that allowed them to file for licenses. For example, in Oregon, the law stated that marriage is a "civil contract entered into in person by males at least 17 years of age and females at least 17 years of age." Since the law did not state that males had to marry females, gay and lesbian marriages were never technically against the law. Marriage licenses were also issued in counties in California, New Jersey, New York, and Washington. In San Francisco, California, Mayor Gavin Newsom challenged the state law and allowed city officials to wed same-sex couples. Ultimately, the gay and lesbian marriages and marriage licenses in all states other than Massachusetts were ruled illegal and invalid.

The court ruling that paved the way for same-sex marriage in Massachusetts opened a firestorm of controversy. Supporters heralded the decision as a step toward equality for all Americans. Opponents of gay and lesbian nuptials spoke out against the redefinition and destruction of traditional marriage. Then President George W. Bush endorsed a constitutional amendment that would define marriage as being between a man and a woman saying that "the sacred institution of marriage should not be redefined by a few activist judges."

Several years earlier, President Bill Clinton had signed the Defense of Marriage Act (DOMA), which stated that states were not required to recognize same-sex marriages performed in other states. Nevertheless, supporters of the constitutional amendment believe DOMA is not enough to keep courts from redefining traditional marriage. Gay rights supporters oppose the amendment, which they feel unjustly writes discrimination into the Constitution. Even many conservatives oppose the amendment because they believe it to be too strong of a federal intrusion into the rights of states. In February 2011, President Barack Obama ordered the Department of Justice to stop defending DOMA against legal challenges, as he felt it was unconstitutional. However, the Republicans in the House of Representatives, led by Speaker John Boehner, have moved to defend DOMA.

Since Massachusetts's landmark decision in 2004, six additional states, Connecticut, California, Iowa, Vermont, and New Hampshire, New York, as well as the District of Columbia have legalized same-sex marriage. However, California's legalization of same-sex marriage was short-lived after voters narrowly approved "Proposition 8," reinstating the ban on gay marriage. A series of rulings upheld the validity of marriages performed before the passage of Proposition 8, while stopping further same-sex marriages, leaving the future of same-sex marriage undecided. At the time of this writing, the decision is currently being appealed. The state government of Maine also legalized same-sex marriage, but a voter referendum led to the repeal of the law before it could take effect.

In the following essays, the Human Rights Campaign (HRC) answers common questions about same-sex marriage and the law, religion, and family. The HRC also reviews the benefits that same-sex marriages could potentially have for gay and lesbian couples and society. Thomas J. Dailey, senior fellow for policy at the Family Research Council, argues that allowing same-sex marriage would go against thousands of years of human social norms and would be a "counterfeit" version of traditional, other-sex marriage. He states that legalized same-sex marriage will lead to an attack on those whose values are not in line with that of supporters.

Questions About Same-Sex Marriage

Since the rise of a national discussion about marriage rights for same-sex couples, many straight friends and family members have been asking important questions about the issue. This section provides some basic answers to those questions, such as:

Why Do Same-Sex Couples Want to Marry?

Many same-sex couples want the right to legally marry because they are in love—many, in fact, have spent the last 10, 20 or 50 years with that person—and they want to honor their relationship in the greatest way our society has to offer, by making a public commitment to stand together in good times and bad, through all the joys and challenges family life brings.

Many parents want the right to marry because they know it offers children a vital safety net and guarantees protections that unmarried parents cannot provide. And still other people—both gay and straight—are fighting for the right of same-sex couples to marry because they recognize that it is simply not fair to deny some families the protections all other families are eligible to enjoy.

Currently in the United States, same-sex couples in long-term, committed relationships pay higher taxes and are denied basic protections and rights granted to married straight couples. Among them:

- **Hospital visitation.** Married couples have the automatic right to visit each other in the hospital and make medical decisions. Same-sex couples can be denied the right to visit a sick or injured loved one in the hospital.
- **Social Security benefits.** Married people receive Social Security payments upon the death of a spouse. Despite paying payroll taxes, gay and lesbian partners receive no Social Security survivor benefits—resulting in an average annual income loss of $5,528 upon the death of a partner.
- **Immigration.** Americans in bi-national relationships are not permitted to petition for their same-sex partners to immigrate. As a result, they are often forced to separate or move to another country.
- **Health insurance.** Many public and private employers provide medical coverage to the spouses of their employees, but most employers do not provide coverage to the life partners of gay and lesbian employees.

Gay and lesbian employees who do receive health coverage for their partners must pay federal income taxes on the value of the insurance.

- **Estate taxes.** A married person automatically inherits all the property of his or her deceased spouse without paying estate taxes. A gay or lesbian taxpayer is forced to pay estate taxes on property inherited from a deceased partner.
- **Family leave.** Married workers are legally entitled to unpaid leave from their jobs to care for an ill spouse. Gay and lesbian workers are not entitled to family leave to care for their partners.
- **Nursing homes.** Married couples have a legal right to live together in nursing homes. The rights of elderly gay or lesbian couples are an uneven patchwork of state laws.
- **Home protection.** Laws protect married seniors from being forced to sell their homes to pay high nursing home bills; gay and lesbian seniors have no such protection.
- **Pensions.** After the death of a worker, most pension plans pay survivor benefits only to a legal spouse of the participant. Gay and lesbian partners are excluded from such pension benefits.

Why Aren't Civil Unions Enough?

Comparing marriage to civil unions is a bit like comparing diamonds to rhinestones. One is, quite simply, the real deal; the other is not. Consider:

- Opposite-sex couples who are eligible to marry may have their marriage performed in any state and have it recognized in every other state in the nation and every country in the world.
- Couples who are joined in a civil union, for example in Vermont, New Jersey or New Hampshire, have no guarantee that its protections will travel with them to other states.

Moreover, even couples who have a civil union and remain in Vermont, New Jersey or New Hampshire receive only second-class protections in comparison to their married friends and neighbors. While they receive state-level protections, they do not receive any of the more than 1,100 federal benefits and protections of marriage.

In short, civil unions are not separate but equal—they are separate and unequal. And our society has tried separate before. It just doesn't work.

Marriage:	Civil Unions:
• State grants marriage licenses to couples.	• State would grant civil union licenses to couples.
• Religious institutions are not required to perform marriage ceremonies.	• Couples receive legal protections and rights under state law only.
	• Civil unions are not recognized by other states or the federal government.
	• Religious institutions are not required to perform civil union ceremonies.

"I believe God meant marriage for men and women. How can I support marriage for same-sex couples?"

Many people who believe in God—as well as fairness and justice for all—ask this question. They feel a tension between religious beliefs and democratic values that has been experienced in many different ways throughout our nation's history. That is why the framers of our Constitution established the principle of separation of church and state.

That principle applies no less to the marriage issue than it does to any other. Indeed, the answer to the apparent dilemma between religious beliefs and support for equal protections for all families lies in recognizing that marriage has a significant religious meaning for many people, but that it is also a legal contract. And it is strictly the legal—not the religious—dimension of marriage that is being debated now.

Granting marriage rights to same-sex couples would not require leaders of Christian, Jewish, Islamic or any other religious leaders to perform these marriages. It would not require religious institutions to permit these ceremonies to be held on their grounds. It would not even require that religious communities discuss the issue. People of faith would remain free to make their own judgments about what makes a marriage in the eyes of God—just as they are today.

Consider, for example, the difference in how the Roman Catholic Church and the U.S. government view couples who have divorced and remarried. Because church tenets do not sanction divorce, the second marriage is not valid in the church's view. The government, however, recognizes the marriage by extending to the remarried couple the same rights and protections as those granted to every other married couple in America. In this situation—as would be the case in marriage for same-sex couples—the church remains free to establish its own teachings on the religious dimension of marriage while the government upholds equality under law.

A growing number of religious communities bless same-sex unions, including Reform Judaism, the Unitarian Universalist Association and the Metropolitan Community Church. The Presbyterian Church (USA) allows ceremonies to be performed but they're not considered the same as marriage. The Episcopal Church, United Church of Christ and the United Synagogue of Conservative Judaism allow individual congregations to set their own policies on same-sex unions.

"I strongly believe children need a mother and a father."

Many of us grew up believing that everyone needs a mother and father, regardless of whether we ourselves happened to have two parents, or two good parents.

But as families have grown more diverse in recent decades, and researchers have studied how these different family relationships affect children, it has become clear that the quality of a family's relationship is more important than the particular structure of families that exist today.

In other words, the qualities that help children grow into good and responsible adults—learning how to learn, to have compassion for others, to contribute to society and be respectful of others and their differences—do not depend on the sexual orientation of their parents but on their parents' ability to provide a loving, stable and happy home, something no class of Americans has an exclusive hold on.

That is why research studies have consistently shown that children raised by gay and lesbian parents do just as well as children raised by straight parents in all conventional measures of child development, such as academic achievement, psychological well-being and social abilities.

That is also why the nation's leading child welfare organizations, including the American Academy of Pediatrics, the American Academy of Family Physicians and others, have issued statements that dismiss assertions that only straight couples can be good parents—and declare that the focus should now be on providing greater protections for the 1 million to 9 million children being raised by gay and lesbian parents in the United States today.

Granting same-sex couples the right to marry, therefore, would enable the millions of same-sex parents raising children today to give their children what every child deserves—the safest, most secure environment possible, with all the legal protections that our country has put in place.

"This is different from interracial marriage. Sexual orientation is a choice."

> *"We cannot keep turning our backs on gay and lesbian Americans. I have fought too hard and too long against discrimination based on race and color not to stand up against discrimination based on sexual orientation. I've heard the reasons for opposing civil marriage for same-sex couples. Cut through the distractions, and they stink of the same fear, hatred, and intolerance I have known in racism and in bigotry."*
>
> —Rep. John Lewis, D-Ga., a leader of the black civil rights movement, writing in *The Boston Globe*, Nov. 25, 2003

Decades of research all point to the fact that sexual orientation is not a choice, and that a person's sexual orientation cannot be changed. To whom one is drawn is a fundamental aspect of who we are.

In this way, the struggle for marriage equality for same-sex couples is just as basic as the successful fight for interracial marriage. It recognizes that Americans should not be coerced into false and unhappy marriages but should be free to marry the person they love—thereby building marriage on a true and stable foundation.

"Won't this create a free-for-all and make the whole idea of marriage meaningless?"

Many people share this concern because opponents of LGBT equality have used this argument as a scare tactic—but it is not true. Granting same-sex couples the right to marry would in no way change the number of people who could enter into a marriage (or eliminate restrictions on the age or familial relationships of those who may marry). Marriage would continue to recognize the highest possible commitment that can be made between two adults, plain and simple.

"How could marriage for same-sex couples possibly be good for the American family—or our country?"

"We shouldn't just allow gay marriage. We should insist on gay marriage. We should regard it as scandalous that two people could claim to love each other and not want to sanctify their love with marriage and fidelity."

—Conservative Columnist David Brooks,
writing in *The New York Times*, Nov. 22, 2003.

The prospect of a significant change in our laws and customs has often caused people to worry more about dire consequences that could result than about the potential positive outcomes. In fact, precisely the same anxiety arose when some people fought to overturn the laws prohibiting marriage between people of different races in the 1950s and 1960s. (One Virginia judge even declared, "God intended to separate the races.")

But in reality, opening marriage to couples who are so willing to fight for it could only strengthen the institution for all. It would open the doors to more supporters, not opponents. And it would help keep the age-old institution alive.

As history has repeatedly proven, institutions that fail to take account of the changing needs of the population are those that grow weak; those that recognize and accommodate changing needs grow strong. For example, the U.S. military, like American colleges and universities, grew stronger after permitting African Americans and women to join its ranks.

Similarly, granting same-sex couples the right to marry would strengthen the institution of marriage by allowing it to better meet the needs of the true diversity of family structures in America today.

"Can't same-sex couples go to a lawyer to secure all the rights they need?"

Not by a long shot. When a gay or lesbian person gets seriously ill, there is no legal document that can make their partner eligible to take leave from work under the federal Family and Medical Leave Act to provide care—because that law applies only to married couples.

When gay or lesbian people grow old and in need of nursing home care, there is no legal document that can give them the right to Medicaid coverage without potentially causing their partner to be forced from their home—because the federal Medicaid law only permits married spouses to keep their home without becoming ineligible for benefits.

And when a gay or lesbian person dies, there is no legal document that can extend Social Security survivor benefits or the right to inherit a retirement plan without severe tax burdens that stem from being "unmarried" in the eyes of the law.

These are only a few examples of the critical protections that are granted through more than 1,100 federal laws that protect only married couples.

In the absence of the right to marry, same-sex couples can only put in place a handful of the most basic arrangements, such as naming each other in a will or a power of attorney. And even these documents remain vulnerable to challenges in court by disgruntled family members.

"Won't this cost taxpayers too much money?"

No, it wouldn't necessarily cost much at all. In fact, treating same-sex couples as families under law could even save taxpayers money because marriage would require them to assume legal responsibility for their joint living expenses and reduce their dependence on public assistance programs such as Medicaid, Temporary Assistance to Needy Families, Supplemental Security Income disability payments and food stamps.

Put another way, the money it would cost to extend benefits to same-sex couples could be outweighed by the money that would be saved as these families rely more fully on each other instead of state or federal government assistance.

For example, two studies conducted in 2003 by professors at the University of Massachusetts, Amherst, and the University of California, Los Angeles, found that extending domestic partner benefits to same-sex couples in California and New Jersey would save taxpayers millions of dollars a year.

Specifically, the studies projected that the California state budget would save an estimated $8.1 million to $10.6 million each year by enacting the most comprehensive domestic partner law in the nation. In New Jersey, which passed a new domestic partner law in 2004, the savings were projected to be even higher—more than $61 million each year.

(*Sources: "Equal Rights, Fiscal Responsibility: The Impact of A.B. 205 on California's Budget," by M. V. Lee Badgett, Ph.D., IGLSS, Department of Economics, University of Massachusetts, and R. Bradley Sears, J.D., Williams Project, UCLA School of Law, University of California, Los Angeles, May 2003, and "Supporting Families, Saving Funds: A Fiscal Analysis of New Jersey's Domestic Partnership Act," by Badgett and Sears with Suzanne Goldberg, J.D., Rutgers School of Law—Newark, December 2003.*)

Where Can Same-Sex Couples Marry Today?

In 2001, the Netherlands became the first country to extend marriage rights to same-sex couples. Belgium passed a similar law two years later. Spain followed suit in July 2005, and in December 2005, the South African Supreme Court ruled that the country had to extend the rights of marriage to same-sex couples by the end of 2006. Some of these countries, however, have strict citizenship or residency requirements that do not permit American couples to take advantage of the protections provided.

In 2003, Ontario became the first Canadian province to grant marriage to same-sex couples, and in July 2005, Canada's federal government passed a law extending marriage equality nationwide.

In November 2003, the Massachusetts Supreme Judicial Court recognized the right of same-sex couples to marry, giving the state six months to begin issuing marriage licenses to same-sex couples. It began issuing licenses May 17, 2004.

In October 2008, the Connecticut Supreme Court recognized the right of same-sex couples to marry. Connecticut began issuing licenses to same-sex couples Nov. 12, 2008.

On Nov. 4, 2008, California voters approved Proposition 8, which amends the state constitution to prohibit marriage by same-sex couples. The amendment overrules a May 2008 decision by the California Supreme Court recognizing marriage equality. California continues to provide rights and responsibilities to registered domestic partners.

Follow the latest developments in California, New Jersey, New Mexico, New York, Oregon, Washington and other communities across the country at the HRC Marriage Center (www.hrc.org/marriage).

Other nations have also taken steps toward extending equal protections to all couples, though the protections they provide are more limited than marriage. Croatia, Denmark, Finland, France, Germany, Iceland, Israel, New Zealand, Norway, Portugal, Slovenia, Switzerland, Sweden and the United Kingdom all have nationwide laws that grant same-sex partners a range of important rights, protections and obligations.

Beginning in December 2005, same-sex couples in the United Kingdom have been able to apply for civil partnership licenses to certify their relationships before the government. These licenses provide same-sex couples hospital visitation rights, pension benefits, the ability to gain parental responsibility for a partner's children and other rights granted to opposite-sex couples.

What Protections Other Than Marriage Are Available to American Same-Sex Couples?

At the federal level, there are no protections at all available to same-sex couples. In fact, a federal law called the "Defense of Marriage Act" says that the federal government will discriminate against same-sex couples who marry by refusing to recognize their marriages or providing them with the federal protections of marriage.

Some members of the U.S. Congress have tried to go even further by attempting to pass a federal marriage amendment that would write discrimination against same-sex couples into the U.S. Constitution. This was defeated twice, in 2004 and 2006.

At the state level, Vermont, New Jersey and New Hampshire offer civil unions (as of 2008), which provide important state benefits but no federal protections, such as Social Security survivor benefits. There is also no guarantee that civil unions will be recognized outside these states. Forty-four states also have laws or state constitutional amendments explicitly prohibiting the recognition of marriages between same-sex partners.

Domestic partner laws have been enacted in California, Maine, Hawaii, Oregon, Washington and the District of Columbia. The benefits conferred by these laws vary; some offer access to family health insurance, others confer co-parenting rights. Some offer a broad range of rights similar to civil unions.

Timothy J. Dailey  **NO**

Ten Facts About Counterfeit Marriage

1. Homosexual Marriage Degrades a Time-Honored Institution

Homosexual marriage is an empty pretense that lacks the fundamental sexual complementariness of male and female. And like all counterfeits, it cheapens and degrades the real thing. The destructive effects may not be immediately apparent, but the cumulative damage is inescapable. The eminent Harvard sociologist, Pitirim Sorokin, analyzed cultures spanning several thousand years on several continents, and found that virtually no society has ceased to regulate sexuality within marriage as traditionally defined, and survived.

2. Homosexual Marriage Would Radically Redefine Marriage to Include Virtually Any Sexual Behavior

Once marriage is no longer confined to a man and a woman, and the sole criterion becomes the presence of "love" and "mutual commitment," it is impossible to exclude virtually any "relationship" between two or more partners of either sex. To those who scoff at concerns that gay marriage could lead to the acceptance of other harmful and widely-rejected sexual behaviors, it should be pointed out that until very recent times the very suggestion that two women or two men could "marry" would have been greeted with scorn. The movement to redefine marriage has already found full expression in what is variously called "polyfidelity" or "polyamory," which seeks to replace traditional marriage with a bewildering array of sexual combinations among various groups of individuals.

3. Homosexual Marriage Is Not a Civil Rights Issue

Defining marriage as the union of a man and a woman would not deny homosexuals the basic civil rights accorded other citizens. Nowhere in the Bill of Rights or in any legislation proceeding from it are homosexuals excluded from the rights enjoyed by all citizens—including the right to marry. However, no

.citizen has the unrestricted right to marry whomever they want. A person cannot marry a child, a close blood relative, two or more spouses, or the husband or wife of another person. Such restrictions are based upon the accumulated wisdom not only of Western civilization but also of societies and cultures around the world for millennia.

4. Upholding Traditional Marriage Is Not "Discrimination"

Discrimination occurs when someone is unjustly denied some benefit or opportunity. But it must first be demonstrated that such persons deserve to be treated equally regarding the point in question. For example, FAA and airline regulations rightly discriminate regarding who is allowed into the cockpit of an airplane. Those who are not trained pilots have no rightful claim to "discrimination" because they are denied the opportunity to fly an airplane. Similarly, the accumulated wisdom of thousands of years of human history, as expressed in virtually all cultures, has defined marriage as between a man and a woman. Homosexual activists conveniently avoid the question of whether homosexual relationships merit being granted equality with marriage. Although not strictly comparable, radically altering the definition of marriage can also pose dangers to society in much the same way as permitting unqualified individuals to fly airplanes.

5. Any Comparison with Interracial Marriage Is Phony

Laws against interracial marriage sought to add a requirement to marriage that is not intrinsic to the institution of marriage. Allowing a black man to marry a white woman, or vice versa, does not change the fundamental definition of marriage, which requires a man and a woman. Homosexual marriage, on the other hand, is the radical attempt to discard this most basic requirement for marriage. Those who claim that some churches held interracial marriage to be morally wrong fail to point out that such "moral objection" to interracial marriage stemmed from cultural factors rather than historic and widely-accepted biblical teaching.

6. Homosexual Marriage Would Subject Children to Unstable Home Environments

Many homosexuals and their sex partners may sincerely believe they can be good parents. But children are not guinea pigs for grand social experiments in redefining marriage, and should not be placed in settings that are unsuitable for raising children.

- **Transient relationships:** While a high percentage of married couples remain married for up to 20 years or longer, with many remaining wedded for life, the vast majority of homosexual relationships are short-lived and transitory. This has nothing to do with alleged "societal oppression." A study in the Netherlands, a gay-tolerant nation that has legalized homosexual marriage, found the average duration of a homosexual relationship to be one and a half years.

- **Serial promiscuity:** Studies indicate that while three-quarters or more of married couples remain faithful to each other, homosexual couples typically engage in a shocking degree of promiscuity. The same Dutch study found that "committed" homosexual couples have an average of eight sexual partners (outside of the relationship) per year. Children should not be placed in unstable households with revolving bedroom doors.

7. Homosexual Activists Have a Political Agenda: To Radically Redefine the Institution of Marriage

Homosexual activists admit that their goal is not simply to make the definition of marriage more "inclusive," but to remake it in their own hedonistic image. Paula Ettelbrick, former legal director of the Lambda Legal Defense and Education Fund, states, "Being queer means pushing the parameters of sex, sexuality, and family, and . . . transforming the very fabric of society." Homosexual writer and activist Michelangelo Signorile rejects monogamy in favor of "a relationship in which the partners have sex on the outside often . . . and discuss their outside sex with each other, or share sex partners."

8. If Victorious, the Homosexual Agenda Will Lead to the Persecution of Those Who Object on Moral or Religious Grounds

If homosexual marriage becomes the law of the land, then children in public schools will be taught that homosexuality is a normative lifestyle, and that gay households are just another "variant" style of family. Those who object may find themselves on the wrong side of the law. Unbelievable? This Orwellian situation has occurred in Massachusetts, which legalized homosexual marriage in 2004. In April 2005, David Parker, the parent of a six-year-old boy, protested to the Lexington elementary school after his son was taught about homosexual "families" in his kindergarten class. At a scheduled meeting at the school, when Parker refused to back down from his request that the school honor the Massachusetts parental notification statute, he was arrested for "trespassing," handcuffed, and put in jail overnight. The next morning Parker was led handcuffed into court for his arraignment, and over the next several months endured two subsequent court appearances before the school district backed down and decided to drop all charges against him. In 2007, Parker's lawsuit against the Lexington school officials was dismissed by a federal judge who refused to uphold his civil rights and to enforce the Massachusetts parental notification statute. Parker's shocking story will become commonplace in a society that forces the acceptance of homosexual marriage as normative.

9. Polls Consistently Show that the Majority of Americans Reject Same-Sex Marriage

Public opinion remains firmly opposed to the redefinition of marriage. A May 2008 Gallup Poll asked the question: "Do you think marriages between same-sex couples should or should not be recognized by the law as valid?" Respondents opposed homosexual marriage by a margin of 56 percent (opposed) to 40 percent (agreeing). Respondents to a CNN/Opinion Research Corporation poll in October 2007 rejected same-sex marriage by the same margins.

10. Support for Traditional Marriage Translates into Ballot Initiatives and Laws around the Country

Because of strong public support for traditional marriage, same-sex marriage advocates have attempted to circumvent public opinion by redefining marriage through the courts. Despite some victories, such as in Massachusetts and California where the courts have mandated same-sex marriage, there is a strong national movement to protect traditional marriage. A total of 45 states have instituted protections for traditional marriage either through state constitutional amendments or through laws:

- 26 states prohibit same-sex marriage in their state constitutions.
- 19 states currently prohibit same-sex marriage through statute only.

In addition, in 2008–9 several more states will be considering ballot initiatives to protect traditional marriage, including Florida and California. Others, such as Indiana and Pennsylvania, will be voting to institute laws defining marriage as between one man and one woman.

POSTSCRIPT

Should Same-Sex Marriage Be Legal?

As of this writing, 10 countries have legalized same-sex marriage: the Netherlands, Belgium, Spain, Sweden, Portugal, Iceland, Norway, South Africa, Argentina, and Canada. Same-sex marriage is legal in parts of other countries, but is limited to certain states, territories, or localities.

In the United States, attitudes remain divided, although trends clearly indicate a shift in attitude. According to a Gallup poll conducted in July 2004, 62 percent of Americans believed that same-sex marriages should not be recognized. By May 2008, the number had fallen to 56 percent. In 2011, Gallup found that, for the first time ever, a majority of Americans (53 percent) were in support of same-sex marriage.

Support is also strong for civil unions, which are recognized in a handful of states. Civil unions are intended as a legal equivalent to marriage, in all but name. While some regard civil unions as an acceptable compromise to this divisive debate, others regard such arrangements with memories of the "separate but equal" days of racial segregation.

Opponents of same-sex marriage frequently rely on biblical references to condemn the practice. They cite passages that describe marriage as between man and woman (1 Cor 7:2), and others that denounce homosexuality in general (Lev 18:22; Cor 6:9; 1 Tim 1:9–11). Yet, if the Bible is to be relied on for enacting marital legislation, other biblical passages may give legislators pause, such as those that endorse polygamy (Gen 29:17–28; 2 Sam 3:2–5) and a man's right to have concubines (2 Sam 5:13; 1 Kings 11:3; 2 Chron 11:21), or those that prohibit divorce (Deut 22:19; Mark 10:9) or mandate female virginity in order for a marriage to be valid (if a wife is not a virgin, she can be executed, the Bible says) (Deut 22:13–21).

Notwithstanding biblical references and implications, the Human Rights Campaign states that fully recognized same-sex marriages are essential to ensure the same legal protections and benefits available to heterosexual married couples. Do you agree? Do you believe civil unions are a just substitution? Why or why not?

Dailey believes that claims of discrimination lobbed at those who oppose same-sex marriage are akin to say the law discriminates against untrained passengers because "they are denied the opportunity to fly an airplane." Do you find this example to be logical? He also argues that, since many heterosexual marriages last over 20 years, same-sex marriages could not provide a similar stability when raising children. Do you agree? Are same-sex relationships less "stable" than other-sex relationships? Would having the right to marry increase or decrease the "stability" of same-sex relationships?

How do you view the argument to amend the U.S. Constitution? What potential benefits or difficulties do you foresee resulting from this action? Finally, what do you believe is the *purpose* of marriage? Is marriage primarily about love, rights, children and family, monogamy, and other considerations? Do you regard it as primarily a religious institution or a legal institution? Is there any *single, predominant* purpose of marriage, or are there many purposes worthy of consideration?

Suggested Readings

S. Chapman, "Gay Marriage Gains, But Fight Isn't Over," *Chicago Tribune* (May 26, 2011).

J. Cornyn, "In Defense of Marriage," *National Review* (July 2004).

A. Liptak, "A Tipping Point for Gay Marriage," *The New York Times* (April 30, 2011).

F. Newport, "For First Time, Majority of Americans Favor Legal Gay Marriage," *gallup.com* (May 20, 2011), http://www.gallup.com/poll/147662/First-Time-Majority-Americans-Favor-Legal-Gay-Marriage.aspx

J. Solomonese, "Athletes Stand up for Gay Marriage," *cnn.com* (May 24, 2011), http://www.cnn.com/2011/OPINION/05/23/solmonese.gaymarriage.athletes/ S. Somashekhar, "Same-Sex Marriage Gains GOP Support," *Washington Post* (August 27, 2010).

ISSUE 16

Do Reality TV Shows Portray Responsible Messages about Teen Pregnancy?

YES: Amy Kramer, from "The REAL Real World: How MTV's '16 and Pregnant' and 'Teen Mom' Motivate Young People to Prevent Teen Pregnancy," an original essay for this edition (2011)

NO: Mary Jo Podgurski, from "Till Human Voices Wake Us: The High Personal Cost of Reality Teen Pregnancy Shows," an original essay for this edition (2011)

ISSUE SUMMARY

YES: Amy Kramer, director of entertainment media and audience strategy at the National Campaign to Prevent Teen and Unplanned Pregnancy, argues that reality television shows engage teens in considering the consequences of pregnancy before they are ready for it and motivate them to want to prevent it.

NO: Mary Jo Podgurski, founder of the Academy for Adolescent Health, Inc., argues that although such television shows have potential benefits, they inadequately address the issue and may even have a negative impact those who participate in them.

Television (TV) has evolved during the past five decades. Just 50 years ago, families could gather around one immovable set with a limited number of channels and observe Desi Arnaz and Lucille Ball occupy different beds in the wildly popular sitcom "I Love Lucy." Considered prudent for TV standards at the time, it would strike many today as an odd family life arrangement for the famous couple—who were married both off-the-air and in-character! Fast forward two decades, and we see Mike and Carol Brady sharing the same bed on "The Brady Bunch," but neither one apparently very interested in sex. (And Mike peculiarly and persistently absorbed in reading *Jonathan Livingston Seagull* in bed.)

Today's TV has a much more substantial representation of sexual relationships and themes. Leaps and bounds from then-landmark events such as William Shatner's and Nichelle Nichol's "first interracial kiss" on TV's "Star

Trek," Ellen DeGeneres coming out on-the-air in the mid-1990s, and Kerr Smith's and Adam Kaufman's "first gay male kiss" on primetime TV in 2000, many of today's TV programs include overtly sexual messages and a greater range of sexual identities and orientations. Indeed, many shows rely and bank on sexual innuendo, humor, and steamy scenes. Although the representation is greater, the *accuracy* of the portrayals is questionable. Is the infrequent gay character actually a *caricature* manifesting common stereotypes? Is sex so closely and frequently tied to crime as portrayed in various crime dramas? Does the constant use of sexual humor mirror and reinforce society's discomfort with sex? Do sexual scenes in prime time dramas make sex appear seamless—and only for the young and beautiful? (Note the hilarious response to 90-year-old Betty White discussing her "Dusty Muffin" on "Saturday Night Live.")

Another way in which TV has changed is with the emergence of the so-called "reality TV show" genre. Popularized with the success of MTV's "The Real World" and CBS's "Survivor," many reality TV shows have followed, so much so that there is even a reality TV show network! Perhaps it was inevitable that the worlds of reality TV and sexuality would collide; new shows addressing specific sexual themes emerged in the last few years. Some shows address issues of pregnancy and family life. In 2007, we were introduced to the family life of parents of octuplets on Discovery Health's "Jon and Kate Plus 8." Later, MTV introduced the real-life teen-focused pregnancy dramas "16 and Pregnant" and "Teen Mom," which follow the lives of real young people dealing with teen pregnancy. VH-1 also airs "Dad Camp," a show in which young men go through "boot camp-style group therapy" in preparing them to take responsibility for fatherhood.

Some sexuality educators, looking for ways to connect with students in authentic, meaningful ways, have embraced the popularity of these shows for their potential as teachable moments. Educators can show a clip to build discussion questions themed around the premise, "What would you do if . . .?"

Other sexuality educators express concern over the reality and impact of the shows. Do the networks do an adequate job of portraying all the hardships of teen pregnancy, or will students perceive the characters as TV stars to be admired and emulated?

In the following selections, Amy Kramer, the director of entertainment media and audience strategy at The National Campaign to Prevent Teen and Unplanned Pregnancy, describes the positive potential these shows can have as allies in sexuality education. She explains how the shows help motivate young people to want to prevent pregnancy before they are ready to be parents. Mary Jo Podgurski, founder of the Academy for Adolescent Health, Inc., who routinely works with pregnant and parenting teens, explains her reasons for declining the opportunity to work with "16 and Pregnant" when producers approached her. Although noting the potential benefits of such shows, she expresses reservations about the impact the shows might have on the teens who appear on a national stage.

YES

Amy Kramer

The REAL Real World: How MTV's "16 and Pregnant" and "Teen Mom" Motivate Young People to Prevent Teen Pregnancy

Like it or not, media is a huge influence in the lives of young people. Teens spend more hours each week in front of a screen than they do in a classroom.[1] Many teens know a lot more about their favorite shows than they do about any academic subject, and characters on television are often more familiar than neighbors. What young people learn in sex ed, if they have sex ed at all, is a fraction of what pop culture serves up on a daily basis. Which is why parents and educators alike should be thankful that MTV has emerged as a sort of accidental hero in the campaign against teen pregnancy.

Thanks to the reality shows "16 and Pregnant" and "Teen Mom," millions of young people are now thinking and talking about teen pregnancy. These shows were developed as nothing more than good entertainment but they have succeeded in ways public health initiatives have not—that is getting young people to stop, pay attention, consider, and discuss what happens when someone becomes a parent before they're ready.

Although we know how to avoid teen pregnancy—get teens to avoid having sex at all or to use contraception carefully and consistently when they do have sex—prevention isn't always as easy as it looks. Getting young people to commit to waiting or protecting themselves is tough. After all, they're kids. The consequences of their actions might not seem as likely as the benefit of the risks. Nearly half of teens admit they've never thought about how a pregnancy would change their lives[2] and most girls who get pregnant say they never thought it would happen to them. It's no wonder young people don't always take precautions to prevent pregnancy—if you never consider that something might happen to you, or what life would be like if it did, why would you consider taking steps to prevent it?

But "16 and Pregnant" and "Teen Mom" seem to be changing that. These shows are bringing the reality of too-early pregnancy and parenthood smack into the middle of the lives and minds of young people in powerful and important ways. Teens come to these shows on their own and they say they come away with a new appreciation for some of the consequences of unprotected sex. In fact, in a nationally representative poll conducted by The National

Campaign to Prevent Teen and Unplanned Pregnancy in 2010, 82% of teens who had seen "16 and Pregnant" said that watching the show "helps teens better understand the challenges of pregnancy and parenthood." Only 17% said the show makes teen pregnancy look glamorous.[3] Already, the fact that young people are tuning in week after week makes what MTV is doing more successful than many PSA campaigns could ever hope to be.

* * *

Rates of teen pregnancy and birth are higher in the United States than in any other industrialized nation. The teen birth rate in the U.S. is more than three times higher than the rate in Canada, and nearly twice that of the United Kingdom (which has the highest rate in Europe). One out of every ten babies born in the U.S. is born to a teen mother. Three out of every ten girls in the U.S. get pregnant before their 20th birthdays—750,000 girls each year. That's 2,000 girls getting pregnant *every day*. These numbers—as shocking as they are—actually represent dramatic improvements. In the past two decades, rates of teen pregnancy and childbearing in the U.S. have dropped by more than one-third.[4]

According to the National Center for Health Statistics, in early-1990s America, 117 out of every 1,000 girls ages 15–19 got pregnant, and 62 out of every 1,000 girls ages 15–19 gave birth. Not even twenty years later those rates are down to 72 per 1,000 teens getting pregnant and 39 per 1,000 teens giving birth. Put another way, teen pregnancy has declined by 38% and teen births are down by one-third. Still too high, but a remarkable improvement on an issue once thought to be intractable.

To what do we owe this astonishing decline in teen pregnancy and teen births? Quite simply and perhaps not surprisingly, it's a combination of less sex and more contraception. According to the National Survey of Family Growth (NSFG), a household-based nationally representative survey conducted periodically by the Centers for Disease Control and Prevention to study families, fertility, and health in the U.S., in 1988, 51% of girls and 60% of boys ages 15–19 had ever had sex. In 2006–2008 those numbers had declined to 42% of girls and 43% of boys. Condom use increased during that time as well: In 1988, 31% of girls and 55% of boys who had sex in the past 90 days said they used a condom the last time they had sex. In 2006–2008, those numbers had grown to 53% for girls and 79% for boys. So, for a complicated array of reasons, teens have been doing the only two things you can do to prevent pregnancy: delaying sex and being better about contraception when they do have sex.

It's also important to note that abortions to teens declined as well over that same time period. In 1988, 39% of pregnancies to teens ended in abortion, in 2006, it was 27%, meaning that the decline in teen births was not due to an increase in terminations.[5]

* * *

Consider the following: While rates of sexual activity, pregnancy, birth, and abortion among teens were declining enormously, the media was growing exponentially and becoming coarser and more sexualized. There are hundreds of channels now and an infinite number of websites. Finding sexually suggestive content on television and explicit content online—or it finding you—is a fact of life for many young people. If media influence on teens' decisions about sex is so direct and so negative, why might it be that teen sexual behavior has gotten more responsible at exactly the same time the media and popular culture has become more sexualized? Simply put, the media can't be solely to blame for teens having sex, or having babies. However, the media can help write the social script and contribute to viewers' sense of what's normal and acceptable—and can make sex seem casual, inconsequential, or serious. In fact, polling for The National Campaign to Prevent Teen and Unplanned Pregnancy shows that year after year 8 in 10 teens say they wish the media showed more consequences of sex (not less sex).[6]

So television alone doesn't cause teen pregnancy, but could it actually help prevent it? Teens themselves suggest that it can. Most teens (79% of girls, 67% of boys,) say that "when a TV show or character I like deals with teen pregnancy, it makes me think more about my own risk of becoming pregnant/causing a pregnancy, and how to avoid it," according to the National Campaign to Prevent Teen and Unplanned Pregnancy.[7] "Thinking about my own risk" is an important piece of the prevention puzzle.

In that same study from The National Campaign, three-quarters of teens (76%) and adults (75%) say that what they see in the media about sex, love, and relationships can be a good way to start conversations about these topics. Communication between parents and teens about their own views and values regarding these issues is critical. Children whose parents are clear about the value of delaying sex are less likely to have intercourse at an early age. Parents who discuss contraception are also more likely to have children who use contraception when they become sexually active.[8] These conversations can be awkward and intimidating (on both sides), but they are important. So anything that encourages such talk, or makes it easier to start the conversation, is valuable.

MTV's "16 and Pregnant" is a conversation starter. Certainly among teens, but also within families. In a 2010 study of more than 150 teenagers involved with Boys & Girls Clubs after-school programs in a southern state, 40% of teens who watched "16 and Pregnant" with their group at the Club, and then talked about it in a facilitator-led discussion, also talked about it again afterward with a parent. One-third discussed it with a boyfriend/girlfriend. More than half discussed it with a friend.[9] That 40% went home and talked about with mom or dad is particularly exciting—because the more opportunities parents have to discuss their own ideas and expectations about pregnancy and parenting, the better. Teens talking about these shows—articulating their own thoughts about a teen parent on MTV or a situation depicted in an episode—brings them one step closer to personalizing it, which is an important step along the behavior change continuum, and the path to prevention.

Educators and leaders in youth-serving organizations are using the MTV shows as teaching tools. A social worker in the Midwest who frequently speaks at schools in both urban and rural areas, has used episodes of "16 and Pregnant" in her work: "With the boys, we had great discussion about what makes a man a 'father'." Boys were a little defensive about the portrayal of the teen dads, but after talking it through, began to empathize more with the young women." A teacher in the South incorporated the series into high school lesson plans: "I use it as part of a unit on teen parenting and parenting readiness to discourage teen pregnancies and to encourage students to wait until they are older and 'ready' before having children. . . . Students enjoy watching the 'real-life' stories of teens and are able to really identify with them." A private special education teacher who works with a teen population especially vulnerable to abusive relationships and pregnancy has also watched the series with students: "The kids were very much engaged because it was something they would watch at home. Some of them had seen the episodes already but looked at them differently once viewed in a group, clinical setting. The conversations were often very serious and enlightening for the students. They were able to put themselves into the girls' shoes and talk about how they would feel, react, respond in each of the situations that came up." Staff at a county juvenile detention center in the Southwest includes the show in teen pregnancy prevention programs and calls it "heavy-hitting and impactful": "They cater to the very media-driven nature of teens today—they aren't dry book material, but rather a great combination of reality and entertainment in a condensed format. . . . A whole year in the life of these teen parents in just an hour of viewing."[10]

* * *

Television shows like MTV's "16 and Pregnant" and "Teen Mom" are created for entertainment purposes with the hope of attracting viewers and keeping them engaged. By that measure, these shows are indisputably successful. Millions of people tune in to each new episode—and the ratings are among the highest on the cable network. Recent episodes have drawn more viewers than even the major broadcast network competition. Public attention to the storylines extends beyond the episodes themselves and into internet discussion forums, where theories and speculation about the lives depicted on the shows are rampant.

Thanks to these very real reality programs, teen pregnancy is no longer a mysterious topic to millions of young people. Viewers have seen in the most vivid way possible what happens when contraception fails, when babies arrive, when boyfriends leave, when money is tight, when parents are disappointed, and when graduating from high school is impossible. Conversations are happening around dinner tables and in carpools, allowing parents and teens to explore their own opinions and behavior. Parents now have an opportunity to discuss their own values and expectations as they pertain to family formation and romantic responsibility. Friends, siblings, and partners are talking to each other about what happens when young people become parents before they're ready. Maybe they're even talking about how to prevent it from happening in the first place.

Every episode of "16 and Pregnant" includes a scene in which the expectant teenager talks about how she got pregnant. Many weren't using any protection at all, others had problems remembering to take their pills every day, some found out that prescribed antibiotics can interfere with the effectiveness of birth control pills, a few missed their Depo shot appointments, others stopped using a method after a break-up and then never returned to its use after reconciliation, etc. This information is presented honestly and in peer-to-peer terms, inviting viewers to listen and learn, and perhaps explore a type of contraception they hadn't previously known about. On "Teen Mom" viewers see the young parents taking steps to prevent subsequent pregnancies: cameras have captured the girls' discussions with their doctors about the vaginal ring, IUDs, and other long-acting methods of contraception. Even the "reunion" episodes devote time to discussion about birth control between updates on the babies and the relationship drama.

Watching what happens to girls who "never thought it would happen to them" encourages viewers to assess their own risk. When teenage fans of the shows see time and again that having a baby as an adolescent often means educational goals are abandoned, family relationships erode, financial challenges become insurmountable, and romantic fantasies are dashed, the prospect of early parenthood in their own lives becomes far less attractive. Rosier depictions of teen pregnancy and its consequences from movies, scripted television shows, and daydreams start to look silly in comparison. Seeing that teen pregnancy happens in the lives of girls from every sort of background (even a familiar one) reminds viewers that it could happen to them and it pushes them to figure out how to avoid a similar fate.

Separate from the shows themselves is the tabloid coverage they receive, though it is so pervasive right now it deserves mention here. That the tabloid media have decided to treat these struggling young mothers like celebrities is certainly unfortunate. That the real-life people around the teen mothers have obviously decided to cooperate with the tabloids (in the form of photos, tips, and other information) is sadder still. However, the bulk of even that coverage focuses on the turmoil in their lives. These are young mothers agonizing over money, men, family drama, health issues, the law, and the unending responsibility of parenthood. Followers of this often repugnant news stream may know even more about the chaos that swirls around young parents than do mere viewers of the show. Coverage does not necessarily equal glamorization. Bottom line: if you sit through a full episode, any episode, of "16 and Pregnant" or "Teen Mom," glamour is totally absent.

* * *

MTV's "16 and Pregnant" and "Teen Mom" are not evidence-based teen pregnancy prevention programs. They aren't a substitute for talented teachers or comprehensive sex ed curricula. These shows aren't more meaningful than traditions of faith. They aren't more important than access to quality healthcare or relevant health information. They aren't more powerful than engaged parents willing to talk openly about tough topics. But teen pregnancy prevention needs to happen everywhere, including in the popular media teenagers love to consume. Everyone who cares about teens, babies, and the next generation of Americans needs to do their part to keep rates of teen pregnancy on a downward trajectory. Families, schools, health care professionals, businesses big and small, religious communities, and yes, the media, all have a role to play. Teen pregnancy prevention requires sustained effort over time by all sectors. This isn't an issue where a vaccine or a cure will lead to a drop in incidence. Even new and better methods of contraception won't do the trick if young people aren't motivated to use them. Making headway on this complex topic requires young people to make better choices over and over again. Any way they can get the message that the teen years are not the appropriate time for parenthood matters.

MTV is doing more than most—even if inadvertently—with "16 and Pregnant" and "Teen Mom." Millions of young people tune in each week and four out of five viewers say that doing so "helps teens better understand the challenges of pregnancy and parenthood." Anyone who cares about reducing rates of teen pregnancy and teen birth should listen to what teens themselves are saying and tune out the rest.

Footnotes/Sources

1. Kaiser Family Foundation, (2010). *Generation M2: Media in the Lives of 8- to 18-Year-Olds.* http://www.kff.org/entmedia/upload/8010.pdf

2. National Campaign to Prevent Teen and Unplanned Pregnancy, (2007). *With One Voice 2007: America's Adults and Teens Sound Off About Teen Pregnancy.* http://www.thenationalcampaign.org/resources/pdf/pubs/WOV2007_fulltext.pdf

3. National Campaign to Prevent Teen and Unplanned Pregnancy, (2010). *With One Voice 2010: America's Adults and Teens Sound Off About Teen Pregnancy.* http://www.thenationalcampaign.org/resources/pdf/pubs/WOV_2010.pdf

4. National Campaign to Prevent Teen and Unplanned Pregnancy, various fact sheets. http://www.thenationalcampaign.org/resources/fact-sheets.aspx

5. Guttmacher Institute, (2010) *U.S. Teenage Pregnancies, Births and Abortions: National and State Trends and Trends by Race and Ethnicity.* http://www.guttmacher.org/pubs/USTPtrends.pdf

6. National Campaign to Prevent Teen and Unplanned Pregnancy, (2007, 2004, 2002). *With One Voice 2007/2004/2002: America's Adults and Teens Sound Off About Teen Pregnancy.* http://www.thenationalcampaign.org/resources/pdf/pubs/WOV2007_fulltext.pdf http://www.thenationalcampaign.org/resources/pdf/pubs/WOV_2004.pdf http://www.thenationalcampaign.org/resources/pdf/pubs/WOV_2002.pdf

7. National Campaign to Prevent Teen and Unplanned Pregnancy, (2010). *With One Voice 2010: America's Adults and Teens Sound Off About Teen Pregnancy.* http://www.thenationalcampaign.org/resources/pdf/pubs/WOV_2010.pdf

8. Blum, R.W. & Rinehard, P.M. (1998). *Reducing the Risk: Connections that make a difference in the lives of youth.* Center for Adolescent Health and Development, University of Minnesota. Minneapolis, MN.

9. Suellentrop, K., Brown, J., Ortiz, R. (2010) *Evaluating the Impact of MTV's '16 and Pregnant' on Teen Viewers' Attitudes about Teen Pregnancy,* The National campaign to Prevent Teen and Unplanned Pregnancy, Washington DC. http://www.thenationalcampaign.org/resources/pdf/SS/SS45_16andPregnant.pdf

10. Telephone interviews and email inquiries by the author.

Till Human Voices Wake Us: The High Personal Cost of Reality Teen Pregnancy Shows

Having a baby young took away my childhood and there's no way I'll ever get it back.

—16–year-old mother

I wouldn't be alive today if I hadn't had her. She's the reason I'm still alive.

—15–year-old mother

The "voices" above are direct quotes from the video I produced in 1998 entitled *Voices: The Reality of Early Childbearing—Transcending the Myths*. The video was marketed nationally by Injoy Productions until 2009 and is still used in the Lamaze teen program Creativity, Connection and Commitment: Supporting Teens During the Childbearing Year (Lamaze International, 2010). Over the course of a year my team interviewed and videotaped young parents with the intent of using their voices and wisdom as an catalyst for teen pregnancy prevention. I share these voices to underscore an acute need to protect teens. When editing the film I discovered that the teen mothers consistently wanted to reveal very intimate aspects of their lives. Data including early drinking, number of sexual partners, an incestuous relationship, nonconsensual sex, and sexual experimentation were all freely revealed. I cautioned them to think of the future. Would their children relish such revelations a decade later? Were these details pertinent to their messages? I persisted, and only information that was truly educational and not sensationalized remained in the film. I believed then that 16-year-old parents could provide a priceless service to other teens as peer educators; I continue to believe such teaching is effective and significant. I simply refused to expose the truly personal details of their lives to scrutiny. I was interested in education, not drama.

My staff and I remain in contact with many of the teen parents in *Voices*. More than ten years after its production they are in 100% agreement: our careful screening spared their children (now young teens) embarrassment.

The young parents I've served have taught me to put a face on the statistics surrounding teen pregnancy; while I will always strive to educate all young people about the risks associated with bearing children young, I am deeply cognizant of the price a teen parent pays when offering his or her life as a lesson plan.

The last 30 years of my life have been dedicated to providing comprehensive sexuality education to young people; our programs reach over 18,000 youth a year in all 14 Washington County school districts. Concurrently I've mentored young parents. I served as a doula (providing labor support) for my first adolescent in the '70s; that young mother became one of many. My staff and I provide educational services and support for nearly 100 pregnant and parenting teens annually. When the MTV program "16 and Pregnant" was in its planning stages I was approached by the producers and asked to provide teens for the show. I declined after much soul searching. This article explores my rationale for that decision.

Why Rethink Reality TV Using Teen Parents?

As an educator I seek teachable moments in everyday life. I am thrilled to have the opportunity to teach; I consider the field of sexuality education a vocation and am blessed to be in a role where life-affirming information is at my disposal and I am free to convey it to teens. I don't deny the impact reality shows like "16 and Pregnant" and "Teen Mom" (now "Teen Mom 2") can have on teens. The April 10, 2011, edition *of The New York Times* reports anecdotes of teachers using the shows as a part of curriculum in life skills and parenting classes (Hoffman, 2011, April 10). The National Campaign to Prevent Teen and Unplanned Pregnancy has distributed DVDs and teacher guides on "16 and Pregnant" and these materials seem to be well received by educators. I also am not deterred by fears that these reality shows glamorize teen pregnancy. The Campaign conducted a national telephone poll of young people ages 12 to 19; 82% said that the shows aided their understanding of the reality of teen pregnancy. Only 17% stated that the shows gave pregnancy a glamorous spin (Albert, 2010). In the hands of a skilled educator the shows' influence can be directed away from glamour to empathic awareness. There is no doubt that there are lessons to be learned from these shows, but at what price?

My primary concern with reality TV shows like "16 and Pregnant" and "Teen Mom" deals with the human cost of these lessons. Young parents, like most young people, are not immune to the appeal of fame. I question a teen's ability to give full permission to a life-changing activity that will reframe his or her identity on a national stage. I am concerned that these young people cannot developmentally grasp the far-reaching implications of their decision to participate. Exploitation is a strong word and I use it with a caveat; I do not believe the shows aim to exploit. I believe that their intentions are good; it is society that removes all boundaries and exposes tender lives to the scrutiny of tabloids and the manipulation of the media. When I filmed *Voices* I stressed the need for discretion; in ten or twenty years, I said, would your baby want to be known for the things you now reveal? In a decade and more, how will the babies in "16 and Pregnant" view their lives? How will they react to their parents, their families, and their infancy and toddler years exposed for posterity?

I am also troubled by a nagging sense that these shows hope to provide a simple solution to the problems associated with adolescent sexuality in America. There are no Band-aids that can be applied to the multi-faceted, complicated situations that arise when teens are sexually involved, yet our culture consistently seeks an easy fix. I was afforded the privilege of attending an Advocates for Youth European Study Tour in 2001. As part of that experience I was exposed to European approaches to sexuality education. In contrast to American culture, European culture does not deny the fact that teens need education that helps them achieve sexual health; comprehensive sexuality education is the norm. Are reality TV shows that focus on the lives of young parents yet another simplistic answer that distracts from the need to mandate comprehensive sexuality education to all of our children?

No Band-Aids

Research points to antecedents to early pregnancy and risky behavior; I question whether the teen parents in reality TV shows reflect those antecedents or are selected for their "camera" quality and the appeal of their families' dramas. I also ponder the use of dollars to develop these TV shows instead of creating programs that would target youth that evidence-based data show are at risk.

Dr. Doug Kirby's work (2002, 2007) alone and with colleagues (Kirby, Lepore, & Ryan, 2006) is considered seminal in the areas of comprehensive sexuality education and teen pregnancy antecedents. Research into the role of siblings in early childbearing from East and associates (1996 through 2007) is pivotal to understanding generational teen pregnancy (East, Reyes, & Horn, 2007; Raneri & Constance, 2007). Kristen Luker (1999, 2006) is considered a founding theorist of the sociological and political theories surrounding early childbearing and linked poverty to teen pregnancy as an antecedent, not a consequence of the pregnancy. Young people who are survivors of sexual and physical abuse (Boyer & Fine, 1992) are at risk for early childbearing, as are children in placement or foster care (Kirby, Lepore, & Ryan, 2006) and children living with domestic violence, drug/alcohol abuse or incarcerated parents (Coyle, 2005; Goode & Smith, 2005; East & Khoo, 2005; Jekielek, Moore, Hair, & Scarupa, 2002). Do the teens in reality TV reflect these antecedents?

Research at the University of Arkansas showed that girls are more likely to experience teen pregnancy if they live with internal poverty (measured as a low locus of control and future expectations) as well as external poverty (Young, Turner, Denny, Young, 2004). Internal poverty "describes a person's lack of internal resources, such as attitudes and beliefs that attribute outcomes to individual effort, high future expectations, and few perceived limitations for life options" (Coles, 2005, 10). Certainly internal and external poverty are antecedents in the pregnancies of some reality TV participants; at any time are those teens given guidance that will help them develop the skills and self-efficacy they need to succeed?

Antecedents to teen pregnancy in the United States lead dedicated sexuality educators to explore the need for education that affects behavioral change. Dr. Michael A. Carrera's Children's Aid Society is a well-respected and researched youth development approach that targets the whole child through early intervention (Children's Aid Society, 2010). On a much smaller scale, my team and I have tried to emulate his efforts. Although we remain committed to comprehensive sexuality education, we first approached teen pregnancy prevention through pro-active education in 1999 with the initiation of an early intervention educational mentoring program entitled Educate Children for Healthy Outcomes (ECHO). ECHO provides one-on-one mentoring to young people who have been identified as at risk for engaging in high-risk behavior. Specifically, we target girls in grades 2–12 who have experienced sexual abuse, abandonment issues, placement problems, truancy, early sexual acting out, and/or familial teen pregnancy and provide them with a supportive, consistent, empowering educator and role model. Our advisors educate participants on youth development topics that guide them in making healthy life choices. Our program topics include: decision making, refusal, communication, and problem solving skills, assertiveness training, anger management, conflict resolution, puberty education, socialization skills, life skills, and prevention education. We strive to empower families to communicate well with each other, help children avoid risky behavior during their adolescent years, and strengthen the family unit as a whole. Only three of the 511 high-risk girls we've mentored since 1999 experienced a pregnancy, and all three of those young women were older than 18 when they gave birth.

Reality shows target all teens without the capacity to address the real and complicated issues that may lead to actual teen pregnancy. Focusing on sexual health for all young people is vital; providing personalized instruction to teens at highest risk, while costly, could maximize positive outcomes.

Voices to Break the Cycle: A Phenomenological Inquiry into Generational Teen Pregnancy

I completed my doctoral work late in life; my dissertation was not only informative but also humbling. I looked at the lived experiences of women who gave birth as adolescents to investigate how these adults might help their pubertal aged children avoid teenage pregnancy. Research participants gave birth as teens (defined as under 19 years of age) and were parenting their biologic children ages 10–15. A key criteria for selection in the study was generational teen pregnancy; participants in the study came from families with a history of teen pregnancy through at least one generation prior to the former teen mother's birth. The study reinforced the antecedents of poverty, foster placement, sexual abuse and familial patterns of early childbearing (Podgurski, 2009).

Stigmatizing women who conceive and bear children during adolescence is common in American culture and can lead to social inequalities (McDermott & Graham, 2005). Data reinforces young mothers' continuing need for support while teens (Pai-Espinosa, 2010) and as their lives move forward beyond adolescence (Jutte et al., 2010). The voices of former teen mothers in my study also revealed lives deeply affected by their adolescent pregnancies. Many women expressed a desire to move away from the community in which they gave birth; 30% of the former teen mothers in the study did relocate. One participant in the study stated: "When I got married I left the area. I found it easier to reinvent myself than deal with people who had labeled me as that pregnant girl. My life here is better than it would have been if I'd stayed where I was." Where can a teen parent whose life has been exposed on a national reality TV show relocate?

Adult empathic understanding and compassion for the lives of teen parents was not common among the participants in my study; over 80% described self-reported disrespectful treatment during their births, upon their return to school, or while seeking employment. If, as the National Campaign for Teen and Unplanned Pregnancy reports, 41% of adults report the show "16 and Pregnant" glorifies teen pregnancy (Albert, 2010), will that compassion diminish?

Till Human Voices Wake Us

What is the effect of fame on the young parents made into instant celebrities by reality TV? What do they and their children sacrifice to the altar of TV ratings?

To examine the possible long-term effects of fame and celebrity status on young parents, it is illustrative to look at fame as it is perceived in youth culture. Halpern (2007) surveyed 5th to 8th grade students in Rochester, New York, and found 29% of males and 37% of females selected fame over intelligence as a desired trait. The study participants viewed at least five hours of TV daily; that figure is consistent with other studies of youth screen time (defined as TV and computer time). For example, Burnett and her research team (2008) found that 60% of teens spent an average of 20 hours in screen time, a full third spent closer to 40 hours per week and 7 percent were exposed to greater than 50 hours of viewing time weekly. Perhaps most significantly, Halbern's work showed that 17% of the students felt that celebrities owed their fame to luck, and believed that TV shows had the power to make people famous. If fame is valued over intelligence and luck is perceived as a better indicator of future well-being than industry among average children, would pregnant and parenting teens buy into that delusion as well?

An intense desire for fame can lead reality TV participants to believe that "every reality show is an audition tape for future work" (Wolk, 2010, p. 32). If adults are affected by fame hunger that directs their actions and choices, how can adolescents avoid influence from reality TV fame? The sad drama of Amber, violence, and child custody revealed on the show "Teen Mom" was popular among tabloids, magazines, and advertisers. As an educator I am troubled. Did Amber receive guidance or were her actions considered fodder for higher ratings? One need go no further than the cover story of a current *OK! Magazine* to read that "More Teen Mom Babies!" are planned, including one baby that is being conceived to save a relationship (2011, April 18). The same issue proclaims that Amber and Gary will reunite. What type, if any, relationship skill education do these young "reality celebrities" receive as their lives are broadcast nationally?

Putting a Face on the Numbers

The names of the young parents in the following anecdotes are fiction but their stories are not. Any of these young people would produce high ratings on a reality TV show. Protecting their anonymity is a fundamental educational task. Ethical treatment of pregnant and parenting youth demands that respect is rendered at all times.

Picture Tracy: This lively young woman was a National Honor Society student when she found she was pregnant at the age of 16. Articulate, empathetic, and soft-spoken, she is now a caring social worker completing her master's degree in counseling. Tracy did not disclose her history of sexual assault until the baby she birthed as a teen was four years old; she now uses her life experiences to help her connect with young women at risk for early childbearing.

Nina is a bright, intelligent 27 year old. Her hair color and body piercings change often but her striking hazel eyes and determined expressions remain constant. She is perceptive, a hard worker, and one of the most resilient young people I've ever known. Nina is also the parent of a 12 year old. She lived in a series of foster homes while pregnant and parenting; her mother gave birth to her as a 15 year old and her grandmother had her first pregnancy as a 16 year old. Nina was born into poverty and continues to struggle to make ends meet. She left school at 17 and hasn't completed the GED (General Equivalency Diploma) she frequently talks about. She often bemoans the fact that her daughter "does without" things she too was denied as a teen. She is proud that she has been her child's only parent and that her daughter has never been in foster care. Like her own parents, Nina fights addiction to alcohol and drugs and has been in and out of rehab several times.

Meet Samantha: Sammy planned her baby to prove that she was heterosexual. Her first kiss at 11 was with a girl; she reacted violently to the fear that she was lesbian in a homophobic family and made a conscious decision to conceive a baby to a man ten years her senior. She was only 12 when her pregnancy was discovered; she didn't tell anyone until she was in her third trimester. She came out when her son was two years old and is currently in a five-year relationship with her female partner.

Jodi gave birth as a tenth grader but only disclosed her step father as her baby's daddy when he starting hitting on her younger sister. Her baby was two years old at the time. Disclosure led to her stepfather's arrest and incarceration for over four years of sexual abuse. Her five siblings were divided and sent to three different foster homes. While Jodi is intermittently proud of her disclosure, she blames herself for the dissolution of her family. She is in a new school district where few know her family's history and is starting to shine academically.

Trevor's father reacted to his girlfriend **Amy's** pregnancy by denying his parentage; within an hour he was homeless at 18. Too old for children and youth services, he wandered from one friend's sofa to another until the single mother of his girlfriend allowed him to move in with her family. The baby is due this spring. Trevor is determined to remain with his partner and states firmly that he will not "be a statistic." His girlfriend's mother, while kind and supportive, is skeptical. She sees Amy's father in Trevor. Although she hopes for the best, she expects him to leave before the baby is two.

It's Not about United States

Those of United States who have committed our lives to supporting, empowering, and educating young people approach this charge in unique ways. I humbly acknowledge that there are many paths to reaching youth. I have learned more from listening to the young people I serve than from any other resource. When I train new staff I reinforce a common theme: our work is not about us, it's about the young people. I am reminded of the old admonition: First, Do No Harm. As adults we are responsible for the needs of all youth, regardless of sexual orientation, gender and gender identity, race, ethnicity, socio-economic status, religion, or level of sexual involvement. I challenge all who serve pregnant and parenting teens to examine the effects adult interventions have upon the lives of these young people and their children, bearing in mind that we do not yet have full knowledge of the long-term implications of national exposure at a time of great vulnerability. When in doubt, protect.

References

Albert, B. (2010). *With one voice 2010: Teens and adults sound off about teen pregnancy.* National Campaign to Prevent Teen and Unplanned Pregnancy. *Retrieved from* http://www.thenationalcampaign.org/resources/pdf/pubs/WOV_2010.pdf

Barnett, T., O'Loughlin, J., Sabiston, C., Karp, I., Belanger, M., Van Hulst, A., & Lambert., M. (2008). Teens and screens: The influence of screen time on adiposity in adolescents. *American Journal of Epidemiology, 172*(3), 255–262.

Boyer, D. & Fine, D. (1992). Sexual abuse as a factor in adolescent pregnancy and child maltreatment. *Family Planning Perspectives, 24*(1), 4–11.

Children's Aid Society. (2010). Dr. Michael A. Carrera, Retrieved from http://www.childrensaidsociety.org/carrera-pregnancy-prevention/dr-michael-carrera

Coles, C. (2005). Teen pregnancy and "internal poverty". *Futurist, 38*(7), 10.

Coyle, J. (2005, September). Preventing and reducing violence by at-risk adolescents common elements of empirically researched programs. *Journal of Evidence-Based Social Work, 2*(3/4), 125.

Goode, W. W. & Smith, T. J. (2005). *Building from the ground up: Creating effective programs to mentor children of prisoners.* Philadelphia, PA: Public/Private Ventures.

East, P. L., & Khoo, S. (2005, December). Longitudinal pathways linking family factors and sibling relationship qualities to adolescent substance use and sexual risk behaviors. *Journal of Family Psychology, 19*(4), 571–580.

East, P. L., Reyes, B. T. & Horn, E. J. (2007, June). Association between adolescent pregnancy and a family history of teenage births. *Perspectives on sexual and reproductive health, 39*(2), 108–115.

Halpern, J. (2007). *Fame junkies: The hidden truth behind America's favorite addiction.* New York: Houghton Mifflin Company.

Hoffman, J. (2011, April 10). Fighting teen pregnancy with MTV stars as Exhibit A. *The New York Times,* p. ST 1, 11.

Jekielek, S. M., Moore, K.A., Hair, E. C., & Scarupa, H.J. (2002, February). Mentoring: A promising strategy for youth development. *Child Trends Research Brief.* Retrieved from www.mentoring.ca.gov/pdf/MentoringBrief2002.pdf

Jutte, D., Roos, N., Brownell, M., Briggs, G., MacWilliam, L., & Roos, L. (2010). The ripples of adolescent motherhood: social, educational, and medical outcomes for children of teen and prior teen mothers. *Academic Pediatrics, 10*(5), 293–301.

Karcher, M. (2005). The effects of developmental mentoring and high school mentors' attendance on their younger mentees' self-esteem, social skills and connectedness. *Psychology in the Schools, 42*(1), 65–77. Retrieved from www.adolescentconnectedness.com/media/KarcherPITS_mentoring&conn.pdf

Kirby, D. (2002). Antecedents of adolescent initiation of sex, contraceptive use, and pregnancy. *American Journal of Health Behavior, 26*(6), 473.

Kirby, D. (2007). *Emerging answers: Research findings on programs to reduce teen pregnancy and sexually transmitted diseases.* Washington, DC: National Campaign to Prevent Teen Pregnancy.

Kirby, D., Lepore, G., & Ryan, J. (2006). *Sexual risk and protective factors—Factors affecting teen sexual behavior, pregnancy, childbearing and sexually transmitted disease: Which are important? Which can you change?* Scotts Valley, CA: ETR Associates.

Lamaze International. (2010). *Creativity, connection and commitment: Supporting teens during the childbearing year.* Retrieved from http://www.lamaze.org/ChildbirthEducators/WorkshopsConference/SpecialtyWorkshops/SupportingTeensDuringtheChildbearingYear/tabid/494/Default.aspx

Luker, K. (1997). *Dubious conceptions: The politics of teen pregnancy.* Boston: Harvard University Press.

Luker, K. (2006). When sex goes to school: Warring views on sex – and sex education since the Sixties. New York: W. W. Norton & Company.

McDermott, E. & Graham, H. (2005). Resilient young mothering: social inequalities, late modernity and the 'problem' of 'teenage' motherhood. *Journal of Youth Studies, 8,* 59–79.

(2011, April 18) More teen mom babies. *OK! Magazine, 16,* 32–35.

Pai-Espinosa, J. (2010). Young mothers at the margin: why pregnant teens need support. *Children's Voice, 19*(3), 14–16.

Podgurski, MJ. (2009). *Voices to break the Cycle: A phenomenological inquiry into generational teen pregnancy.* (Doctoral dissertation). University of Phoenix, Phoenix, AZ. Raneri, L., & Constance, M. (2007, March).Social ecological predictors of repeat adolescent pregnancy. *Perspectives on Sexual & Reproductive Health, 39*(1), 39–47.

Young, T., Turner, J., Denny, G., Young, M. (2004, July). Examining external and internal poverty as antecedents of teen pregnancy. *American Journal of Health Behavior, 28*(4), 361–373.

Wolk, J. (2002). Fame factor. *Entertainment Weekly,* (665), 32.

POSTSCRIPT

Do Reality TV Shows Portray Responsible Messages about Teen Pregnancy?

In her essay, Amy Kramer highlights the importance of teen pregnancy reality television (TV) shows in teen pregnancy prevention efforts. She comments on the popularity of these shows, and the way they engage teenage viewers. As the MTV programs both entertain and educate, Kramer describes how they spark conversation among young people, how parents can utilize the shows as a starting point for discussions about their values, expectations, and how to prevent an unplanned pregnancy. Have you seen a teen pregnancy reality TV program? What about them did you find to be realistic or unrealistic? What kind of discussions did you have with friends, parents, or teachers about the show? Can you imagine them having an impact on a person's sexual decisions?

Kramer notes that the shows depict realistic consequences of sexual activity and teen pregnancy without glamorizing these outcomes. She says, "Families, schools, health care professionals, businesses big and small, religious communities, and yes, the media, all have a role to play." Do you agree with her assessment of the role of various institutions, including the media in addressing teen pregnancy prevention?

Mary Jo Podgurski does not dispute the potential benefit that reality TV shows about teen pregnancy can have. She notes their merits and their good intentions. However, she is concerned about the potential for teens who appear on the show to be exploited. She says that, developmentally, teens can't fully "grasp the far-reaching implications of their decision to participate." What might be some examples of far-reaching implications? Think back to when you were 15 or 16. How prepared do you think you would be to share your life story on national TV, if you experienced early pregnancy or became a teen parent?

Noting that young people may be blinded by fame, Podgurski also commented on how participants on the show may be selected for their "camera quality." What do you think she meant, and how do you think this might be problematic? Podgurski also expressed concern about society applying a "Band-aid" solution to a complex, multifaceted issue, and that perhaps money would be better invested in programs that actually address the variety of antecedents to early pregnancy and risky behavior. Is there room for *both* evidence-based teen pregnancy prevention programs *and* media-driven shows that open the door for discussion between parents and children? Is one approach better than the other? If you were in a position to award a million-dollar teen pregnancy prevention project, would you invest in both approaches or would you support one more than the other?

Suggested Readings

J. Chang and J. Hopper, "Pregnancy Pressure: Is MTV's 'Teen Mom' Encouraging Pregnancy for Fame?," *ABC News* (February 11, 2011).

L. Dolgen, "Why I Created MTV's '16 and Pregnant,'" *CNN.com* (May 4, 2011).

A. Stanley, "Motherhood's Rough Edges Fray in Reality TV . . . And Baby Makes Reality TV," *The New York Times* (January 21, 2011).

Internet References . . .

Alliance for Marriage

Alliance for Marriage is a nonprofit research and education organization dedicated to promoting marriage and addressing the epidemic of fatherless families in the United States. It educates the public, the media, elected officials, and civil society leaders on the benefits of marriage for children, adults, and society.

http://www.allianceformarriage.org

Alternatives to Marriage Project

The Alternatives to Marriage Project advocates for equality and fairness fo unmarried people, including people who choose not to marry, cannot marry, or live together before marriage.

http://www.unmarried.org

American Family Association

The American Family Association is a national nonprofit organization that advocates for "traditional family values" through activism aimed at media outlets and advertisers, including those on the Internet.

www.afa.net

Electronic Frontier Foundation

The Electronic Frontier Foundation works to educate the press, policymakers, and the general public about civil liberties issues related to technology.

http://www.eff.org.

Federal Communications Commission (FCC)

The FCC is a United States government agency charged with regulating interstate and international communications by radio, television, wire, satellite, and cable.

http://www.fcc.gov

The Alan Guttmacher Institute

The Alan Guttmacher Institute is a nonprofit organization focused on sexual and reproductive health research, policy analysis, and public education.

www.guttmacher.org

The Coalition Against Trafficking in Women–International

The Coalition Against Trafficking in Women is an international organization focused on ending sexual exploitation, including the sex trafficking of women and girls.

www.catwinternational.org

Sex and Reproduction

Some of the most contentious modern debates involve reproduction: Should abortion be legal and accessible? Should abortion be restricted at some stages of embryonic or fetal development? Should parents be encouraged to space the births of their culture? Is the use of contraception a moral decision for people who do not wish to become parents? Should people avoid sex that does not result in the possibility of pregnancy? If so, does this include sex between same-sex partners? Does that mean that all oral sex, anal sex, or masturbation is illicit? Does it mean no sex should take place when a woman is beyond menopause, or if one or both partners are infertile? In this section, we examine four contemporary issues that involve reproductive choice.

- Should Pharmacists Have the Right to Refuse Contraceptive Prescriptions?

- Is Abortion Moral?

- Should There Be Restrictions on the Number of Embryos Implanted During In Vitro Fertilization?

- Should Parents Be Allowed to Select the Sex of Their Baby?

ISSUE 17

Should Pharmacists Have the Right to Refuse Contraceptive Prescriptions?

YES: Eileen P. Kelly, from "Morally Objectionable Work Assignments: Catholic Social Teaching and Public Policy Perspectives," The Catholic Social Science Review (vol. 12, 2007)

NO: National Women's Law Center, from "Pharmacy Refusals 101" (July 2010)

ISSUE SUMMARY

YES: Eileen Kelly, a professor of Management at Ithaca College, argues that conscience clauses are necessary to protect the religious liberty and rights of pharmacists and others in the workplace.

NO: The National Women's Law Center, a national organization that works to promote issues that impact the lives of women and girls, highlight laws and public opinion while stressing that free and unrestricted access to contraception is in the best interest of women's health.

After the Supreme Court's 1973 decision on *Roe v. Wade* that legalized abortion, the Church Amendment was passed. The amendment, deemed a "conscience clause," was seen as a way to protect health care providers from being required to take part in procedures they may object to, despite the legality of the service. Essentially the Church Amendment "prevents the government (as a condition of a federal grant) from requiring health care providers or institutions to perform or assist in abortion or sterilization procedures against their moral or religious convictions. It also prevents institutions receiving certain federal funds from taking action against personnel because of their participation, nonparticipation, or beliefs about abortion or sterilization" (Sonfield, 2005).

Over the years, additional federal conscience clauses have been enacted dealing not only with abortion services, but also education about abortion and training in abortion or sterilization procedures (Feder, 2006). Additionally, nearly all states have enacted their own conscience clauses. Most states allow individuals the right to refuse to participate in abortion services. Others protect objectors from participating in sterilization and contraceptive services as well (Sonfield, 2005). More recently, more attention has been given to the impact these clauses have in allowing pharmacists to refuse to fill prescriptions for birth control based on their beliefs. State laws differ on how much protection is provided for pharmacists. In some cases, the pharmacist must offer to transfer the prescription to a willing pharmacy. In other states, there is no such requirement (Sonfield, 2008).

How far should conscience clauses be allowed to reach? Is pharmacy refusal without a referral to another pharmacy acceptable? Or should pharmacists who oppose contraception be forced to refer a customer to a pharmacist that does not share their values? Is part of being a doctor or pharmacist providing the best services and information available regardless of belief? If a medication is approved by the Food and Drug Administration (FDA), should a licensed pharmacist, trained and licensed to dispense these medications, be able to pick and choose which prescriptions they fill?

Across the country, several "pro-life" pharmacies have opened—these pharmacies refuse to stock condoms, hormonal birth control, or emergency contraception (Stein, 2008). Is this an acceptable compromise? Should such pharmacies be required to inform potential customers that they do not stock such items by posting the information on the door?

Supporters of the conscience clauses stress that they are simply living their ethics, and that they should not be punished for their religious beliefs. Opponents warn that such laws interfere with women's access to health care, and that refusal to fill a prescription can be used as an attempt to shame and humiliate.

In her essay, "Morally Objectionable Work Assignments: Catholic Social Teaching and Public Policy Perspectives," Eileen Kelly argues that conscience clauses are a necessary protection of civil rights. The National Women's Law Center, in a document titled "Pharmacy Refusals 101," zeros in on the effects of such refusals on women's health and what can be done to prevent them.

References

J. Feder, "The History and Effect of Abortion Conscience Clause Laws," accessed at https://www.policyarchive.org/bitstream/handle/10207/3696/RS21428_20060227.pdf?sequence=2 (2006).

A. Sonfield, "Rights vs. Responsibilities: Professional Standards and Provider Refusals," *The Guttmacher Report on Public Policy* (vol. 8, no. 3, August 2005), accessed at http://www.guttmacher.org/pubs/tgr/08/3/gr080307.html

A. Sonfield, "Provider Refusal and Access to Reproductive Health Services: Approaching a New Balance," *Guttmacher Policy Review* (vol. 11, no. 2, Spring 2008), accessed at http://www.guttmacher.org/pubs/gpr/11/2/gpr110202.html

R. Stein, "Pro-Life Drugstores Market Beliefs. *The Washington Post,* accessed at http://www.washingtonpost.com/wp-dyn/content/article/2008/06/15/AR2008061502180.html?sid=ST2008082103218 (2008)

YES

Eileen P. Kelly

Morally Objectionable Work Assignments: Catholic Social Teaching and Public Policy Perspectives

This article examines the increasing problem of health care employees other than physicians and nurses, especially pharmacists, facing discipline or termination for refusing to engage in immoral practices such as dispensing contraceptives. The article considers the limitations of current anti-discrimination statutes in protecting such employees, and believes that "conscience laws"—which so far only a minority of states have enacted, but many are considering—afford the best possibility for protection.

In Ohio, a pharmacist is fired for refusing to fill a prescription for birth control pills. In Wisconsin, another pharmacist faces a similar fate plus sanctions from the state licensing board for refusing to fill a prescription for emergency contraceptives. In Illinois, an emergency medical technician is terminated for refusing to drive a woman to an abortion clinic. In each instance, the employee is placed in the untenable position of having to choose between providing services that are contrary to their deeply held religious beliefs or facing discipline and discharge for refusing to do so.

In the last several years, there has been a notable increase in the number of incidences of employees placed in such nightmarish dilemmas. Not coincidentally, most of the employees receiving media scrutiny are health care workers, particularly pharmacists. While doctors and nurses have long had the right to refuse morally objectionable work under state statutes, pharmacists and other health care workers have not. The statutory right of refusal has only recently been extended by a minority of states to other categories of health care employees.

Catholic Social Teaching

A vigorous and contentious national debate is now occurring over whether health care professionals have the right to withhold services for procedures they find morally objectionable. Advances in medical technology, coupled with the overall decline in morality in society, make the outcome of this debate critical

From *Catholic Social Science Review*, vol. 12, 2007, pp. 425–430. Copyright © 2007 by Society of Catholic Social Scientists. Reprinted by permission.

for society's long term welfare. Morally objectionable procedures and practices that were unthought-of in previous generations are now commonplace and either legally sanctioned or conceivably will be in the not too distant future.

Embryonic stem cell research, euthanasia, physician assisted suicide, abortion, abortifacients, artificial birth control, sterilization and artificial insemination are just a few of the procedures and practices that contribute to the "culture of death" enveloping society. The Catholic Church has consistently upheld the value and dignity of each human life and taught that life must be unequivocally protected in all its various stages. John Paul II persuasively articulated the gospel of life in *Evangelium Vitae*. In doing so, he underscored long-standing Church teaching. As the *Catechism* notes, abortion has been condemned by the Church since the first century.

Rational employees do not accept jobs or undertake professions that are opposed to their religious beliefs. In short, no morally upright person is going to voluntarily work for Don Corleone or become an abortionist. More commonly, employees enter into employment relationships that subsequently force them to make choices in morally compromising situations. In extreme scenarios, the employee may be compelled to leave a job to maintain his or her moral integrity. What is particularly pernicious with the current moral crisis facing the health care professions is that most employees enter into those professions with the understanding that they are embarking on a noble and moral career to help others. In most instances, the employee invests a great deal of time and expense getting an education for his or her profession. Increasingly, Catholic health care workers are now being confronted with having to choose between their jobs or their religious beliefs. In some cases, they may even have to leave their profession.

Existing public policy is somewhat muddled in both protecting and encroaching on the employee's right to refuse morally objectionable work. While there is some legal protection for an employee's right of refusal, that protection is very limited. Employees who refuse to perform morally objectionable work have essentially two legal avenues of recourse open to them. First, they can seek protection under existing federal and state discrimination laws. Second, if they live in a state with a "conscience law" covering their particular job, they can seek protection under it. On the other hand, there is a movement afoot to pass state statutes requiring certain health care providers to provide morally objectionable services.

Anti-Discrimination Statutes

Title VII of the Civil Rights Act of 1964 makes it illegal for a non-sectarian employer to discriminate against an applicant or employee on the basis of religion. All fifty states have similar prohibitions in their respective state anti-discrimination laws, as well as some municipalities. In addition to prohibiting employers from discriminating on the basis of religion, Title VII and related statutes require that the employer reasonably accommodate the religious beliefs and practices of their employees to the extent that it does not create an undue hardship on the business. There are essentially three common types of accommodations that employees seek. The first is accommodation for religious observances or practices, such as asking time off for Sabbath observance. The second is grooming and dress code accommodation, such as a Muslim woman asking to wear a hijab. The third and most contentious is accommodation for conscientious objections to assigned work which is in opposition to an employee's religious beliefs, such as a pharmacist requesting not to dispense emergency contraceptives.

Notably, the employer's duty to accommodate the religious beliefs and practices of their employees is not an absolute one. Rather, the employer has only a duty to reasonably accommodate an employee's request to the extent that it does not create an undue hardship on the business. Unlike disability cases, the Supreme Court ruled in *TWA v. Hardison,* 432 U.S. 63 (1973) that the obligation to accommodate religious beliefs and practices is a *de minimis* one. The Supreme Court held in *Ansonia Board of Education v. Philbrook,* 55 USLW 4019 (1996) that once the employer offers any reasonable accommodation, they have met their statutory burden. Notably, that accommodation need not be the most optimal one or the employee's preferred one. The determination of undue hardship is at issue only when the employer claims that it is unable to offer any reasonable accommodation without such hardship. The definition of undue hardship is essentially any accommodation that would be unduly costly, extensive, substantial, disruptive, or that would fundamentally alter the nature or operation of the business. Factors that would be taken into account in assessing undue hardship would be the nature of the business, the cost of the accommodation, the nature of the job needing accommodation, and the effect of the accommodation on the employer's operations. No bright line rule exists to determine precisely what constitutes an undue hardship. Rather the determination is made on a case-by-case basis contingent upon the particular factual scenario of each situation.

The limited nature of an employer's *de minimis* legal obligation to accommodate an employee's religious beliefs and practices has serious implications for employees requesting to refrain from morally objectionable work assignments. In many instances, an employer could readily demonstrate undue hardship. For example, a pharmacist may request reasonable accommodation for his or her religious beliefs by being allowed not to fill customer prescriptions for emergency contraceptives. The employer can readily demonstrate undue hardship if the pharmacy normally has only one pharmacist on duty. It is impossible to foresee when a customer may appear at the counter with a prescription for emergency contraceptives. Thus only three practical accommodations could be made. First, the pharmacy could hire another pharmacist to be on site with the conscientious objector pharmacist. This obviously would entail extra expense. Second, the customer could be directed by the objecting pharmacist to another pharmacy. Third, the objecting pharmacist could direct the customer to return when a non-objecting pharmacist is on duty. The latter two alternatives would both entail possible lost revenue, customer alienation, bad publicity and lawsuits. Thus the employer could readily meet its *de minimis* obligation and demonstrate that it would create an undue hardship to accommodate the pharmacist with religious objections.

Because the bar is set so low for an employer to meet its duty of reasonable accommodation for religious beliefs and practices, existing federal and state anti-discrimination statutes provide inadequate legal protection for employees with moral and religious objections to assigned work. More often than not, such employees would find themselves disciplined or discharged with scant legal recourse. Because of this inadequate statutory protection, many observers believe that conscience laws are needed to provide more substantive protection to employees.

Conscience Laws

Conscience laws are laws that grant an employee a statutory right to refuse to perform work or provide services that violate their religious or moral beliefs (see: Dennis Rambaud, "Prescription Contraceptives and the Pharmacist's Right to Refuse: Examining the Efficacy of Conscience Laws," *Cardozo Public Law, Policy and Ethics Journal* (2006), 195–231). Conscience laws are also referred to as conscience clauses or right of refusal clauses. Conscience laws first appeared in the aftermath of *Roe v. Wade, 410 U.S. 113* (1973) when state laws were passed which permitted doctors and other direct providers of health care services the statutory right to refuse to provide or participate in abortions. In general, conscience laws would prevent an employer from taking coercive, adverse or discriminatory action against an employee who refuses to perform assigned work for reasons of conscience. Depending on the particular text of the statute, conscience clauses may additionally protect the worker from civil liability and from adverse action by licensing boards.

More recent conscience clauses have focused on pharmacists, although some have broader coverage. The impetus for the flurry in state legislative action was the FDA approval of the morning-after pill. In the wake of that approval, pharmacists who refused to dispense the drug on moral grounds increasingly faced discipline, discharge and confrontations with state licensing boards. The current status of state conscience laws and pending bills is constantly in flux as more legislatures consider such laws. According to the National Conference of State Legislatures at the time of this writing, Arkansas, Georgia, Mississippi and South Dakota have passed statutes which permit a pharmacist to refuse to dispense emergency contraception because of moral convictions. Four other states (Colorado, Florida, Maine and Tennessee) enacted conscience clauses that are broader in nature and do not specifically mention pharmacists. California has enacted a more restrictive conscience clause which permits a pharmacist to refuse to fill a prescription only if the employer approves the refusal and the customer can still have the prescription filled in a timely manner (see: National Conference of State Legislatures, "Pharmacist Conscience Clauses: Laws and Legislation," [October 2006] . . .). At least 18 states are contemplating some 36 bills with varying scope and protection. Among those, nine states are considering conscience clauses that cover a broad array of health care workers. A few states are even considering bills that would permit insurance companies to opt out of providing coverage for morally objectionable services (see: Rob Stein, "Health Workers' Choice Debated," *Washington Post* [January 30, 2006], A01).

Needless to say, the surfeit of proposed state protective legislation has created an outcry among pro-choice and Planned Parenthood proponents. Some of this backlash is being translated into state law. In Illinois for example, the governor passed an emergency rule that requires a pharmacist to fill prescriptions for FDA-approved contraception. Several Illinois pharmacists have been fired for refusing to fill such prescriptions.

On the federal level in 2004, President Bush signed into law the Weldon Amendment which bars federal funding of any government program that subjects any institutional or individual health care provider to discrimination on the basis that the health care provider does not provide, pay for, provide coverage of, or refer for abortions. The U.S. Conference of Catholic Bishops has gone on record supporting the amendment. The State of California has filed a lawsuit challenging the constitutionality of the amendment.

Conscience laws seek to provide a balance between protecting workers compelled to choose between their livelihood and their religious beliefs and the public welfare. Whether American society will support this compromise or instead insist on forcing compliance by employees with moral objections to work assignments remains to be played out in the legal system.

Pharmacy Refusals 101

Prescription Contraception Is Basic Health Care for Women

- Family planning is central to good health care for women. Access to contraception is critical to preventing unintended pregnancies and to enabling women to control the timing and spacing of their pregnancies. Contraceptive use in the United States is virtually universal among women of reproductive age. A woman who wants only two children must use contraception for roughly three decades of her life. Also, women rely on prescription contraceptives for a range of medical purposes in addition to birth control, such as regulation of cycles and endometriosis.

- Emergency contraception (EC), also known as the morning after pill, is an FDA-approved form of contraception that prevents pregnancy after sexual intercourse. EC is a time-sensitive medication that has great potential to prevent unintended pregnancies. Currently, there are several options for emergency contraception available, one that requires a prescription and two that are available without a prescription for individuals 17 and older.

Refusals to Dispense Contraception Are Increasing

- Reports of pharmacist refusals to fill prescriptions for birth control—or provide EC to individuals who do not require a prescription—have surfaced in at least twenty-four states across the nation, including: AZ, CA, DC, GA, IL, LA, MA, MI, MN, MO, MT, NH, NY, NC, OH, OK, OR, RI, TN, TX, VA, WA, WV, WI.

- These refusals to dispense prescription contraceptives or provide EC are based on personal beliefs, not on legitimate medical or professional concerns. The same pharmacists who refuse to dispense contraceptives because of their personal beliefs often refuse to transfer a woman's prescription to another pharmacist or to refer her to another pharmacy. These refusals can have devastating consequences for women's health.

- Despite the fact that two brands of EC are available without a prescription to certain individuals, refusals based on personal beliefs are still a problem. Non-prescription EC must be kept behind the counter, so individuals seeking it must interact with pharmacists or other pharmacy staff who may have personal beliefs against providing the drug.

- Some examples of refusals in the pharmacy:
  - November 2010: Adam Drake attempted to purchase non-prescription EC at a Walgreens in **Houston, Texas** and was turned away, despite the fact that the federal Food and Drug Administration (FDA) has approved that brand of EC for sale to *men and women* aged seventeen and older.
  - March 2010: A pro-life pharmacy refusing to stock or dispense contraceptives in **Chantilly, Virginia,** closed due to lack of business. When it opened in October 2008, staff at the pharmacy refused to provide referrals or help individuals find contraception elsewhere.
  - January 2010: A mother of two in **Montclair, California** went to her local CVS to purchase EC after she and her fiancé experienced a birth control failure. The pharmacist refused to dispense EC to her, even though it was in stock, and told her to "come back in two and a half days," at which point it would no longer be effective.
  - May 2007: In **Great Falls, Montana,** a 49-year-old woman who used birth control to treat a medical condition went to her local pharmacy to fill her latest prescription. She was given a slip of paper informing her that the pharmacy would no longer fill any prescriptions for birth control. When she called back to inquire about the policy change, the owner of the pharmacy told her that birth control was "dangerous" for women.
  - January 2007: In **Columbus, Ohio,** a 23-year-old mother went to her local Wal-Mart for EC. The pharmacist on staff "shook his head and laughed." She was told that even though the store stocked EC, no one on staff would sell it to her. She had to drive 45 miles to find another pharmacy that would provide her with EC.
  - December 2006: In **Seattle, Washington,** a 25-year-old woman went to her local Rite-Aid to get non-prescription EC after she and her fiancé experienced a birth control failure. The pharmacist told her that although EC was in stock, he would not give it to her because he thought it was wrong. The woman had to repeatedly insist that the pharmacist find her another pharmacy in the area that would provide her with EC.
  - January 2006: In **Northern California,** a married mother of a newborn baby experienced a birth control failure with her husband. Her physician called in a prescription for EC to her regular pharmacy, but when she went to pick it up, the pharmacist on duty not only refused to dispense the drug, which was in stock, but also refused to enter the prescription into the pharmacy's computer so that it could be transferred elsewhere.
  - January 2005: In **Milwaukee, Wisconsin,** a mother of six went to her local Walgreens with a prescription for emergency contraception. The pharmacist refused to fill the prescription and berated the mother in the pharmacy's crowded waiting area, shouting "You're a murderer! I will not help you kill this baby. I will not have the blood on my hands." The mother left the pharmacy mortified and never

had her prescription filled. She subsequently became pregnant and had an abortion.

- April 2004: In *North Richland Hills, Texas,* a 32-year-old mother of two went to her local CVS for her regular birth control prescription refill. The pharmacist refused to refill her prescription because of his personal beliefs. The pharmacist said he would not fill the prescription because oral contraceptives are "not right" and "cause cancer."
- January 2004: In *Denton, Texas,* a rape survivor seeking EC was turned away from an Eckerd pharmacy by three pharmacists, who refused to fill the time-sensitive prescription due to their religious beliefs. The pharmacists' refusal put the survivor in danger of becoming pregnant due to the rape.

The Legal Landscape: What Governs the Practice of Pharmacy?

- The laws governing pharmacists vary from state to state. Pharmacists must abide by state laws and regulations, which are written by the state legislature and the state Pharmacy Board.
- The laws and regulations in most states do not specifically speak to the issue of pharmacist refusals based on personal beliefs. States that provide general guidance about when pharmacists may refuse to dispense tend to limit the reasons for such a refusal to professional or medical considerations—such as potentially harmful contraindication, interactions with other drugs, improper dosage, and suspected drug abuse or misuse—as opposed to personal judgments.
- Many pharmacist associations that have considered this issue, including the American Pharmacists Association, have issued policies requiring that patient access to legally prescribed medications is not compromised—for example by either filling valid prescriptions or transferring them to another pharmacist who can. Although such policies are not legally binding, they encourage pharmacists to meet consumers' needs.

Legislative and Administrative Responses to Refusals in the Pharmacy

Fewer than half of the states in the country explicitly address the issue of refusals to provide medication to patients in the pharmacy.

Prohibiting or Limiting Refusals

- *Existing State Laws and Policies:*
  - **Eight states**—CA, IL, ME, MA, NV, NJ, WA, WI—explicitly require pharmacists or pharmacies to provide medication to patients. In April 2011, a court prevented the Illinois regulation from being enforced against two pharmacists and the pharmacies they own.
  - In **seven states**—AL, DE, NY, NC, OR, PA, TX—pharmacy boards have issued policy statements that allow refusals but prohibit pharmacists from obstructing patient access to medication.

- *State Legislation*: Thus far in the 2011 legislative session, **seven states** (AZ, IN, MO, NJ, NY, OK, and WV) have considered **eleven bills** to prohibit or limit refusals. These bills would prevent pharmacists or pharmacies from denying access to contraception based on personal beliefs, including **seven bills** that apply to non-prescription EC.

Permitting Refusals

- *Existing State Laws and Policies:* **Six states**—AZ, AR, GA, ID, MS, and SD—have laws or regulations that specifically allow pharmacies or pharmacists to refuse for religious or moral reasons without critical protections for patients, such as requirements to refer or transfer prescriptions. However, a state court prevented Arizona's law allowing pharmacy and pharmacist refusals from going into effect pending litigation and it is therefore not currently enforceable.
- *State Legislation:* Thus far in the 2011 legislative session, **three states** (IN, MO, and PA) have considered **three bills** that could permit pharmacists or pharmacies to refuse to dispense certain drugs and devices without protecting patient access. The Missouri bill incorrectly classifies EC as an abortifacient despite the fact that the FDA approved it as a form of birth control.

Public Opinion

- According to surveys, the public is overwhelmingly opposed to allowing refusals in the pharmacy that prevent women from obtaining contraception.
  - A national survey of Republicans and Independent voters conducted in September and October 2008 on behalf of the National Women's Law Center and the YWCA found that 51% *strongly* favor legislation that requires pharmacies to ensure that patients get contraception at their pharmacy of choice, even if a particular pharmacist has a moral objection to contraceptives and refuses to provide it. That includes 42% of Republicans and 62% of Independents.
  - In a national opinion survey released in July 2007, which was conducted for the National Women's Law Center and Planned Parenthood Federation of America by Peter D. Hart Research Associates, 71% of voters said that pharmacists should not be allowed to refuse to fill prescriptions on moral or religious grounds, including majorities of every voter demographic such as Republicans (56%), Catholics (73%), and evangelical Christians (53%). Even more respondents (73% overall) supported requiring pharmacies to dispense contraception to patients without discrimination or delay.
  - A poll conducted in May 2007 by Lake Research Partners found that 82% of adults and registered voters believed that "pharmacies should be required to dispense birth control to patients without discrimination or delay."
  - An August 2006 poll conducted by the Pew Research Center on People and the Press found that 80% of Americans believe that pharmacists should not be able to refuse to sell birth control based on their

religious beliefs. This was true across party lines and religious affiliations. Particularly notable was the poll's finding that "No political or religious groups express majority support for this type of conscience clause."

- A November 2004 *CBS/New York Times* poll showed that public opinion disfavoring pharmacist refusals was strong regardless of party affiliation. 78% of Americans believe that pharmacist refusals should not be permitted, including 85% of Democrat respondents and 70% of Republican respondents.

How to Respond to a Refusal in the Pharmacy

- File a complaint with your state's pharmacy board to get sanctions against the pharmacist or pharmacy.
- Communicate your story to the press.
- Ask the state pharmacy board or legislature to put in place policies that will ensure every consumer's right to access legal pharmaceuticals.
- Alert the pharmacy's corporate headquarters; some pharmacies have policies that protect women's right to receive contraception in store, without discrimination or delay.
- Get EC today, before you need it!

POSTSCRIPT

Should Pharmacists Have the Right to Refuse Contraceptive Prescriptions?

Imagine, for a moment, that you (or your partner or friend) have just received a prescription for hormonal contraceptives. You take the prescription to your local pharmacy and hand it to the pharmacist on duty. Now imagine that the pharmacist hands the slip of paper back to you, stating that he or she will not fill your prescription because doing so would violate his or her religious or ethical beliefs. When you ask the pharmacist to call the other local pharmacy, which is about a 30-minute drive across town, he or she again refuses, citing that this is a right under state law. How would you feel?

Now, picture yourself as a pharmacist in another state. Your religious beliefs are such that you feel any attempt to prevent pregnancy goes against God's will. However, you fear that refusing to fill prescriptions for contraception could cost you your job. You like your job and your short commute, which allows you to spend more time with your family. If you lost your job, you would have to try your luck with another pharmacy, and there would be no guarantee that they would support your religious beliefs either. How would you feel if your manager insisted you fill prescriptions for birth control, or risk being fired?

In the final days of his second term as president, George W. Bush expanded the reach of federal "conscience clauses" through the Provider Refusal Rule. Supporters, including the United States Conference of Catholic Bishops and the group Pharmacists for Life, praised the president for protecting the religious freedom of those who work in the health care fields, from surgeons to ambulance drivers. Opponents, including the American Medical Association and Planned Parenthood, stressed that ideology should not trump patient care. In February 2011, President Barack Obama partially rescinded the Provider Refusal Rule, asserting that contraception cannot be equated with abortion and clarifying language that could have denied service to individuals based on "lifestyle."

The two essays selected for this issue present a compelling contrast between the rights of employees and the rights of patients. Both provide examples of scenarios with minor citations. Are these types of examples useful or does the lack of clear citation damage their effectiveness? Kelly presents her side from the perspective of Catholic social teaching. It is important, however, to understand that followers of particular religions are not completely homogeneous in their beliefs and practices. While Christian organizations like the U.S. Conference of Catholic Bishops and the Christian Medical and Dental

Association support broadening the reach of conscience clauses, other religious organizations like Catholics for Choice and the The United Methodist General Board of Church and Society have encouraged President Obama to reverse Bush's expansion of the clause. Similarly, not all who support the expansion of the "right of refusal" are religiously identified.

The National Women's Law Center provides a set of statistics showing widespread opposition to pharmacists' refusal of contraception. Were any of the statistics surprising? Why or why not? The group also provides a set of steps to take if a prescription is refused. Would you feel comfortable taking any of these steps? How are these steps similar or different to those presented by the American Family Association in Issue 11?

Where do you stand on this issue? Most people agree that freedom of religion is a valuable part of our democratic society. But does that freedom have limits? And what about other medications? If a pharmacist's religion adheres to the belief that antidepressants are not the best way to treat depression, should the pharmacist be allowed the right of refusal? Why do you think much of the controversy over pharmacist refusals have focused on contraception and not other medications? The Provider Refusal Rule also covers other health care workers—should pharmacy technicians be allowed to refrain from ordering contraceptives during their routine inventory checks? Should an EMT be allowed to refuse to drive the ambulance to the hospital if he or she fears an abortion may be necessary in order to save the patient's life?

Suggested Readings

H. Clinton & C. Richards, "Blocking Care for Women," *New York Times* (September 18, 2008)

G. Cook, "The Battle Over Birth Control," *Salon* (April 27, 2005)

J. Feder, "The History and Effect of Abortion Conscience Clause Laws," accessed at https://www.policyarchive.org/bitstream/handle/10207/3696/RS21428_20060227.pdf?sequence=2 (2006)

J. Jacobson, "Obama Administration Repeals Portions of Bush Provider Conscience Rules," *RH Reality Check* (February 18, 2011)

A. Sonfield, "Rights vs. Responsibilities: Professional Standards and Provider Refusals," *The Guttmacher Report on Public Policy* (vol. 8, no. 3, August 2005), accessed at http://www.guttmacher.org/pubs/tgr/08/3/gr080307.html

A. Sonfield, "Provider Refusal and Access to Reproductive Health Services: Approaching a New Balance," *Guttmacher Policy Review* (vol. 11, no. 2, Spring 2008), accessed at http://www.guttmacher.org/pubs/gpr/11/2/gpr110202.html

R. Stein, "Pro-Life Drugstores Market Beliefs," *The Washington Post*, accessed at http://www.washingtonpost.com/wp-dyn/content/article/2008/06/15/AR2008061502180.html?sid=ST2008082103218

ISSUE 18

Is Abortion Moral?

YES: Jennifer Webster, from "Choosing Abortion is Choosing Life," an original essay written for this volume (2009)

NO: Douglas Groothuis, from "Why I Am Pro-life: A Short, Non-sectarian Argument," adapted from http://theconstructivecurmudgeon .blogspot.com/2009/03/why-i-am-pro-life-short-nonsectarian.html (2009)

ISSUE SUMMARY

YES: Jennifer Webster, projects coordinator for the Network for Reproductive Options, asserts that the choice of abortion is a multi-factoral decision that always expresses a moral consideration.

NO: Douglas Groothuis, author and professor of philosophy at Denver Seminary, draws on the philosophical tradition to present his moral argument against abortion.

Women have abortions for a variety of reasons. Financial concerns, health issues, relationship problems, family responsibilities, and the desire to attend or remain in school or pursue a career path are but a few (Finer et al., 2005). Abortions have been practiced all around the world and throughout history (Jones & Lopez, 2006). Until the onset of modern surgical techniques, folk methods such as ingesting plant compounds (Riddle, 1992) or inserting chemicals or sharp objects into the vagina or uterus were used to induce abortion (Jones & Lopez, 2006). Information about contraception and abortion was passed from woman to woman through generations of oral history, thanks in part to religious and legal prohibitions against transmitting written instructions or information (Riddle, 1992).

Discussions about abortion are often framed as a matter of "rights," in other words, a woman's right to reproductive autonomy versus the right of the unborn to be born. The right to an abortion is essentially determined by the laws in one's area. In the United States, Comstock Laws formalized the illegal status of abortion in 1873. During the late 1960s and early 1970s, several states began to loosen their restrictions (Jones & Lopez, 2006). The year 1973 brought the cases of *Roe v. Wade* and *Doe v. Bolton*, which legalized abortion on the federal level. They established the "trimester framework," essentially legalizing first trimester abortions on demand, allowing states to regulate second trimester procedures with regard to the mother's health, and allowing states to prohibit abortion during the third trimester, unless the mother's health is at risk (Hatcher et al., 2007).

As the legality of abortion changed over time, individual states enacted legislation to restrict access to abortion. In many states, antiabortion advocates have imparted restrictions on abortion rights through an array of tactics including restricting federal funding for abortion, enacting waiting periods, and requiring counseling for those seeking abortions (Hatcher et al., 2007). The Supreme Court upheld the "Partial-Birth Abortion Ban Act of 2003" in 2007, which made dilation and extraction procedures illegal without regard for a woman's health (Hatcher et al., 2007).

According to the Guttmacher Institute (2008), about 40 percent of unintended pregnancies are terminated. About one-third of women will have had an abortion by the age of 45. The number of abortions in 2005 was 1.21 million, down from 1.31 million in 2000. The number of abortions per 1,000 women ages 15–44, per year, has fallen from 29.3 in the early 1980s to 19.4 in 2005. Fifty percent of abortions are obtained by women over age 25. Thirty-three percent are obtained by women between the ages of 20 and 24. Teenagers account for 17 percent of abortions. Almost 90 percent of abortions occur during the first 12 weeks of pregnancy (Guttmacher, 2008).

For many, the decision of whether to have an abortion, or to support or deny access to abortion procedures, has little to do with law or statistics. Certainly, laws can make accessing an abortion provider easier or more difficult, but abortions still take place in countries where abortion is illegal. For many, the question often boils down to morality. And our concepts of morality are often based on our worldviews (Lakoff, 2002). For people with different worldviews, it can be hard to see eye to eye on any number of issues. Is abortion immoral? If your worldview holds that abortion kills an innocent life, the answer is probably always "yes." If your worldview emphasizes the well-being and autonomy of women, the answer may often be "no." And many people have much more complex and nuanced beliefs that are based on a variety of factors that do not allow for an easy answer to the question "Is abortion a moral or immoral decision?"

In the following essays, Jennifer Webster, project coordinator for the Network for Reproductive Options, asserts that choosing abortion is always a moral decision based on a multitude of factors. Douglas Groothuis, a professor of philosophy at Denver Seminary, presents the case for the immorality of abortion while arguing for the status of a fetus as a living human being.

References

Alan Guttmacher Institute, *Facts on Induced Abortion in the United States* (July 2008), accessed November 26, 2008, at http://www.guttmacher.org/pubs/fb_induced_abortion.html

L. Finer et al., "Reasons U.S. Women Have Abortions: Quantitative and Qualitative Perspectives, *Perspectives on Sexual and Reproductive Health* (vol. 37, 2005).

R. Hatcher et al., eds., *Contraceptive Technology*, 19th ed. (New York: Ardent Media, 2007).

R. Jones and K. Lopez, *Human Reproductive Biology*. (Boston: Academic Press, 2006).

G. Lakoff, *Moral Politics: How Liberals and Conservatives Think* (Chicago: University of Chicago Press, 2002).

J. Riddle, *Contraception and Abortion from the Ancient World to the Renaissance* (Cambridge, MA: Harvard University Press, 1992).

YES

Jennifer Webster

Choosing Abortion
Is Choosing Life

I think it is a measure of how well the anti-abortion movement has been able to influence thinking and discussion of abortion in this country that when I sat down to write this essay I found myself confounded and conflicted on what I see as a fairly straightforward question. Can abortion be moral? Yes. Absolutely, without question, choosing an abortion is always a moral decision.

I say this and immediately I hear all the objections of the anti-abortion movement, what about the rights of the innocent baby, abortion is murder, women shouldn't be allowed to use abortion as birth control. Even I, who ought to know better, hear these voices and feel compelled to answer them. For nearly four decades we have allowed those most vehemently opposed to abortion to control the public debate and claim the moral high ground on abortion.

Women have abortions for lots of reasons.

- A senior in college has an abortion after one night celebrating with her boyfriend.
- A woman raped by her brother-in-law chooses to have an abortion, contrary to her Catholic upbringing, because she knows that this baby will cause her to re-live the the horror of the attack she suffered every day that she is pregnant and perhaps for the rest of her life.
- A young woman just moved to a new city with her husband who is finishing his master's degree and is overwhelmed by the needs of her 10-month-old baby; she chooses an abortion because she knows her son will suffer if she has a second baby so soon.
- A mother of three who lost her job, pregnant by the man who is divorcing her, chooses an abortion to enable her to care for the three kids she has.
- A woman trying to get out of an abusive relationship gets an abortion because she doesn't want to be tied to her abuser for the rest of her life and doesn't feel she is emotionally capable of caring for his child.

These are just a handful of stories that women seeking abortions tell everyday. They are by no means the only stories. Often a woman simply knows she does not have the emotional, social, or material resources to nurture and care for a child.

According to a study by the Guttmacher Institute,[1] approximately 3 million United States women become pregnant unintentionally every year. Nearly half of those women were using some form of birth control and of those 3 million pregnancies, about 1.3 million will end with an abortion. Among women choosing abortion, 60% are already mothers. By far, the most common reason women give for terminating pregnancies is they feel that now is not a good time for them to have a baby, because, for whatever reason, they are not able to provide for a child the way that child needs and deserves to be provided for. Women choose to have abortions because they want to be good mothers. Women who choose to have an abortion are making a moral decision for their own welfare and for the welfare of their children and family. As one young woman put it, "Choosing an abortion, for me, was choosing life. It was the first time I acted as if my life mattered."[2]

One reason abortion is not seen as a moral decision in our society is the historical discounting of women as moral agents. It is only recently that women have been recognized as capable of thinking, reasoning and making moral decisions. Take the story of a young married woman in the 1940s. She and her husband decided to postpone having children because of their limited income, need to finish school and no desire to live with their parents. They use a diaphragm to prevent conception, but it fails and she becomes pregnant. Her doctor tells her he can recommend someone who will perform a safe, although illegal, abortion but she must first get written permission from her husband and her father.[3] Is it even possible to imagine a medical procedure for which a man would need to get permission from his wife and mother?

There is a lot of complexity in the decision to terminate a pregnancy (as there is in virtually every moral decision we face in our lives). Abortion is the only moral deliberation that we, as a society, reduce to the black and white question of whose life is valued. It is only because women are the primary moral agents in abortion decisions that we allow it to be seen in such absolute terms.

When we collectively deliberate on the morality of any issue, we have to look at all the factors. The only way to look at abortion as an immoral decision is to see the unborn fetus as having an absolute right to life and to discount or erase the life of the woman faced with the decision. If you look at the preceding stories of women who have chosen abortion, who can say that those women made the wrong choice? Do those women deserve to be punished? No, those women made brave decisions to protect their welfare and to improve the welfare of their families. Women who choose abortions are making a moral decision by choosing to protect the lives of the already-born.

There are vast social and economic inequities in our society that impact on women's reproductive decision-making. Women living at or below the Federal Poverty Level are four times more likely to get an abortion than women who live at 300% above the Federal Poverty Level. Women in certain communities of color are more likely to choose to terminate a pregnancy, probably because they are more likely to be living in poverty. These women also tend to have less access to contraception, health care and educational opportunities. This lack of access is part of a larger system of social and economic inequality that abortion opponents rarely, if ever address. By ignoring a woman's life and circumstances, we erase her history, her autonomy and her right to self-determination.

In a society filled with racism, sexism, poverty, war and violence, in a country where half a million children live in foster care, four children die every day from abuse and 28 million children live in poverty[4], we have much more pressing moral concerns than the question of when life begins and the rights of fetuses. It is the height of arrogance, or perhaps just misplaced priorities, to question the morality of abortion decisions, when so many members of our communities don't enjoy access to their basic human rights.

What is truly immoral and unjust are the attempts by courts and legislatures to restrict women's access to abortion. Everything from requiring parental notification/consent, mandatory waiting periods, mandated counseling with medically inaccurate information are all attempts to restrict abortion access and disproportionately impact young women, women of color and low-income women.

These attempts at restricting women's access to abortion are particularly troublesome in light of a 2007 study by the Guttmacher Institute[5]. The study found that abortion rates were lowest in the countries in which abortion was the most accessible. In countries where abortion is legal, free and available, such as the Netherlands, abortion rates are among the lowest in the world. Likewise, in countries as diverse as Peru, the Philippines or Uganda, where abortion is illegal, abortion rates are only slightly higher than the United States. The countries with the lowest abortion rates were also the countries in which contraception is readily available and sexuality education is comprehensive and evidence-based, two things that the anti-abortion movement also generally opposes.

The Guttmacher study clearly indicates that the best way to reduce the number of abortions performed was to reduce the need for abortion. The history of abortion in the United States vividly illustrates that restricting access to abortion does little to stop abortions. Despite this overwhelming evidence, the anti-abortion movement continues to seek to restrict women's access to abortion, which raises a lot of questions about the motivations and true purpose of the anti-abortion movement.

The abortion debate in the United States is a tiring one. For decades now, both sides have argued for their position and given little ground. Life is pitted against Choice and there seems to be no way to move forward. What gets lost in this endless debate is the reality of women's lives. The decision of what to do with an unintended pregnancy is a morally complex one and women faced with the decision weigh their responsibilities carefully to examine what they have to offer to a new child. The issue is not so much a woman's right to choose to have an abortion, as a woman's right to choose her life.

Until women are seen as equal to men, with full complement of human rights, discussing the morality of abortion is specious. If we truly believed in women's autonomy, moral authority and right to self-determination, if we believed that only women can rightly make the decisions that will shape their lives, then we would recognize abortion for what it is: a safe medical procedure that is sometimes necessary for some women. If we lived in a society that valued women and women's lives this debate would go away. We would all work to prevent unintended pregnancy, to support women and the children they choose to have, recognizing that a woman's fundamental right to choose her own life is the first step to creating a morally just society.

Notes

1. Heather Boonstra, Rachel Benson Gold, Cory Richards and Lawrence Finer, *Abortion in Women's Lives* (Guttmacher Institute, 2006).

2. Anne Eggebroten, *Abortion: My Choice, God's Grace, Christian Women Tell Their Stories* (New Paradigm Books, 1994, p. 32).

3. From Helen Forelle, *If Men Got Pregnant, Abortion Would Be a Sacrament* (Canton, SD: Tesseract Publications, 1991).

4. Child Welfare Information Gateway. . . .

5. "Induced Abortion: Rates and Trends Worldwide," a study by the Guttmacher Institute and the World Health Organization authored by Gilda Sedgh, Stanley Hensha, Susheela Singh, Elisabeth Aahman and Iqbal Shah, published in *The Lancet,* October 13, 2007.

Douglas Groothuis  **NO**

Why I Am Pro-life:
A Short, Nonsectarian Argument

Abortion is the intentional killing of a human fetus by chemical and/or surgical means. It should not be confused with miscarriage (which involves no human intention) or contraception (which uses various technologies to prohibit sperm and egg from producing a fertilized ovum after sexual inter-course). Miscarriages are natural (if sad) occurrences, which raise no deep moral issues regarding human conduct—unless the woman was careless in her pregnancy. Contraception is officially opposed by Roman Catholics and some other Christians, but I take it to be in a moral category entirely separate from abortion (since it does not involve the killing of a fetus); therefore, it will not be addressed here.[1]

Rather than taking up the legal reasoning and history of abortion in America (especially concerning *Roe vs. Wade*), this essay makes a simple, straightforward moral argument against abortion. Sadly, real arguments (rea-soned defenses of a thesis or claim) are too rarely made on this issue. Instead, propaganda is exchanged. Given that the Obama administration is the most pro-abortion administration in the history of the United States, some clear moral reasoning is called for at this time.

The first premise of the argument is that human beings have unique and incomparable value in the world. Christians and Jews believe this is the case because we are made in God's image and likeness. But anyone who holds that humans are special and worthy of unique moral consideration can grant this thesis (even if their worldview does not ultimately support it). Of course, those like Peter Singer who do not grant humans any special status will not be moved by this.[2] We cannot help that. Many true and justified beliefs (concerning human beings and other matters) are denied by otherwise intelligent people.

Second, the *burden of proof* should always be on the one taking a human life and the *benefit of doubt* should always be given to the human life. This is not to say that human life should never be taken. In an often cruel and unfair world, sometimes life-taking is necessary, as many people will grant. Cases include self-defense, the prosecution of a just war, and capital punishment. Yet all unnecessary and intentional life-taking is murder, a deeply evil and repugnant offense against human beings. (This would also be acknowledged by those, such as absolute pacifists, who believe that it is never justifiable to take a human life.)

Third, abortion nearly always takes a human life intentionally and gratuitously and is, therefore, morally unjustified, deeply evil, and repugnant—given what we have said about human beings. The fetus is, without question, a *human being*. Biologically, an entity joins its parents' species at conception. Like produces like: apes procreate apes, rabbits procreate rabbits, and humans procreate humans. If the fetus is not human, what else could it possibly be? Could it be an ape or a rabbit? Of course not.

Some philosophers, such as Mary Anne Warren, have tried to drive a wedge between *personhood* and *humanity*. That is, there may be persons who are not human (such as God, angels, ETs—if they exist), and there may be humans that are not persons (fetuses or those who lose certain functions after having possessed them). While it is true that there may be persons who are not humans, it does not logically follow that there are humans who are not persons. The fetus is best regarded as a person with potential, not a potential person or nonperson.[3]

When we separate personhood from humanity, we make personhood an achievement based on the possession of certain qualities. But what are these person-constituting qualities? Some say a basic level of consciousness; others assert viability outside the womb; still others say a sense of self-interest (which probably does not obtain until after birth). All of these criteria would take away humanity from those in comas or other physically compromised situations.[4] Humans can lose levels of consciousness through injuries, and even infants are not viable without intense and sustained human support. Moreover, who are we to say just what qualities make for membership in the moral community of persons?[5] The stakes are very high in this question. If we are wrong in our identification of what qualities are sufficient for personhood and we allow a person to be killed, we have allowed the wrongful killing of nothing less than a person. Therefore, I argue that personhood should be viewed as a substance or essence that is given at conception. The fetus is not a lifeless *mechanism* that only becomes what it is after several parts are put together—as is the case with a watch or an automobile. Rather, the fetus is a living human *organism,* whose future unfolds from within itself according to internal principles. For example, the fertilized ovum contains a complete genetic code that is distinct from that of the mother or father. But this is not a mere inert blueprint (which is separable from the building it describes); this is a living blueprint that becomes what its human nature demands.

Yet even if one is not sure when personhood becomes a reality, one should err on the side of being conservative simply because so much is at stake. That is, if one aborts a fetus who is already a person, one commits a deep moral wrong by wrongfully killing an innocent human life. Just as we do not shoot target practice when we are told there may be children playing behind the targets, we should not abortion fetuses if they may be persons with the right not to be killed. As I have argued, it cannot be disputed that abortion kills a living, human being.

Many argue that outside considerations experienced by the mother should overrule the moral value of the human embryo. If a woman does not want a pregnancy, she may abort. But these quality of life considerations always involve issues of lesser moral weight than that of the conservation and protection of a unique human life (which considers the sanctity or innate and intrinsic value of a human life).[6] An unwanted pregnancy is difficult, but the answer is not to kill a human being in order to end that pregnancy. Moreover, a baby can be put up for adoption and bring joy to others. There are many others who do want the child and would give him or her great love and support. Furthermore, it is not uncommon for women to experience deep regrets after aborting their offspring.

The only exemption to giving priority to the life of the fetus would be if there were a real threat to the life of the mother were the pregnancy to continue. In this case, the fetus functions as a kind of intruder that threatens the woman's life. To abort the pregnancy would be tragic but allowable in this imperfect world. Some mothers will nonetheless choose to continue the pregnancy to their own risk, but this is not morally required. It should be noted that these life-threatening situations are extremely rare.

This pro-life argument does not rely on any uniquely religious assumptions, although some religious people will find it compelling. I take it to be an item of natural law (what can be known about morality by virtue of being human) that human life has unique value. A case can be made against abortion by using the Bible (only the Hebrew Bible or both the Hebrew Bible and New Testament combined) as the main moral source, but I have not given that argument here.[7] Rather, this essay has given an argument on the basis of generally agreed upon moral principles. If the argument is to be refuted, one or more of those principles or the reasoning employed needs to be refuted.

Although at the beginning of this essay I claimed I would not take up the legal reasoning related to abortion, one simple point follows from my argument. In nearly every case, abortion should be illegal simply because the Constitution requires that innocent human life be protected from killing.[8] Anti-abortion laws are not an intrusion of the state into the family any more than laws against murdering one's parents are an intrusion into the family.

Notes

1. See Scott Rae, *Moral Choices,* 3rd ed. (Grand Rapids, MI: Zondervan, 2009), 288–291.

2. For an exposition and critique of Singer's thought, see Gordon R. Preece, ed., *Rethinking Peter Singer* (Downers Grove, IL: InterVarsity Press, 2002).

3. See Clifford Bajema, *Abortion and the Meaning of Personhood* (Grand Rapids, MI: Baker Books, 1974). This book is on line. . . .

4. On the dangerous implications of his perspective, see Francis A. Schaeffer and C. Everett Koop, *Whatever Happened to the Human Race?*, revised ed. (Wheaton, IL: Crossway Books, 1983).

5. For a developed philosophical and legal case for including the unborn in the moral community of human beings, see Francis Beckwith, *Defending Life: A Moral and Legal Case Against Abortion Choice* (Cambridge University Press, 2007); and Robert P. George and Christopher Tollefsen, *Embryo: A Defense of Human Life* (New York: Doubleday, 2008).

6. On the distinction between a quality of life ethic and a sanctity of life ethic, see Ronald Reagan, "Abortion and the Conscience of a Nation." . . . This was originally an article in the Spring 1983 issue of *The Human Life Review*.

7. See Rae, 129133.

8. See Beckwith, Chapter 2.

POSTSCRIPT

Is Abortion Moral?

Recent years have seen a shift in attitudes toward abortion. A 2009 Gallup poll found that 51 percent of Americans considered themselves "pro-life" on abortion, compared with 42 percent who described themselves as "pro-choice." This poll marked the first time that a majority of Americans have taken a "pro-life" position since the Gallup poll began asking the question in 1995. Why do you think there has been a shift in attitudes? How would you define the terms "pro-life" and "pro-choice"? How do these terms differ with alternate descriptors, such as "pro-abortion," "anti-abortion," and "anti-choice"? It is interesting to note that further polling by the Gallup group found that 53 percent of people said that abortion should be legal under certain circumstances. Under what circumstances, if any, do you think abortion should be legal?

Groothuis describes President Barack Obama's administration as "the most pro-abortion administration in the history of the United States." Early in his first term, Obama rescinded the "global gag-rule," enacted by former President George W. Bush, which restricted federal funding for abortion related services (including providing information) in other countries. Despite this, Obama has stated publicly that he would "like to reduce the number of unwanted pregnancies that result in women feeling compelled to get an abortion or at least considering getting an abortion." Secretary of State Hillary Clinton has stated repeatedly that she believes abortion should be "safe, legal, and rare."

This wording—"safe, legal, and rare"—concerns people on both sides of the abortion debate. Ardent pro-choice advocates question why abortions need "rarely" occur, if they are both legal and safe. Pro-life activists assert abortion can never be "safe" because abortion harms innocent life.

Groothuis presents three premises to advance his opposition to abortion. Do you agree with his logic? Groothius did make an exception for allowing abortion if the mother's life is at risk because of the child's birth (which he posits is a rarity). But what if the child's birth would keep the mother and her other children in poverty? Could staying in poverty be seen as immoral when you have other children to care for? Webster presents a variety of scenarios in which women may seek an abortion. Do you feel that abortion could be an appropriate decision in each of these situations? Is it more or less of a moral decision for a senior in college who "has an abortion after one night celebrating with her boyfriend" or for "a woman raped by her brother-in-law?" Or are they equally moral decisions?

To what extent does either description of morality—Groothuis's or Webster's—represent your own? What nuances, exceptions, or other reasons help to establish your own viewpoints on abortion? Finally, in a speech given at Notre Dame in 2009, President Obama called for a continued dialogue about abortion that includes "open hearts, open minds, and fair-minded words." Two weeks later, Dr. George Tiller, who provided late-term abortions at his clinic in Wichita, Kansas, was shot and killed by an anti-abortion activist. With his call for open minds and fair-minded words, what was the president saying about the history of the public discourse on abortion? In what ways have Americans' hearts and minds been closed, or their words unfair? How well do Groothuis and Webster succeed at responding to the president's invitation for civil dialogue?

Suggested Readings

D. Barstow, "An Abortion Battle, Fought to the Death," *The New York Times* (July 25, 2009).

J. Baumgardner and T. Todras-Whitehill, *Abortion and Life* (New York: Akashic Books, 2008).

Alan Guttmacher Institute, *Facts on Induced Abortion in the United States,* accessed July 6, 2011, at http://www.guttmacher.org/pubs/fb_induced_abortion.html (May 2011).

D. Marquis, "Why Abortion Is Immoral," *The Journal of Philosophy* (vol. 86, no. 4, 2009).

A. Sanger, *Beyond Choice: Reproductive Freedom in the 21st Century* (New York: Public Affairs, 2004).

L. Waddington, "American Pendulum Swings Back in Favor of a Woman's Right to Make Reproductive Choices," *The Iowa Independent* (May 23, 2011).

S. Wicklund and A. Kessleheim, *This Common Secret: My Journey as an Abortion Doctor.* (New York: Public Affairs, 2008).

J. Williams, "Obama Urges Dialogue, Not Demonization, on Abortion," *Boston Globe* (May 18, 2009).

ISSUE 19

Should There Be Restrictions on the Number of Embryos Implanted during In Vitro Fertilization?

YES: Charalambos Siristatidis and Mark Hamilton, from "Single Embryo Transfer," *Obstetrics, Gynecology, & Reproductive Medicine* (June 2007)

NO: William Saletan, from "Crocktuplets: Hijacking the Octuplets Backlash to Restrict IVF." Accessed May 01, 2009, at http://www.slate .com/id/2212876/

ISSUE SUMMARY

YES: Charalambos Siristatidis, an obstetrician, and Mark Hamilton, a gynecologist, advocate for restrictions on the number of embryos implanted during IVF, arguing the reduction of risk to mother and child.

NO: William Saletan, national correspondent for slate.com and author, acknowledges the risks of multiple embryo transfer but argues that any attempts to legislate the practice must consider women's reproductive autonomy.

$\mathbf{A}$ variety of assisted reproduction technologies (ART) have helped millions of women become pregnant and give birth. Over the past 30 years, in vitro fertilization (IVF) has become a popular choice for those who have had trouble becoming pregnant through traditional means. IVF allows egg cells to be surgically removed and fertilized by sperm cells in a laboratory, then are transferred into the woman's uterus in hopes of pregnancy and birth (CDC, 2008).

In the United States, fertility clinics have typically transferred more than one fertilized embryo to increase the chances of success. Because of this, between 35 and 42 percent of pregnancies through IVF result in multiple births (Jones, 2006). Although some expecting parents see this as an added bonus, many medical experts warn that the increased risks (to both mother and child) involved in multiple births make the implantation of more than one embryo too risky to be considered ethical.

In 2009, headlines were made when Nadya Suleman gave birth to octuplets, born as a result of IVF. The births were considered miraculous, and brought accolades for the delivery team. The media speculated over which companies would step up to provide free products, as had been the trend with other recent multiple births. However, the good will quickly turned to criticism, as it was revealed that Suleman, dubbed "Octomom" was already the mother of six children, all produced via IVF. She was also unemployed and living with her mother. Critics wondered where she got the money for the procedure and how she could afford to care for 14 children.

According to the American Society for Reproductive Medicine guidelines, the transfer of one embryo is ideal, no more than two should be transferred under normal circumstances for women under the age of 35. For women over 40, the maximum number of embryos implanted should be five. Although these guidelines are from a respected organization, they are not law, and at the time of this writing, the doctor who performed Suleman's IVF awaits a ruling by California's medical board that will determine the fate of his medical license.

From an efficiency and safety standpoint, the guidelines make sense. Researchers have found that single embryo implantation resulted in higher pregnancy rates than double embryo implantation (Fiddelers et al., 2009; Veleva et al., 2009). So why would doctors not follow the guidelines? In many cases leaving embryos frozen, or having them donated to infertile couples is unimaginable. These concerns raise ethical questions of what is to be done with frozen embryos.

Questions arose in the aftermath of the "Octomom" controversy. How would the mother meet the needs of her children? Would the government have to pay for their welfare to the unemployed mother? This was a question asked by state legislators in Georgia and Missouri, who quickly pushed forward bills that would regulate the number of embryos implanted via IVF.

In the following selections, Siristatidis and Hamilton present evidence for the reduction of risk to mother and child through the practice of SET. Saletan challenges the introduction of legislation that supposedly protects women's health through outlawing multiple embryo transfer, but in reality restricts their reproductive options.

Suggested Readings

Centers for Disease Control and Prevention (CDC), "2006 Assisted Reproductive Technology (ART) Report: Commonly Asked Questions," accessed at http://www.cdc.gov/ART/ART2006/faq.htm (2008); "2008 Assisted Reproductive Technology Report," accessed at http://www.cdc.gov/art/ART2008/index.htm (2010).

A. Fiddelers, et al., "Cost-Effectiveness of Seven IVF Strategies: Results of a Markov Decision-Analytic Model," *Human Reproduction* (vol. 1, no. 1, 2009).

M. Hennessy-Fiske, "Octomom Doctor Could Still Lose Medical License," *Los Angeles Times* (February 9, 2011).

R. Jones and K. Lopez, *Human Reproductive Biology* (Burlington, MA: Academic Press, 2006).

Z. Veleva, et al., "Elective Single Embryo Transfer with Cryopreservation Improves the Outcome and Diminishes the Costs of IVF/ICSI." *Human Reproduction* (vol. 1, no. 1, 2009).

V.C. Wright, et al., "Assisted Reproductive Technology Surveillance—United States, 2005," accessed at http://www.cdc.gov/mmwr/preview/mmwrhtml/ss5705a1.htm (2008).

YES

**Charalambos Siristatidis
and Mark Hamilton**

Single Embryo Transfer

Abstract

Multiple pregnancies present significant problems for mothers and babies. The incidence of twin pregnancies has increased dramatically in the last 30 years, linked to the development of assisted reproductive technologies including *in vitro* fertilisation (IVF). The occurrence of multiple pregnancies after IVF is directly related to the number of embryos replaced during treatment. Policies to reduce the number of multiple pregnancies through limiting the numbers of embryos transferred have been successfully introduced in some parts of Europe. Anxieties that pregnancy rates would decline significantly after introduction of a policy of single embryo transfer have not been realised, particularly when the pregnancies derived from the transfer of additional cryopreserved embryos are taken into consideration. Obstacles to the introduction of such a policy in the UK relate to the commissioning arrangements for IVF and the competitive commercial environment in which IVF is provided. Continued high multiple pregnancy rates are not acceptable. IVF children should be given the best chance possible of safe delivery, at term, as singletons.

Introduction

One in seven couples has infertility problems. For many, the only effective treatment is *in vitro* fertilisation (IVF). Each year in the UK, over 40,000 such treatment cycles are undertaken, resulting in the birth of more than 10,000 babies. Many of the babies born arise from multiple pregnancies. More than half of all twin pregnancies in the UK result from fertility treatment. The observed secular trends in the incidence of multiple pregnancies over the last 25 years are thus a direct consequence of the increased use of IVF in infertility care.

The Burden of Multiple Pregnancy

The number of twin births in the UK has risen dramatically over the last 30 years, from just under 6000 in 1975 to over 9000 in 2004. Multiple pregnancies pose major risks for both women and children. Obstetric complications such as haemorrhage, pre-eclampsia, diabetes and pre-term delivery are common. Neonatal consequences are often profound, with significantly increased

From *Obstetrics, Gynaecology and Reproductive Medicine*, 17(6), June 2007, pp. 192–194.
Copyright © 2007 by Elsevier Health Sciences. Reprinted by permission via Rightslink.

risks of death and cerebral palsy. The long-term consequences of extremely pre-term birth may impose a major health burden on the child, and the costs incurred through such birth complications can be extremely high. In addition, there are often health and social consequences for the families concerned.

Risk Reduction

The link between the number of embryos transferred to the uterus during IVF and the likelihood of multiple pregnancy is irrefutable. In 2001, the Human Fertilisation and Embryology Authority (HFEA), the regulator of treatment centres in the UK, limited the number of embryos allowed to be transferred, other than in exceptional circumstances, to two. This policy was toughened in 2004, allowing no exceptions below the age of 40 years. The consequence of this has been a massive reduction in the incidence of triplet pregnancies but little effect on the number of twins. Further restrictions on embryo transfer practice merit consideration. Intuitively, since most twin pregnancies in IVF are dizygotic, a unilateral move to elective single embryo transfer (eSET) for all patients would virtually abolish the problem. Inevitably, matters are not as simple as this because patients, many of whom are funding their treatment themselves, are concerned to have the maximum chance of a pregnancy, and restriction of embryo transfer numbers might prejudice the one opportunity they have to conceive. Furthermore, it is likely that not all patients have the same prospect of successful treatment and thus, when considering restrictive embryo transfer policies, it is necessary to identify the patients in whom the chance of pregnancy is greatest and the embryos with the highest chance of implantation.

Experience of Single Embryo Transfer

To date, single embryo transfer is widely practiced only in Scandinavia, Holland and Belgium. Randomised controlled trial evidence suggests that the pregnancy rates per cycle after eSET are lower than in double embryo transfer (DET) cycles. These trials have been conducted in patients deemed to have a good prognosis regarding the woman's age and the number and quality of available embryos. Analyses, as summarised in a recent Cochrane review, suggest that, compared with eSET, DET in fresh IVF/intracytoplasmic sperm injection cycles leads to a higher live birth rate (OR 1.94, 95% CI 1.47–2.55; $p < 0.00001$). The multiple pregnancy rate, however, was significantly higher in women who underwent DET (OR 23.55, 95% CI 8.00–69.29; $p < 0.00001$). These and other trials have also examined the influence on overall pregnancy rates if the use of any additional cryopreserved embryos derived from the same ovary stimulation cycle is taken into account. The difference in pregnancy rate is eliminated when pregnancies following a subsequent frozen/thawed transfer cycle are added.

It can be deduced from these data that the introduction of a single embryo transfer policy involving fresh followed by frozen single embryo transfers, in patients with a good prognosis, can virtually abolish the risk of multiple pregnancy while maintaining a live birth rate similar to that achieved by transferring two fresh embryos.

Defining the good-prognosis patient is a requirement for a successful eSET policy. Further research in this area will be required, but at present studies take into account the age of the woman (usually <36 years), previous failed IVF attempts (usually first cycle), basal follicle-stimulating horome (<10 IU/l) and number of good-quality embryos available (usually at least two).

The experience in Sweden merits particular attention. Persuaded by the trial evidence, a national policy has evolved based on the principle that only one embryo should be replaced, apart from in exceptional circumstances. In practice, 70% of all IVF cycles are now eSET cycles. Importantly, perhaps as embryological expertise has increased, pregnancy rates have been maintained and the twin rate resulting from treatment has decreased from 25% in 1999 to 5% in 2004.

The Patient's Perspective

While the cumulative pregnancy rates achieved through eSET policies match those of DET, the need for additional cycles of care is not attractive to patients. More embryo transfers cost more money, and entail more time off work and more trips to hospital. The emotional strain caused by extra cycles associated with disappointment is an issue. For many patients, the experience of a failed cycle is akin to bereavement. Additional exposure to risk of failure may be interpreted by some as compounding their anguish. Clinics need therefore to strike a balance between a desire to maximise the chance of conception for the patient and minimising the risk of multiple pregnancy. Both aspirations have the intention of maximising the chance of a safe live birth of a healthy child.

Embryo Selection

The future success of single embryo transfer policies will be influenced by our ability to improve culture conditions for embryos, and the development of techniques to determine with confidence the best embryo to select for transfer; that is, the embryo with the greatest potential for implantation. At present, embryo selection is determined on morphological grounds, which is a relatively crude technique in terms of predicting the genetic competence of individual embryos. Research into more sophisticated techniques such as biochemical and genetic screening may prove fruitful. Extended culture to the blastocyst stage may be a useful method of determining the embryo with the maximum implantation potential.

Commissioning Care

An examination of the way in which IVF is commissioned in countries where eSET has become the norm is informative. In Belgium, a reimbursement system has been introduced that links the funding of six IVF cycles for a patient to the compulsory use of eSET in the patient's first cycle. Further eSET is required if the patient's age and available embryo quality are favourable. In contrast, no legislative proscription on IVF care has been imposed in Sweden, Denmark or Norway, yet the sector, perhaps through peer pressure, has largely moved to eSET as the default position. Experience in the UK suggests that proscription rather than appeal to clinical sensibility is more likely to result in a change in practice. Implementation in full of the guideline on the assessment and treatment for people with fertility problems issued by the National Institute for Clinical Excellence in 2004, in which three cycles of treatment were recommended, including transfer of fresh and all frozen embryos per cycle, would help to facilitate a change in practice. The way in which IVF data is presented to the public, both by the regulatory authority and by clinics, could also make a difference. Outcome per cycle, as currently used, tends to be a disincentive to good clinical practice rather than a more responsible description of cumulative pregnancy rates. The HFEA, and the infertility sector itself, has a major role to play in changing the mind-set of patients and clinics regarding how embryo transfer is conducted. In a commercially driven marketplace derived from inadequate state funding of IVF, this is a significant challenge.

Conclusions

The evidence base linking the practice of multiple embryo transfer and the consequent establishment of pregnancies at high risk of serious complications is irrefutable. The health benefits to children, the reduction in distress for families and the enormous cost savings for society that would be achieved through a reduction in the need for immediate and long-term health care for affected children make an overwhelming case for change in this area of clinical practice. Modification of embryo transfer practice through careful patient and embryo selection can significantly reduce the risk of such hazards.

To quote a recent important document from the HFEA: "The fertility sector has for too long been responsible for the creation of children with complex needs. IVF children deserve the best possible chance to be born at full term and as healthy singletons. The only way this can be achieved is by making eSET the norm."

Practice Points

- Twin pregnancies carry much higher obstetric risks for women
- Multiple birth is the single biggest risk to the health and welfare of children born after IVF
- Modification of embryo transfer practice through careful patient and embryo selection can significantly reduce the risk of such hazards

 **NO**

Crocktuplets: Hijacking the Octuplets Backlash to Restrict IVF

No more octuplets! That's the rallying cry for Georgia Senate Bill 169, which faces a committee hearing Thursday morning. The bill's lead sponsor, state senator Ralph Hudgens, says he believes in "less government," "more personal responsibility," and "greater individual freedoms." Supposedly, that's what galls him about Nadya Suleman, the now-infamous woman who had six kids and, through in vitro fertilization, just gave birth to eight more. "Nadya Suleman is going to cost the state of California millions of dollars over the years; the taxpayers are going to have to fund the 14 children she has," Hudgens told the *Wall Street Journal*. "I don't want that to happen in Georgia." Georgia Right to Life, which helped Hudgens draft his bill, puts a gentler spin on it. The Suleman case shows that "the fertility industry needs governmental oversight," the group argued in a press release two weeks ago. Its president explained that S.B. 169 "is written to help reduce the attendant harm that could come to the mother and her children through the creation and implantation of more embryos than is medically recommended." The release was titled "Georgia Right to Life Introduces Legislation to Protect the Mother and Child."

So which rationale should we believe? The one about protecting taxpayers or the one about protecting women?

Neither. Never trust the press release. Always read the bill.

S.B. 169 does limit the number of embryos you can implant in an IVF patient to two or three, depending on whether the patient is younger or older than 40. But it also does several things that have nothing to do with saving tax money or protecting women from the risks of carrying multiple fetuses. It forbids the sale of eggs or sperm, bans therapeutic human cloning, and prohibits any stem-cell research involving the destruction of leftover embryos.

"This bill would limit the number of embryos transferred in any given cycle to the same number that are fertilized," says the Georgia Right to Life press release. But that's not what the bill says. Here's the actual text of the legislation:

> In the interest of reducing the risk of complications for both the mother and the transferred in vitro human embryos, including the risk of preterm birth associated with higher-order multiple gestations, a person or entity performing in vitro fertilization shall limit the number of in vitro human embryos created in a single cycle to the number to be transferred in that cycle.

In other words, if you're 39, your doctor is forbidden to fertilize more than two of your eggs per treatment cycle. Take all the hormones you can stand, make all the eggs you want, but you get two shots at creating a viable embryo, and that's it.

How does this restriction "protect the mother" and "reduce the risk of complications" for her? It doesn't. If you wanted to protect the woman, you might limit the number of embryos that could be transferred to her womb, not the number that can be created in the dish. In fact, by limiting the number that can be created, you increase her risk of complications. The fewer eggs you fertilize, the lower your chances of producing an embryo healthy enough to be transferred and carried to term. That means a higher failure rate, which in turn means that women will have to undergo more treatment cycles, with the corresponding risks of ovarian hyperstimulation and advancing maternal age.

So why limit the number of embryos created per cycle? Because the bill's chief purpose isn't really to help women. It's to establish legal rights for embryos. That's why it bans cloning and embryo-destructive stem-cell research. And if the woman and her husband get into a legal battle over what to do with their embryos, guess which of them has the final say? Neither. According to the bill's text, "the judicial standard for resolving such disputes shall be the best interest of the in vitro human embryo."

From the standpoint of respecting embryos, this is all wonderful stuff. But it doesn't serve the health interests of women seeking IVF, and it certainly doesn't protect taxpayers. "A living in vitro human embryo is a biological human being who is not the property of any person or entity," the bill declares. "The fertility physician and the medical facility that employs the physician owe a high duty of care to the living in vitro human embryo." Guess who's going to foot the bill for that "high duty of care"? With half a million embryos already frozen and thousands more accumulating every year, a declaration of medical rights for embryos would be one of the biggest entitlement programs in history.

Oh, and if you like what Suleman did, you'll love S.B. 169. By requiring doctors to "limit the number of in vitro human embryos created in a single cycle to the number to be transferred," the bill logically requires them to transfer every embryo created. That's exactly what Suleman did. She loved her babies too much to leave any of them behind. Enough with the opportunism about the octuplets. Respecting embryos is a noble idea. But it won't be safer for women, and it won't come cheap.

POSTSCRIPT

Should There Be Restrictions on the Number of Embryos Implanted during In Vitro Fertilization?

Siristatidis and Hamilton state the benefits of single embryo transfer. Although guidelines are in place that recommend this practice, do you feel that laws should be created in order to reduce multiple transfers? Saletan does not disagree with the health benefits of single embryo transfer. However, he feels that much of the legislation currently being discussed is intended to restrict women's reproductive freedom more than protect her health. Is there a way to legislate IVF without infringing on a woman's reproductive autonomy? Is there a line that should be drawn between the desires of the patient and concern for their safety? Should couples who undergo fertility treatments have restrictions placed on the number of children they can ultimately have? Is any attempt to reduce the options available unfair to women and hopeful couples?

And what, as many commentators asked, about the welfare of the children after their release from the hospital? Should parents who opt to have more than one embryo transferred be required to undergo background screenings? These kinds of questions make some reproductive rights advocates nervous. They see the possibility of restrictions a form of modern-day eugenics. In the early 1900s, the eugenics movement pushed for reduced reproduction among groups, including the poor, minorities, and the disabled, who were thought to possess negative hereditary traits. Should the government have a say in who gets to be a mother? Or how many children she can give birth to at once? On what criteria would the mother or couple be judged? Should there be different rules if the mother is single, in a same-sex marriage, or in a relationship; wealthy or poor; suffering from depression; or developmentally disabled? Is legislation that limits an individual's right or ability to reproduce a form of eugenics? Should the decision of Suleman and her doctor impact the reproductive choices of others?

Suggested Readings

Centers for Disease Control and Prevention (CDC), "2006 Assisted Reproductive Technology (ART) Report: Commonly Asked Questions," accessed at http://www.cdc.gov/ART/ART2006/faq.htm (2008).

Centers for Disease Control and Prevention (CDC), "2008 Assisted Reproductive Technology Report," accessed at http://www.cdc.gov/art/ART2008/index.htm (2010).

A. Fiddelers et al. "Cost-effectiveness of Seven IVF Strategies: Results of a Markov Decision-Analytic Model," *Human Reproduction,* advance access, published online on March 24, 2009.

"Georgia 'Octomom Bill' Would Limit Embryo Implants," *CNN* (March 3, 2009).

M. Hennessy-Fiske, "Octomom Doctor Could Still Lose Medical License," *Los Angeles Times* (February 9, 2011).

"IVF Limits Could Reduce Newborn Deaths: Study," Reuters, *The Vancouver Sun* (May 16, 2011).

R. Jones and K. Lopez, K., *Human Reproductive Biology* (Burlington, MA: Academic Press, 2006).

Z. Veleva et al., "Elective Single Embryo Transfer with Cryopreservation Improves the Outcome and Diminishes the Costs of IVF/ICSI," *Human Reproduction,* Advance Access, published online on March 24, 2009.

V.C. Wright et al., "Assisted Reproductive Technology Surveillance—United States, 2005," accessed at http://www.cdc.gov/mmwr/preview/mmwrhtml/ss5705a1.htm (2008).

ISSUE 20

Should Parents Be Allowed to Select the Sex of Their Baby?

YES: John A. Robertson, from "Extending Preimplantation Genetic Diagnosis: Medical and Non-medical Uses," *Journal of Medical Ethics* (vol. 29, 2003)

NO: Marcy Darnovsky, from "Revisiting Sex Selection: The Growing Popularity of New Sex Selection Methods Revives an Old Debate," http://www.gene-watch.org/genewatch/articles/17-1darnovsky.html (January–February 2004)

ISSUE SUMMARY

YES: Law professor John A. Robertson argues that preimplantation genetic diagnosis (PGD), a new technique that allows parents-to-be to determine the gender of their embryo before implantation in the uterus, should be permissible. Robertson argues that it is not sexist to want a baby of a particular sex and that the practice should not be restricted.

NO: Marcy Darnovsky, associate director of the Center for Genetics and Society, argues that by allowing PGD for sex selection, governments are starting down a slippery slope that could create an era of consumer eugenics.

T he practice of selecting the sex of a child is nothing new. Historically, couples who wanted a child of a specific sex might abandon an unwanted boy or girl in wilderness, leave the baby on the doorstep of a church or orphanage, or kill the unwanted baby. Although these practices still continue in some societies today, sex selection has also changed in significant ways. The development of ultrasound technology, for example, allows expecting parents to determine the sex of the baby before it is born, and some might consider abortion if the child is not of the desired sex. Parents might feel additional pressure to make this decision in countries like China, which has a "one child" policy, whereby additional children receive no governmental support—a critical consideration in a country that has traditionally placed a higher value on male infants than females.

For many Americans, the idea of sex selection by abandonment, abortion, or infanticide would be considered unethical, if not appalling. But in other areas of the world, the practice is carried out routinely to help parents meet strong cultural preferences to produce a male child. Such actions are based in the entrenched sexism of these male-dominated societies.

A seemingly more ethical technique that sortes sperm before conception has offered about a 50–85 percent effectiveness rate at predetermining sex for the past 30 years. More recently a new development in medical technology known as preimplantation genetic diagnosis (PGD), previously used to screen embryos for markers that may signal diseases like cystic fibrosis, now allows people using in vitro fertilization to select the sex of an embryo, with 99.9 percent accuracy. In this procedure, egg cells that have been fertilized in a laboratory are tested for specific markers before being implanted into the uterus. To many satisfied customers, this has provided the opportunity to "balance" a family by adding a child of the other sex, evening out the number of male and female children. In some cases, first-time parents simply desire a child of one sex or the other.

While the use of PGD for medical reasons, such as screening for Down syndrome, in an embryo are generally seen as acceptable, there is less consensus concerning its use for nonmedical reasons, including sex selection. Is wanting to choose the sex of your child sexist? Does it reflect or perpetuate a gender bias in society? If selecting the sex of your unborn child is possible and legal, what about predetermination of other characteristics, such as eye color? Height? Musical ability? Sexual orientation?

In the following selections, John A. Robertson, professor at the University of Texas School of Law, argues that using PGD for sex selection in certain instances is not inherently sexist, and that it—and perhaps other nonmedical types of PGD should not be regulated based on the fear of what could possibly happen at some future time. Marcy Darnovsky, associate director of the Center for Genetics and Society, argues that by allowing PGD for sex selection, governments are starting down a slippery slope that could create an era of consumer eugenics.

YES

John A. Robertson

Extending Preimplantation Genetic Diagnosis: Medical and Non-Medical Uses

PGD and Its Prevalence

PGD has been available since 1990 for testing of aneuploidy in low prognosis in vitro fertilisation (IVF) patients, and for single gene and X linked diseases in at risk couples. One cell (blastomere) is removed from a cleaving embryo and tested for the genetic or chromosomal condition of concern. Some programmes analyse polar bodies extruded from oocytes during meiosis, rather than blastomeres.[1] Cells are then either karyotyped to identify chromosomal abnormalities, or analysed for single gene mutations and linked markers.

Physicians have performed more than 3000 clinical cycles of PGD since 1990, with more than 700 children born as a result. The overall pregnancy rate of 24% is comparable to assisted reproductive practices which do not involve embryo or polar body biopsy.[1] Four centres (Chicago, Livingston (New Jersey), Bologna, and Brussels) accounted for nearly all the reported cases. More than 40 centres worldwide offer the procedure, however, including other centres in the United States and Europe, four centres in London and centres in the eastern Mediterranean, Southeast Asia, and Australia.

More than two-thirds of PGD has occurred to screen out embryos with chromosomal abnormalities in older IVF patients and in patients with a history of miscarriage. About 1000 cycles have involved single gene mutational analysis.[1] Mutational analysis requires additional skills beyond karyotyping for aneuploidies, including the ability to conduct the multiplex polymerase chain reaction (PCR) of the gene of interest and related markers.

Several new indications for PGD single gene mutational analysis have recently been reported. New uses include PGD to detect mutations for susceptibility to cancer and for late onset disorders such as Alzheimer's disease.[2,3] In addition, parents with children needing hematopoietic stem cell transplants have used PGD to ensure that their next child is free of disease and a good tissue match for an existing child.[4] Some persons are also requesting PGD for gender selection for both first and later born children, and others have speculated that selection of embryos for a variety of non-medical traits is likely in the future.

PGD is ethically controversial because it involves the screening and likely destruction of embryos, and the selection of offspring on the basis of expected

From *Journal of Medical Ethics*, vol. 29, 2003, pp. 213(4). Copyright © 2003 by Institute of Medical Ethics. Reprinted by permission of BMJ Publishing Group.

traits. While persons holding right to life views will probably object to PGD for any reason, those who view the early embryo as too rudimentary in development to have rights or interests see no principled objection to all PGD. They may disagree, however, over whether particular reasons for PGD show sufficient respect for embryos and potential offspring to justify intentional creation and selection of embryos. Donation of unwanted embryos to infertile couples reduces this problem somewhat, but there are too few such couples to accept all unwanted embryos, and in any event, the issue of selecting offspring traits remains.

Although ethical commentary frequently mentions PGD as a harbinger of a reproductive future of widespread genetic selection and alteration of prospective offspring, its actual impact is likely to be quite limited.[5,6] Even with increasing use the penetrance of PGD into reproductive practice is likely to remain a very small percentage of the 150,000 plus cycles of IVF performed annually throughout the world. Screening for susceptibility and late onset diseases is limited by the few diseases for which single gene predispositions are known. Relatively few parents will face the need to conceive another child to provide an existing child with matched stem cells. Nor are non-medical uses of PGD, other than for gender, likely to be practically feasible for at least a decade or more. Despite the limited reach of PGD, the ethical, legal, and policy issues that new uses raise, deserve attention.

New Medical Uses

New uses of PGD may be grouped into medical and non-medical categories. New medical uses include not only screening for rare Mendelian diseases, but also for susceptibility conditions, late onset diseases, and HLA matching for existing children.

Embryo screening for susceptibility and late onset conditions are logical extensions of screening for serious Mendelian diseases. For example, using PGD to screen out embryos carrying the p53 or BRCA1&2 mutations prevent the birth of children who would face a greatly increased lifetime risk of cancer, and hence require close monitoring, prophylactic surgery, or other preventive measures. PGD for highly penetrant adult disorders such as Alzheimer's or Huntington's disease prevents the birth of a child who will be healthy for many years, but who in her late 30s or early 40s will experience the onset of progressive neurological disease leading to an early death.

Although these indications do not involve diseases that manifest themselves in infancy or childhood, the conditions in question lead to substantial health problems for offspring in their thirties or forties.[7] Avoiding the birth of children with those conditions thus reflects the desire of parents to have offspring with good prospects for an average life span. If PGD is accepted to exclude offspring with early onset genetic diseases, it should be accepted for later onset conditions as well.

PGD for adult onset disorders does mean that a healthy child might then be born to a person with those conditions who is likely to die or become incompetent while the child is dependent on her.[8] But that risk has been tolerated in other cases of assisted reproduction, such as intrauterine insemination with sperm of a man who is HIV positive, IVF for women with cystic fibrosis, and use of gametes stored prior to cancer therapy. As long as competent caregivers will be available for the child, the likely death or disability of a parent does not justify condemning or stopping this use, anymore than that reproduction by men going off to war should be discouraged.

A third new medical indication—HLA matching to an existing child—enables a couple to have their next child serve as a matched hematopoietic stem cell donor for an existing sick child. It may also ensure that the new child does not also suffer from that same disease. The availability of PGD, however, should not hinge on that fact, as the Human Fertilisation and Embryology Authority, in the UK, now requires.[9] A couple that would coitally conceive a child to be a tissue donor should be free to use PGD to make sure that that child will be a suitable match, regardless of whether that child is also at risk for genetic disease. Parents who choose PGD for this purpose are likely to value the new child for its own sake, and not only for the stem cells that it will make available. They do not use the new child as a "mere means" simply because they have selected HLA matched embryos for transfer.[10,11]

Non-Medical Uses of PGD

More ethically troubling has been the prospect of using PGD to screen embryos for genes that do not relate to the health of resulting children or others in the family. Many popular accounts of PGD assume that it will eventually be used to select for such non-medical traits as intelligence, height, sexual orientation, beauty, hair and eye colour, memory, and other factors.[5,6] Because the genetic basis of those traits is unknown, and in any case is likely to involve many different genes, they may not be subject to easy mutational analysis, as Mendelian disease or susceptibility conditions are. Aside from gender, which is identifiable through karyotyping, it is unrealistic to think that non-medical screening for other traits, with the possible exception of perfect pitch, will occur anytime soon.

Still, it is useful to consider the methodology that ethical assessment of non-medical uses of PGD, if available, should follow. The relevant questions would be whether the proposed use serves valid reproductive or rearing interests; whether those interests are sufficient to justify creating and destroying embryos; whether selecting for a trait will harm resulting children; whether it will stigmatise existing persons, and whether it will create other social harms.

To analyse how these factors interact, I discuss PGD for sex selection and for children with perfect pitch. Similar issues would arise with PGD for sexual orientation, for hair and eye color, and for intelligence, size, and memory.

PGD for Gender Selection

The use of medical technology to select the sex of offspring is highly controversial because of the bias against females which it usually reflects or expresses, and the resulting social disruptions which it might cause. PGD for gender selection faces the additional problem of appearing to be a relatively weak reason for creating and selecting embryos for discard or transfer.

The greatest social effects of gender selection arise when the gender of the first child is chosen. Selection for first children will overwhelmingly favour males, particularly if one child per family population policies apply. If carried out on a large scale, it could lead to great disparities in the sex ratio of the population, as has occurred in China and India through the use of ultrasound screening and abortion.[12,13] PGD, however, is too expensive and inaccessible to be used on a wide scale for sex selection purposes. Allowing it to be used for the first child is only marginally likely to contribute to societal sex ratio imbalances. But its use is likely to reflect cultural notions of male privilege and may reinforce entrenched sexism toward women.

The use of PGD to choose a gender opposite to that of an existing child or children is much less susceptible to a charge of sexism. Here a couple seeks variety or "balance" in the gender of offspring because of the different rearing experiences that come with rearing children of different genders. Psychologists now recognise many biologically based differences between male and female children, including different patterns of aggression, learning, and spatial recognition, as well as hormonal differences.[14,15] It may not be sexist in itself to wish to have a child or children of each gender, particularly if one has two or more children of the same gender.

Some feminists, however, would argue that any attention to the gender of offspring is inherently sexist, particularly when social attitudes and expectations play such an important role in constructing sex role expectations and behaviours.[16] Other feminists find the choice of a child with a gender different from existing children to be morally defensible as long as "the intention and consequences of the practice are not sexist", which is plausibly the case when gender variety in children is sought.[17] Desiring the different rearing experiences with boys and girls does not mean that the parents, who have already had children of one gender, are sexists or likely to value unfairly one or the other gender.[18]

Based on this analysis the case is weak for allowing PGD for the first child, but may be acceptable for gender variety in a family. With regard to the first child, facilitating preferences for male firstborns carries a high risk of promoting sexist social mores. It may also strike many persons as too trivial a concern to meet shared notions of the special respect due preimplantation embryos. A proponent of gender selection, however, might argue that cultural preferences for firstborn males should be tolerated, unless a clearer case of harm has been shown. If PGD is not permitted, pregnancy and abortion might occur instead.

The case for PGD for gender variety is stronger because the risk of sexism is lessened. A couple would be selecting the gender of a second or subsequent children for variety in rearing experiences, and not out of a belief that one gender is privileged over another. Gender selection in that case would occur without running the risks of fostering sexism and hurting women.[18]

The question still arises whether the desire for gender variety in children, even if not sexist, is a strong enough reason to justify creating and discarding embryos. The answer depends on how strong an interest that is. No one has yet marshalled the evidence showing that the need or desire for gender variety in children is substantial and important, or whether many parents would refrain from having another child if PGD for gender variety were not possible. More evidence of the strength and prevalence of this need would help in reaching a conclusion. If that case is made, then PGD for gender variety might be acceptable as well.[19]

The ethics committee of the American Society of Reproductive Medicine (ASRM) has struggled with these issues in a series of recent opinions. It initially addressed the issue of PGD for gender selection generally, and found that it "should be discouraged" for couples not going through IVF, and "not encouraged" for couples who were, but made no distinction between PGD for gender selection of first and later children.[20] Subsequently, it found that preconception gender selection would be acceptable for purposes of gender variety but not for the first child.[18]

Perceiving these two positions to be inconsistent, a doctor who wanted to offer PGD for gender selection inquired of the ethics committee why preconception methods for gender variety, which lacked 100% certainty, were acceptable but PGD, which guaranteed that certainty, was not. Focusing only on the sexism and gender discrimination issue, the chair of the ethics committee, in a widely publicised letter, found that PGD for gender balancing would be acceptable.[21] When the full committee reconsidered the matter, it concluded that it had not yet received enough evidence that the need for gender variety was so important in families that it justified creating and discarding embryos for that purpose.[19] In the future if such evidence was forthcoming then PGD for gender variety might also be acceptable.

What might constitute such evidence? One source would be families with two or more children of one gender who very much would like to have another child but only if they could be sure that it would be a child of the gender opposite of existing children. Given the legitimacy of wanting to raise children of both genders, reasonable persons might find that this need outweighs the symbolic costs of creating and discarding embryos for that purpose.

Another instance would be a case in which a couple has had a girl, but now wants a boy in order to meet cultural norms of having a male heir or a male to perform funeral rituals or play other cultural roles. An IVF programme in India is now providing PGD to select male offspring as the second child of couples who have already had a daughter.[22] Because of the importance of a male heir in India, those couples might well consider having an abortion if pregnant with a female fetus (even though illegal in India for that purpose). In that setting PGD for gender selection for gender variety appears to be justified.

PGD for Perfect Pitch

Perfect or "absolute" pitch is the ability to identify and recall musical notes from memory.[23] Although not all great or successful musicians have perfect pitch, a large number of them do. Experts disagree over whether perfect pitch is solely inborn or may also be developed by early training, though most agree that a person either has it or does not. It also runs in families, apparently in an autosomal dominant pattern.[23] The gene or genes coding for this capacity have not, however, been mapped, much less sequenced. Because genes for perfect pitch may also relate to the genetic basis for language or other cognitive abilities, research to find that gene may be forthcoming.

Once the gene for perfect pitch or its linked markers are identified, it would be feasible to screen embryos for those alleles, and transfer only those embryos that test positive. The prevalence of those genes is quite low (perhaps three in 100) in the population, but high in certain families.[23] Thus only persons from those families who have a strong interest in the musical ability of their children would be potential candidates for PGD for perfect pitch. Many of them are likely to take their chances with coital conception and exposure of the child to music at an early age. Some couples, however, may be willing to undergo IVF and PGD to ensure musical ability in their child. Should their request be accepted or denied?

As noted, the answer to this question depends on the importance of the reproductive choice being asserted, the burdens of the selection procedure, its impact on offspring, and its implications for deselected groups and society generally. The strongest case for the parents is if they persuasively asserted that they would not reproduce unless they could select that trait, and they have a plausible explanation for that position. Although the preference might appear odd to some, it might also be quite understandable in highly musical families, particularly ones in which some members already have perfect pitch. Parents clearly have the right to instill or develop a child's musical ability after birth. They might reasonably argue that they should have that right before birth as well.

If so, then creating and discarding embryos for this purpose should also be acceptable. If embryos are too rudimentary in development to have inherent rights or interests, then no moral duty is violated by creating and destroying them.[24] Some persons might think that doing so for trivial or unimportant reasons debases the inherent dignity of all human life, but having a child with perfect pitch will not seem trivial to parents seeking this technique. Ultimately, the judgment of triviality or importance of the choice within a broad spectrum rests with the couple. If they have a strong enough preference to seek PGD for this purpose and that preference rationally relates to understandable reproductive goals, then they have demonstrated its great importance to them. Only in cases unsupported by a reasonable explanation of the need—for example, perhaps creating embryos to pick eye or hair colour, should a person's individual assessment of the importance of creating embryos be condemned or rejected.

A third relevant factor is whether musical trait selection is consistent with respect for the resulting child. Parents who are willing to undergo the costs and burdens of IVF and PGD to have a child with perfect pitch may be so overly invested in the child having a musical career that they will prevent it from developing its own personality and identity. Parents, however, are free to instill and develop musical ability once the child is born, just as they are entitled to instill particular religious views. It is difficult to say that they cross an impermissible moral line of risk to the welfare of their prospective child in screening embryos for this purpose. Parents are still obligated to provide their child with the basic education and care necessary for any life plan. Wanting a child to have perfect pitch is not inconsistent with parents also wanting their child to be well rounded and equipped for life in other contexts.

A fourth factor, impact on deselected groups, is much less likely to be an issue in the case of perfect pitch because there is no stigma or negative association tied to persons without that trait. Persons without perfect pitch suffer no stigma or opprobrium by the couple's choice or public acceptance of it, as is arguably the case with embryo selection on grounds of gender, sexual orientation, intelligence, strength, size, or other traits. Nor is PGD for perfect pitch likely to perpetuate unfair class advantages, as selection for intelligence, strength, size, or beauty might.

A final factor is the larger societal impact of permitting embryo screening for a non-medical condition such as perfect pitch. A valid concern is that such a practice might then legitimise embryo screening for other traits as well, thus moving us toward a future in which children are primarily valued according to the attractiveness of their expected characteristics. But that threat is too hypothetical to justify limiting what are otherwise valid exercises of parental choice. It is highly unlikely that many traits would be controlled by genes that could be easily tested in embryos. Gender is determined by the chromosome, and the gene for pefect pitch, if ever found, would be a rare exception to the multifactorial complexity of such traits. Screening embryos for perfect pitch, if otherwise acceptable, should not be stopped simply because of speculation about what might be possible several decades from now.

PGD for Other Non-Medical Traits

The discussion of PGD for perfect pitch illustrates the issues that would arise if single gene analysis became possible for other traits, such as sexual orientation, hair or eye colour, or height, intelligence, size, strength, and memory. In each case the ethical assessment depends on an evaluation of the importance of the choice to the parents and whether that choice plausibly falls within societal understandings of parental needs and choice in reproducing and raising children. If so, it should usually be a sufficient reason to create and screen embryos. The effect on resulting offspring would also be of key moral importance. Whether selection carries a public or social message about the worth of existing groups should also be addressed.

Applying this methodology might show that some instances of non-medical selection are justified, as we have seen with embryo selection for gender variety and perhaps for having a child with perfect pitch. The acceptability of PGD to select other non-medical traits will depend on a careful analysis of the relevant ethical factors, and social acceptance of much greater parental rights to control the genes of offspring than now exists.

Conclusion

Although new indications are emerging for PGD, it is likely to remain a small part of reproductive practice for some time to come. Most new indications serve legitimate medical purposes, such as screening for single gene mutations for late onset disorders or susceptibility to cancer. There is also ethical support for using PGD to assure that a child is an HLA match with an existing child.

More controversial is the use of PGD to select gender or other non-medical traits. As with medical uses, the acceptability of non-medical screening will depend upon the interests served and the effects of using PGD for those purposes. Speculations about potential future non-medical uses should not restrict new uses of PGD which are otherwise ethically acceptable.

References

1. International Working Group on Preimplantation Genetics. Preimplantation genetic diagnosis: experience of 3000 clinical cycles. Report of the 11th annual meeting, May 15, 2001. *Reprod Biomedicine Online* 2001;3:49–53.

2. Verlinsky Y, Rechitsky S, Verlinsky O, et al. Preimplantation diagnosis of P53 tumor suppressor gene mutations. *Reprod Biomedicine Online* 2001;2:102–5.

3. Verlinsky Y, Rechitsky S, Schoolcraft W, et al. Preimplantation diagnosis for fanconi anemia combined with HLA matching. *JAMA* 2001;285:3130–3.

4. Verlinsky Y, Rechitsky S, Verlinsky O, et al. Preimplantation diagnosis for early-onset alzheimer's disease caused by V717L mutation. *JAMA* 2002;283:1018–21.

5. Fukuyama F. *Our postmodern future: consequences of the biotechnology revolution.* New York: Farrar, Strauss, & Giroux, 2002.

6. Stock G. *Redesigning humans: our inevitable genetic future.* New York: Houghton Mifflin, 2002.

7. Simpson JL. Celebrating preimplantation genetic diagnosis of p53 mutations in Li-Fraumeni syndrome. *Reprod Biomedicine Online* 2001;3:2–3.

8. Towner D, Loewy RS. Ethics of preimplantation diagnosis for a woman destined to develop early-onset alzheimer disease. *JAMA* 2002;283:1038–40.

9. Human Fertilisation and Embryology Authority. Opinion of the ethics committee. Ethical issues in the creation and selection of preimplantation embryos to produce tissue donors. London: HFEA, 2001 Nov 22.

10. Pennings G, Schots S, Liebaers I. Ethical considerations on preimplantation genetic diagnosis for HLA typing to match a future child as a donor of haematopoietic stem cells to a sibling. *Hum Reprod* 2002;17:534–8.

11. Robertson JA, Kahn J, Wagner J. Conception to obtain hematopoietic stem cells. *Hastings Cent Rep* 2002;32:34–40.

12. Sen A. More than 100 million women are missing. *New York Review of Books* 1990;37:61–8.

13. Eckholm E. Desire for sons drives use of prenatal scans in China. *The New York Times* 2002 Jun 21: A3.

14. Jaccoby EE, Jacklin CN. *The psychology of sex differences.* Palo Alto: Stanford University Press, 1974.

15. Robertson JA. Preconception gender selection. *Am J Bioeth* 2001;1:2–9.

16. Grubb A, Walsh P. Gender-vending II. *Dispatches* 1994;1:1–3.

17. Mahowald MB. *Genes, women, equality.* New York: Oxford University Press, 2000: 121.

18. American Society of Reproductive Medicine, Ethics Committee. Preconception gender selection for nonmedical reasons. *Fertil Steril* 2001;75:861–4.

19. Robertson JA. Sex selection for gender variety by preimplantation genetic diagnosis. *Fert Steril* 2002;78:463.

20. American Society of Reproductive Medicine, Ethics Committee. Sex selection and preimplantation genetic diagnosis. *Fertil Steril* 1999;72:595–8.

21. Kolata G. Society approves embryo selection. *The New York Times* 2001 Sept 26: A14.

22. Malpani A, Malpani A, Modi D. Preimplantation sex selection for family balancing in India. *Hum Reprod* 2002;17:11–12.

23. Blakeslee S. Perfect pitch: the key may lie in the genes. *The New York Times* 1990 Nov 30: 1.

24. American Society of Reproductive Medicine, Ethics Committee. Ethical considerations of assisted reproductive technologies. *Fertil Steril* 1994; 62(suppl):32–7S.

Marcy Darnovsky  **NO**

Revisiting Sex Selection: The Growing Popularity of New Sex Selection Methods Revives an Old Debate

In the United States and a few other prosperous, technologically advanced nations, methods of sex selection that are less intrusive or more reliable than older practices are now coming into use. Unlike prenatal testing, these procedures generally are applied either before an embryo is implanted in a woman's body, or before an egg is fertilized. They do not require aborting a fetus of the "wrong" sex.

These pre-pregnancy sex selection methods are being rapidly commercialized—not, as before, with medical claims, but as a means of satisfying parental desires. For the assisted reproduction industry, social sex selection may be a business path toward a vastly expanded market. People who have no infertility or medical problems, but who can afford expensive out-of-pocket procedures, are an enticing new target.

For the first time, some fertility clinics are openly advertising sex selection for social reasons. Several times each month, for example, the *New York Times'* Sunday Styles section carries an ad from the Virginia-based Genetics & IVF (in-vitro fertilization) Institute, touting its patented sperm sorting method. Beside a smiling baby, its boldface headline asks, "Do You Want To Choose the Gender Of Your Next Baby?"

Recent trends in consumer culture may warm prospective parents to such offers. We have become increasingly accepting of—if not enthusiastic about—"enhancements" of appearance (think face-lifts, collagen and Botox injections, and surgery to reshape women's feet for stiletto heels) and adjustments of behavior (anti-depressants, Viagra, and the like). These drugs and procedures were initially developed for therapeutic uses, but are now being marketed and normalized in disturbing ways. When considering questions of right and wrong, of liberty and justice, it is well to remember that the state is not the only coercive force we encounter.

This constellation of technological, economic, cultural, and ideological developments has revived the issue of sex selection, relatively dormant for more than a decade. The concerns that have always accompanied sex selection debates are being reassessed and updated. These include the prospect that selection could reinforce misogyny, sexism, and gender stereotypes; undermine the well-being of children by treating them as commodities and subjecting them to excessive parental expectations or disappointment; skew sex ratios in local populations; further the commercialization of reproduction; and open the door to a high-tech consumer eugenics.

Sex Selection Debates in the United States

Sex selection is not a new issue for U.S. feminists. In the 1980s and early 1990s, it was widely discussed and debated, especially by feminist bioethicists. This was the period when choosing a boy or girl was accomplished by undergoing prenatal diagnostic tests to determine the sex of a fetus, and then terminating the pregnancy if the fetus was of the undesired sex.

Ultrasound scanning and amniocentesis, which had been developed during the 1970s to detect, and usually to abort, fetuses with Down's syndrome and other conditions, were on their way to becoming routine in wealthier parts of the world. Soon they were also being openly promoted as tools for enabling sex-selective abortions in South and East Asian countries where the cultural preference for sons is pervasive. Opposition in these countries, especially strong in India, mounted in the early 1980s and remains vibrant today.

Throughout the 1980s and early 1990s, feminists and others in the U.S. who addressed the issue of sex selection were—almost universally—deeply uneasy about it. Not all opposed it equally, but none were enthusiastic or even supportive.

Some, like Helen Bequaert Holmes, pointed out that the deliberate selection of the traits of future generations is a form of eugenics.[1] Many deplored the practice as a symptom of a sexist society, in effect if not always in intent. In a book-length treatment of these concerns, published in 1985, philosopher Mary Anne Warren asked whether the practice should be considered an aspect of what she dubbed 'gendercide'—"no less a moral atrocity than genocide"— and published an entire book on the topic in 1985.[2]

But there was also broad consensus among feminists that any effort to limit sex-selective abortions, especially in the U.S., would threaten reproductive rights. Warren, despite her misgivings, argued that choosing the sex of one's child was sexist only if its intent or consequence was discrimination against women. She concluded that "there is great danger that the legal prohibition of sex selection would endanger other aspects of women's reproductive freedom," and considered even moral suasion against the practice to be unwarranted and counterproductive.

By the mid-1990s, the discussion had reached an impasse. No one liked sex selection, but few were willing to actively oppose it. Sex selection largely faded as an issue of concern for U.S. feminists, especially outside the circles of an increasingly professionalized bioethics discourse.

Separating Sex Selection from Abortion Politics

The new technologies of sex selection (and, perhaps, their potential profits) have prompted some bioethicists to argue in favor of allowing parents to choose their offspring's sex. As in past debates on other assisted reproductive procedures, they frame their advocacy in terms of "choice," "liberty," and "rights." John Robertson, a lawyer and bioethicist close to the fertility industry, is one of the leading proponents of this approach. In a lead article of the Winter 2001 issue of *American Journal of Bioethics,* Robertson wrote, "The risk that exercising rights of procreative liberty would hurt offspring or women—or contribute to sexism generally—is too speculative and uncertain to justify infringement of those rights."[3]

Robertson's claims are based on a world view that gives great weight to individual preferences and liberties, and little to social justice and the common good. As political scientist Diane Paul writes in a commentary on Robertson's recent defense of "preconception gender selection," "If you begin with libertarian premises, you will inevitably end up having to accept uses of reprogenetic technology that are even more worrisome" than sex selection.[4]

Definitions of procreative liberty like Robertson's are expansive—indeed, they often seem limitless. They are incapable, for example, of making a distinction between terminating an unwanted pregnancy—that is, deciding whether and when to bear children—and selecting the qualities and traits of a future child. However, sex selection and abortion are different matters, especially when a pregnancy is not involved.

Since new sex selection technologies are used before pregnancy, political discussions and policy initiatives which address them need not directly affect women's rights or access to abortion. In fact, many countries already prohibit "non-medical" sex selection, with no adverse impact on the availability or legality of abortion. One such nation is the United Kingdom, where, in November, 2003, after a comprehensive reconsideration of the issue, their Human Fertilization and Embryology Authority recommended that sex selection for social reasons continue to be prohibited, and that the Authority's purview be expanded to include regulation of sperm sorting technologies as well as other sex selection procedures. Even in the United States, where abortion rights are imminently threatened, the emergence of pre-pregnancy technologies should make it far easier than before, when sex determination meant selective abortion, to consider sex selection apart from abortion politics.

Eugenics: Is the Slope Becoming More Slippery?

When Mary Anne Warren considered sex selection in 1985, she summarily dismissed concerns of its contribution to a new eugenics as "implausible" on the grounds that "[t]here is at present no highly powerful interest group which is committed to the development and use of immoral forms of human genetic engineering."[5]

However, less than two decades later, a disturbing number of highly powerful figures are in fact committed to the development and use of a form of human genetic engineering that huge majorities here and abroad consider immoral—inheritable genetic modification, or manipulating the genes passed on to our children. These scientists, bioethicists, biotech entrepreneurs, and libertarians are actively advocating a new market-based, high-tech eugenics.

Princeton University molecular biologist Lee Silver, for example, positively anticipates the emergence of genetic castes and human sub-species. "[T]he GenRich class and the Natural class will become . . . entirely separate species," he writes, "with no ability to cross-breed, and with as much romantic interest in each other as a current human would have for a chimpanzee."[6] Nobel laureate James Watson promotes redesigning the genes of our children with statements such as, "People say it would be terrible if we made all girls pretty. I think it would be great."[7]

Silver's and Watson's remarks (and all too many similar ones) refer to technologies that are being used routinely in lab animals, but have not been applied to human beings. However, pre-implantation genetic diagnosis (PGD), the most common new sex selection method, is very much related to these technologies. It was introduced in 1990 as a way to identify and discard embryos affected by serious genetic conditions, and thus prevent the birth of children with particular traits. Though PGD is touted as a medical tool, disability advocates have pointed out that many people who have the conditions it targets live full and satisfying lives. PGD, they say, is already a eugenic technology.

In recent years, PGD has begun to be used to screen for more and more genetic attributes—late-onset conditions, tissue types suitable for matching those of a future child's sick sibling, and sex. Advocacy of even greater permissiveness in the use of PGD is beginning to pepper the professional literature. Bioethicist Edgar Dahl recently published an essay arguing that if a "safe and reliable genetic test" for sexual orientation were to become available, "parents should clearly be allowed" to use it, as long as they are permitted to select for homosexual as well as heterosexual children.[8] Bioethicist Julian Savulescu even baits disability advocates with the argument that we "should allow people deliberately to create disabled children."[9]

Concern about consumer eugenics and the commodification of children looms large for critics of social sex selection. As part of a recent campaign aimed at the Human Fertilization and Embryology Authority, the UK-based bioethics group Human Genetics Alert writes, "If we allow sex selection it will be impossible to oppose 'choice' of any other characteristics, such as appearance, height, intelligence, et cetera. The door to 'designer babies' will not have been opened a crack—it will have been thrown wide open."[10]

Another British NGO, Gene Watch UK [*no relation to* GeneWatch *magazine—ed.*] puts it this way: Allowing sex selection "would represent a significant shift towards treating children as commodities and [subjecting] the selection of a child's genetic make-up . . . to parental choice, exercised through paying a commercial company to provide this 'service'."[11]

Some researchers, bioethicists, and fertility practitioners have publicly opposed such uses of PGD, and expressed alarm at what the new push for social sex selection seems to portend. In September, 2001, Robertson, then acting chair of the Ethics Committee of the American Society for Reproductive Medicine (ASRM), issued an opinion that overturned the organization's opposition to PGD for social sex selection. The *New York Times* reported that this "stunned many leading fertility specialists." One fertility doctor asked, "What's the next step? . . . As we learn more about genetics, do we reject kids who do not have superior intelligence or who don't have the right color hair or eyes?"[12]

In the US, several women's organizations and other NGOs drafted a letter, signed by nearly a hundred groups and individuals, urging the ASRM not to loosen its recommendations on sex selection. Several months later, the ASRM affirmed its opposition to the use of PGD for "non-medical" sex selection. (The organization does not oppose sperm selection to select the sex of a child for "family balancing.") The spread of social sex selection and the ASRM episode were described in an *Atlantic Monthly* article titled "Jack or Jill? The era of consumer-driven eugenics has begun." Author Margaret Talbot concluded,

> [I]f we allow people to select a child's sex, then there really is no barrier to picking embryos—or, ultimately, genetically programming children—based on any whim, any faddish notion of what constitutes superior stock. . . . A world in which people (wealthy people, anyway) can custom-design human beings unhampered by law or social sanction is not a dystopian sci-fi fantasy any longer but a realistic scenario. It is not a world most of us would want to live in.[13]

A Transnational Issue and a Preference for Girls

In 1992, Nobel Prize-winning economist Amartya Sen estimated the number of "missing women" worldwide, lost to neglect, infanticide, and sex-specific abortions, at one hundred million. Similarly shocking figures were confirmed by others.

Many in the global North are distressed by the pervasiveness and persistence of sex-selective abortions in South and East Asia, and believe bans on sex selection procedures may be warranted there. At the same time, some of these people believe sex selection in countries without strong traditions of son preference may not be so bad.

This double standard rests on shaky grounds. The increased use and acceptance of sex selection in the U.S. would legitimize its practice in other countries, while undermining opposition by human rights and women's rights groups there. Even *Fortune* recognized this dynamic. "It is hard to overstate the outrage and indignation that MicroSort [a sperm sorting method] prompts in people who spend their lives trying to improve women's lot overseas," it noted in 2001.[14]

In addition, there are also large numbers of South Asians living in European and North American countries, and sex selection ads in *India Abroad* and the North American edition of *Indian Express* have specifically targeted them.[15] South Asian feminists in these communities fear that sex selection could take new hold among immigrants who retain a preference for sons. They decry the numerous ways it reinforces and exacerbates misogyny, including violence against women who fail to give birth to boys. If these practices are unacceptable—indeed, often illegal—in South Asia (and elsewhere), should they be allowed among Asian communities in the West?

In contrast to sex selection in South and East Asia, however, a preference for girls may be emerging in North America and Europe. Anecdotal evidence—based on reports from companies offering various methods for sex control and on perusal of the "Gender Determination" message board . . ., which has over a quarter million postings—tends to confirm that of North Americans trying to determine the sex of their next child, many are women who want daughters.

That North Americans may not use new technologies to produce huge numbers of "extra" boys does not, however, mean that sex selection and sexism are unrelated. One study, by Roberta Steinbacher at Cleveland State University, found that 81% of women and 94% of men who say they would use sex selection would want their firstborn to be a boy. Steinbacher notes that the research literature on birth order is clear: firstborns are more aggressive and higher-achieving than their siblings. "We'll be creating a nation of little sisters," she says.[16]

Observers of sex selection point to another discriminatory impact: its potential for reinforcing gender stereotyping. Parents who invest large amounts of money and effort in order to "get a girl" are likely to have a particular kind of girl in mind. As a mother of one of the first MicroSort babies recalled, "I wanted to have someone to play Barbies with and to go shopping with; I wanted the little girl with long hair and pink fingernails."[17]

There are many reasons people may wish for a daughter instead of a son, or a boy rather than a girl. In a sympathetic account, *New York Times* reporter and feminist Lisa Belkin described some of the motivations of U.S. women who are "going for the girl."

"They speak of Barbies and ballet and butterfly barrettes," she writes, but "they also describe the desire to rear strong young women. Some want to recreate their relationships with their own mothers; a few want to do better by their daughters than their mothers did by them. They want their sons to have sisters, so that they learn to respect women. They want their husbands to have little girls. But many of them want a daughter simply because they always thought they would have one."[18]

Wishes and Consequences

Compelling though some of these longings may be, sex selection cannot be completely understood or appropriately confronted by evaluating the right-ness or wrongness of parental desires. The preferences of prospective parents are obviously relevant in child-bearing matters, but so are the well-being of future children, and the social consequences of technologies—especially those that are already being aggressively marketed.

Wishing for a girl, or for a boy, is cause for neither shame nor condemnation. But as legal scholar Dorothy Roberts points out, it is important to "scrutinize the legal and political context which helps to both create and give meaning to individuals' motivations."[19]

If wishes, choices, and preferences are to be appropriately balanced with social justice and the common good, they cannot be unthinkingly transformed into protected liberties, much less codified rights. Isolated from social consequences, both wishes and liberties are at best naïve.

Notes

1. Humber and Almeder, eds. "Sex Preselection: Eugenics for Everyone?" *Biomedical Ethics Reviews,* 1985

2. Mary Ann Warren. *Gendercide: The Implications of Sex Selection.* Rowman & Littlefield, 1985

3. John A. Robertson. "Preconception Gender Selection," *American Journal of Bioethics,* Winter 2001

4. Dian Paul. "Where Libertarian Premises Lead," *American Journal of Bioethics,* Winter 2001

5. Mary Ann Warren. *Gendercide: The Implications of Sex Selection.* Rowman & Littlefield, 1985

6. Lee Silver. *Remaking Eden.* Avon, 1997

7. Shaoni Bhattacharya. "Stupidity should be cured, says DNA discoverer," *New Scientist,* February 28, 2003 . . .

8. Edgar Dahl. "Ethical Issues in New Uses of Preimplantation Genetic Diagnosis," *Human Reproduction,* Vol. 18 No. 7

9. Julian Savunescu, from the title of a November 25, 2003 presentation in London. . . .

10. "The Case Against Sex Selection," December 2002 . . .

11. "GeneWatch UK Submission to the HFEA Consultation on Sex Selection," January 2003

12. Gina Kolata. "Fertility Ethics Authority Approves Sex Selection," *The New York Times,* September 28, 2001

13. Margaret Talbot. "Jack or Jill? The era of consumer-driven eugenics has begun," *The Atlantic Monthly,* March 2002

14. Meredith Wadman. "So You Want A Girl?," *Fortune,* February 2001

15. Susan Sachs. "Clinics' Pitch to Indian Émigrés," *New York Times,* August 15, 2001

16. Lisa Belkin. "Getting the Girl," *The New York Times Magazine,* July 25, 1999

17. "Choosing Your Baby's Gender," . . . November 7, 2002

18. Belkin.

19. Dorothy Roberts, *Killing the Black Body: Race, Reproduction, and the Meaning of Liberty,* New York: Vintage Books, 1997, p. 286

POSTSCRIPT

Should Parents Be Allowed to Select the Sex of Their Baby?

Imagine yourself in the position of being able to choose the sex of your future children. What would be the benefits of having a daughter as opposed to a son, or vice versa? How much of these benefits rest on your expectations of your future child's personality? Are these traits inherently tied to their sex? Can you be certain that the child's gender will "match" their sex?

Now imagine the way your future children look. How tall are they? What color eyes do they have? What color is their hair? Is your child athletic, artistic, or intelligent? In the near future, it may be possible to make your "dream family" come true—for a fee. If you had the economic means, would you consider purchasing certain characteristics for your child? Why or why not?

Is there something about yourself that you consider unique? Is it a physical ability or talent, or even a physical feature that sets you apart from the crowd? Did it come from your mother or father—or is it distinctive from all of your family members? Now imagine that your parents told you that they wanted you to have this feature so bad that they "selected" it while you were still an embryo. Would you feel any less unique? What if they simply said they wanted you to be a certain sex? Would that change the way you feel about yourself? Would you feel different about a friend whose athletic talent was thanks in part to their parents' design, rather than nature's (although athletic ability, unlike eye color, e.g., would still require discipline and hard work to cultivate)?

In early 2011, the Food and Drug Administration (FDA) required a clinic in Virginia to stop using a different technique, a sperm sorting technology known as MicroSort, to predetermine the sex of a child unless there is a specific risk of sex-related illness. The technology is still under review by the FDA and a final decision on the use of MicroSort for sex selection is, at the time of this writing, yet to be made. Why might the government restrict the use of some forms of sex selection, but not PGD?

Do you consider it acceptable to use PGD (or other techniques) to predetermine the characteristics of your baby? Is it acceptable to screen for hereditary debilitating conditions and diseases? What did you make of Darnovsky claim that allowing PGD for sex selection could pave the way for "designer babies"?

Robertson challenged the "slippery slope" argument by stating, "Speculations about potential future nonmedical uses should not restrict new uses of PGD which are otherwise ethically acceptable." Do you agree? Is genetic sex selection medically ethical? Is preferring a child of one sex inherently sexist? If genetic markers are found for musical ability, intelligence, sexual orientation, or any other trait, will companies begin to offer the selection or deselection of these traits to potential parents and customers? Should these types of procedures be regulated or restricted even if they do not yet exist?

Suggested Readings

S. Baruch, "Sperm Sorting and the FDA," *Generations Ahead Blog*, accessed at http://www.generations-ahead.org/blog (April 20, 2011).

E. Dahl, "FDA Bans Gender Selection Procedure," *Ethical Technology,* accessed at http://ieet.org/index.php/IEET/more/dahl20110517 (May 17, 2011).

A. R. Fahrenkrog. "A Comparison of International Regulation of Preimplantation Genetic Diagnosis and a Regulatory Suggestion for the United States," *Transnational Law & Contemporary Problems* (vol. 15, no. 2, Spring 2006).

D. Grady, "Girl or Boy? As Fertility Technology Advances, So Does an Ethical Debate," *New York Times* (February 6, 2007).

L. Harris, "Choosy Moms Choose Their Babies' Sex?" *Salon* (February 26, 2009).

S. Matthew Liao, "The Ethics of Using Genetic Engineering for Sex Selection," *Journal of Medical Ethics* (vol. 31, no. 2, February 2005).

S. Puri and R. D. Nachtigall, "The Ethics of Sex Selection: A Comparison of the Attitudes and Experiences of Physicians and Physician Providers of clinical sex selection services," *Fertility & Sterility* (vol. 93, no. 7, May 2010).

B. Trivedi, "Boy or Girl? Embryo Tests Give Parents the Choice," *New Scientist* (September 30, 2006).

Contributors to This Volume

EDITORS

WILLIAM J. TAVERNER, M.A., CSE, is the editor-in-chief of the *American Journal of Sexuality Education* and is the director of The Center for Family Life Education, the nationally acclaimed education division of Planned Parenthood of Greater Northern New Jersey. He has coauthored many sexuality education resources, including *Making Sense of Abstinence; Older, Wiser, Sexually Smarter; Sex Ed 101; Streetwise to Sex-Wise;* and eight editions of *Taking Sides: Clashing Views in Human Sexuality.* A trainer of thousands throughout the United States who has twice advocated for sexuality education at U.S. Congressional briefings, he has received several awards recognizing his leadership in the field, including the first "Schiller Prize" given by the American Association for Sexuality Educators, Counselors, and Therapists; the "Golden Apple Award," given by the Association for Planned Parenthood Leaders in Education; and a "Sexual Intelligence" award that called him "one of the country's preeminent sex educators, trainers, and sex education theorists." He can be reached at sexedjournal@hotmail.com.

RYAN W. MCKEE, M.S., is a doctoral candidate in the Human Sexuality Education Program at Widener University. He was the winner of the Student Paper Award at Eastern Region Meeting of the Society for the Scientific Study of Sexuality. He teaches courses on human sexuality and health issues at Montclair State University and Kean University. While earning his M.S. degree in sociology from Virginia Commonwealth University, McKee worked as a research assistant on numerous projects including the Virginia Transgender Health Initiative, the Virginia Teen Pregnancy Prevention Initiative, the Youth Risk Behavior Survey, and the Virginia Community Youth Survey. He has written for Columbia University Health Services' award winning GoAskAlice! Web page (www.goaskalice.columbia.edu) and was recently published in the four-volume *Sexuality Education: Past, Present, and Future* anthology. He can be reached at ryan@ryanmckee.com.

AUTHORS

THE ADMINISTRATION FOR CHILDREN AND FAMILIES works within the United States Department of Health and Human Services and is responsible for federal programs that promote the economic and social well-being of families, children, individuals, and communities.

FUAMBAI S. AHMADU works for the National Institutes of Health (NIH) in Maryland. After receiving her doctorate from the Department of Anthropology at the London School of Economics in 2005, she completed a two-year postdoctoral fellowship at the Department of Comparative Human Development, University of Chicago.

MERCEDES ALLEN is the founder of AlbertaTrans.org, a network designed to help foster and support the transgender community in Edmonton, Calgary, and rural Alberta, Canada.

THE AMERICAN FAMILY ASSOCIATION advocates for traditional family values, focusing primarily on the influence of television and other media—including pornography—on American society.

MEGAN ANDELLOUX, a certified sexologist and sexuality educator, is the director of the Center for Sexual Pleasure and Health, a sexuality resource center for adults in Pawtucket, Rhode Island. Ms. Andelloux lectures at major universities, medical schools, and conferences on issues surrounding sexual freedom and the politics of pleasure.

ELOKIN CAPECE is a health educator with Planned Parenthood Greater Memphis Region. She holds an MA in Women's Studies from the University of Memphis and has an undergraduate degree in history, Greek and Roman studies, and education.

PATRICK J. CARNES is a nationally known speaker on the topic of sex addiction. He is the author of numerous books, including *Facing the Shadow: Starting Sexual and Relationship Recovery* and *In the Shadows of the Net: Breaking Free of Compulsive Online Sexual Behavior.*

RHONDA CHITTENDEN is a regional educator for Planned Parenthood of Greater Iowa and is a regular columnist for *Sexing the Political,* an online journal of Gen X feminists on sexuality.

TIMOTHY J. DAILEY is senior fellow for Policy at Family Research Council.

MARCY DARNOVSKY is the associate executive director of the Center for Genetics and Society in Oakland, California.

DONALD DYSON, MSS, Ph.D., is an asssociate professor in the Widener University Program in Human Sexuality, and serves as the director of doctoral studies in the Center for Education. He also serves as an adjunct faculty member at Widener's Center for Social Work Education.

J. PAUL FEDOROFF is director of the Forensic Research Unit at the Institute of Mental Health Research, University of Ottawa, and director of the Sexual Behaviours Clinic at the Royal Ottawa Hospital.

NORA GELPERIN is the director of training and education for Answer at Rutgers University and has presented workshops at local, state, and national conferences.

DOUGLAS GROOTHUIS is professor of philosophy at Denver Seminary and the author of 10 books, including *Truth Decay* (InterVarsity Press, 2000).

REBECCA HAGELIN is a public speaker on family and culture and is the author of *30 Ways in 30 Days to Save Your Family*.

MARK HAMILTON is the chair of the British Fertility Society and a consulting gynecologist with Aberdeen Maternity Hospital, Scotland.

DONNA M. HUGHES is the Eleanor M. and Oscar M. Carlson Endowed Chair at the University of Rhode Island and one of the world's leading researchers on sex trafficking.

HUMAN RIGHTS CAMPAIGN is the largest national lesbian, gay, bisexual, and transgender civil rights organization, representing a grassroots force of over 750,000 members and supporters nationwide.

MAUREEN KELLY is the vice president for education and training for Planned Parenthood of the Southern Finger Lakes in Ithaca, New York.

EILEEN P. KELLY is a professor at Ithaca College and teaches courses in applied ethical issues in management, labor relations, strategic management, and employment law.

AMY KRAMER is the director of entertainment media and audience strategy at The National Campaign to Prevent Teen and Unplanned Pregnancy.

SUSAN A. MILSTEIN is an associate professor in the Health Department at Montgomery College and is the lead consultant for Milstein Health Consulting and an advisory board member for the Men's Health Network.

NATIONAL WOMEN'S LAW CENTER is a nonprofit organization that works to expand the possibilities for women and focuses on family economic security, education, employment opportunities, and health, with special attention given to the concerns of low-income women.

CONNIE B. NEWMAN is an endocrinologist and adjunct associate professor of medicine at New York University School of Medicine, New York.

PAMELA PAUL is a journalist and an author. Her books include *Parents, Inc.,* and *Pornified: How Pornography is Damaging Our Lives, Our Relationships, and Our Families*.

WAYNE V. PAWLOWSKI is an independent consultant, trainer, and clinical social worker based in the Washington, DC, area, with more than 20 years in sexuality education, reproductive health, and family planning.

MARY JO PODGURSKI is the founder of the Academy for Adolescent Health, Inc., in Washington, Pennsylvania (www.healthyteens.com). She is an adjunct professor in the Department of Education at Washington and Jefferson College.

LARA RISCOL is a freelance writer who explores societal conflicts and controversies surrounding sexuality. She has been published in *AlterNet, The Nation,* and *Salon* and other media outlets worldwide, and is working on a book called *Ten Sex Myths That Screw America.*

A. M. ROSENTHAL is a clinical psychology doctoral student at Northwestern University. His research focuses on sexual orientation, and he is advised by J. Michael Bailey.

JOHN A. ROBERTSON holds the Vinson & Elkins Chair at The University of Texas School of Law at Austin. A graduate of Dartmouth College and Harvard Law School, he has written and lectured widely on law and bioethical issues.

WILLIAM SALETAN is a national correspondent for *Slate* magazine and is the author of *Bearing Right: How Conservatives Won the Abortion War.*

BRENT A. SATTERLY, Ph.D., LCSW, CSE is associate professor and BSW program director at Widener University's Center for Social Work Education as well as adjunct faculty in Widener's Human Sexuality Program. Dr. Satterly specializes in experiential education and training, providing strengths-based clinical care to the GLBTQ community, survivors of sexual trauma, families, and people with HIV/AIDS.

RICHARD A. SHWEDER is a cultural anthropologist and the William Claude Reavis Distinguished Service Professor of human development at the University of Chicago. His recent research examines the scope and limits of pluralism and the multicultural challenge in Western liberal democracies.

LAWRENCE A. SIEGEL is the president and CEO of the Sage Institute for Family Development in Boynton Beach, Florida.

RICHARD M. SIEGEL is the vice president of education, training, and counseling services for Planned Parenthood of South Palm Beach & Broward Counties, Inc., in Boca Raton, Florida.

CORY SILVERBERG is a certified sexuality educator, author, and consultant. He received his M.Ed. from the Ontario Institute for Studies in Education and teaches on topics including sex and technology, sexual pleasure, and sex and disability across North America. Cory can be found online at http://sexuality.about.com, where he writes and blogs about sexual politics, education, culture, and health.

CHARALAMBOS SIRISTATIDIS is affiliated with the Assisted Reproduction Unit, part of the Department of Obstetrics and Gynaecology at Aberdeen Maternity Hospital in Scotland.

DORIAN SOLOT is the executive director of the Alternatives to Marriage Project (www.unmarried.org) and coauthor of *Unmarried to Each Other: The Essential Guide to Living Together as an Unmarried Couple.*

LEONORE TIEFER is a clinical associate professor of psychiatry at New York University School of Medicine and the author of *Sex is Not a Natural Act.*

JENNIFER WEBSTER is the projects coordinator for the Network for Reproductive Options, a grassroots feminist organization seeking to ensure reproductive justice for the women of Oregon.

KELLEY WINTERS, formerly under pen-name Katherine Wilson, is a writer on issues of transgender medical policy, founder of GID Reform Advocates, and an advisory board member for the Matthew Shepard Foundation and TransYouth Family Advocates.

WORLD HEALTH ORGANIZATION is the directing and coordinating authority for health within the United Nations system. It is responsible for providing leadership on global health matters, shaping the health research agenda, setting norms and standards, articulating evidence-based policy options, providing technical support to countries, and monitoring and assessing health trends.